Into the LONELINESS

ELEANOR HOGAN is a literary non-fiction writer with a professional background in Indigenous policy research. Her writing, including her previous book, *Alice Springs*, published by NewSouth in 2012, draws strongly on her experience in central Australia, where she has lived and worked since 2000. She was winner of the Peter Blazey Fellowship 2017 and the Hazel Rowley Literary Fellowship 2019 for biographical writing.

I responded to this book with every cell in my body, neuron in my brain and beat of my heart. A stunning achievement of epic storytelling, historical enquiry and elegant analysis. Eleanor Hogan has resurrected Hill and Bates as Australian icons, women as complex, compelling and deeply flawed as the nation itself.

CLARE WRIGHT

Into the Loneliness is a fascinating biographical study of two significant and intriguing women who were in many ways ahead of their time, yet reflective of it in their artistic endeavours. Using a sophisticated structure and interconnected narratives, this impressive biography reconceptualises the shifting, complex, relationships between Daisy Bates, Ernestine Hill and Indigenous Australians.

JENNY HOCKING

Into the Loneliness presents a relationship between two remarkable but flawed women, one with profound, ongoing consequences for Indigenous people. It's a book about sexism, about writing, and the nature of friendship. It's a study of white Australian attitudes that persist to this day. And it's an astonishing true story that leaps off the page

JEFF SPARROW

A meticulous unveiling of the enigmatic Daisy Bates and her writing companion Ernestine Hill. Tracking her subjects across the Nullarbor, Hogan strips away layer after layer of dissimulation as she unpicks their writing partnership.

BILL GARNER

To my mother, Enid Gordon, for introducing me to Australian women writers from the interwar period, and to my father, Roger Hogan, for sharing his love of bushwalking and camping, and never being afraid to take the family Kingswood down an unsealed road.

Into the LONELINESS

The unholy alliance of
Ernestine Hill and Daisy Bates

ELEANOR HOGAN

NEWSOUTH

This book reproduces certain historical terms commonly used in 19th and 20th-century writing and public discourse, which are now recognised as racially pejorative or misogynistic. Generally, inverted commas signal their first reference in the text; their offensive nature should be assumed for subsequent references. There has been much debate over recent decades about the appropriate naming of Australia's first nations peoples, which reflects the country's fractured history since colonisation. 'Aboriginal people' is mainly used to refer to Australia's first inhabitants and custodians throughout the book, in preference to the more outdated and essentialist term, 'Aborigine'. 'Anangu' specifically refers to people from the western desert area, as the name they commonly use when referring to themselves.

Warning: Aboriginal and Torres Strait Islander people should be aware that this book contains words and descriptions written by non-Indigenous people in the past that may be confronting and would be considered inappropriate today. It also contains the names and images of deceased Indigenous people and graphic descriptions of historical events that may be disturbing to some readers.

A NewSouth book

Published by
NewSouth Publishing
University of New South Wales Press Ltd
University of New South Wales
Sydney NSW 2052
AUSTRALIA
newsouthpublishing.com

© Eleanor Hogan 2021
First published 2021

10 9 8 7 6 5 4 3 2 1

This book is copyright. Apart from any fair dealing for the purpose of private study, research, criticism or review, as permitted under the *Copyright Act*, no part of this book may be reproduced by any process without written permission. Inquiries should be addressed to the publisher.

A catalogue record for this book is available from the National Library of Australia

ISBN   9781742236599 (paperback)
         9781742245058 (ebook)
         9781742249575 (ePDF)

Internal design Josephine Pajor-Markus
Cover design Lisa White
Cover images Ernestine Hill's caravan in Mundrabilla country, c 1947 (SLSA). Australia pictorial exploration map, c 1967. Cartographer: Sheila Leacock (NLA). Top left: Ernestine Hill and her caravan, 1949. Photographer: Douglas Glass (NAA). Top right: Daisy Bates at Sunny Brae farm, Westall, 1947. Photographer: Robert Hill (NLA).

All reasonable efforts were taken to obtain permission to use copyright material reproduced in this book, but in some cases copyright could not be traced. The author welcomes information in this regard.

UNSW Press Literary Fund wishes to acknowledge the generous support of its donors.

Contents

Pitjantjatjara glossary	ix
Map of locations	x
Prologue	xii
Introduction	1

I | WANDERING

1	A confirmed wanderer	17
2	A wandering sickness	55
3	Great wide spaces	82

II | PASSING

4	An uneasy alliance	115
5	The Passing of the Aborigines	135

III | GHOSTING

6	A wraith, flitting by	165
7	Derelict on the Nullarbor	204
8	The lady living over the hill	231

IV | HOMING

9	Gypsying to windward	247
10	The great-great-grandmother of that welfare mob	280

V | DREAMING

11	A surrealist's madness	309
12	This little breathlessness	334
13	A fleeting project	352
14	Inside the breakwind	366

Notes	375
Abbreviations	400
References	401
Acknowledgements	412
Index	416

Pitjantjatjara glossary

Anangu	people
churinga	(also spelt tjuringa and tjurunga) sacred object
inma	singing; ceremony
kata kura	funny in the head
kungka	woman
mala	rufous hare-wallaby
mamu	harmful spirit being
minyma	mature woman
pana	earth, dirt, land
Pila Nguru	Spinifex people
tjilpi	old
uwa	yes
walypala	white people
wana	women's digging stick
wanampi	water snake guarding water holes; rainbow serpent
waru	fire
watjilyitja	half-caste
watu	wombat
wiltja	shade shelter
wiya	no

SOURCE *Pitjantjatjara/Yankunytjatjara to English Dictionary*, 2nd edn, IAD Press, Alice Springs, 1996.

Map of locations

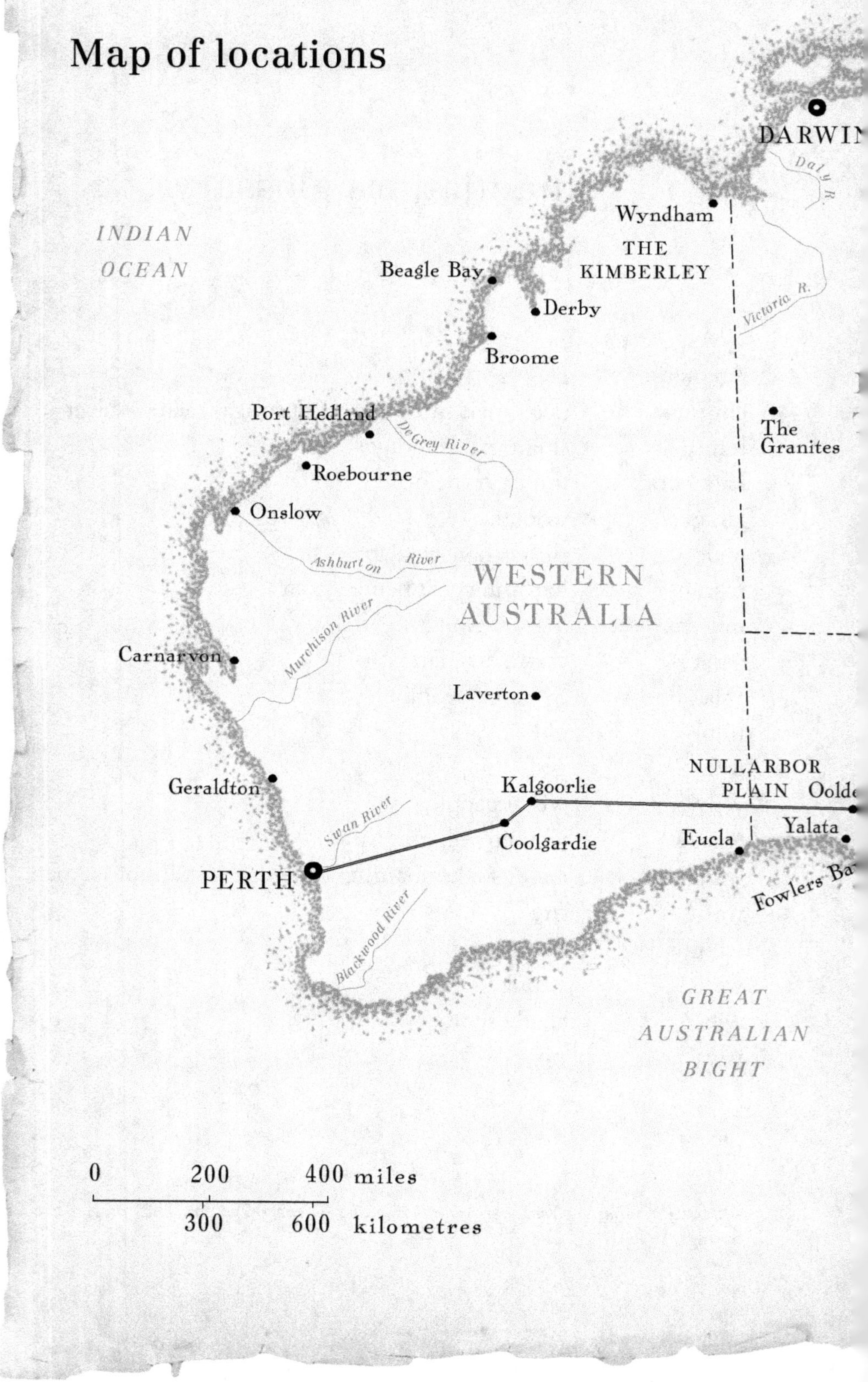

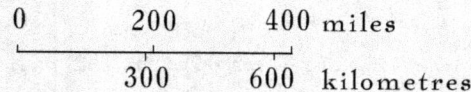

Prologue

In 1930 the woman who called herself Mrs Hill caught the Old Trans across the Nullarbor. She sat with a notebook propped on her knees, her suitcase, typewriter and thin swag slung in the rack overhead, revelling in the train's front-stall view of the weird and mournful wilderness all around. Strewn with saltbush, the treeless plains glinted faintly silver, becoming almost too dazzling to watch at noon, waxing pink and grey as a galah's breast at dawn and dusk.

A freelance correspondent for the Sydney *Sun*, Ernestine Hill was combing the country's vast open spaces for stories to take to the breakfast table newspapers in the nation's coast-clinging capitals. Wearing Oxford bags or shorts, stockman's boots and a broad-brimmed hat, she styled herself as a New Woman, stepping out full of courage and brio – a grand way of saying she dressed for comfort, practicality and ease of movement, and, if she was honest, for camouflage. She prided herself on blending in with the men around her, wearing this outfit like the name 'Mrs Hill' as a flimsy talisman to ward off whatever might cross her path. For most of the trip, she was the only woman of her kind, as she was on all her journeys. 'You could travel a thousand miles in the north without seeing a sheet or a towel,' she wrote in her notebook, '– or a white woman or child.'

It was the Depression, and men were roaming the continent for work. The Trans-Australian Express was a marginally safer way to travel across the south-west than the Eyre Highway, which had been a madman's track for decades. Hitchhikers jumped the rattlers and trudged from one squatter's lot to the next, their bare feet stamping the road into being across the Bight. The detritus of grand visions and schemes, many of them had helped lay the Overland Telegraph and the transcontinental rail after the gold rushes at Coolgardie and Kalgoorlie had subsided. Their ranks had been swelled by men returning from the Great War, haunted trampers like sleepwalkers from a nightmare that would never end, from the trenches to this – a landscape that stretched like endless nothingness before their eyes.

'Water was scarce for 1000 miles, they walked with their boots round their necks to government tanks full of dead rabbits and birds, hanging around the stations for food and work,' Hill observed. 'There was no friendliness for men or women, no settlement whatever along the coast.'

But if their predicament seemed harsh, that of another diaspora of people – the 'real Australians', as she called them – seemed much lonelier. Their traditional lands grazed to stubble, their soaks and waterholes drained, those whom the missions hadn't scooped up gathered along the railway lines. Hill saw them camping near soaks and government tanks along the East–West Line between Kalgoorlie and Port Augusta, thronging the Trans as it pulled into sidings, begging for food, clothing and coins, bartering with boomerangs and carved artefacts. Passengers pelted them with shillings, apples and old hats; fettlers taunted them with stale bread, cheap sweets, offal, billies of flour, tea-leaves and plate scrapings in exchange for favours.

It was time, Ernestine announced in her notebook, 'Time to talk with them all', although she needed a focus, something or someone, to shape her scraps of observations about life along the line into a *Sun* feature.

While the train idled at Ooldea siding on the Nullarbor's edge, a passing comment the conductor made pricked her attention, suggesting a possible subject. Somewhere out there in the 118 degree Fahrenheit heat, he said, Mrs Daisy Bates was in her camp over the dunes, doing 'so much for the blacks'.

Hill craned her neck out the window, squinting in the glare, but saw nothing beyond the weary upturned, imploring faces outside the carriage and the scatter of sheds around the platform except a gritty shoulder of sand. She tucked the anecdote away, thinking little more of it until she heard the name again where she least expected it. Later in Perth while dining with the ladies of the Karrakatta Club, they regaled her over strawberries and cream with tales about a former member, Mrs Daisy Bates, who'd once dragged a barefoot Aboriginal woman into their exclusive preserve as her guest of honour. When they'd complained, Bates had protested that the woman they called a 'disreputable old gin' was none other than Fanny Balbuk, one of the city's original landlords, and 'actually hostess to them all with the Karrakatta Club thrown in'.

Bates had been a mystery to them, a lady journalist camping without husband or family near outcast 'blacks' at Ma'amba Reserve on Perth's fringes. What exactly she'd been doing, they weren't sure – making postcards of Aboriginal people to sell, writing newspaper stories or some such – but she and her tents had been a reliable source of novelty, somewhere to take visiting officials and their wives on a Sunday outing. No-one had seen her since she'd taken off in a steamer to camp on the Bight almost two decades ago, although it seemed she'd dug herself in at Ooldea, if her articles about life with her 'natives' were to be believed.

Hill was fascinated. Bates lingered in her mind like a question mark, and two years later Ernestine caught the Trans back to Ooldea, convinced the woman was the stuff of great story. She didn't warn anyone at the siding of her visit, fearing that Daisy, like some rare and untamed quarry, might 'take fright or fly'. Bates was notoriously difficult to approach. Reclusive to the point of eremitic, she withdrew from fellow whites, preferring the company of Aboriginal people at her camp; it was rumoured 'she was mad, & had an open grave by her tent door & hated men'.[1]

Alighting at the platform with her port, camera and typewriter, Hill momentarily felt stranded as she watched the Trans disappear like a mirage down the tracks. Then a woman, broad as she was tall, emerged from a fettler family's donga near the siding. On hearing Ernestine's mission, she said that Mrs Bates lived in the blacks' camp but she'd be along soon to collect her mail from the train, and motioned at the dunes beyond the station. Hill followed the flap of her hand and saw a white spot emerging among the gravel and saltbushes on the sandy slope.

Bates shimmered into view among the mulga and the mallee in the midday heat haze, an apparition from another era, taut and straight-backed in prim, Victorian rig, shading herself with a large black umbrella. The fettler woman called her over, and as she drew closer, a gloved finger pushed back frayed mesh from an old straw boater to reveal a sharply alert gaze and skin desiccated by sun and time. Her voice came as a surprise – soft, gentle, lilting, Irish – quietly firm, not the commanding imperial tones one might expect. Regarding Ernestine with prickly uncertainty, Bates asked her purpose, softening when she realised the girl had dropped from the skies, as it were, to visit her. Brushing off the fettler woman's suggestion that her guest stay the night on her donga's verandah, she invited Ernestine to take tea at her camp and see if she cared to 'share my very primitive life'.

Privately thrilled, Hill left her luggage at the siding. Unencumbered, she still struggled to keep up with Bates's deft clip a mile or more over scalding sands, although her host was surely in her seventies.

'Tawny-dark sandhills rippled with wind stretching to the desolate north,' Ernestine wrote of the view from their climb, 'like ploughed land and then the deep blue of low hills ... Ooldea itself is a jumble of helter-skelter hills ... kicked up by wallaby.'

They descended into a wind-blasted dust bowl, the bare branches of trees clutching at the blanched sky as if signalling distress. They were on the banks of Yuldilgabbi, Bates explained, a great soak that had once been a small oasis, a delta of Aboriginal trading routes. For centuries, Aṉangu – the local Kokatha people, the Mirning and Wirangu from the coast, the Ngalea and Pindiini from inland and beyond – had travelled hundreds of miles to exchange resources and perform ceremony by the soak. Food had been abundant; a gauzy mantle of shrubs had covered its slopes, attracting mala to graze and watu to burrow and forage.[2] Observing the promise of water, Aṉangu had bored holes in Yuldilgabbi's surface, tapping into the reservoirs honeycombing the limestone beneath the Nullarbor Plain. Explorers had imitated them, then engineers, who'd drilled deeper, more intrusive wells, channelling its underground reserves through pipes over the dunes to the railway siding. People now drifted in from the desert to find that Yuldilgabbi was no more, its flanks parched, devoid of their former life.

Bates led Hill to a small enclosure on the dunes bounding the eroded soak. Two tents, one blown to a ruin, and a couple of bough sheds were barricaded with a breakwind of mulga trees with prickle bushes across the entrance – to keep out wild dogs, Daisy said, although rabbits, small marsupials and birds took no notice, as far as Ernestine could see. The centrepiece was an eight-by-ten canvas, which she boasted Western Australian premier John Forrest had given her when she commenced her tent life outside Perth. Crammed with notebooks, manuscripts, clothes and camping gear, there was hardly any space for Daisy's small bed with its roo-skin rug. An old water tank, upended on its side, was stuffed with maps, papers and books, including a dozen volumes of Dickens, which she'd read so often she could recall passages at will. Further up the slope behind the tents was a bough shed that served as an observatory, a ladder propped against it that Daisy scrambled up at night to plot the constellations whose stories Anangu told her.

Inside the breakwind, Hill knelt beside her host by a campfire where a potato glowed, hidden, 'black-fashion', in its embers. Bates subsisted on the staples of white civilisation, which she shared with her natives – sugar, flour and 'always tea – my panacea for all ills'. Often she made a meagre damper, supplementing it with porridge, boiled rice, a potato or the occasional treat of an egg. It was no wonder she was still wasp-waisted, skinny as a sprite, living on this diet and practising 'physical jerks' such as jumping rope as well as dragging a barrow named Augusta (after the port) to the siding every day.

Photographs Hill took on this visit show Bates in a white shirt, tie and ankle-length navy serge skirt topped off with a dust coat, gloves and a hat with a shroud-like mesh, as if she's about to handle a beehive or hazardous chemicals. Armed with her black umbrella, she dispenses 'Empire Clothing' from her barrow, doling out sheets and billies of tea, pulling white shirts over Aboriginal men's heads. This was her work; why she had come to Ooldea back in 1919. A self-taught ethnologist, she boasted to Hill that she'd learned 'to think black', mastering 115 dialects by camping alongside Aboriginal people. She'd begun by listening to the disenfranchised locals at Ma'amba Reserve in Perth speak in their own languages, jotting down words, stories, lore. Later she'd sailed to Eucla on the Bight's western edge and pitched her tents again, hoping to distil more about Aboriginal life and culture from talking to people in the south-west. She'd camped several times on the Bight, continuing her practice of listening and writing, scribbling on whatever came to hand – cellophane newspaper wrappings, old soup tin labels, telegram pads. She'd gravitated to Ooldea after hearing what was happening along the rail line. Over time Bates had supplemented her language work with ad hoc acts of mercy, feeding and clothing Aboriginal people, convinced they were dying out, to 'give them tranquillity and peace in their last moments'.[3]

Hill was, as far as she knew, the first person past the breakwind, sleeping in a bough shed inside Bates's tiny compound. She only experienced five days of 'tent life', but it was long enough for her to hammer out two features, one based on a story Bates told her about a local Aboriginal woman, which grabbed the *Sunday Sun*'s banner headlines. Later Ernestine would be ashamed of this article, calling it the work of 'a wicked and ruthless young journalist'.[4] Yet the memory of camping with Bates stayed with her long afterwards, a cipher for what might be possible – indeed, for a white woman – in the land's vast loneliness.[5]

Introduction

Late in the autumn of 1945, the first letter came.

> Dear Ernestine Hill,
>
> I miss you greatly here in Adelaide, I wonder if I shall ever see you here again …
>
> Are you returning South? & when? I am not going back to tent life but am here in Adelaide & about to begin new script – this time to write up my blacks' life & mine with them, & to note for future Australians, their customs, laws, their whole daily lives, ways, foods, legends, & to make broadcasting (or 'broadcast-able') script of them all, as well as making a book or booklets.[1]

Daisy Bates was at the Queen Adelaide Club where Ernestine had brought her a decade earlier to record stories about her life working with remote Aboriginal people. At the time, Hill was employed at the *Advertiser* and she'd persuaded Bates to leave her camp of sixteen years on the Nullarbor and put herself and trunkloads of her precious notes on the Adelaide train so they could write her memoirs together. The pair had sequestered themselves in an *Advertiser* office, Daisy as prophet dictating to Ernestine as scribe, producing a series of articles, 'My Natives and I', which was syndicated across the major city newspapers. The serial had been repackaged as a book, *The Passing of the Aborigines*, in 1938, and had soon become an international bestseller.

Now it seemed Bates had publishing plans of her own. In 1941 the national archives had housed ninety folios of her notes on Aboriginal life – laws, customs, stories and glossaries for over 100 languages – but she still had more material 'to preserve for future Australians'. The Commonwealth government had furnished her with an office and a secretary in Adelaide, but she declared them no use. Who better to enlist than Ernestine Hill, who not only had superlative shorthand and typing skills but shared her passion for bringing 'the world of Australia and the Empire the wonderful unique knowledge … of Northern Australia?'[2]

Hill was by then a well-known journalist and the author of several books, including *The Great Australian Loneliness*, a lushly descriptive travelogue that had consolidated her reputation as a leading commentator on 1930s outback Australia. During the Second World War, she'd become an ABC commissioner, edited the *ABC Weekly* women's pages and given broadcast talks.

Bates prevailed on her old friend, sensing the potential of new media such as radio programs and film documentaries, of which Hill with her ABC experience was surely aware. 'I want you near me,' her letter continued, 'to share, & share my "material", your broadcasting knowledge & a possibility of doing something with the many old photographs taken since 1899. There is a name for photo-broadcasting but I forget it.' Perhaps she imagined them pulling together something photo-broadcast-able from her snapshots and illegible, flyblown notes. 'What do you think? You'll tell me fully and clearly, I know. My love for you is unalterable, but I think my youth is going.' She was eighty-five. 'Let me know what you think.'[3]

Introduction

Ernestine was camping at Borroloola when she received Daisy's first plaintive request. She and her son Bob had headed north not long before the war's end, planning to research a history she was writing of the Northern Territory. 'Here where the world is quiet, we are trying to finish the Territory book,' she wrote to Sydney friend and literary mentor George Mackaness, 'where now I am content in the leafy shadow of a tent and the cool of a bough shade … My symphony concert is corroboree, my only other callers the shirtless philosophers of this forgotten shore.'[4]

Hill was weary, ground down by wartime privations and the relentless schedule she'd kept as a single mother supporting herself and her child. Early in 1942 she'd been laid off from editing the *ABC Weekly*'s women's pages after war-driven staffing cuts. Later that year, she was appointed ABC commissioner and had travelled far beyond the railway lines to interview people across the country about what they wanted from radio programming. It was a role she'd relished but had resigned from after two years, pleading ill health, worn out not only by her constant circumnavigation of the country but from fighting for Bob, her only child, to be spared from military conscription. As the Hills boiled a billy and cooked damper seasoned with the occasional morsel of goat over a campfire at Borroloola, they must have been reluctant to give up their hard-won peace. Nor may Ernestine have wanted to plunge a couple of thousand miles down the Centralian corridor to reprise her earlier role as glorified secretary to Bates in the *Advertiser* office.

Daisy's letters kept coming, although her address changed to Streaky Bay, a town some 700 kilometres west of Adelaide on the South Australian coast. She bolted there after receiving treatment for an ulcer at an Adelaide hospital, planning to resume her tent life among Aboriginal people on the Nullarbor, although she'd been alarmed to find after a brief reconnaissance that 'it was now "whitefella" country' with 'only the third generation of settlers in this bleak area and no natives anywhere'.[5]

At eighty-seven, she was really too frail to camp so she boarded with a local farmer and his family in a sleep-out behind their stone farmhouse at Westall, near Streaky Bay. She did light chores such as making her own bed and kindling the fire, but she could 'do no more skipping rope business or running up stairs & down'.[6] Her world had shrunk to the walls of a galvanised iron room and, with rain dripping and wind whistling between its seams, was no substitute for life in her tents on the Nullarbor's hot dry plains.

'If I could "scrounge" 2 jeeps and bring them to W.A. would you live in one with me? In some quiet area?' she asked Hill, as if suggesting they play hooky. She kept up the pressure over the next couple of years, entreating Ernestine in 1947 to 'get a big Double Caravan of some kind – I asked the Govt for one but my letter was not even answered.' The Secretary of the Department of the Interior wrote to Hill, seeking clarification about 'just what Mrs. Bates has in mind' after she'd written requesting 'a quiet simple little camp, or tent, or room, just as I had my 16 years' tent at Ooldea'.[7]

'[P]athetic little letters were coming to me from Daisy Bates, who is 88, imploring me to come back to see her,' Hill later told George Mackaness, 'So I did.'[8] In June 1947 she and Bob drove south to Melbourne then headed west, 'gypsying to windward with Buggy and Caravan' which they'd bought specially for the trip, planning to deliver Bates to 'the dreaming of her beloved "Joobaitch" in the Bibbulmun country in Western Australia' where she'd camped in the early 1900s.[9] But when they arrived at Westall Farm, they found that Bates was failing more than they'd

Introduction

anticipated; a caravan trip was definitely out of the question. Instead, Ernestine sat on the only chair in Bates's room, listening as she'd first done inside the breakwind at Ooldea to Daisy while she held forth from the bed, 'talking all the time about the old days and the blacks and their legends'.[10]

Bates's voice, summoning Ernestine to rescue her in a caravan from an iron shed at wind-ravaged Westall Farm, arrested me when I first read her letters to Hill. Sometimes wheedling, cajoling, sentimental verging on cloying, her voice at times was eerie and unnerving, haunting, with a dreamlike delusional quality. Her letters also possessed an intensity, a surety that she could tug on the thread of friendship and Hill would travel thousands of kilometres at her bidding. What hold did this desert eccentric have over a popular journalist almost forty years her junior? I wondered. I'd heard of Daisy Bates as the contentious foremother of Australian anthropology, but I had no idea she'd been associated with Ernestine Hill. What did they have in common? What interests and experiences had bonded them?

I came across this sheaf of Bates's correspondence unexpectedly while I was rummaging through archival boxes in the Ernestine Hill Collection at Queensland University's Fryer Library. I visited the collection after reading *The Great Australian Loneliness*, wanting to learn more about its author, the jaunty young woman who 'first set out, a wandering "copy-boy" with swag and typewriter … dangling from a camel-saddle, jingling on a truck' in July 1930, hitching a lift on any available transport.[11] Delighting in Hill's lighthearted, girl's-own-adventure romp across outback Australia, I marvelled at her daring in venturing to isolated areas some still might consider risky for a woman to travel alone. I'd wandered myself as an Indigenous policy researcher across northern Australia for almost two decades, and many of the places she described – Borroloola, Broome, Coober Pedy, Arnhem Land, Tennant Creek, Alice Springs – clicked by familiar as worn beads on a rosary.

Something of Hill's desire to escape 'the rhythm of the "big machine" and the sameness of cities' spoke to me.[12] I'd lived in Alice Springs during the noughties and had relocated to Melbourne for work in 2010, although I still travelled back regularly to central Australia as a researcher. Cloistered under Melbourne's grey skies, I knew what it was to tire of house-hemmed horizons and long to see distance wherever you looked. I'd picked up a copy of the *Loneliness* from a book barrow at Swinburne University where I was working, curious to read a woman journalist's perspective on life in remote Australia during the 1930s. By 21st-century standards, I often found Hill's style twee and sentimental, her outlook and preoccupations dated, sometimes racist and offensive; I cringed equally at her purple prose and patronising descriptions of 'exotic others'. But I was struck by Hill's facility as a journalist and travel writer in straddling the boundary of popular and middle-brow writing to communicate the diversity of experience in remote Australia to metropolitan readers during her era. Through her writing, she sought to loosen a southern urban stranglehold on national identity by exposing life beyond its 'six, and now alarmingly seven, big cities of premature birth' with a proto-multicultural vision 'of smug, colour-conscious White Australia below the twentieth parallel, and black, white and brindle struggling above it'.[13]

This impetus behind *The Great Australian Loneliness* resonated with my experience of living and working in central Australia – so much so that I visited Hill's collection at the Fryer Library, wanting to know what had driven her wandering. Although I found signs of a diverse and varied life in its boxes – manila folders

Introduction

bulging with notes, unfinished drafts of novels and plays, letters to family and friends, photographs of camels, pearl luggers and troglodyte mining towns – there were few traces of the wandering copy-boy from the *Loneliness*, only fragmentary notes of Hill's roaming that had informed this book, some in an exercise book titled, 'From the first old Centre notebook 1932'. I opened it to discover a list of Aboriginal words, 'Oodnadatta Language', with their English counterparts on the first page, then extracts of typescript in red ink pasted on other pages. They featured shadowy remnants of encounters with people in central Australia whose names I recognised – of Hill rigging a tent between trees at Boggy Hole, finding artists Rex Battarbee and John Gardner living on ducks and rabbits while painting at a waterhole, meeting Pastor Albrecht at Hermannsburg mission, where 'educated blacks' complained their rations were "fowl's food". As Australia's first landlords they objected. Compelled to chew.'[14] The exercise book was a literal palimpsest, reflecting the collection's conglomerate of different textured artefacts – scraps of Aboriginal language, Hill's own inscrutable shorthand and cramped copperplate, typescripts of her notes and facsimiles of lost originals.

Often I enjoyed the rawness of this mosaic dross from Hill's itinerant lifestyle more than I did the curlicues and flourishes of her published prose. Some of her jottings possessed a telegrammatic poetry: 'Nobody hides in the great wide spaces and everyone answers a shout.'[15] She tended to be franker in these random notes than in *The Great Australian Loneliness*, as if here she could admit what was unsayable at the time: 'He always employs blacks – he pays them nothing a week and they feed themselves.'[16] Scribbling ideas and observations in notebooks is a common enough practice of writers and journalists, and I have a bad habit of buying a new notebook, writing a few pages of ideas for yet another project, then abandoning it in a bottom drawer. But Hill's note-taking had a

7

compulsive aura of a writer snared in her own web of semiosis, endlessly scribing yet unable to articulate her vision, scrambling to shore up her fragments against the tide of time.

Sifting through her collection, trying to piece together fragments of her life, was like looking at the messy underside of an embroidery sampler. Inside the first box was a series of slim foolscap diaries, covered in wrapping paper: candy stripes, Aboriginal motifs, tall ships, daisies. On top was a yearbook, which outlined Hill's colour-coding for her notebooks: 'Yellow – Central deserts. Inland sea. Aboriginal road, Blue with galleons – W.A. pearling/ Broome, Daisies – Daisy, Aboriginal folk lore – red and black', and so forth. She constructed typologies, prefacing a New Index Work Book: 'Folk Lore Lists and Synopses, of my own gathering throughout Australia, to be classified into aboriginal and white Australia.' A spreader as well as a cataloguer, her mind flew off at tangents – 'Folk-Lore: Wonders, Explorers, Opals – Harlequinade. Sapphire, Feathers' – as if she couldn't channel her thoughts about the country. My heart lurched in my chest. It was hard not to feel the pathos of a once-celebrated journalist wrapping up her treasures in Christmas paper, but it seemed like crazy old lady territory, the rambling logic of a near vagrant woman.

Hill's fortunes were waning by the time she left for Streaky Bay in 1947. She had already published four travelogues and a novel; *The Territory* came out in 1951 and her last book, *Kabbarli*, a memoir of Bates, a year after her death in 1972. These last two volumes bookended two decades in which she puddled about, writing notes for various projects, redrafting chapters of novels she promised would be her best yet. Most of the Hill collection's material is from this period. Her correspondence depicts a writer, boxed up in a guesthouse or hotel room, wiring friends and relatives for money, fending off publishers' requests for completed manuscripts: 'No good collecting and collecting – they want the books.'

Introduction

She struggled with emphysema and 'nervous dyspepsia, also a puffiness and at times a weariness and melancholy submission to circumstance'. Reading her letters from these years, I was confronted with the boredom, the repetitiveness of much of her life. The Great Australian Monotony. Her words, not mine: one of the titles she floated in her notes for *The Great Australian Loneliness*.

In her final years, Hill struggled to preserve her 'sixty years of travel and memories within Australia … to leave a picture of my native land as close as possible to truth'. She'd always been 'an avid collector … of words – notes of stories, of historical data, of personalities, natural history, descriptions of the country', which accompanied her in trunks wherever she went.[17] Hill feared leaving behind 'sixty years of fragments that nobody can make out fully' and contemplated seeking assistance of the sort the Commonwealth government had given Bates to archive her manuscripts in Canberra, telling Bob Hill her material was 'too good for Australia to be left behind or thrown out'.[18] Her desire to give her notes a significant resting place after her death indicates she thought that it was, like Bates's collection, in the national interest.

As I read Bates's letters urging Ernestine to help write up her observations of camping with Aboriginal people 'to note for future Australians', they suggested a key to understanding Hill's desire to shore up her own sixty years of fragments. In *The Many Worlds of RH Mathews*, historian Martin Thomas uses the word 'ethnomania' to describe the 'frantic energy' that gripped laypeople such as Mathews and Bates in the early 20th century in studying races and civilisations before anthropology was institutionalised as a discipline in Australia.[19] Hill caught the ethnomanic impulse from Bates, who claimed she'd been 'bitten with the virus of research'.[20]

Despite protesting she was 'no anthropologist', Ernestine felt a similar urgency about preserving 'these stray notes of mine' which she'd gathered 'mainly from blacks and from a few observant whites in many days and many ways of roaming', because of what she'd witnessed during the decades after roads, railway and telegraph lines had scored the continent, disrupting Aboriginal dreaming tracks and country.[21] In *The Great Australian Loneliness*, she recalls sitting 'on an upturned petrol tin under the stars', attempting to capture corroboree dances before they disappeared: 'there was always something to scribble in my note-book by the light of those crackling fires'.[22] She did not restrict herself to observations of Aboriginal people; her stories included the 'shirtless philosophers' – pioneering bushmen. 'I have magnificent and incredible copy of the old days and these,' she wrote. 'It is incredible the way these people are left. I must write their stories, the story of the great sandhills, in a novel.'[23] She sought to capture the essence of an Australia she thought was quickly passing but had universal resonances that needed to be preserved as a Great Australian Imaginary or bicultural dreaming.

Hill's project, like Bates's before her, was audacious; I was intrigued, if disquieted, by their sense of a mandate for their ethnomanic activities. The idea that they must play scribe for Aboriginal people was framed by their era's self-justificatory belief that colonisation was inevitable because the First Australians were dying out. Neither woman was trained in anthropology or any similar discipline, yet they thought they could distil the essence of another culture to ground a fledgling national identity. Who does that? I asked myself. At the same time, I could not help admiring their nomadic chutzpah and the extreme lengths they went to, to accomplish their creative and intellectual ventures. What kind of woman, especially in the early 20th century, crosses the country by caravan or camel, or camps by a railway siding on the Nullarbor?

Introduction

Originally, I'd been drawn to the Hill collection to understand what had driven Ernestine's compulsive wandering through remote Australia, but its material hadn't yielded the answers to questions or disclosed the secrets that I'd expected. Instead, Hill's friendship with Bates had emerged as a way of interpreting the salvage operation of Australia's tangled Aboriginal and settler history Ernestine hoped to accomplish by archiving her recollections from her roaming. But I was nervous about Hill's alliance with the disconcerting Daisy Bates, whom she later described as 'a queerly difficult woman', and what seemed like Daisy's thrall over her. I remembered Bates from a Women's Studies course on anthropology in which I'd learned that while she had been 'first in her field', pioneering ethnographic fieldwork for women like Olive Pink and Ursula McConnel, she was an embarrassment to the sisterhood, someone to be mentioned with a shudder because of the misery she'd inflicted on the people she purported to serve.

Anthropologist Isobel White told a story about Bates drawn from her fieldwork at Yalata Aboriginal Reserve on the Great Australian Bight during the 1970s that illustrates these tensions for settler feminist scholars. Some older people at Yalata had been brought down from Ooldea during the Maralinga testing in the 1950s. When she asked them about Bates, she was disappointed by their focus on her eccentricities – 'the curious figure she cut with her old-fashioned clothes and her parasol'. Even worse, one day 'when we were talking about her, I realised that the children were dancing around us reciting "Daidj Bate mamu". Mamu means ghost or devil, which suggested to me that Mrs Bates's name was used to scare the children as a sort of bogey!'[24]

This discomfiting picture of the earnest white female anthropologist who finds her discipline's foremother is the subject of Aboriginal children's taunts presents the conundrum of Bates. A woman of science and a nonconformist who lived alongside

Aboriginal people unseen by the usual eyes reserved for white women in her era, Bates commands some respect for her perspicacity as a trailblazer for European feminists and anthropologists. She attracted derision not only because of her idiosyncrasies, her anachronistic Victorian attire and high-handed ways, but more seriously because of her active loathing of mixed-descent children and her scandalous reporting on Aboriginal cultural practices. Most notoriously, Bates published stories contending that Aboriginal people practised cannibalism – a claim that was contested and discredited within her own era.

For Ernestine Hill, jumping the train at Ooldea one searing day in 1932, 'the little Dresden figure and the moving tent were a surprise in the primeval scene, a question mark'.[25] Like others of her era, she was preoccupied with questions of what kinds of existence were possible for women – typically European ones – in Australia's vast open spaces, which were thought unfit for 'civilised' habitation. If any woman epitomised outback self-sufficiency for her, it was Bates, living in apparent solitude by a remote railway siding. Gaining an audience with the bluestocking at Ooldea was more than an opportunity for a scoop for Hill; it marked the beginning of a lifelong obsession, although she later distanced herself from aspects of Bates's views about Aboriginal people. The ideal Ernestine Hill presented in her writing of 'a woman always alone' on the desert's rim, and indeed of her ever-mobile self with her typewriter, suitcase and swag, crested a wave of women who travelled, worked and lived, sometimes in pairs – as nurses, teachers and missionaries – in outback Australia last century. Their activities spearheaded a phenomenon, in which I've participated, of secular missionaries who set out to do good in remote areas, often in Aboriginal communities.

Uncomfortable though Bates's and Hill's legacies were, I was curious about how they may have shaped perceptions and experiences of remote life, especially for women. How had they, and other women like them, made their way in isolated and remote areas when roads, railway and telegraph lines had just been laid? More to the point, how had these women grounded themselves not just physically but psychologically in the 'loneliness'? Although Hill and Bates's friendship had been intense and volatile, as I was to discover, it had nevertheless been a significant source of connection and support for them both, not least in their literary and ethnographic pursuits. Had similar alliances and connections sustained other women in remote Australia? How had Bates's and Hill's activities and writing influenced generations of settler women encountering the 'otherness' of Australia?

These lines of inquiry led me to Hill's then Bates's archives, and later back to remote Australia to visit some of the places they'd inhabited. Although I'd travelled throughout northern and central Australia, I hadn't spent much time in the south-west, so I hired a campervan, planning to follow Hill's route when she visited Bates at Streaky Bay before crossing the Nullarbor. I was curious to see what might remain of Bates's Ooldea campsite and whether it was as remote and desolate as Hill had reported. Was Daisy a woman alone, as Ernestine insisted, on the desert's rim, and how had she managed, given her age and deteriorating health? I wondered whether anyone, Aboriginal or otherwise, who had met these women was still alive and whether they might have memories and reflections to share. Travelling west out of Melbourne, I hoped to gain insights into how Hill and Bates had sustained themselves and what imprints they'd left for other women in negotiating what they called the country's loneliness.

I | WANDERING

1
A confirmed wanderer

*'I was a confirmed wanderer,
a nomad even as the aborigines.'*[1]

Ernestine Hill kicks off *The Great Australian Loneliness* with a gust of bravado, describing the many conveyances in which she travelled across 'the painted deserts and the pearling seas, by aeroplane and camel and coastal-ship, by truck and lugger and packhorse team and private yacht ... across five years and 50,000 miles, a trail of infinite surprises'.[2] A caravan isn't mentioned on this list, although it's one of her most iconic modes of transport, probably because of the well-known photograph in which she appears, a stern-faced wraith in a pants suit in front of an old-style teardrop van framed by a large gum. But she didn't travel in one until she was in her late forties and then only for a couple of years. In my drive across the Nullarbor, I wanted to catch a glimmer of what it had been like for Bates roughing it in her tent and Hill swagging it on the road, though, being of a similar age to Hill when she purchased her van, I was perhaps more attracted to caravanning. I did have a swag – indeed, I prefer sleeping in one under the stars to a tent's fuggy, claustrophobic atmosphere – but I'd only ever camped with friends. Several years earlier I'd ridden a mountain bike on the Gibb River Road from Kununurra to Derby with a friend from Alice, and we'd slept by creeks or the side of the road in sleeping bags on thermarests we carried in trailers behind our bikes. But although my journey wasn't as long, risky or rugged as any of Bates's or Hill's had been, I wasn't game to commit to such a flimsy and precarious existence over a long period by myself.

    I shopped around online for a van I could afford to hire and found a company that rented out older models cheaply. My designated vehicle was an early noughties Toyota HiAce Hi-Top camper on the verge of retirement, which came with a few challenges. I spent an anxious ten minutes after leaving the hire company's office, driving the van around the backstreets, trying to get used to this new snail shell's dimensions before taking it onto the highway. I had to heft half my body weight into putting it into first gear or reverse, which was disconcerting in city traffic. The lock on the driver's door was so worn it needed to be jemmied open with the key. But it was marvellously handy; a cubbyhouse on wheels, as caravanning poet Beth Spencer puts it.[3] You could stop almost anywhere to boil a kettle or make a meal. The end-of-the-day rigmarole associated with camping of choosing a site, pitching a tent then building a fire to cook dinner was greatly reduced. I folded down the van's main bed permanently (the pull-out table was too old and erratic to grapple with), and it became a comfortable haven where I could read my Kindle or watch a DVD on my laptop at night. It also provided a ready-made cubicle in which to write, although as a taller person I often tired of its ergonomics. After typing for a while lying on my stomach on the fold-out bed, I'd shift to work in a café, a roadhouse or against the comforting white noise of machines churning in a laundromat. But the van combined a basic level of domestic comfort with greater proximity to the natural environment than most motels and roadhouses offered; even at a caravan park, you could often score a site abutting a beach, lake or bushland.

    'A glorious thing it is to live in a tent in the infinite,' Daisy cries in *The Passing of the Aborigines*. Was I glamping it, I wondered, travelling in a van rather than camping in a tent like Bates, who eschewed the many conveniences of the Hills's caravan when they arrived at Streaky Bay. Or like Ernestine, who unfurled her swag, 'foam weltering over me', on the deck of a lugger that was 'practically falling to pieces' while sailing round the Gulf of Carpentaria?[4] 'Caravanning is not camping,' historian Bill Garner states in *Born in a Tent*. Originally marketed 'by appeals to luxury and "all the conveniences of home"'

> A caravan is a permanent structure built to defeat the weather in a way that a tent never can. It is designed to be able to separate the occupants from both the environment and their neighbours. Cooking and washing take place inside and the van has a rigid, lockable perimeter. It is a small house on wheels.[5]

It was exactly because I wanted the protection of a van's 'rigid, lockable perimeter' that I didn't simply pack a tent in my bike panniers or my runabout's boot. As a lone woman, caravanning appealed to me as a safe, pragmatic and economic way of travelling autonomously, of avoiding being locked into scheduled bookings and potentially pricey but uninspiring accommodation. Hill also admired the comfort and convenience of caravan life. 'Having suffered all sorts of strain and stress,' she wrote, 'bumpy roads and windy camps and knocking at desolate doors after 200 miles and more in the day to be told "no accommodation," and this for a long long time – we now have a pleasant little caravan.'[6] Like her, I found it offered 'a great little shelter from the winds that blow',[7] especially in the south-west, when my trip was punctuated by storms. But the overwhelming reason I chose a van over a tent wasn't shelter or convenience but because it might afford a modicum of protection from the things women worry about – or are cautioned to – casting about by themselves.

Late one September after a winter of rain, I headed west out of Melbourne in the campervan. Across the first border, I found the South Australian fields much lusher than my memory of the silvery pale-green haze of crops on dry plains. This all changed when I joined the Eyre Highway and began passing through low flat-topped hills edged with saltbush plains. The landscape had an uneasy sense of familiarity: it was enough like central Australia for me to feel a guilty tug, as if bumping into a relative I hadn't seen for a while. The Eyre was not as lonely or isolated as roads I'd driven in the Territory. Vans, Winnebagos and motorhomes toiled along what had been a dirt highway when the Hills bumped their buggy and caravan over it in the late 1940s. Various governments tarmacked strips but the new Eyre wasn't completely sealed from Port Augusta to Norseman until after Hill's death. The old Eyre, the 'struggle of self-made road' she saw from the Trans in 1930, still runs rogue as a four-wheel-drive track from the Nullarbor Roadhouse to the Western Australian border.[8]

I was planning to trace the route Hill had taken when she'd visited Bates in 1947, detouring to Streaky Bay before crossing the Nullarbor to Perth, a distance I'd never travelled before by road. I'd entertained thoughts of using 'Australia's Home', the notes for a travel book Ernestine had been trying to write on her trip, as a guide, although it petered out, narratively disappointed perhaps by Bates's lack of fitness to join the Hills. My interest had also been piqued by photographs from their journey in 'Along the Eyre Highway with Ernestine Hill', an online album featuring arresting black-and-white images of desolate rocks, solitary stone cottages marooned in sand, the Hills's caravan ploughing through tundra-like shrubs and of Perth friend, Henrietta Drake-Brockman, waving from a sweep of dune.[9]

Nothing prepared me, however, for the Great Australian Bight's ferocious beauty. I had my first glimpse of the Bight at Streaky Bay, where I drove straight from Adelaide, cutting across the top of the Eyre Peninsula, before swinging out from the main highway to the coast. Streaky Bay is itself a handsome town, with elegant, well-preserved sandstone buildings, including the original hotels where Bates stayed, flanking a grid of waterfront streets leading down to a jetty. A dusky mantle of cloud was settling over the bay when I arrived, pink and mauve tones stippling the corrugated sands beneath its broad watery flats, the inspiration for the name Flinders gave it from the *Investigator* in 1802: 'And the water was much discoloured in Streaks … and I called it Streaky Bay.'[10]

Before leaving Melbourne, I'd sought directions over the phone from a local at Streaky Bay's museum to the farmhouse at nearby Westall where the Hills had visited Bates in exile, as it were, after receiving her woebegone entreaties to rescue her. The local said the farmhouse was about 20 kilometres out of town but easy enough to find at the end of the first left-hand turn-off on Westall Way Loop.

I drove out to Westall on a firm sandy road cutting through salt lakes glinting like mirrors in the softening light, pocked with dark maroon tussocks of grass like sea anemones and hemmed with banks of barley bowing in the breeze. Swerving onto what I thought was the correct turn-off, I found myself ploughing up a dirt track with jagged limestone protruding from corrugations, almost running my vehicle aground. Barbed wire fences bounded the crops, but I couldn't see any sign of a stone cottage. Waves broke on wide beaches edged with granite below the headland. Bob, who'd tagged along after a farmer on his rounds, trying to paint some watercolours, described how 'the cliffs ran down in rust red colours to the turquoise shallows'.[11] The water retained its aqua tones, but the stony shoreline was blanched beneath the greying sky; the colour contrast would be more dramatic in sharp daylight.

Then I realised I'd driven in the wrong direction: the farmhouse was probably on the other side of the loop. I backed down onto Westall Way and continued circling cautiously, cursing myself for my dreadful habit of trying to cram too much into any allotted time. Light was fading; the area would soon be wrapped in darkness. I wondered how much I'd be able to see. I drove past a couple of resorts and eco-farms, as well as more conventional agricultural properties, often with signs forbidding entry. When I'd almost completed the loop, I flagged down a farmer on a tractor and asked for directions.

I wasn't far off, the farmer said. He pointed out a road that was little more than muddy tyre tracks through the paddocks. At its end, a rusted old Dodge truck and a weather-beaten rowboat were marooned among the nodding, yellow heads of barley in front of a boxy blond sandstone cottage. Glassless windows, like empty eye sockets, stared seawards; strips of corrugated iron flanked the remnants of a main door. I walked around the side of the house, looking for a safe entry point and for where Bates might have stayed, peering through a pane-less window into a small room with old bed bases propped against the fireplace's carved wooden frame, floorboards splintering around them like Blitz rubble. I didn't fancy my chances of a safe landing if I scrambled through the window frame. I continued to the back, where I found a door hanging from one rusty hinge, and picked my way inside the house past an old generator and a peeling set of doors. Hardly any floorboards were left beyond the remaining struts of the hallway, white-anted no doubt for firewood. I edged into abandoned rooms, trying to map out the likely patterns of habitation: the living-room-cum-kitchen with its wide fireplace, where Bates boiled tea before anyone rose, and the small, poky rooms out the back where the farmer's children had slept. Most of the iron roof was still intact; strips of browning plaster hung from beams, waving like disconsolate pennants in the evening breeze: go back! The ghosts have long departed.

Behind the farmhouse, I found the raised stone-and-concrete foundations of another dwelling, a shed or perhaps a sleep-out tacked on like an afterthought. Was it the remains of something similar to the iron shed where Daisy had waited in death's anteroom, drinking tea, consorting with Dickens's characters, reciting Irish rhymes from her childhood or Bibbulmun lore, aware that not only Aboriginal life as she'd witnessed it but the ways of the Victorians, her own generation, were passing?

My next port of call was the Streaky Bay National Trust Museum, where I'd organised to meet Rae Brewster, the local who'd given me directions to Westall over the phone. The museum is an early 20th-century sandstone schoolhouse, and holds some Bates material along with other memorabilia from the town's history. Most of Bates's personal effects, much of which I'd seen, have been dispersed to institutions in Adelaide and Canberra and I was more interested in meeting Rae herself, who remembered both Ernestine and Daisy from her teenage years, when she'd worked as a sandwich hand in the local delicatessen in the late 1940s. Bates had been a familiar figure about town, once giving young Rae a pound of apples for helping her cross the road because she was too blind to see where she was going. Rae had also served the Hills when they came into the deli one day with Daisy and their dog, Jarrah. Ernestine had described researching *My Love Must Wait* to Rae, who admitted she still had the book at home but had never finished it because she 'found it heavy going'.

Rae Brewster was easily identifiable at the museum: a short, bluff woman with white powder puff hair and cornflower blue eyes, the sort that become more piercing with age. Clearly the lifeblood of the place, she was holding court among several mid-aged volunteers behind the counter when I entered, which impressed me, given she must have been in her early eighties. Once I'd introduced myself, she told me that many came to the museum because they were interested in Daisy Bates. Only recently, when some Aboriginal people from Western Australia had visited, they'd said, 'She didn't do a whole lot for us.' She doubted any of the Aboriginal locals had direct memories of Daisy Bates; most of those who'd known her were probably dead.

Another of the volunteers, who'd had some contact with local Aboriginal people, added that the current generation didn't much like Bates. 'They hate her. It was because of her emphasis on the pure blood, you see. She used to play favourites against each other and cut dead half-caste people in the street.'

Rae led me to some display cases in another room where some oddments from Bates's tent life were corralled: a walking stick, an Arthur Mee book, a small book of days, a kerosene lamp, a fan, a pocketbook and some knick-knacks. The most striking items were Daisy's clothes: a stiff black jacket and a long skirt with huge hooks and stays, and an ankle-length, grey-green gabardine overcoat that she'd worn around Adelaide. The skirt's waist was about the width of my hand span: it would hardly fit any of my friends' primary-school-age children. Daisy was malnourished when she was treated in hospital in the mid-1940s, but the slightness of her frame also spoke of her impoverished childhood, born on the back of the Great Famine in Ireland, in 1859.

Rae's eyes were red-rimmed and she spoke with a slight tremor; she'd had a virus for two weeks. She wound up her spiel diplomatically by declaring Daisy an 'enigma': a word some researchers use when they hit a roadblock to explaining the tangle of motivations and circumstances behind Bates's life course. Then she paused, leaning on a display case.

'Vida Thompson had guests for dinner once,' she said, 'and Daisy Bates told them a story about an Aboriginal mother eating her baby! About how she was scared the woman would eat another child when she left the camp.'

The Thompsons were one of the families with whom Bates boarded at Streaky Bay. I imagined Daisy, then in her late eighties, taking centre stage at the kitchen table, with her hollowed-out eyes and mad tumbleweed of hair, rattling Mrs Thompson's respectable visitors with some gruesome, exotic Other tales. I'd first read one of these stories in Bates's letters to Ernestine: Daisy kept looping back to Hill's visit to Ooldea in 1932, reminding her of how she 'barged in from the skies – that fine day & were here to help Minmilla who had killed & eaten her baby', as if the memory of this repellent tale would entice her to visit.[12] I hadn't been sure what to make of it; Bates's letters were so rambling, repetitive and circuitous, I'd wondered whether she was suffering from dementia. I'd hoped the cannibal story was something of a delusional aberration, but when I read Bates's correspondence to anthropologists, chief scientists, bishops and state premiers during the 1920s and 1930s, I found it was a constant preoccupation of hers while she was at Ooldea.

'I don't know whether that story's true or not,' Rae said.

'A lot of people didn't think it was true at the time,' I said, 'and said so publicly.'

'Why would she say a thing like that then? It's very distressing.'

'I think she began peddling these tales because she was running out of money. It was a way of drawing attention to her situation at Ooldea – of how dire circumstances were along the East–West line.'

'Daisy thought she was special,' Rae said. 'She thought the government should pay for her. She wanted recognition.'

My guide was flagging. She wanted to sit down and have a cup of tea; I could hardly blame her and besides it's what Hill and Bates would have recommended. I returned to browsing the displays. Rae was from my mother's generation, and beneath her invective about Daisy I heard the plain-spoken stoicism of those born between the wars: that one should not think more highly of oneself than one ought. But I was glad she used the word 'recognition'. I'd reached the same conclusion after reading Bates's correspondence: that more than anything else, she wanted recognition.

Bates had lobbied to be acknowledged and paid for her work with Aboriginal people under various titles – Woman Justice, Woman Inspector, Protectress, Woman Protector – at first at Eucla in Western Australia, where she'd been appointed an honorary protector in 1912, and later in South Australia as she shifted her camps further along the Bight. She had supporters, women's societies prominent among them, who'd been petitioning the same authorities since 1912. I'd seen a thick wad of letters in South Australian Records from people and organisations as diverse as Bishop Gibney of Perth, the Catholic Women's League, the Travellers' Aid Society, the Women's National Club, the Women's Christian Temperance Union, and the Women's Non-Party ~~Political~~ Association of SA (they dropped 'Political' to underline their lack of partisanship but were too frugal to invest in new letterhead). Beneath Bates's attention-seeking antics is the cry of the self-taught woman who fought to gain equivalent acknowledgement of her work by her male contemporaries. But it hardly warrants putting about nasty scuttlebutt about people whose best interests she claimed to have at heart, such as the story of Minmilla. Indeed, why would she say such a thing?

A confirmed wanderer

In 1899 Bates had stepped off the SS *Stuttgart* onto the Fremantle docks, boasting that she had a commission from the London *Times* to investigate allegations that pastoralists were mistreating Aboriginal people in north-west Australia. Her curiosity had been seeded by a letter to its editor from an Englishman, describing the brutality he'd witnessed while working in the north-west. No record of a formal assignment from the *Times* exists; it seems Bates volunteered to write an article on the subject, saying she was a journalist bound for Western Australia. This hint of a potential scoop also gave her a grand cue for re-entering the country.

It wasn't Daisy's first time in Australia: she had a husband there, a stockman named Jack Bates, and a teenage son, Arnold, who was in a Perth boarding school. She'd seen neither for five years. Jack had written, urging her to return, saying he'd set his sights on some pastoral leases up north. Bates had been in London on a mental health break of sorts. Her funds had quickly run low, and to support herself she'd found work as an assistant to WT Stead, the editor of the *Review of Reviews*, an acclaimed literary and political monthly. He'd recognised her mental and verbal ability, and offered her a stint as a subeditor on *Borderland*, a journal of psychic research he published. A strong-willed, sharp-thinking woman, Daisy had no truck with its contents but took the job for the opportunity it presented – an apprenticeship as a reporter.

Arriving in Perth, Daisy contrived to find a Parisian tailor, whom she ordered to whip up an ensemble, one that wouldn't date and in which she could greet royalty, suitable for her new life. Early in 1900, she freighted a horse and buggy on a lugger, which she accompanied up the west coast to Roebourne, where she met Jack, who'd travelled ahead of them. They drove for 800 miles, visiting properties, Daisy becoming that rare creature, one of the first white women to broach the Kimberley. Six months later she'd laid her original mission to rest, reporting to the *Times* that she'd found no signs of deliberate cruelty in pastoralists' treatment of Aboriginal people in the north-west.

Resting afterwards at a Roebuck Plains Station, Bates became fascinated by the intricacies of the kinship system regulating family relationships among Aboriginal people. Observing how the Yawuru people had classified local settlers within this system, she was delighted when they gave her a 'skin' name, affiliating her with a kinship group. Later in the year, she travelled up to Beagle Bay on the Dampier Peninsula in response to a commission from Bishop Matthew Gibney to write a series of articles about the Trappist mission he'd established there ten years earlier. Dean Martelli, an Italian priest, whom she'd met on the SS *Stuttgart*'s decks, had introduced her to Gibney in Perth. Bates stayed with the monks in a peculiar dispensation granted by the abbot, since 'no woman except a queen could be allowed within its walls'.[13] She was not too queenly for hard work; she took a hoe and tilled sugarcane and banana plantations with the monks and Aboriginal people. Toiling alongside her, they explained more of the local kinship system's complexities to her. She was intrigued, her interest flaming into passion.

She returned to Perth where the WA registrar-general offered her a job in 1904 collating information about local languages and practices from a questionnaire that had been despatched to police, station owners, missioners and postmasters across the state. It was a 'Vanishing race' initiative: since 'West Australia possessed no standard literature of her fast fading aboriginal population, it was deemed desirable that a work should be compiled from all the existing records which should stand as a book of reference for ethnologists and philologists in their study of our interesting aborigines.'[14] Bates found the quality of the surveys variable, complaining they hadn't been completed meticulously enough and that there were discrepancies between them. Offering to undertake a mop-up operation, she spent eight months riding across the south-west as far as Laverton: 'wherever there was a strange dialect, I filled in the vocabulary as best I could in the limited time at my disposal. The result is the acquisition of some 40 dialects, all of which will be of infinite value to the philological world.'[15] She proposed writing a grander work – a comprehensive grammar and vocabulary of the tribes of Western Australia before they passed into memory, although she couldn't present a faithful record without going into the field herself. The premier, John Forrest, who'd grown up among Nyoongar people near Bunbury, was sympathetic to her plans. He not only approved her request to camp with the remaining 'derelicts', as they were called, at Ma'amba Reserve on Perth's outskirts, but sent men with canvas to erect her first tent.

'I was specially fortunate in mastering my ABC amongst the remnants of these groups,' Bates wrote. Daily she listened to Joobaitch, the '1st Perth native man & last of his Area Group', and his niece, Fanny Balbuk, jotting down all she could glean about Bibbulmun culture.[16] She camped alongside them for a winter and a summer, 'until privation brought on congestion of the lungs', a shadow of the reason she'd left Ireland in 1882: a spot on a lung that might have been tuberculosis, the disease that had killed her mother when Daisy was only four.[17] Still, she tended to ride herself hard, taking little care for practical matters like when she might rest or what she might eat. RH Mathews, an east coast surveyor who had, like her, become addicted to observing the first Australians' ways, chastised her once for living on 'biscuits etc'. 'You were too enthusiastic in your work that you knocked yourself about too much and did not get proper food …' he wrote in 1907. 'The next time you go camping you should take more care of yourself and have good nourishing food.'[18]

After five weeks' absence, Bates returned to Ma'amba Reserve to collect material for a paper she was researching on kinship subdivisions among the south-west Australian natives. It was read out on her behalf at a Royal Geographical Society meeting in London and later published, bringing her work to the attention of anthropologist Northcote Thomas and folklorist Andrew Lang in England, who offered to revise her book for publication. 'It is ahead of every other work on the Australian aborigines,' Bates wrote.[19] Anthropology was in its early days as an academic discipline, and its overwhelmingly male professional practitioners in institutional settings used second-hand reports such as questionnaires or made only brief visits to reserves, unlike amateur folk ethnologists like Bates and Mathews. Daisy had no qualms about self-promotion and thought her practices gave her research greater veracity, arguing that she had 'lived amongst the natives and with them, not for a month or so, but for years, and so the work will have the native personal tone that all previous works have missed'.[20]

The Western Australian government had only given Bates a minor clerk's salary to assemble the vocabularies, and she requested a further £200 to complete the manuscript. Instead, they offered her a new post as protector of Aborigines on the Great Australian Bight in 1912. It was honorary and unpaid, but the Karrakatta Bibbulmun, the custodians of the Swan River, were dying, Balbuk and Joobaitch among them. Attracted by the opportunity to spend time with Aboriginal people further south-east, whose lives and culture were potentially more traditional than those around Perth, she steamed off to Eucla, a telegraph station and port on the Bight near the South Australian border, declaring herself a 'confirmed wanderer, a nomad even as the aborigines'.[21] She camped in a clump of mallee near the telegraph line, 2 miles west of the tiny township, so as not to be too 'far away from civilisation – of sorts' yet close enough to Aboriginal people gathering in the area to resume her observations.[22]

Two years later she thundered across the Bight in a camel buggy driven by an Aboriginal woman, Gauera, and her fourteenth husband (yet another husband joined them along the way) to the eastern port of Fowlers Bay. She sailed to Adelaide to deliver an address on Aboriginal social networks at the conference of the British Association for the Advancement of Science. Women's organisations thronged her with speaking invitations, and she appeared before the Royal Commission into the condition of Aborigines in South Australia.

No, Bates told the Royal Commission, she did not think that Aboriginal people benefited from being in contact with white civilisation; it was 'much better for the natives to be left by themselves'.[23]

Had she any thought of bettering their conditions or bringing them to a better state of life?

> I think I have. I have just adopted them. It seems to me they are my poor relations. I am not missionising. I make my own life amongst them and they cannot help being moral when I am in the camp … they think my being as decent as I am amongst them is due to the fact that I must have been a native some time ago.[24]

She lobbied for a camel buggy so she could continue her work, riding from camp to camp, arguing the sheer presence of a white woman would prevent the immorality – prostitution, disease, drunkenness – occurring as Aboriginal women came in contact with European men. Backtracking 400 kilometres to Eucla to collect her canvas and paraphernalia, she rode back across the Bight to pitch her tents near Fowlers Bay, waiting while South Australian women's guilds lobbied her cause. But neither a paid protectorate nor a camel buggy was forthcoming. Bates shuffled her tents about this accusing finger of a promontory for the next five years, pitching herself as a protector to various governments.

'Her work was and is largely "hush-hush" work,' she stated in a pamphlet to promote herself to Adelaide worthies, writing in the third person to create an aura of objectivity, 'yet she always felt she was doing Empire work even when tending the sick or burying the dead.'[25]

Her focus shifted beyond social observation and learning languages to caring for 'my natives', as she called them, a term commonly used in the decades around the turn of the 20th century by white officialdom to refer to Aboriginal people. The SA government gave her rations to distribute in the country around Fowlers Bay and further west on the Bight. She began making more dramatic statements about the turn her work was taking among local Aboriginal people. Once she nursed a young woman dying from venereal disease, dosing her with brandy to numb the pain. Another time, she chased after a demented, blind man who'd wandered off into the bush and slung all 6 foot of him over her narrow shoulders, carrying him back to her camp where he died. Later she claimed that she'd dug a grave for him all by herself.

Drained of funds and living on the barest of essentials, her health broke in 1919, so she took a brief respite in Adelaide. Her marriage to Jack Bates had dissolved after her foray to the north-west; they had never officially parted but he'd stayed up north, managing properties, after she returned to Perth in 1902. He'd signed over several pastoral leases to her, but any income she received from them dribbled away over time. She eked out a living, dashing off newspaper articles about aspects of remote Aboriginal life such as native shepherding, astronomy, myths and rainmaking.

Increasingly her reports had become smoke flares of anxiety from the Bight, with titles like 'More about the Aborigines. Why they are dying out.'[26]

In 1919 William South, the chief protector of Aborigines in South Australia, offered her a position as matron of a convalescent home in Adelaide for wounded soldiers returning from the Great War. It was a cushy option after living rough for over a decade and her only paid appointment. South may have hoped to put her out of the game – she was sixty, he and his successor deemed her 'now old and feeble and suffer[ing] from bad sight'.[27] But Bates could never endure city life for long and she tired quickly of 'matronage'. Hearing rumours that Aboriginal children were begging along the recently constructed East–West Line, especially near the large siding at Ooldea where the two spans of the rail from Kalgoorlie and Port Augusta had met in 1917, she decided to take the situation in hand. What the place needed, she thought, was 'a woman J.P. installed just as a mild deterrent'.[28] In September 1919, she shipped her canvases, trunks and tin hatboxes along with her ageing but relentless self on the train up to Ooldea.

Anthony Bolam, the stationmaster at Ooldea, snapped a photograph of Bates at her new camp south of the railway tracks. A group of Aboriginal people, some sitting and squatting, some standing, are framed in her tent fly like a family portrait. Daisy stands off to one side, slightly stooped, arms outstretched as if in benediction.

Not long after she arrived, Bates began petitioning South Australian authorities – the premier, the chief protector and the commissioner of public works – to give her rations to dispense to Aboriginal people at Ooldea. Anangu were gathering by the station, humbugging passengers on the train because they were starving, she told them, having found Yuldilgabbi, the large soak a mile or so away, drained of its resources. She alone was attending to their needs, handing out flour and old clothes from her paltry supplies, spending her own scant funds on their welfare.

South had provided rations for the police to dole out at Ooldea and neighbouring sidings six months earlier. When he asked whether there was any substance to Bates's claims, the local constable tartly replied: 'I see them almost every day, and find none sorely in need of care and attention, as Mrs Bates puts it.' She, on the other hand, was 'scarcely doing anything for the Natives but … all she possibly can to tempt them to camp in the vicinity of her camp … by telling them that she is the one in authority over the Natives'.[29]

'My main concern is to make their passing as easy as it is in my power to make it,' Bates wrote, 'to give them a little heaven on earth, so that at the moment of their passing I commend them to my Father.'[30] Words that reflect official late 19th- and early 20th-century protection era policy that Aboriginal people were a primitive and therefore doomed race, and needed to be looked after in the face of encroaching white civilisation. This approach was encapsulated by the phrase, 'smoothing the pillow of the dying race', popularly attributed to Bates but coined by a missionary, JS Needham, in 1925.[31]

Others, like the local constable at Ooldea, were unconvinced that Bates's ministrations were necessary. Several years earlier when she'd requested her protectorate at Eucla be subsidised to extend east across the Bight to Fowlers or Streaky Bay, South had mooted paying her £2 per week. Pastor Wiebusch, the superintendent of Koonibba mission near Ceduna, challenged this proposal, saying that police officers stationed on the Bight did more for Aboriginal people than Mrs Bates, who 'encouraged idleness, instead of teaching them to earn their own living'. Rather than dying out, Aboriginal people were making their own livelihood by hunting, and selling pelts and artefacts along the line. Like the local constable and railway officials, Wiebusch thought Bates's protectionist approach encouraged dependency rather than self-sufficiency. Others, such as a visiting missionary, suggested Bates's own pillow needed smoothing: 'When I saw her at Ooldea three years since she was nearly blind and needing care and protection herself.'[32]

South was suspicious and visited the line in 1920 to investigate these claims. Bates had shifted her tents north of the siding to Yuldilgabbi to be closer to Anangu as they came in from the desert and camped around the soak. South was only too aware of her ambitions and concluded that she was encouraging Aboriginal people 'to infest the lines' so she could observe them for research rather than any humanitarian purposes. Again she pleaded with him for a paid role, this time as protectress of Aboriginals, but he was not to be swayed, instead warning the minister and the commissioner for public works against giving her rations: 'I fear Mrs. Bates is inducing the aborigines to muster at Ooldea for the purpose of furthering her requests for an appointment in the Department.'[33]

Then there was the matter of her outlandish claims: 'Mrs. Bates has written some astounding articles for the press concerning cannibalism among the Aboriginals and in letters to many influential people even to His Majesty the King has stressed the cannibalistic habits of the natives,' the SA chief protector wrote the year before Ernestine Hill's visit to Ooldea. 'Her reports are not corroborated by other writers and authorities and I think it would be very unwise to grant her an appointment and so give official status to her extravagant statements.'[34]

During his 'wanderings in wild Australia', anthropologist Charles Mountford encountered Aṉangu at Ooldea. Recalling Bates's stories about their cannibalism in his 1940 diary, he wrote: 'No doubt, [these] brought her a few pounds for articles, and gave some kick to her book, but [were] perfectly untrue. Not that she herself did not hear about it, she undoubtedly did, but with her training as an ethnologist, she knew or should have known that the members of a distant tribe always do all sorts of terrible things, in the minds of the locals.'[35]

He'd heard people at Kata Tjuṯa near Uluru describing the cannibalistic activities of fierce, anthropomorphic ancestral creatures, the Pungalunga men. In *Brown Men and Red Sand*, he recounted how, when he asked Aṉangu during his expeditions to central Australia, 'if any of their tribe had ever eaten human flesh', they recoiled in horror. After denying they'd ever engaged in such a practice, they pointed to other people 'to the south, that live along the railway line' – which included the mobs near Ooldea – indicating they 'were man-eaters, and hunted the tribes to the north of them'.[36] Mountford was unconvinced, musing, 'It is always the distant folk, the foreigners who do the cruel and terrible things.' It was also difficult to 'find out whether one's informants are speaking of the long-distant past or of present-day events', which had 'confused some investigators and convinced them that the eating of human flesh is a normal practice among the aborigines'.[37] Bates was the 'worst offender' when it came to presenting gossip and hearsay as truth. Rather than old and confused, he thought she was wilful and opportunistic.

Bates reported first encountering 'cannibals' during her visit to the Trappist mission at Beagle Bay in an *Australasian* article she published two decades later in 1921. When she asked the abbot whether cannibalism was a local practice, he'd pointed out a woman who had reputedly 'eaten her newborn baby'. Bates's commentary is deadpan but the woman's response sounds like a classic piece of leg-pulling: 'When she was asked how she could kill and eat her wee baby, she replied, "I only ate one, that woman ate three".'[38]

'Is cannibalism known to exist in district?' was one of the questions on the survey that the Western Australian government provided Bates and others in 1904 for collecting Aboriginal vocabularies. Anecdotal reports of cannibalism flared up from a lunatic frontier fringe of sorts during the century's early years, but by the 1920s and 1930s anthropological authorities such as Herbert Basedow, AP Elkin and Ted Strehlow had discounted claims about such practices, with the exception of mortuary rituals performed by some Aboriginal groups.[39] Bates observed in her field notes that 'Cannibalism was a custom, & at certain times & with certain parts of human flesh it was a rite', but it wasn't until she began camping at Ooldea that she persistently advocated this practice was rife across the country.[40]

In 1920 Bates described tracking Nyan-ngauera, a pregnant Aboriginal woman, after she'd left the camps by Ooldea Soak early one morning with her daughter. Nyan-ngauera had eluded Bates, who'd given up after following her for 12 miles, fearing heat exposure, although she later claimed the young woman had given birth then killed and shared the baby with her surviving child. To support her story, she freighted a box of bones to the South Australian Museum, whose staff discounted its contents as the remains of a feral cat. She wrote to JB Cleland, chair of the University of Adelaide's Board for Anthropological Research, in 1930 saying that a woman had eaten her newborn baby at Ooldea, and promised to post him the bones. In another letter, she reported the same incident had occurred 40 kilometres away, although she admitted she hadn't been to the exact site or seen the bones. Cleland was sceptical about her accounts and whether the remains he received were human in origin. Nevertheless, he advised her to parcel up any other suspicious bones and send them to him, which she did in 1932. Historian Tom Gara states that some remains in the museum were identified in 2003 'as being those of a human infant, but there is no documentation relating to them, and it is not known whether they relate to the 1930 incident or another one.'[41] Given the Aboriginal people's precarious situation, battling for food and resources at the depleted soak, there were other plausible causes for the child's death. Bates's assertion that nearly every central desert woman had eaten at least one of her children, Gara writes, can be 'dismissed simply on the basis of population dynamics'.[42] It would have been unsustainable for cannibalism to be such a widespread practice.

Bates was frustrated by the official disavowal of what she saw as a crisis situation, complaining that, despite the evidence she'd posted to the museum, 'the Adelaide Govt like the man who first saw the hippopotamus, still refuses to believe it.'[43] But the authorities took her reports of cannibalism at Ooldea seriously. When Chief Protector South visited the East–West Line in 1920, he concluded that 'No evidence could be obtained from either white or blacks' about these practices.[44] In 1924 the South Australian Aborigines Department sent Constable Lodge, who was stationed at Tarcoola, a larger settlement closer to Port Augusta, to investigate after Bates published another article on the subject, but neither the stationmaster nor the local rations issuer at Ooldea were convinced that any cannibalistic activities had occurred. After Bates's correspondence with Cleland in 1930, the SA police despatched Lodge to Ooldea again. The 'reports are exaggerated', he informed his department, 'all the young gins at the Ooldea camp were carrying healthy looking babies on their backs.'[45]

What was happening on the East–West line?

In 1920 a delegation from the SA Women's Non-Party Association visited Protector South and the commissioner for public works to lobby them on Bates's behalf. None of the women had visited Ooldea, but they'd met and corresponded with Daisy and were concerned that not only were people starving, but about the situation of Aboriginal women and girls. Bates had published an article in the Adelaide *Register* claiming they were becoming prostitutes at Tarcoola station further east on the line, some bearing children to white men. Several years earlier she'd entreated the South Australian government to respond because 'the telegraph master or station owner there will not compel the white men to give up their native women or half-caste children owing to the fear of creation of unfriendly feeling amongst the white men'.[46] Appointing a female protector, she argued, would do away with such an anomaly – a conviction the women's societies shared.

'They are of the opinion that there is no one like a woman to attend to the needs of women and children. They can talk to them where a man could not,' South wrote to the commissioner of public works, who assured the delegation that officials regularly provided local Aboriginal people rations, reminding them of Bates's ambitions – that she was after the position of 'lady protectress'.[47] Privately South told the commissioner that Daisy had misled the Women's Non-Party Association about the rationing situation at Ooldea: 'she is evidently a disappointed [sic] and hysterical woman determined to avenge herself on me and the Ooldea Constable'.[48] Bates had no doubt enlisted women's and other organisations in her campaign to become protector. South's language here is particularly vehement: she'd struck a boys' club raw nerve.

Constance Cooke, the convener of the Women's Non-Party Association's Aboriginal Welfare Committee, travelled on the

Ghan from Adelaide to Oodnadatta in 1926 and was 'appalled by the misery, the want and degradation that I saw' among Aboriginal people.[49] The year before she gave a speech to the Anti-Slavery and Aboriginal Protection Society in London, agitating for the creation of an Aboriginal state to prevent the first Australians from dying out: 'we have taken the land away from the original owners, and reduced them to a state of serfdom.'[50] Along with members of the Aborigines Protection League, she'd petitioned federal Parliament for a self-governing state for Aboriginal people where they could continue to live according to their own laws and traditions. Mary Bennett, an Australian living in London, was so stirred by Cooke's speech that she dedicated her life to working with Aboriginal people, and left England to teach at Mount Margaret mission near Laverton in Western Australia during the 1930s.

Cooke and her associates were largely urban-based and relied on frontline updates, as it were, from Bates and others, and on sources such as JW Bleakley's 1929 report, *The Aboriginals and Half-Castes of Central Australia and North Australia*. The report was a damning exposé of the tacitly ignored issue of 'combo-ism': settler men's use of Aboriginal women for sex, at best as common-law wives; at worst, in cases of child rape. Bleakley observed that semi-starvation led to the prostitution of Aboriginal women, often in what he called 'gin sprees' where 'car loads of men from bush townships and construction camps … had given trouble on stations even 100 miles distant'.[51] In response the federal government invited mission, welfare and other humanitarian representatives such as Cooke to speak at a conference in Melbourne in April 1929 to address the matters the report had raised. Cooke lobbied for the need to appoint women protectors to safeguard Aboriginal women and girls against the excesses of white men, challenging the police's control in Aboriginal welfare. In 1930 she presented a paper, 'The status of Aboriginal Women in Australia', which made the abuse of Aboriginal women and girls in northern Australia the welfare committee's main concern.

Annie Lock at the United Aborigines Mission in Alice Springs was another of the Women's Non-Party Association's informants. 'I quite agree with you that the Policemen are not the right ones to be Protectors of Aborigines,' she wrote to Bennett in 1929:

> Many of them are as bad as any other white men with the young lubras ... The greatest trouble is that the white men seem to delight to get the young girls from ten years up and will even come and ask for them and offer money, tobacco and all sorts of things to the women for the girls.[52]

Lock described how Aboriginal people were camping near the telegraph line 'for protection since the shooting of the natives out West'.[53] She'd seen Aboriginal people's fear of the police for herself, after Constable George Murray and local men made vigilante-style attacks on camps near Coniston station in central Australia during the previous year.

Assertions that 'nothing was happening' on the railway line, on the fringes of townships and on pastoral stations in response to complaints from Bates, Lock, the Women's Non-Party Association, Bleakley and others sound suspiciously like a case of what in 1935 anthropologist Olive Pink called the 'sex solidarity' among men that stopped them from acknowledging the inferior treatment of Aboriginal people, especially that of women. 'The attitude of all the graziers and white men generally was to draw a distinct and ungiving colour-line,' Hill observed, 'even when living with an aboriginal woman – the man who "knocked about with the blacks" was a "wamba" and held in contempt. "gone native." "combo." The Boss was the Sahib. They were left to their own devices when not at work. "never talk to your blacks," was the motto. Taking their part was "a queer."'[54]

'(white man father)', Bates wrote in 1917 at Fowlers Bay. 'The poor black women come to me, but they do not want their condition known, & how can I attend them in the midst of White people. I am nearly heartbroken. I can only tell them what to do, given them linen & sundries, & trust to them to do what is necessary.'[55] She was well aware of how white men were 'visiting native camps for immoral purposes' and how they were 'keeping Native women'.[56] When she addressed the Royal Aborigines Commission in 1914, she reported that at Fowlers Bay 'a native girl procured abortion and killed her half-caste child before it was born'.[57]

'If South Australia continues her policy of non-interference between white men and native women,' she wrote to Protector South, 'the number of 'caste children will form a very serious problem. Half-castes are often extremely prolific.'[58] She believed that interracial sex led to the diminution of individual races, eroding racial stock, and that the birth of 'half-castes' was a moral problem, a symptom of failed standards of racial purity. Bates's views were in keeping with those of her era; anxiety was mounting among policymakers, anthropologists and other commentators such as Bleakley, Walker and Baldwin Spencer during the 1920s and 1930s about the extent of miscegenation.[59] After travelling through remote Australia in the late 1920s, Adelaide physician WD Walker proclaimed 'the advent of the White man sounds the death knell of the black man – if not in this generation, in the next – and all that survives him is a pitiable horde of half-castes'.[60] Many children were sent to missions and to 'half-caste homes' like the Bungalow in Alice Springs and Colebrook Home near Quorn as the notion that being 'rescued' from Aboriginal camps and given opportunities for vocational training and education was in their best interests hardened into government policy. Even proposals by Spencer, Pink, Bennett and others to ensure Aboriginal people's survival through the creation of reserves advocated segregating full-descent Aboriginal people to maintain racial 'purity' and preserve cultural practices.

Bates was trenchant in her disavowal of miscegenation. At Ooldea she banished children of mixed descent and their parents – anyone whom she suspected had associated with 'low whites', the trampers and fettlers on the railway line – from her camp, saying she would prefer to keep them 'in perpetual Coventry', priding herself that in 'those 16 years there was not one halfcaste begotten at my camp – a unique record'.[61] She was sceptical about their potential for assimilation into mainstream white society, which became official policy after her death in the 1950s. In a vociferous exchange with William Harris, a mixed-descent Aboriginal activist, in the *Sunday Times* in 1921 she claimed that, even with early training, 'with very few exceptions the only good half-caste is a dead one. The Aborigines are unmoral [sic], the half-castes are immoral, and to breed our own population as under the present system we are now doing is an ugly reflection on all of us.'[62]

Although Bates lobbied authorities about these issues, she only despatched a few articles about the perils of miscegenation to the newspapers. Cannibalism, with its sensationalistic and saleable content, was more palatable to white mainstream readers and became one of her journalistic mainstays. Gara estimates she wrote forty or fifty articles on the subject during this period – roughly a quarter of her overall newspaper publications.[63] Historian Bob Reece suggests Bates may have been reluctant to castigate white – and indeed her fellow Irish – men publicly for their behaviour, and that it was easier to fall back on the standards of the day in condemning women, especially non-Anglo-Celtic ones, for children born outside of marriage. Bates also cast women rather than men as the agents of cannibalistic practices: 'Cannibal infanticide is confined wholly to the women of the tribe – no grown man will ever consent to eat children.'[64] It's no coincidence she shunted the blame onto Aboriginal women, the ultimate outsiders of colonial society, in both situations. Her claims about cannibalism acted as a smokescreen, a displacement of the cause of so many lost children and disappearing babies. In *Finding Eliza: Power and Colonial Storytelling*,[65] Aboriginal legal academic Larissa Behrendt observes that the Eliza Fraser myth of a white woman surviving 'among cannibals' provided a vehicle for projecting frontier violence onto Aboriginal people: a trope that Bates literally mobilised for her own self-aggrandisement in her reports of cannibalism as the woman who lives alone with the blacks.

In 1931 Bates wrote to Cleland, badgering him to pay for a parcel of stories she'd sent him, admitting that the newspaper editors who usually published her articles had returned £30 worth of them, struggling with their own financial difficulties. 'I have been absolutely dependent on the newspapers for some time,' she told him. 'The "homing" of my articles is like pigeon homing. And so, as I say, I want £50 to carry me through this stress.'[66] She was in her early seventies, and her other meagre income streams – donations from supporters, the capital from her leases – had dried up.

A year later, when Ernestine Hill 'dropped from the skies' at Ooldea, Bates saw an opportunity, informing Cleland that: 'being a quick & clever journalist, a good shorthand writer & typist, she obtained day-by-day notes that I am sure she will make good use of'. As a Queenslander working for a Sydney newspaper, Hill was outside the Perth and Adelaide establishments whose patience Bates had exhausted. 'I wonder if her cannibal articles will silence the Adelaide Pardiggles, Honeythunders and Jellabys-ite?' Daisy mused to Cleland about the sceptics and interfering moralists down south.[67]

On 19 June 1932 the *Sunday Sun's* front page featured an article by Ernestine Hill under the headline, 'Cannibalism on East–West', garlanded with even more lurid subtitles: 'Black baby saved from being eaten. Grisly feasts persist – Story of white woman who intervened. Mother's awful loss'. It opened with a disconcerting statement: 'Last week, when Minmilla disappeared from camp – another child was expected – the white woman was horror-stricken, anticipating that it, too, would go the way of the others.'[68] The article explained that while Hill was camping with Bates behind her breakwind at Ooldea, Daisy had told her she was worried about Minmilla, a pregnant Aboriginal woman who'd left the camp a week earlier to give birth. She wasn't merely concerned about the woman's safety and wellbeing: she feared Minmilla had killed and eaten her baby. It was an everyday event, she said. Cannibalism was rife everywhere, from the Kimberley to Eucla, but especially at Ooldea because the parched soak no longer attracted fresh game. Bates proposed tracking Minmilla as she'd once followed Nyan-ngauera, another expecting mother.

It was a scoop beyond Hill's wildest expectations. 'Minmilla aged 30, Gooinmurdo's wife, small son Thannana aged eight has helped her eat three daughters, one brother,' she wrote coolly on a sheaf headed 'Cannibal Notes', as if taking down a case history.[69] Her raison d'être was to follow the story, claiming 'your true journalist is a little more, or a little less, than human, a child taking notes' who knew 'no partialities, no class-distinction, no creed distinction, nor colour-line, nor bias, nor loyalty, save to the story'.[70] She was mere carbon paper scratched by a pen's impressions, absolved of any responsibility other than to report what she saw and heard as she scrambled after Bates over the dunes hunting their quarry of a story.

Hill's article went viral, taking out newspaper front pages across the country. As a rising, east coast journalistic star, she mainstreamed Bates's story, lending credence to the reports that had been issuing from the elderly eccentric on the Nullarbor's edge. But Ernestine Hill's 'startling revelations' weren't received without question. 'Civilised Australians, born and bred in the cities and settled country areas, find it almost impossible to credit that such practices actually flourish in their own country,' the editor reassured readers in the next *Sunday Sun*. Hill later regretted her role in perpetuating this 'sensational' story's claims, presenting herself in her 1973 memoir, *Kabbarli*, 'interrupt[ing] Mrs Bates's fluent monologue, asking for proof of her statement'. She admitted rushing her copy from Ooldea to the *Sun* in 1932 without pause for thought or fact-checking. At the time, she'd been too trusting, taking Bates's 'fluent monologue' and assertion that the 'evidence' was in the Adelaide Museum at face value, but since then her own 'careful research' hadn't revealed any 'official record of cannibal customs'. Nor had she entertained any doubts when Minmilla 'turned up in the camp next day with a bouncing baby boy in her wooden scoop and with Thannana by the hand – a reformed cannibal, Daisy insisted' or queried the incident's fortuitous timing during her visit to Bates's camp.[71] She would not have despatched the story, she protested later in *Kabbarli*, had she known the child was unharmed, but she did know: this incident appears in the original 1932 article. In *The Great Australian Loneliness*, she also reports 'thinking, purely as a journalist, that God and Daisy Bates had robbed me of a thundering front-page story' when Minmilla and child reappeared. At thirty-three she was searching for stories to make her reputation; the article was one of several she published in the same year that brought her dubious acclaim, whose lack of professional rigour she would regret.

A week after 'Cannibalism on East–West' appeared in the *Sun*, Hill published 'Woman of Ooldea', a hagiographic profile of Bates accompanied by a photograph of Daisy poised for action, brandishing an umbrella outside her tent. 'Romantic tales of white women among the Australian blacks have become the sensation of the moment,' the article opened, although this was the 'only authentic story … a white woman who has voluntarily given up 32 years of her life to wandering with the nomad tribes of half a continent'.[72]

'Long long walks alone to the Soak in the night-time over the lonely undulating sandhills,' Hill wrote in her notes for this portrait. 'Tiny high-heel tracks left in lonely places.'[73]

Ooldea was undeniably isolated, a blur of tents and sheds around a matchbox siding, but no-one living there during the 1920s and 1930s was entirely alone. Up to 150 Aboriginal people might be camping near the soak, and around 200 'low whites' – the stationmaster, the rations officer, the fettlers and their wives – were at the siding in its heyday. When Protector South visited Ooldea in 1920, he observed that although several officials' wives were housed near the station, 'Mrs Bates will not associate with any but the Aborigines. She is considered most eccentric.'[74]

'I have to keep alert always to see and nip in the bud the very slightest approach to familiarity of the white women,' Bates wrote.[75] Privacy was important. At her first camp at Ma'amba Reserve, she'd allowed the governor inside her tent one day to see her 'gadgets'. Afterwards the Bibbulmun, thinking the governor was the brother of the white peoples' King, told her that only he could visit but 'no other man can go into any woman's hut or shelter unless he is her husband'. Bates 'kept their law throughout', claiming not only to detain men but 'all my white visitors outside the breakwind of bushes surrounding my various camps'.[76]

At Ooldea Bates went above and beyond the Bibbulmun's dictum of not permitting men to enter her tents: 'No native ever allowed inside, no white man, very rarely siding women.'[77] A model of long-gone Victorian rectitude, so much energy, so much control – the gloves, the dust coat, the veil, the glare glasses, the breakwind that few could pass – went into patrolling the boundaries between self and others.

'I occupy a different place in the native mind,' she told Cleland, claiming to stay apart from others for field work purposes, to keep up appearances as a spirit creature, 'Kabbarli. Dhoogur, – ancestral dream-time. Māā'mu. Sexless to the natives'. She traded on her age, ghostly whiteness and apparent sexlessness so she could chant 'in those corroborees in which it is death for a woman to see': men's business. 'When I go to these night dances I go as Māā'mu Kabbarli ("spirit", "magic" grandmother), so that I shall still, <u>in the natives' minds</u>, keep my apartness from them. & I find that they all feel this apartness.'[78]

Daisy was alone by the standards of the day, a woman without family around her, refusing to define herself as someone's wife in any more than title. For decades she'd been referring to Jack Bates as 'late'; even so, there were rumours of other men, including husbands.

She'd been popular with the fellows when she was young, the quick-witted, dark-haired, milk-skinned beauty, an Irish governess who'd arrived at Townsville on the SS *Almora* in 1883. Like many poor Irish and Scots in the 19th century, Daisy had taken advantage of the Queensland government's offer of free passage to increase its stock of labourers and domestic servants. She'd begun working on properties near Charters Towers, where she gained a reputation as a pretty, clever sort of girl who could be relied upon to enliven any social occasion. She had a great sense of fun and enjoyed male attention, although coquetry was more than gaming on her behalf. She used flirtation as a weapon, knowing that if she was to amount to anything in the new country, to move beyond the rank of governess, she must marry.

What happened at Charters Towers was something she always held close; it seemed as unlikely as a fairy story as time passed. There'd been a man, easy on the eye and a fine rider like her, one they'd called the Breaker because he could tame any wild horse. He'd courted Daisy with ballads, called himself a gentleman, claiming his father was an admiral in the Royal Navy; they shared a facility with poetic licence. She'd persuaded herself to believe him, pretending to be Anglican so that they could marry. But not long after their wedding, he went droving, trailing debts behind him. She gave up waiting for him to return and travelled further south. Crossing state boundaries, you could leave a past behind you, forget your religion, conceal your marital status, tweak your name and birthdate, and start afresh in those days.

Daisy roamed about New South Wales, governessing at properties, dancing at woolsheds, attending country shows. One day she caught sight of a man, buck-jumping an outlaw colt at a rodeo. Handsome in a wide-brimmed hat, wearing a white silk neckerchief, Crimea shirt, cummerbund and Canton moles, radiant in the midday sun, Jack Bates dazzled her in that moment.

'I'll marry that man!' Daisy called out to anyone who'd listen.[79] Jack heard and took her on as a challenge like the brumby colt. When he was sure of winning her, he galloped her up to a small church in Nowra where he commanded the minister to marry them with bystanders as witnesses. Their courtship was as heated and impulsive as Daisy liked, but love of horses and a flair for drama was not enough to keep a union going. Daisy soon realised she'd married another man 'who had not even begun to carve his name on the world's roll – a drifting aimless irresponsible human'. Jack cast about the eastern seaboard, picking up work as a stockman on stations, droving wherever he could. While he was away Daisy entertained herself with another charade of marriage, this time to an old flame from home, a seaman whose ship had docked in Sydney.

Once the seaman's boat pulled out of the port, she patched over her differences with Jack and followed him half-heartedly around the backblocks of New South Wales. In August 1886 she found herself lumbered with a child, Arnold Hamilton Bates. She hadn't recognised the signs of pregnancy till childbirth was almost upon her; nor had she been warned of its pain. Afterwards she swore off lovemaking, continuing to drift in this listless life with Jack and her son, feeling the distance between them growing. In 1894 she boarded the *Macquarie* as a solo passenger bound for London on the flimsy pretext that she was suffering from a mysterious case of 'nostalgia', for which doctors had prescribed a trip back 'home'.

Five years later when Jack wrote to her, saying he planned to purchase some pastoral leases in the north-west, she returned, this time to Perth, hoping he'd become a husband she could be proud of marrying, a man of property in the new colony. But disappointment swept over her when she spied him waiting for her on the Fremantle docks:

> God! What a shock the meeting was! A series of shocks tumbling one upon each other in the first month of their reunion! This creature with the weak overhanging lip! The man who was to win success for her! ... His very form and

features had moulded themselves to his character, and had become loose and flabby and common – above all common.⁸⁰

Any attraction was long gone. She delayed settling back into married life for as long as she could, galloping across the Kimberley to investigate claims of settler cruelty to blacks and sojourning at Beagle Bay Mission with Trappist monks At the end of 1901 Daisy took Arnold out of school in Perth, and reluctantly they travelled up the coast to join Jack Bates on the property he was managing at Roebuck Plains.

Several months later the family drove a thousand head of cattle well over 1000 kilometres south to Murchison, where Jack had taken out three leases. It was a gruelling journey for all concerned. Two hundred cattle wandered off along the way to slake their thirst in disused wells. Shrouding herself in layers of clothing to prevent sunburn, Daisy suffered from heat prostration, declaring the ride had taken fifteen years off her life. Jack had let her name the property beforehand, and she'd called it Glen Carrick, a moniker evoking the gentrified pastoral life of her Anglo-Irish childhood. He'd also promised to build her a house of 'creaking corrugated iron to beat the white ants'; instead, she arrived to find nothing but a simple bough shed.

Daisy had not yet 'acclimatised to the poverty and the loneliness', Hill later observed. The habit of loneliness was something to be learned, although Bates 'had no desire to be a housewife, Mrs Station Owner, hard-working auxiliary to a hard-working man. Marriage was not enough'.⁸¹

She could certainly never ride 'double harness'. She chafed at Jack's uncouthness and the 'vague feeling of inferiority which took possession of her as he noticed her continuance of all the niceties of demeanour so long unpractised by him … These were part of <u>her</u> being – they had become entirely apart from <u>him</u>; forgotten, lapsed through misuse.' Besides, he didn't understand her interest in the blacks, why she wanted to spend so much time at Glen Carrick with them rather than with him, learning their words and their stories, tracing their networks. One day he went too far in his contempt, striking an Aboriginal man with a white-hot iron he was using to brand calves in the cattleyard. The man dropped like a log in the yard and lay there till sundown.

Daisy quit the bare excuse of a homestead and returned to Perth, depositing Arnold back at boarding school. The fifteen-year-old she'd met on her return from London had been a familiar stranger, 'with a character aimless and lax as that of his father', a party to Jack Bates's 'listless quest'.[82] She had tried to 'eradicate the taint of incompetence and laziness' from her son by dragging him up to Glen Carrick, although she'd known it was a futile exercise, as it was to pretend any life was left in their family. But she was forty-five, an age at which a woman could respectably direct her energies away from childbearing, cast aside the moorings of convention and go under canvas at Ma'amba Reserve to study the Bibbulmun.

'So many little things, little in themselves, have to be watched and guarded against.'[83] It was important for Daisy to set herself apart at Ooldea, not just so that Anangu might believe she was a genderless spirit creature, but to avoid letting any little thing slip in front of the low whites. She let Ernestine Hill believe she was the first journalist to cross her breakwind's threshold, although she wasn't the only white woman Bates had admitted into her domicile. In 1921 Miss Ruxton, a fellow Irishwoman from Perth, had visited Ooldea, intent on researching an article about Bates for the *Sunday Times*. Daisy had put her up for five days in a tent a few yards from hers, explaining 'I'm very jealous about my privacy.' Five years later 'a jolly little artist visitor' blew into her camp – Olive Pink, who was to emulate Bates's Edwardian costume as well as her field work practice in central Australia. 'She cooked and did for me and for herself,' Bates wrote, 'and had her little tent home and was as private as if she was in her own home.'[84]

But she could tell things to Ernestine Hill. Bates almost babbled in her excitement at being in the company of someone who shared similar bearings. The girl – and she was one to Daisy – leaned forward listening intently, her long pale face luminous in the campfire's flickering light, straight fine hair close enough to touch. Reflected in Ernestine's dark, unwavering gaze, Bates could see she believed it all. Not just the tales of being a white woman among cannibals like Eliza Fraser but of her life before she left Plymouth on the SS *Almora*. Of how she'd been born in Ballychrine in Tipperary, at Ashbury House, an estate that had been in her mother's family, the Hunts, for generations. Of how a local banshee 'must have wailed' at her birth because her mother died soon afterwards. She and her two older siblings, Kathleen and Jim, were sent to live with Grandmother Hunt, to whom they listened of an evening spinning tales as she wove the household's linen on a wheel by a peat fire. By day Daisy and her curly-haired brother Jim tumbled about fairy forts and ruins, chasing imaginary leprechauns and clurichauns from Granny Hunt's lore. Both sides of their family were strictly Church of Ireland; their neighbours in Ballychrine were Anglo-Irish gentry. So well connected were the Hunts that when Daisy got a splinter in her eye as a child, they took her to London to be treated by Kidd, Disraeli's doctor.

Then Granny Hunt died, and the family was divided. Kathleen and Jim were sent to Dublin, and Daisy boarded with a Mrs Goode, the dean of Ripon's widow, near Conway Castle in Wales. Fate kept on happening, as Ernestine later observed.

Sir Francis and Lady Outram invited the teenage Daisy on a Continental pilgrimage as a companion for their six children. They travelled to 'the gay and dainty Paris of the "seventies"', bound for Switzerland and then Rome, where they had a private audience with the Pope. En route, Daisy befriended a niece of Napoleon's in Antwerp. They returned to Scotland, staying near Balmoral Castle, where Daisy bumped into Queen Victoria, making a hasty yet charming curtsey – an encounter that left her starry eyed about royalty for life. Soon afterwards, she ran into the Prince of Wales, the future King Edward VII, while visiting a friend of Florence Nightingale.

So dazzling and precocious was young Daisy that much older men and women 'invariably took a fancy to me because I was boisterous and irrepressible, vibrant with vitality'. She credited this 'bright thread of beautiful friendships' with making her the woman of service she later became in her 'solitary tent in the sandhills'.[85] Hers was an incredulity-straining rollcall of brushes with fame and royalty, none of which the devoted Ernestine ever appears to have doubted. Instead, she was glamoured by 'D.B. Herself', flattered that this unusual woman who straddled the threshold of two cultures at Ooldea Soak drew her into her confidence. 'The name of Daisy Bates will go down in Australian history as that of a new Hester Stanhope,' Hill wrote, poised to usher in the mythologising of that woman living 'unafraid in the great loneliness'.[86]

2

A wandering sickness

*'I have suffered, or circumstances have forced me into …
a sort of wandering sickness.'*[1]

Ernestine Hill went shopping for a gun before she set off to discover what lay beyond the railway lines. Good-humoured shopkeepers and an ex-missionary told her she wouldn't need one; that the outback was safe enough to push a perambulator across – a suitable metaphor to offer a white woman concerned about domesticating the interior. She took their advice and left Perth in July 1930 with her typewriter and a swag, armed with a 'badly sharpened lead-pencil' to confront the unknown.[2]

Fear nagged at me during my early days alone in a van. I found myself slouching towards androgyny at road stops and campsites, clamping a broad-brimmed hat over my hair, hunching under baggy shirts that I wore over jeans teamed with a pair of elastic-sided boots – Dr Martens, which if anything probably marked me as something of a city slicker. Despite being a tall, broad-shouldered woman, I doubt my instinctive attempt at disguise fooled anyone. I didn't dress this way to imitate Hill; it was more of an unconscious slide, although it probably stemmed from similar practical and protective reflexes as hers in adopting what was regarded in her time as masculine attire.

As much as I wanted to entertain a gung-ho, girl's own adventurous spirit like Ernestine Hill on taking to the road, I was paralysed by the basic fear, to paraphrase Margaret Atwood's often-quoted observation, that women are afraid men will kill them. A certain kind of man embodied this anxiety for me while I was living in the Territory, especially when I travelled to unfamiliar towns and communities for work. Searching for a pub meal at the end of the day, I'd startle at the occasional white man with bloodshot eyes, wearing stubbies and a singlet, lurching out of the dusk haze ahead of me on the road. One evening while swimming in a motel pool, I looked up at the end of a lap to see several lone men on separate balconies, drinking tinnies, watching me. This type, the solitary white working-class man, the sinister gender flipside of the jaunty adventurous identity I wanted to claim, is a cliché that has long been knocking about in the Australian unconscious. Try as I might to rationalise away the likelihood of encountering *Wolf Creek*'s Mick Taylor or Bradley John Murdoch – that these were unfortunate exceptions, that the Falconios were unlucky, that I was too old to be preyed upon – this phantasm was all-too-readily jolted into my awareness.

Yet the challenges I encountered crossing the Nullarbor or on my later journeys were rarely what I expected. If anything, I was more at risk from my own practical ineptitude than a malevolent white male battler. One of the first intimations of extremity on my drive west was a sign warning 'No fuel for 129 km' soon after I turned onto the Eyre. My stomach sinking, I realised that while wandering about in a podcast-induced stupor looking for a decent coffee at my last stop in Port Augusta, I'd forgotten to refill my tank. Miscalculate how much fuel you have and you could be stranded for ages in a remote area. I had about a quarter of a tank left, which might be just enough since I was averaging about 400 to 500 kilometres between refills. Dropping to a slower pace, I crawled on a knife-edge of anxiety to Kimba, where I refuelled at a petrol station sporting an 8-metre-high galah.

Initially, I stayed at caravan parks, although I soon began to experiment with free-range camping. I resented expending so much mental energy on my safety as a solo female camper: that I couldn't free park with the same abandon as a man, a couple, a family or a group. In choosing a campsite, I would arrive well before nightfall to check out who was there so I would have enough time to find another place if I had any qualms or niggling doubts. Another woman, a flock of grey nomads, a man with young children were reassuring signs. After parking my van, I would muse about what item to grab to defend myself if confronted by intruders: would I slug them with a gas container, the fire extinguisher, a Prosecco bottle? I first camped wholly alone on a clifftop overlooking a sparkling, unpopulated beach. I took courage after chatting earlier with a man who'd been roasting fish over a campfire with some kids near a caravan on the cliff. They were locals, he told me; no one much knew about the campground and there was hardly any crime in the area so I'd be safe. His assurances turned out to be true enough but I spent most of the night twisting in my bed, startling at the slightest sound, refusing to be soothed by the lapping of distant waves.

I can't exactly pinpoint when, but my anxiety about being a lone woman on the road gradually receded and became outweighed by a Micawberish optimism that somehow everything would pan out. That if I locked myself out of the van in the middle of nowhere, a grey nomad would step out from a Winnebago with a bent coathanger, or if my vehicle broke down, it would provide a secure shell to camp in until help arrived. I became more at ease about camping behind a natural breakwind of bushes by the roadside, in a bay in a national park or overlooking a beach. I began to avoid staying at any of the major caravan park chains, except when I was desperate for a shower or could not find an alternative in the area.

This transition was psychological rather than a response to any external events; more a matter of gaining a sense of self-possession, of feeling I could inhabit space on and off the road. Had a similar shift occurred for Bates and Hill, I wondered, or had they adopted a carefree swagger, setting off in more isolated times when most roads were unsealed, telephony was limited and services such as the Royal Flying Doctor were in their infancy? Ernestine later felt embarrassed, scarcely knowing 'whether to laugh or cry', whenever she remembered her misguided gun-shopping episode, pronouncing it an insult to the people she'd met in the 'real Australia', instead finding 'black and white, they were all friends'.[3] After a year's farmstay on a Nullarbor sheep station in 1913, Bates reported being 'glad to get under canvas again' in the sandhills at Eucla.[4] If anything, these statements suggest the transition happened more quickly for them; that of necessity they acquired a confident, survivalist optimism rather than be swamped and immobilised by fear about travelling alone as a woman in the outback.

Hill called herself a 'hobohemian', a whimsical title invoking what landscape writer Robert Macfarlane calls 'the wilful wanderer, the Borrovian or Whitmanesque walker, out for the romance of the way'.[5] Her lifestyle was a romantic echo of the archetypal swagman's, although her ethic was more in keeping with early-20th-century youth movements such as the *Wandervogel*, who hiked and camped as 'a protest against the tedium and convention of bourgeois life' before these activities were commercialised as popular leisure pursuits. Philosopher Theodor Adorno writes: 'People had to "get out", in both senses of the phrase. Sleeping out beneath the stars meant that one had escaped from the house and from the family.'[6] Hill's constant wandering became her singular protest against what she saw as the oppressive nature of urban life in contrast to the wonderland within the country's vast open spaces.

Her ability as a European woman to negotiate what was then often referred to as the Australian interior had a curio value which she capitalised on through her romantic portrayal of herself and her travel. 'Ernestine Hill, woman wanderer of the Out-back,' a 1933 by-line read, 'brilliant and sympathetic recorder of its dramas, gives you another great life story.'[7] She circumnavigated the continent relentlessly, claiming to have clocked up 50 000 miles in the first five years of her reporting and to have travelled around Australia twice 'in varying routes in hard monotony of miles' when she completed *The Territory* in 1951.[8] Indeed, her willingness to put her trunks on a train and scrounge a lift by whatever transport available over long distances in the service of 'the story' became a reflex response. But where this impetus came from bemused Hill herself.

'I've been tossed hither and yon since childhood,' Ernestine wrote to a friend during her final weeks. 'Sometimes, wistfully, I wonder why. Seems inevitable and hereditary.' Several stanzas of a lullaby scratched in her uneven copperplate accompany the letter. 'Lonely I wander,' it begins, 'Neath tropic suns and starry skies'. Ernestine's father, Robert Hemmings, composed these lyrics and set them to a German folk song for his wife to sing to his daughters while he was away, travelling for work. 'Father must not wander,' the final verse concludes. 'He must come to us at home, Abiding with the ones he loves, His Ernestine and Ray.'[9] Strains of this lullaby, with yearning for absent people, its melancholy *Wandervogel* ethos, its ornate language and attraction to exotic climes, echoed throughout Ernestine's life.

During Ernestine's childhood, the Hemmings shifted up and down the Queensland coast, a restless second-generation Anglo-Celtic family trying to make their own livelihood. Both her parents had mobile occupations. Her father was a 'northern traveller', a sales representative for GR Ryder & Co. Ltd, a British box-making company, and Finney Isles & Co., an Irish-founded drapery business in Brisbane. Her mother, Margaret Foster-Lynam, or 'Madge', was a teacher originally from Townsville who'd begun her career in Rockhampton. The family moved between Mackay and Thursday Island during Ernestine's early years, an experience that left her with 'infinite memories, comparisons of ways of motion'.[10] Seeing 'the Chinese processions and the bubonic plagues and all sorts of doings even the elders have not the faintest idea about', hearing Melba sing and attending *Hamlet* in Townsville also imprinted a love of the north's cultural diversity in the young girl's psyche.[11]

The Hemmings were older parents when they married in 1898: Madge was in her late thirties and Robert was in his mid-forties. Hemmings's people were English and had come out during the mid-19th-century gold rushes, whereas Madge's family was Irish, from Tipperary – a bond for Hill with Bates. Robert was said to be a widower and brought a daughter, Ray, to the marriage. But when a later generation of family members searched for a birth certificate for Ray, they couldn't find one and suspected she was illegitimate. The Hemmings's only child, Mary Ernestine, was born in Rockhampton on 21 January 1899, the year that Daisy sailed from Southampton to Fremantle. Having older parents meant that Ernestine was at home with Victorians such as Bates and Mary Gilmore, with whom she later formed significant relationships. The Dickens-toting Daisy shared a similar literary sensibility to Robert and Madge Hemmings, who were well versed in 19th-century classics and loved attending the theatre. Hill's father also had journalistic aspirations and contributed freelance articles to *The Age*.

Queensland education department records describe Madge Hemmings as hard-working, energetic but nervous and 'difficult to manage' – a combination of qualities that made for an 'over-fond and proud mother', ambitious for her only daughter.[12] Madge brought up Ernestine to be a child prodigy type, reputedly making her read all the classics by the age of ten and encouraging her to write poetry. When Ernestine was first enrolled at a Catholic state school in Townsville, she entertained other students by writing caricatures of teachers in verse and passing them round. The nuns scolded her but they recognised her ability, urging her to buckle down and focus on her studies. Which she did, receiving the first bursary in the Queensland State School examination, enabling her to board at the more prestigious All Hallows' Convent School in Brisbane. Madge continued to cultivate Ernestine's literary interests from the sidelines, sometimes undermining the nuns' authority by taking her daughter out to the theatre. But the convent made deep inroads into Ernestine's psyche, compounding her tendencies to modesty and self-effacement.

Not long after Ernestine began boarding at All Hallows', Robert Hemmings died from a heart attack. She was only eleven at the time and felt his passing deeply. 'All the years are vivid memories when one is old,' she later wrote but it was his memory to which she returned at the end of her life.[13] A gentle, romantic personality like Ernestine, Hemmings had a more moderate and nurturing influence on his daughters than Madge. His death precipitated another family absence. Financially stretched without her husband's earnings, Madge resumed working as a teacher in Brisbane and sent Ray to board with an aunt. The pair had a tense relationship – Ray found her stepmother 'domineering and resented her' – and the move provided her with enough distance to pursue another life.[14] She met and married young an American, leaving soon afterwards with him for the United States, correspondence to her family petering out. Ernestine always missed Ray, her childhood playmate, even though a significant age gap existed between them. Although she later hoped that publicity from sales of her books in America would bring them back in contact, she never saw her half-sister again. The only photograph she possessed of Ray was a postcard her cousins sent her – a flat black-and-white image of a miniature woman, hands clasped in front of her, eyebrows quizzically raised, her gaze unfocussed as if lost in thought – dated 1910, the year of their father's death.

Ernestine Hemmings published her first poem at the age of thirteen in Brisbane's *Catholic Advocate* and became a regular contributor to its Children's Page. In 1916 the Brisbane Hibernian Newspaper Company, the *Advocate*'s publisher, produced *Peter Pan Land*, a volume of her poetry, under the imprimatur of Archbishop Duhig. Local literati lavished praise on the 'Queensland girl poet par excellence', whom they heralded as a 'genius unspoiled': 'Doubt was expressed as to the work coming from the brain of a child of 14', or whether it was 'that of some sympathetic ghost of maturer years'.[15] Newspaper photographs show a solemn-faced girl, with a high forehead and long jaw tapering to a pointed chin. Her large, dark eyes are her most arresting feature: they almost quiver on the page. Lank hair hangs round her shoulders; in one photo, taken when she was sixteen, it's cropped in the helmet-like bob with its abrupt fringe she wore as an adult. A simple white smock falls just below her knees, revealing wishbone-thin calves in black stockings. 'She is still young for her age, both in appearance and manner,' one reporter observed. 'In repose her face is rather wistful and sad; but when you talk to her of the things that interest her … her big brown eyes shine with fire and imagination.'[16] A childlike, fey creature, she was everything you might want in a girl poet.

That the *Catholic Advocate* directed the proceeds of *Peter Pan Land*, which sold at the modest price of 1s 6d per copy, towards further education for Ernestine suggests recognition not only of her talent but of ongoing family hardship. There was a stronger than usual emphasis on the need to educate young women to support themselves during the Great War, as well as more opportunities to study and practise in traditionally male-dominated occupations such as law. As a scholarship girl, Ernestine knew her family and teachers might presume she was on the fast track to study for a Master of Arts or law if they 'had been able absolutely to crush her ambitions and imagination'.[17] Instead, she left school after completing her Junior exams and enrolled in Stott and Hoare's Business College in Brisbane with her cousin, Catherine Roy, known to the family as 'Coy'. The daughter of Madge's only brother, Coy was three years younger than Ernestine and took on a sisterly role in Ray's absence. Madge tutored the girls, and they both won secretarial scholarships – Ernestine a 12-month one, and Coy a six-month one. Hemmings continued to distinguish herself, gaining high passes in shorthand and typing, skills suited to a journalistic career. She knew writing was her real talent, confessing that she'd given up on the idea of studying law because 'It means too much hard work, and in my case, I don't think it would be worth it. No doubt I will eventually drift into journalism.'[18] Her first job was in the Brisbane Stamp Office, but within eighteen months she was promoted to the position of librarian in the Justice Department. This might have seemed just the thing for a bookish girl, but a local reporter observed she was bored, complaining 'bitterly of the monotony and stillness of life … despite the fact that admirers of her work visit … frequently to offer her advice and cheer'.[19]

What was it that 'made the name of this girl poet stand out in relief from among a host of others chanting their songs to an ungrateful muse' in wartime Brisbane? Ernestine Hemmings pondered similar questions after taking a '*Bulletin* bard' to task for publishing doggerel trivialising female poets. 'Twenty per cent of women, at some period of their lives,' she wrote in an opinion piece titled 'Australian poetesses', 'develop a craze for writing verse but that of these about two per cent write anything resembling poetry. Only two per cent know anything of originality of theme, of melody, of thought and expression, of the music of beautiful words.' Poetry was for emerging writers then what memoir is today – a vehicle for personal expression and literary experimentation. 'But one thing is certain', she concluded, 'the women of Australia are able and ready to take a prominent place in the twentieth century literature, as in anything else.'[20] Ernestine was too modest to draw attention to her own poetry, which demonstrated technical proficiency for a teenager but was, as a critic observed, Anglified, 'a trifle bookish', 'light and fanciful, and as delicate as the fairies it depicts'.[21] Yet it displayed the flair for detailed, descriptive observation that would consolidate her profile as a leading narrative journalist of the interior, although her writing would continue to be mocked for its exuberant flights of fancy and purple prose.

On their way to spend Christmas with relatives in Melbourne in 1918, Ernestine and Coy daringly visited JF Archibald at his Sydney office. One of the founders of the *Bulletin*, which had been influential in Australian literary and political life for several decades, Archibald had recently been appointed editor of the literary pages for *Smith's Weekly*, a new satirical tabloid pitched at returned servicemen. He had a reputation for encouraging young talent, scrawling 'PLEASE CALL' on rejected manuscripts if he thought the writer showed promise, fossicking for gems from the 'spectres of poets and artists drifting up the narrow rickety stairs'[22] to Smith's offices above the Imperial Arcade. The girls' visit may have been inspired by his open door policy as well as work prospects. What Ernestine self-mockingly referred to as a 'childish verse' had appeared in the *Bulletin*, and she'd framed the cheque of 12/6 she'd received in payment as an imprimatur of her literary aspirations. The poem was published when she was still at boarding school, when Archibald was no longer the *Bulletin*'s editor so he may not have been aware of her talent. However, she so impressed him at their first meeting that he offered her a job as his secretary. Coy joined *Smith*'s as a typist at her cousin's urging, and the young women flatted together in Kirribilli.

Working for an independent paper publishing the likes of Kenneth Slessor, Bartlett Adamson and Colin Wills was a gift to Ernestine after the monotony of Brisbane's state offices and brought her closer to her ambition of being a journalist on a metropolitan newspaper. Along with poems, she began publishing opinion pieces in Brisbane's *Daily Mail* and *Catholic Advocate*, followed by southern publications such as the *Australian Worker* and the *Bulletin*, industriously laying the foundations for a writing career. She also came in contact with members of Sydney's bohemia such as the Lindsays, an illustration by Norman Lindsay accompanying one of her poems, although Bob Hill later commented that 'the life she led was I think a slightly more ladylike version of the story told in The Roaring Twenties'.[23]

If Sydney was a place of opportunity for Ernestine, it was also challenging. Archibald promoted her to subeditor on *Smith's Weekly* midway through 1919, but his mentorship of Miss Hemmings was short-lived. On 10 September 1919 he was rushed to St Vincent's Hospital, where he died suddenly and unexpectedly, Ernestine and his chauffeur by his bed. A vignette of hers, 'The city of everlasting no', published in Brisbane's *Catholic Advocate* early in 1918 about her initial impressions of Sydney, belies her wonder and discomfort as a newcomer to the southern capital. Sydney is 'little short of a harrowing disenchantment … over-crowded, heterogenous, noisy nasty-selling, careless, blatantly swift'; if it were a woman, it would be 'a flapper, pert, flippant, happy-go-lucky, a little artificial perhaps'. Brisbane, on the other hand, is the 'quiet little school girl, neat and pretty, but very unsophisticated', suggesting her shy, other-worldly and slightly priggish self.[24] The contrast here between these northern and southern cities displays an unease with life in the urban south, typified by Sydney, that would harden into outright dislike. But this piece is also infused with an undercurrent of sexuality absent from her 'childish verse', hinting at the naïve schoolgirl's envy of the flapper: the Harbour City is 'an Eastern princess, mysterious, fascinating, impassioned'. Ernestine Hemmings's girl's own adventure in the big smoke was about to take a more adult turn.

Smith's brought Ernestine into the orbit of Robert Clyde Packer, or 'RC' as he was known, the patriarch of the future Packer dynasty. In his first engagement as a newspaper proprietor, RC managed the weekly that he'd founded with fellow journalist Claude McKay and politician James Joynton Smith, who financed it, hoping it would provide a platform for his views. *Smith's Weekly* upheld the rights of the working man and 'prided itself on being irreverent, funny and anti-authority' and was 'also chauvinistic, nationalistic and fiercely anti-communist', catering to popular masculine pursuits such as horseracing, in which Joynton Smith invested, owning one racecourse and managing two others.[25] In many respects, RC embodied the aspirational profile of the self-made, common man that *Smith's* courted. Born into a second-generation family of Scottish-British immigrants in Hobart, he was rumoured to have bought a ticket to the mainland with the winning flush from a bet he'd placed at twelve-to-one using 10 shillings he'd picked up at a racetrack. A journalist, he climbed as far as he might want locally to become subeditor of the *Tasmanian News*, then worked his way through the newspaper backblocks of Townsville and Dubbo before joining the staff of the *Sunday Times* in Sydney in 1908 and becoming subeditor of the *Sunday Sun* in 1916. In 1903 he married Ethel Maud Hewson, an enterprising Irish immigrant who'd started a typing business in Sydney. They had two children, Kathleen and Frank, their son consolidating RC's work and becoming synonymous with the rise of the Packer media empire.

Packer was a strange mixture of rustic Protestantism – his favourite book, *Self-help*, was about personal discipline – and hedonism; a betting man who enjoyed sport, one of his most notable achievements was to launch the first Miss Australia beauty contest in 1926. Forceful, energetic, turbulent, prone to gusts of rage – 'Packer's the man to roar like hell', an office wag wrote, 'And when he's roaring all is well' – this combination of qualities fostered his ascendancy as 'a pillar of popular journalism'.[26] He possessed a shrewd, tactical intelligence along with 'a keen sense of what readers of the mental age of 15, or less, want in the way of news and stunts'.[27] To Ernestine, the young bookish, cloistered, would-be journalist – 'shy as a Wonga pigeon' – this yachting, golf-playing, roo-shooting animus figure may have represented the qualities she lacked at this stage.[28] Frank Packer, however, described his father as 'a shy and retiring man, and deeply generous',[29] which suggests RC had another, more sensitive side that may also have appealed to her. According to Louise Campbell, Coy's daughter and Ernestine's second cousin, they read poetry together when he visited her Kirribilli flat; a volume of Byron remains in the family with 'Bill', his nickname for her, written on its inside cover.[30] RC was also forty, twice Ernestine's age when she met him, perhaps recalling the roaming freelance journalist father she'd lost nearly a decade earlier.

On 30 October 1924 Ernestine gave birth to a son, Robert David, who would become known as Bob. Two years later the name 'Ernestine Hemmings' appeared in print for the last time, and a Mrs Hill appeared on the Launceston *Examiner*'s literary staff.

Later when asked about the child's father in interviews, Ernestine said that Mr Hill was either overseas or dead. She claimed to have named her son after her father, but Robert was of course RC's first name. Rumours always circulated about the child's paternity. 'There are strange yarns of Ernestine and her son,' Miles Franklin later confided to Katharine Susannah Prichard. 'That he is Packer's, that gave up everything and ran to the wilds to save him, from the slaughter.'[31] In the early 1970s Margriet Bonnin began researching Hill as the potential subject of a postgraduate thesis but found that personal details about Ernestine and the elusive Mr Hill were scant. Thelma Afford, whose husband Max worked at the ABC with Hill during the 1940s, told Bonnin: 'No one seems to have ever met or heard Ernestine discuss her husband', observing that Hill's entry in *Who's Who in Australia 1941* was 'rather extraordinary for it gives no age, nothing at all about her husband, nothing of her own life. One cannot tell from this whether Hill is married or maiden name. It does not even mention her son. She has given away absolutely no personal details at all. It's very strange you know.'[32]

Bonnin cautiously reported that a 'traumatic affair with one of the senior executives of that [i.e. Associated] newspaper group led to the birth of a son'.[33] Packer is the only senior newspaper executive whom she mentions, and she refers to Hill as 'C.R. [sic] Packer's protégé', suggesting identification by association. Bonnin interviewed both the Hills, and her notes reveal that while Ernestine was silent on the subject, Robert believed that RC Packer was his father on the basis of what his mother had told him. Correspondence between Bonnin and Hill's literary friends indicate that Robert Hill's paternity was an open secret among their networks, but that after Ernestine's death they agreed the affair 'would not be mentioned except by implication'.[34]

Robert Hill's family maintained a belief that Packer was his father to the extent that they included RC alongside Ernestine as parents on his death notice. In later life Bob reputedly sent hair and fingernail samples for DNA testing to Kerry Packer, but never received any response or acknowledgement.³⁵ Certainly the 'strange yarns of Ernestine and her son' had reached enough critical mass by 2014 for media historian Bridget Griffen-Foley to report in prefacing her new edition of Frank Packer's biography, *The House of Packer*, that its first two chapters 'must now be read in the context of a likely relationship between RC Packer and Ernestine Hill'. Griffen-Foley states that Robert Hill was born 'in Hobart, where Packer had spent his early life'.³⁶ However, Louise Campbell claims that his birthplace was Belgrave, Victoria, and that Madge Hemmings, aided by her sister, Kitty, took the matter in hand. This seems more likely than Packer despatching his pregnant mistress to a location where she might encounter his kin, although he may have had some hand in Hill's appointment at the Launceston *Examiner*.

Whether RC ever laid eyes on his son is another matter. In one family story, he asked Ernestine to bring the baby to Essendon airport so that he could meet him. But something happened, RC was caught up in business-related matters and, a man among men, he strode across the tarmac without skipping a conversational beat, never or perhaps deliberately not seeing Ernestine holding up the baby against a grey Melbourne sky, hoping to catch his eye. It's tempting to brush off the affair as the story of a schoolgirl crush on a powerful older man but Louise Campbell says Ernestine told her mother, Coy, that RC Packer was the great love of her life.³⁷ When exactly their relationship ended is unclear. Robert Hill speculated to Bonnin that either Packer had been 'very much in love with E.H. & prepared to commit bigamy & marry her to make Bob legitimate' but he'd died before that was possible or that it had been an 'affair which he hoped would blow over'.³⁸ That these two theories are virtually polar opposites, and that Bob himself didn't know the truth of the matter, suggests how hushed up the affair was, even within the family. Whatever the case, his birth changed not only the nature of his mother's liaison but the course of her career and life.

When Ernestine took up the position at the Launceston *Examiner*, Aunt Kitty, one of Madge's unmarried sisters, moved to Tasmania to look after two-year-old Robert. Together with Hill's mother, she supported Ernestine by helping raise her son during his early years, often travelling considerable distances to set up house for them, later to Broome to put Bob through the local primary school. As for the mysterious 'Mr Hill': the origins of this name are unknown. Perhaps it came to Ernestine as she looked out to the hills around Launceston, wondering what had become of her life. But it was a ruse in which Hill's older female relatives colluded, trying to protect the former convent girl in an era where single motherhood was shameful, abortion was dangerous and illegal – an unlikely option for Ernestine and her maternal relatives, given they were Catholic – and illegitimate children were usually put up for adoption.

Professionally, this period marks Hill's transition from girl poet to the grittier figure of the cigarette-toting, slacks-wearing journalist. Her time in Sydney compounded her allegiance to the north and her distaste for the 'City of everlasting no', as the urban south's embodiment – 'a magnified ant-hill, just as commendable, and just as futile'.[39] Nevertheless, according to Bonnin, Robert's birth 'was significant because it accounted in part for both her wandering lifestyle and for the high accord given her stories in *Sun* newspapers'.[40] Psychologically, the experience of bearing a child out of wedlock cemented Hill's retiring qualities into a reluctance to disclose too much or to form bonds with others. 'She was always a mystery to me,' Beatrice Davis, Hill's editor at Angus &

Robertson, wrote, 'hinting at so much and telling nothing about herself'.[41] Even Bob found Ernestine intrinsically unknowable:

> I, who have seen a great deal of mother's life and have always been kept closely advised by her of her movements, her hopes and intentions, since the time when my great-aunt guardian no doubt read me letters from her during her travels around Australia, even during my very early youth, really do not yet know anything definite about mother as a person.[42]

Although it is often difficult for children to see their parents as individuals in their own right, this is an extraordinary statement given the many years Bob spent travelling and living with his mother as an adult. Irene Foster, or 'Rene', a journalist who worked with Hill at the *Advertiser* and corresponded extensively with her, found her 'inelicitible, elusive – a not to be pinned down person', speculating it was 'that first love … that made her seem so often remote, secretive and unwilling to meet people'.[43]

Very little archival material from this period in Hill's life remains, apart from recollections of her travels in the early 1930s. Neither the Fryer nor any other library holds any of Hill's personal letters written before 1939: no confidences or confessions to Coy, Madge, Aunt Kitty or the Duracks, or indeed to RC, exist. Not a whisper to imply that she was anyone except who she claimed to be – the wife of a late Mr Hill – nor any hint of what she might have felt about her lover, erstwhile or otherwise, whom she surely wanted to impress with her daring freelance journalism. Her travel notes, which consist mainly of sketchy outlines, impressions and snatches of dialogue, often seem opaque, as if she doesn't want you to see her, propping her notebook on her swag or crouching on a petrol tin by a campfire, scribbling away in her enigmatic shorthand. Hill is very much the reporter rather than the memoirist in her notes and writing. Although her articles often draw you in with a 'women's page' chatty camaraderie, she's a reticent narrator, a watchful spidery presence, reluctant to put too much of herself into the story, deflecting attention away from herself with tales of outlandish others. 'These "personality" specials are not from me, whose only reward is to be able to do more work,' she told writer Mary Durack. 'Quietly, I am no figure for a pencil or a pen and don't want to be.'[44] Like Bates, she had *little things* to conceal.

One of the first references to a 'Mrs Hill' appears in an October 1930 diary entry of Michael Patrick Durack, the pioneering Irish cattle baron whose sprawling East Kimberley pastoral properties Ernestine visited early in her travels across the country. His daughter Mary later recalled seeing 'a slim dark girl in a wide-awake straw hat and with no luggage but a small suitcase, a thin swag and a typewriter' step 'off the crazy open truck on to the verandah of the Ivanhoe Station homestead'. When her father, 'with his ever ready interest in people who did unusual things', asked what had possessed her to make 'this strange odyssey', Ernestine told them 'it was a line read in the chill of a Tasmanian winter: "The blacks' fires were burning in the Durack Ranges." Native fires in a wild range back of the back of beyond!'[45]

In late 1929 Ernestine Hill returned to the mainland to become a feature writer for the *Sunday Sun* that Packer managed for Associated Newspapers. But the position didn't involve relocation to Sydney: it was a freelance correspondent gig in which she was free to roam outback Australia, wiring back colourful stories to be published in the capital city dailies. According to Bonnin, the new job was 'subsidised by Associated Newspapers, apparently to keep her out of Sydney and as partial compensation for her plight'

– like writing a glowing reference for an employee you want out of the way.[46] Bob Hill thought his mother's story about reading a line about 'glittering bush fires' in the Kimberley was 'always a bit of a cover'; that she was 'shaken to the roots' after her affair with Packer 'then lived a wandering truly Bohemian life', never having a permanent home but camping everywhere.[47] Circumstances had forced on her, Ernestine enigmatically told Mary Durack, 'a sort of wandering sickness'.[48]

Initially, Hill flew with her suitcase and typewriter from Perth to Carnarvon, where she posted articles on anodyne subjects such as the difficulty of getting mail to the north-west, before flying to Roebourne, where she delighted in tracing the Pilbara's pearling history through its local Malay, Japanese and British burials. She stayed at country pubs like the old Jubilee Hotel in Roebourne, fascinated by the 'dusty punkah hanging in disuse' from the dining-room ceiling.[49] Upset by claims that she'd stayed at stations and that stories of her rugged life were all newspaper spin, she protested that she 'didn't believe in doing it'. True, in the early years, the 'business about a swag was theatricalism', she confessed to Margriet Bonnin in 1972. 'I was a stranger to what I was trying to do – I didn't get the true love of the trail in Australia until I got a bit familiar with [it]', although by the time she'd crossed the Kimberley to explore the Top End's mantle of tropics, she'd come to prefer 'rolling my little swag beneath the stars'.

> Meanwhile I was using Australia by and large as my ashtray. I had become past mistress of the art of bath in a billy … in full view of any audience there might happen to be on the great lighted stage of the Australian bush, of offending the men of the party behind a tree and slipping into a creek, night or morning, in performing the morning toilet in a puddle on the road. Taking notes in trucks bouncing over

the ruts, chasing wild men with a camera and digging a hole with my hip in the stones.

Before she set off, Hill bought a camera from Stephen Spurling (a photographer, who had a shop in Launceston), to take photos to illustrate her articles as journalists did in those days – 'never as today – as cub reporter accompanied by a cameraman!' – becoming expert at developing prints in hotel bathrooms. She'd take an empty petrol can and beg a nearby homestead for clean water from their bore, return to her hotel and brew tea while plugging up holes in the bathroom, then develop prints which she'd hang with safety pins on a line in her room while she finished her articles to post the next day.

'I wonder why I did all this. Was I "clean mad"?' she said to Bonnin. 'I'm not sorry.'[50]

Fellow journalist Patricia Kelley said that when she visited Quilpie, 'the people testified that E.H. was quite mad – a woman wandering about on her own asking all sorts of strange questions. But she certainly left her mark out there.'[51] Not only Hill's presence, but her presentation occasionally caught the unsuspecting off-guard. When Lucinda, an Aboriginal woman, told a central Australian station owner that a 'missus' – Ernestine – had been looking for him, she qualified the title with a reference to the white woman's unexpected garb, describing her as 'Not proplyfella missus, missie longa shirt and trousers.'[52] At Finke River, W Thompson, the 73-year-old storeowner, who'd been in the Territory for forty years, told her, 'When I left the world the women were in crinolines, now they're in short trousers.'[53] Hill revelled in the confusion her androgynous attire created, especially among men. Once after she bought a beer for an old prospector at Port Hedland hotel to 'oil him up', she heard him say to his fellow barflies, 'I been having a yarn to the little bloke that's writing a book.'

'[U]naccustomed to the ways of the new woman and deceived by my outback shirt and trousers,' Hill proudly reported, 'Jim had mistaken my sex.'⁵⁴

A New Woman at large, Ernestine was paradoxically at home with white bushmen, who named her 'good old "Ironstone" Hill' after the outcrops of rock flanking the dry creek beds in drought country for her steeliness.⁵⁵ 'And what was paramount above all this,' journalist Rene Foster wrote of her appeal for them, 'was an existence and a passion for the land, perhaps seen in a new light – before which they were confounded'.⁵⁶ Bushmen championed Hill because she shared their ideals and communicated them so vitally through her vision of Australia, although her relationship as a European woman to those living in its remote areas was not without challenges and contradictions.

'Out in the great wide spaces, where "men are men and beer is five bob a bottle"...' Ernestine Hill announced, 'has sprung from the spinifex in the space of a few short weeks a Gold City in embryo, with the faith of Australia and of £1,000,000 behind it.'⁵⁷ It was 1932, the year that set her on the front page of the public mind. Her freelance reporting career acquired momentum as articles based on her travels through Western Australia and the Top End, accompanied by her photos of exotic people and locations, appeared in the Sydney *Sun* and were syndicated to other major city newspapers such as the Melbourne *Herald*, the *West Australian*, and the Adelaide *Mail* and *Advertiser*. By 1935, Hill was regularly publishing pictorial essays in *Walkabout*, a widely read and respected Australian geographic magazine that was distributed internationally, which became a mainstay of her journalistic life. She became recognised among the ranks of popular bush writers, alongside

Ion Idriess, Frank Clune, William Hatfield, Henrietta Drake-Brockman and Mary Durack, who wrote colourful and graphic, if sometimes hyperbolic and unreliable, reports of life in the interior. Hill's early reporting also earned her a reputation for overinflated, inaccurate and dramatic claims, most notoriously in 'Cannibalism on East–West', her story about camping with Daisy Bates, and her contribution to a fake gold rush at The Granites in central Australia through features with titles such as 'Man's fight for desert gold' and 'Granites is Gold City in embryo'.

With its expanses of gritty red earth, punctuated by coarse spinifex, stunted mallee and habitually low rainfall, pastoralists had deemed the area known as 'The Granites', about 550 kilometres north-west of Alice Springs in Warlpiri homelands, as unsuitable for running cattle. Rumours about old-timers finding oddments of gold there and at the Tanami goldfields another hundred kilometres north-west had eddied about since the turn of the century. In 1931 Harold Lasseter died after attempting to locate a massive gold reef he claimed to have sighted on an earlier trip to central Australia. The story, which epitomised so many hopes and fears about prospecting, soon passed into national mythology through Ion Idriess's Depression comfort blockbuster, *Lasseter's Last Ride*. Hill herself later memorialised a version that Paul Johns, reputedly the last man to see Lasseter alive, had told her in a chapbook titled *About Lasseter*. During the Depression in the early 1930s, many hoped for a reversal of fortune such as the emergence of 'a new Coolgardie in the heart of Australia' although gold mining in the Territory had been in decline since the 19th century. Expectations swelled when CH Chapman, a Brisbane well borer, launched an expedition to the Tanami and subsequently paid £5000 to three miners for their claim, 'Burdekin Duck', at The Granites. When the men blew their money on a 'jamboree', the 'wildest tales of chance drill-holes boring into almost solid gold' began to fly.[58] As it was, Chapman, watching from afar in Melbourne, had indulged in a face-saving ruse, compensating the men when the mine provided only a small yield of gold.

After camping with Bates at Ooldea in June 1932, Hill wound her way up the Centralian corridor, sometimes riding the rail, at other times hitching lifts, often with the post, stopping wherever there was a hint of story. She heard news of Burdekin Duck on the wireless at Marree, a small town at the intersection of the Birdsville and Oodnadatta Tracks, and later by 'mulga wire' while she was 'meandering about on camels in the ultimate bush',[59] tracing the Finke River on camel-mail, her most exotic form of transport, from Horseshoe Bend to Hermannsburg. When she arrived at the Lutheran mission hamlet, she waited a week before finding a suitable truck to stow her swag and travel to Alice Springs.

Hill made the Stuart Arms Hotel her base in Alice, holding court with old-timers and would-be prospectors of an evening on its wide verandahs, thrilling in the talk 'of gold and camels and perishes and Tanami and the Telegraph line'.[60] News of the Chapman claim buoyed the hopes of businesspeople in central Australia, who had been feeling the Depression's pinch. With her customary hyperbole, Hill enthused that Alice Springs was 'the seething centre of the gold excitement of the continent', predicting that it would become 'a great and prosperous city'.[61] She was only there a few days before she succumbed to gold fever, bought a miner's right and a water bag, and threw in her lot with a geological expedition heading to The Granites, camping by the roadside and batting away flies while she boiled a quart pot over the fire. 'Flies! What do flies matter?' an old miner greeted her party when they arrived. 'Gold has been found in Australia at a time when gold was needed most.'[62]

'Little Mrs Hill did not know what she had started,' Eric Baume wrote. A New Zealand–born reporter, Baume was a journalistic boy wonder who'd worked for Packer since 1923. 'Indeed, when I arrived at Alice Springs she was amazed. "They've sent you from Sydney!" she said. "Good heavens, they must be keen for a story."'[63]

'They' – Packer and his fellow Associated Newspapers executives – were not only keen for a story. All sorts of disturbing rumours were circulating about how hundreds of unemployed people, often with no more than swags and the clothes on their back, had cadged the fare for the Ghan, now dubbed the 'Gold Express', from Adelaide. Many jumped the rattler, some hitchhiked, and a couple attempted to ride there on pushbikes. They arrived destitute in Alice Springs, ill-equipped to deal with the October heat, the flies, the limited food, water, bad sanitation and accompanying outbreaks of dysentery that plagued the miners. The Granites were another three days' drive on tracks that camels had traversed more often than Land Rovers, with sandy and boggy stretches in which trucks rarely broke 10 miles an hour. Some were so hopeful of finding gold they tried walking the distance.

'The rise of the Granites shares was too swift, too mysterious, too quiet to be all that it might have been,' Cecil Madigan wrote.[64] RC Packer, who'd become managing editor of Associated Newspapers, consulted with Keith Murdoch, the managing director of the Melbourne *Herald*, both of whom felt the situation warranted serious investigation rather than the fuelling of unfounded expectations, leading desperate people into further hardship. Packer commissioned Madigan, a geologist, to provide a more objective, scientific report than a mining company, despatching Baume, recently promoted to an executive position, to accompany him. Frank Packer initially joined them but returned to Sydney to undertake negotiations for his father at Associated Newspapers to acquire the *World*, the Australian Workers' Union daily.

After six days of 'examining, sampling, dollying, and panning' at The Granites, Madigan concluded 'the vein had already given out' and there 'was nothing else of any value to be seen on the field'.⁶⁵ Once his findings echoed across the east coast, the 'boom collapsed as rapidly as it had blazed up' and Granites gold shares plunged from £85 to fourpence in a few days. Mining companies withdrew from The Granites, and the heat moved on to Tennant Creek. Many amateur prospectors were left stranded in central Australia; within a month of her gold rush scoop, Hill chronicled stories of men begging for lifts to Melbourne and Adelaide, 'only too anxious to return to the cities, where there is some system of sustenance and a chance to work'.⁶⁶ No such assistance or opportunities were available in central Australia, and the federal government ultimately bailed them out by paying rail fares.

'Mother had not intended to create a sensation, Bob Hill wrote. 'She always said that the Granite Gold rush was a sensation of the time.'⁶⁷ Hill's breathless account of her visit to The Granites had been fuelled by existing rumours from the Chapman expedition and her mining contacts in Alice Springs. After visiting The Granites, May Brown, the 'Wolfram Queen', who invested in a string of Top End pubs from the proceeds of Wolfram mining during the First World War, criticised Hill and others for 'boom broadcasting' its untested yield. Moreover, as NT historian Sue Harlow comments, the stories Hill and other journalists told 'were embellished with a romantic character making their warnings ineffectual'.⁶⁸ 'We translated gold fever into headlines, and some of their copy was much more feverish than mine ...' Hill later wrote. 'In spite of the warnings our perhaps too picturesque description of dangers and privations – because of it, maybe – men still came from 3000 miles away, to disappointment.'⁶⁹

The Granites had been 'hot news', Baume observed, 'for Ernestine's stories have a punch about them which gets news editors where news editors should be got, and the front page is hers for the asking.' In his monograph *Tragedy Track*, which became the best-known account of The Granites false gold rush, he slated responsibility for the fiasco to 'Little Mrs Hill', as he condescendingly calls her. His preface, with its playground sneer of a title, 'She started it all', launches into a two-page torrent of mansplaining in the guise of critiquing Hill's journalism and her credulity in reporting 'what she heard as news', acting as 'a little mother confessor to those gaunt men of the desert' at the Stuart Arms. He follows with a take-down of Hill:

> She rushed out to the field itself in a shirt, a pair of shorts and a sombrero hat, after having been warned by telegram not to go by papers who did not want to be mixed up with the death from exposure or thirst of a crazy woman journalist who sent wires asking if she could go to The Granites and went before the answer forbidding her to go reached her! She had the time of her life. She met wild Myall blacks, she drank the bad well water and the mess from soaks and rock holes. She ate damper and she drank black tea. She thrilled the wireless operator at The Granites until he worked day and night for her ... She was deliriously happy, with adventure running through her veins like fire and the joy of endless stories permeating her.[70]

It's a blame-shifting, trivialising portrait cashing in on the romantic persona she and Associated Newspapers had created, here as the 'crazy woman journalist' who failed to heed advice from male newspaper executives, becoming swept up in the romance of the adventure at others' expense. Still, you don't have to read too deeply between the lines to feel the heat of jealousy rising from Baume's words: 'I have never seen a woman so adored by these men of the Territory.' Not only was he her rival in the Associated Newspapers stable and the right-hand man of her sometime lover, he aspired to publish his own travel writing. Unlike Hill, however, he wasn't a good camper. Madigan described how Baume 'sagged off' with another group member: 'their eyes were glassy and their faces purple'.[71] Only too happy to quit their Granites expedition early, he hitched a lift to Alice Springs to wire Madigan's findings to their southern media overlords.

Back at the Stuart Arms, Baume heard the clatter of Hill's typewriter in the early hours of the morning. 'She is telling the story of the Territory's heart,' he wrote sarcastically. 'If it is ever published, then it will be the greatest document, of Australians, of the century.'[72] He was busy dashing off his own pot-boiler; *Tragedy Track* was out before Christmas. But he was right to be jealous. Hill *was* writing the articles that would lay the foundations for what would become the bestselling story five years later of not just the Territory's but of the country's heart: *The Great Australian Loneliness*.

3

Great wide spaces

'They don't like the great wide spaces – saying with Pascal "le silence eternal de ces espaces infinis m'effraie".'[1]

At Ceduna, I became aware of passing into a transitional zone. Grittier, more down-market than Streaky Bay, an assortment of thrift, electrical and camping stores along its shopping strip, the town's main tourist drawcard is the plump, juicy local oysters you can buy from a van parked on the outskirts of town, at the pub or at the annual Oysterfest. Otherwise, it's the last port before embracing the Nullarbor's arid plains. I stopped there early one morning to stock up at its supermarket before rejoining the Eyre, where supplies would only be available from the occasional roadhouse.

The morning was brisk, with an icy bite to the air, despite being late September. Aboriginal people clustered along the foreshore's verge, dew glinting on the grass. Some hung around outside local services, waiting for them to open, waving to friends and family members in T-shirts emblazoned with organisational logos walking to work. In Foodland, I almost bumped into a shop assistant wheeling a trolley of frozen roo tails to stack in the fridge section – something I hadn't seen since my last trip to Alice Springs. I'd definitely crossed a metaphorical border.

Like Alice, Derby, Tennant, Katherine and other regional centres, Ceduna is a hub town where coastal and desert mobs can access services and resources. It's often a contact point that government and community organisations use in consultation processes when they sweep across the country, canvassing opinions on Aboriginal policy and service delivery issues. I'd previously made fly-in, fly-out visits to Ceduna for that purpose, the first being to consult for the former Aboriginal and Torres Strait Islander Commission (ATSIC) about regional autonomy – potential governance arrangements for Aboriginal people. That was back in the year 2000, when Indigenous representatives had a formal public profile and optimistic embers burned about self-government and self-determination. I'd hitched lifts with ATSIC officials from Adelaide to Port Pirie and Port Augusta to Ceduna. I remember peering out at dusk through the local hotel's plate glass windows across Murat Bay's reddening tones towards the hulks of container ships and oil rigs, and thinking, beyond that horizon, Antarctica lies. An ATSIC manager – one who told me that he'd never let a woman travel alone and definitely not without a sat phone – reminded me that just out of town, the Nullarbor began. With titles of books like Madigan's *Crossing the Dead Heart* and Mountford's *Brown Men and Red Sand* in mind, I imagined a glassy expanse, an ocean of orange dust. Until I lived in central Australia, I never had a conception of the desert or the arid zone as anything but a sandy wasteland.

Since colonisation, governments have envisaged this 200 000 square kilometre sprawl of land along the Bight in various ways, with proposals of a Nuytsland in honour of the explorer who named the plains 'null-arbor' – no trees – in 1838, and then a goldfield colony called Auralia, to be governed from Kalgoorlie in the late 19th century. The cavalier ease with which they imagined carving up this area issued from the falsehood of *terra nullius*: that the country was 'no-man's land', unoccupied before British colonisation. Central Australia has remained an imaginary state within the delineations of this space; once part of the north–south corridor of Centralia administered from Adelaide, it now comprises the remote cross-border region spanning the Territory's lower half and South and Western Australia. In November 2016 Bernard Salt published a reconfiguration of states and territories 'based not on accidents of history and European settlement but on the community of interests of modern Australians'.[2] In a cap doff to its brief administrative rule of central Australia from 1927 to 1931, Salt reinstated Alice Springs as the inland capital, observing it 'has waited 85 years to regain its title … but this time it will service a far bigger slice of the outback'.[3] In Salt's paradigm, it is to govern the vast region of Outlandia, a sparsely populated quarter of the continent extending from Kalgoorlie to Broken Hill and up to Alice, crossing every existing border except Victoria's. The difficulty in naming this unruly area, and its ever-shifting status, reflects settler discomfort with calibrating it within their idea of Australia.

Hill detected a shortsightedness among southern city-dwellers, a reluctance to look too far into the interior and into themselves. In a stark gloss on what AD Hope characterised as the settler population's tendency to cling to the 'five teeming sores' of its coastal capitals, she observed:

> They don't like the great wide spaces – saying with Pascal 'le silence eternal de ces espaces infinis m'effraie' and they don't like hills and mountains – too much energy needed to conserve the water and make the roads and climb to the top – to see how little is built on the hills take a trip round Australia by air. Mountains near town unclimbed in 100 years – chains of towns at their feet. Only a very few railways and roads spiral and climb the heights – to the spectacular wealth of a few mines. Myopic. They don't like looking far.[4]

The eternal silence of these infinite spaces frightens me. The expanses of the interior and the north were confronting to successive waves of settlers. What Hill saw as the country's loneliness had an existential dimension, bound up in the white pioneering mythology of the bushman, the ethos Russel Ward captured in *The Australian Legend* of the 'specifically Australian outlook that grew up first and most clearly among the bush workers in the Australian pastoral industry'.[5] *The Great Australian Loneliness* evokes solitary battlers toughing it out in a desolate wasteland punctuated by isolated homesteads and the bleached bones of swagmen and prospectors, which was at once familiar and unnerving for Hill's readers, interwar generations of urban Australians who'd become dissociated from the bulk of the country's land mass and the production of wealth sustaining them.

The Great Australian Loneliness, which Hill drew from her reporting across the country, poised her work at the crest of the wave of enthusiasm for writing about 'vast open spaces' or 'great wide spaces' during the 1930s. Notably it was a very masculine genre, pitching the lone male journalist as an offshoot of the solitary bushman. In 1931 Robertson & Mullens published Ion Idriess's *Lasseter's Last Ride* and William Hatfield's *Sheepmates*, whose success established the marketability of this outback-oriented, descriptive travel writing genre. These writers' preoccupations reflected debate about the potential for opening up the continent for economic development through mining and pastoralism in the wake of the Great War and the Depression. Author Patrick White also played on the notion of vast open spaces – the initials echoed in the title of his novel *Voss*, about explorer Ludwig Leichhardt – to allude to a mental or spiritual vacuity at the heart of Australian cultural life, characterising it as the 'Great Australian Emptiness, in which the mind is the least of all possessions'.[6] Although British critics in particular derided the 'surfeit of these dull saltbush sagas' as 'Schoolboy Efforts' because of their lack of literary finesse and mechanical (purple, in Hill's case) prose, the popularity of this genre – which outstripped fiction sales – during the 1930s cannot be underestimated. Author Kylie Tennant comments on how writers and readers looked to the bush for the basis for identity, especially as recreational travel became widespread:

> The publishing factor cannot be overlooked. Angus & Robertson, the dominant firm, found that its book-buyers, city and country, wanted books about the country they were just starting out to explore for themselves – not in official parties of exploration – and any books that told of people who did the travel first were popular.[7]

It was the impact of these books on Australian readers, rather than their literary merit, which was significant. 'Although these so-called middlebrow writers have been frequently scorned by critics and neglected by subsequent Australian literary history,' literary academic Anna Johnson observes:

> in fact they were very influential cultural brokers who mediated debates about place, race, and culture for the interested general reader. Their magazine articles and books provided many Australians with an opportunity to grapple with stories and ideas about the modern nation and to participate in discussions about emerging social formations and national identities.[8]

The backdrop for Hill and her fellow VOS writers was decades of public policy debate about whether the 'empty north', a sparsely populated expanse with potentially untapped agricultural and mineral riches, could be cultivated to provide wealth and security for the south or whether, given its unreliable rainfall and poor soil quality, it was a barren and inhospitable waste beyond redemption. Aboriginal people, who were perceived as nomadic hunter-gatherers doomed to die out, had little purchase in this debate, despite their longstanding connections to country. Neighbouring Asian countries were believed to pose a greater threat to white settlement, the subtext of President Roosevelt's infamous warning in 1905, 'Beware of keeping the Far North empty'.[9] It was a threat that southern politicians and policymakers took seriously in a period when Australia was trying to establish itself as a nation and national identity was synonymous with racial – that is, white – purity. Anxieties were expressed about the high concentrations of Asian people and Pacific islanders living along the northern coastline in Western Australia, the Northern Territory and Queensland, especially in Darwin, where they consistently outnumbered European settlers. A eugenicist notion prevailed that Europeans, let alone their wives and children, were not as constitutionally suited to living in arid and tropical climes as Asians. Debate oscillated between whether immigration policy's white cordon sanitaire should be loosened to admit more Asians to cultivate the country's proverbial fruit bowl or whether only trade should be permitted with Asia, and southern Europeans encouraged as more suitable immigrants to develop the north.

    What constituted the 'north' in these policy dialogues is often as hazy as it is in Hill's writing, where the idea of the 'empty north' frequently blends with that of 'vast empty spaces'. Trying to discuss *The Great Australian Loneliness*'s terrain, I find myself sliding between using 'north', 'central' and 'interior' – does the 'loneliness', for example, encompass northern and central Australia? – then collapsing these categories into 'remote Australia', another nebulous construction that might sweep as far south and wide as Outlandia. In closing the *Loneliness,* Hill tosses the gauntlet to 'smug, colour-conscious White Australia' to consider the struggles of black, white and brindle northerners, clefting the divide at the 20th parallel south. Although this latitude scores the country from Port Hedland through Tennant Creek to Airlie Beach, she reports on South Australian locations well below this line. More recently, consultation for the 2015 *Our North, Our Future: White Paper on Developing Australia* flung the girdle even lower to trace the Tropic of Capricorn, the 23rd parallel south, from Newman to Hill's birthplace, Rockhampton.[10] In the Territory, it was extended down to the South Australian border – a demarcation that drew ire from some WA communities at a similar latitude who perceived themselves as 'northerners'. The vagueness of where the north actually begins and the south ends in these configurations suggests that identification with either side of the divide is not just a matter of geographic co-ordinates but of ethos and affiliation, even a state of mind.

I identified with this state of mind when I first read *The Great Australian Loneliness.* 'The adventure is over. But my heart is out there for good,' Hill writes in opening the book – a melodramatic gesture to be sure, but beyond these words I recognised a restlessness common among those who've been in remote Australia. Dipping in and out of central Australia had become something of a habit for me since my first visit as a public servant from Canberra in the year 2000. I'd flown to Alice Springs and cadged a lift from a woman in a local organisation to attend a meeting at Yuendumu. I don't remember her name, only that she was vocal, cheerful and possessed of what seemed like a fearsome autonomy. We rose before dawn the next morning, and the woman drove at 140 kilometres an hour to reach the community, the LandCruiser juddering about as she tried to avoid potholes and corrugations on dirt roads. I watched mesmerised as the landscape's colours, that Namatjira palette – the subtle mauves, the pistachio greens, the burnt orange – waxed slowly into focus. It was the beginning of a process of seduction, culminating in my relocation to Alice Springs in late 2003. A decade later I left to take up a job in Melbourne, but found myself returning to central Australia every few months, as if I was suffering from a relapsing and remitting condition. This lifestyle of constant momentum is a not uncommon pattern for people who've lived in remote Australia; with it comes an idiosyncratic take on mobility and distance, and a longing to return. It's a form of *das unheimliche* or of unhoming: of having your fundamental sense of home unsettled by exposure to another experience of place, as if once having kicked aside your moorings and lost touch with the familiar, you can never see the country the same way again.

While the north epitomised the extremes of frontier existence for Hill, life above the 20th parallel was about embracing the otherness of being in this country and of what she saw as its loneliness. *The Great Australian Loneliness* is an encyclopaedic ramble retracing her roaming reporting in the 1930s up the Western Australian coast, across the Top End tropics, then through central Australia. The book, which was 'all rushed into a small canvas, and helter-skelter on' by Hill,[11] often writing until 2 am after a day at the Adelaide *Advertiser,* possesses a ragged jauntiness and loose open-endedness in contrast to her later, more polished and cohesive works such as *Flying Doctor Calling* and *Kabbarli*. For me, this is part of its charm and its strength, reflecting the narrator's enthusiasm for her wide-ranging subject matter; you don't go to Hill's writing for historical accuracy but for her poetic vision, her ability to capture the northern zeitgeist.

The *Loneliness*'s vision of remote Australia is paradoxical, offsetting white settlers' isolation in the outback with the narrator's curiosity about the vivid and diverse dramatis personae and geography she encounters on her travels. This tension in Hill's writing, which is the source of her facility in contributing to her era's dialogues about country and identity, stemmed from her personal history as a northerner working for a southern metropolitan newspaper. Her origins as a Catholic born in Queensland, the stronghold of the white working man's paradise and its supremacist racial purity policies, aligned her with the Anglo-Celtic battler, whom her employers at Sydney Associated Newspapers courted. Yet her childhood in Far North Queensland also whet her appetite for the rich variety of life above the 20th parallel. Her genuine interest and sensual delight in the north and what it has to offer in the *Loneliness* contrast with southern policymakers' anxiety about its future and its proximity to Asia.

The questioning, wide-eyed wonder Hill's narrator displays in her enthusiastic embrace of what she often calls remote Australia's 'weirdness' – cultural diversity – is a technique that as a travelling correspondent she's freer to employ than a policymaker, who needs to exert control over perceived social issues. Hers is often a playful, curious flirtation with diversity, a form of protomulticulturalism. As cultural theorist Meaghan Morris observes, Hill 'manifestly enjoyed the experience' of a '"white minority" nation ... She describes the formation of new ways of living together on a daily basis as well as of new multicultural communities emerging over time.'[12] Travelling through northern and central Australia, Hill felt more at liberty to explore living with diversity than she does in what for her did the smug, colour-conscious urban south. This is something of a paradox, then and now, given that the Australian north, like the American South, is often associated with rigid racial boundaries and beliefs. Yet contrary to expectations, in my experience life in the north offers greater proximity and exposure to the issues of negotiating cultural divides philosophised about at length – and great distance – in southern inner-city suburbs. The small population bases and isolation of outback cities and towns make it difficult to avoid whomever you might consider 'other', whether a white battler, a recent immigrant or a traditional owner. The plates of gender identity are also open to shifts. The adoption of a hardy, can-do attitude in the outback can involve women taking on behaviour conventionally seen as masculine, such as the fearless independence of the woman who drove me out to Yuendumu or of Hill travelling solo as a New Woman in her stockman's hat, shorts and boots. But Hill was not without her own contradictions when it came to gender, especially in her optimism about the roles European women might play in ending the isolation of Australia's great wide spaces.

'It takes a great measure of courage and initiative for a woman to set out on such a journey as she has undertaken,' MP Durack observed of Mrs Hill when she visited the Kimberley in 1930.[13] She spent several days with him, his wife Bess and daughter Mary at Ivanhoe Station, waiting for a leak in her vehicle's radiator to be repaired, then accompanied him to the main homestead at Argyle Downs, planning to travel on to Darwin. Durack enjoyed Hill's company; he found her a lively conversationalist, keenly interested in northern settlement. When WR Easton, the NT surveyor-general, joined their party, she quickly drew him into debate, 'contend[ing] that if homes were made more attractive women would be encouraged to come and share hardships with the men. Easton takes the opposite view. Says he would not himself ask women to live in the North.'[14]

'Wives are not encouraged in the wilderness,' Hill laments in the *Loneliness*. The Territory in particular was 'cursed only with the mistakes of misunderstanding and the hoodoo of its loneliness'.[15] She was sailing against the prevailing wind of male prejudice, as her encounter with Easton suggests. Historian Mickey Dewar comments that in early Territorian writing, men opposed the introduction of white women because it meant 'a modification of behaviour from the bush ways', their freedom to revel in 'masculine' vices such as drinking, 'whoring', gambling, racing and so on associated with frontier life.[16]

Yet for Hill, the lone white men – diggers, fossickers and prospectors – she met ostensibly without the comfort of family and domicile in the outback assumed a melancholy nobility. She romanticised their predicament, declaring that 'all Australian bushmen are knights-errant', writing of the '"Gentlemen riders" who became stockmen in the early days in the Territory, and ended up very far out. Most of them too far – hermits – on a beach or by a waterhole, roofless.' Enticing more white women to share the lives of male battlers was for her the panacea to the loneliness and critical to securing civilisation. *The Great Australian Loneliness* is dotted with sightings of isolated women, like Mrs Ratigan, who'd 'lived mostly alone for mostly 35 years' and was 'the only white woman in 250 straight miles' at Halls Creek, and Mrs Shadforth, who'd driven cattle overland for 2000 miles but had 'made a pretty home on the edge of beyond', complete with 'lubras watering the garden'. They were heroic figures 'holding back the North for us, which without them must slip back, ever and again, to a haunted, homeless loneliness'.[17] The problem was how to attract enough European women to fill the 'vast blank melancholy of the Australian bush', with its tense silences.

Hill's most ambitious attempt to grapple with the loneliness occurred in October 1933, when she became the first journalist to enter 'the rim of the Arnhem Land, the triangle of death' after the Caledon Bay crisis. The previous year, Yolŋu had killed five

Japanese fishermen who'd breached Arnhem Land's waters near Caledon Bay; two white men died in a further, related incident at Woodah Island. McColl, the white policeman despatched to investigate, was speared, and Dhakiyarr, the Yolŋu man charged with his murder, was sentenced to hang, although he later successfully appealed this sentence. People feared racially motivated violence might spread to Darwin: there were threats of a police raid to 'teach the blacks a lesson'. Despite these volatile events, the dauntless Hill sailed into Arnhem Land on a supply boat, aware that she was entering a de facto self-governing Aboriginal state, 'the only corner of Australia that has persistently baffled, and even frightened, the white pioneer', where Yolŋu had 'defined the laws of his making, and, with a fierce patriotism, preserved their race intact … they keep their country still'. Part of the lure for her were the 'two "white-fella Lubra"' rumoured to have survived a shipwreck in 1925. She was startled to discover five women 'living many miles from each other, who have faced the danger and the loneliness for many years, unmolested and unafraid'. 'You feel safer when the blacks are about,' they told her. 'It is when they disappear on "walkabout" that the bush grows lonely and frightening.' To Hill, their situation modelled how increasing white women's presence would contribute to peaceful coexistence between Indigenous and non-Indigenous people in the north. Later, on hearing that the Commonwealth government had sent anthropologist Donald Thomson to befriend Yolŋu using 'his experience and bush-craft and sympathy', Hill mused that 'a woman with a swagful of sweets, a bright pretty frock, a gentle voice, and an accordion and a baby in her luggage' would more easily make peace with the locals because a 'woman with a baby, a lubra with a piccaninny, are always sure friends'.[18]

Hill was not alone in claiming that European women could soften the edges of the colonial project. 'Woman is a born

Adventurer', Viola Apsley declared in 1926 – words Ernestine might have written – after she and her husband, a pair of English aristocrats, published *The Amateur Settlers*, a Wodehousian account of their escapades exploring the Australian interior's suitability for British working-class migrants. But Australian travel writers such as Hill, along with William Hatfield and the Price Connigraves, who rhapsodised about the suitability of the north for European female habitation, had another agenda: fear of miscegenation and desire to shore up a white national identity. The 'steadily-increasing propagation of half-breed races' resulting from sexual relations between white men and other ethnicities was the most visible and troubling sign of these 'bush ways' for Australian commentators, especially in the Territory, whose mixed-race population had doubled within the previous decade. The Territory's future was unthinkable 'without the influx of white settlers in large numbers', Hill proclaimed, without which 'the future of White Australia in the north looks very black indeed'.[19]

Along with politicians, bureaucrats, anthropologists and social reformers during the 1920s and 1930s, Hill attributed miscegenation to the greater ratio of white men to white women in northern Australia. In his report *The Aboriginals and the Half-Castes of Central Australia and North Australia*, the chief protector, JW Bleakley, mooted the solution to the 'most difficult problem of all' was to 'encourage white women to brave the hardships of the outback. One good white woman in a district will have more restraining influence than all the Acts and Regulations.' While Hill never mentions Bleakley's report directly, her writing dramatises these social policy concerns. 'Men take strange brides in this lonely land,' she announces in the *Loneliness*, emphasising that these 'weird unions' between European men and Aboriginal women are often born of frustration and 'a fiendish loneliness, that eats into a man's soul'.

Yet she counters the idea that these are always marriages of convenience with vignettes about mutual affection, such as a white man's eagerness to marry an Aboriginal stockwoman legally and 'a black woman who tended a lonely white man through long and desperate illness to become his faithful wife for many years'. When she visits Darwin – 'the scapegoat of white Australia' according to the accepted public policy prognosis – she can't help marvelling at the range of racially diverse relationships she encounters, such as an Aboriginal woman raising a Greek child, a white boy adopted by a Chinese family, 'a Greek wedding with Chinese bridesmaids, and a Manila string band in attendance, and a Chinese-Filipino and a Norwegian-aborigine who are Australians and first cousins'.[20] Hill's fascination with these 'weird unions' and 'grotesque love stories' has a prurient streak, and her cataloguing of exotic others has a freak show quality, but although she is apprehensive about the future of a 'brindle north', she undermines prevailing social dogma by portraying these relationships as non-threatening and benign. Her curiosity about intercultural relationships opens a gap between her allegiance to the official 1930s policy line on miscegenation and her emotional response to what she encounters, her delight in the north's cultural diversity.

Far more fantastical for Hill than the 'strange brides' some white men take is the reverse situation: white women marrying non-European men. The most intriguing of these is Jackie Forbes, known by the disparaging nickname of 'Witchetty', a 55-year-old widow living on 'blackfella tucker' in 'a little village of wurlies' in the Flinders Ranges. A Cockney woman, she was married to an Aboriginal man for eighteen years under both white law and the 'blackfella wedding' firestick ceremony of NSW tribes. Mrs Witchetty had no regrets about this decision or about adopting her husband's lifestyle, wandering from station to station with him and their two sons; indeed, she felt fortunate to live with 'a free, good-hearted people'. Although her husband had been dead a year, she was now part of the mob and received 'a gin's frock of blue galatea and a blackfella's blanket once a year', along with their weekly rations of tea, flour and sugar. As far as Hill knew, Mrs Forbes was the only case of a white woman 'living black'; even Daisy Bates preferred to live near rather than within Aboriginal camps. But if Hill had a sneaking admiration for how Mrs Forbes 'thinks black', she is careful to distance herself from the woman's 'weird life' with light and not-so-light mockery:

> Mentally above the average, writer of very interesting letters, Mrs Forbes, since her unique marriage, has had practically no association with women of her own race ... On the other hand, she knows no inferiority complex. With no housework to do, she spends all her days in reading hair-raising thrillers, blissfully unconscious that she is the most hair-raising thriller of the lot.

Assimilating in the wrong direction, as it were, Mrs Forbes adopted qualities that settlers associated with Aboriginal people, becoming 'lazy and contented like my husband's people'.[21] Perhaps most curiously of all for Hill, Forbes is so comfortable with her adoptive people that she doesn't feel the need to associate with other white women.

The 'strange case of Mrs Witchetty' provides an unexpected answer for Hill about whether it's possible for Europeans to integrate with their new environment – one she implies is a dead end. She didn't foresee the emergence of mixed-descent Aboriginal people, such as Mrs Forbes's sons, who 'speak good English, but better blackfella', as a sign of survival and the continuation of culture. Instead, they bear the tragic burden of miscegenation, living in a no-man's land between two cultures – 'half-way between the Stone Age and the twentieth century'. Hill's views here are in keeping with the pre-assimilationist era's outlook on miscegenation; that the increasing numbers of 'hybrids' were symptomatic of Aboriginal people's inevitable passing, the half-caste being 'the sad futureless figure of this lonely land'.[22]

Aboriginal women come in for particular censure in Hill's commentary on miscegenation, which is frequently patronising and moralising. 'The black woman in sexual contact with the white man is a tragedy that she herself never understands', who 'understands only sex, and that she understands fairly well. She is easy for the taking', and the half-caste girl is no better: 'unmoral as her mother … an easy prey for the unscrupulous white wanderer'. Aboriginal women and girls bear the brunt of white projections of guilt in the *Loneliness*, which portrays settler men 'suffering the full curse of comprehension' of mixed-descent children's future and forfeiting 'any white woman's respect and devotion' as a result of miscegenation. Hill often falls back on stock infantilising, dehumanising stereotypes of Aboriginal women common to her era, as 'extras' in the background of settler life, as laughing, amenable, childlike people who provide comic relief – the 'grinning gargoyle of comedy in the Territory' – and grease the wheels of colonisation: 'a lubra standing behind in the shadows smiling'. She also claims their status is inferior within Aboriginal society, likening a woman in one instance to an old camp dog, howling and scrabbling about, asserting that Aboriginal women don't possess any cultural knowledge – an erroneous idea she probably acquired from Bates, who believed that men were the principal cultural custodians.

Yet Hill makes a startling detour from conventional narratives about European settlement in the *Loneliness*'s second-last chapter, asking readers to consider the country's indebtedness to Aboriginal women. Within white Australia:

The part that the lubra has played in colonizing Australia is never acknowledged, except by a few of the more honest old pioneers. In wild country, where the white man ventures alone, she is always the first to make friends … First to guide him to the secret waterholes, with her quick intelligence she picks up a word or two of his language, and learns that he is ready to barter tasty white flour and the magic tobacco for whatever mad quest he is out on. Time and again her intervention with the tribe has saved his life.

She describes 'instances of their devotion and loyalty' to settlers, comparing Aboriginal women favourably to young men: 'Much more active and intelligent than the boys, in Kimberley and the Territory lubras are even to-day recognized as the best "stockboys" and easily the best trackers, and throughout the courts of the North and Centre, in nine cases out of ten, they are the interpreters.'[23] That said, she frames Aboriginal women mainly in terms of their historical value to white settlers, hinting at, but not elaborating on, the exploitative sexual and economic dimensions of their experience during northern settlement.

Hill was aware of Aboriginal women's 'very considerable part in the colonisation of a country that is actually more closely theirs than our own'; of the drovers boys, dressed as androgynously as herself, with their own brand of invisibility working alongside settler men in the mines and on cattle stations. This is more apparent in snippets of observations within unpublished notes from her travels that I came across in the Fryer Library's Hill collection, such as: 'The lubras, in shirt and trousers, lived in the saddle as horseboys with pack-teams, camels and donkey teams, hard manual labour – goat-shepherd, gardeners housekeepers on the stations, as well as wife till the wives …' 'COLONIZATION ABJECT,' she wrote on another loose-leaf in the Hill Collection headed 'Yellow

Ochre. Anmatjira' – a reference to a mine near Rumbalara in central Australia. She knew that Aboriginal women often worked in mines without rights or payment: 'I have seen the miners of the Territory all lay [sic] on the flat of their backs in bough sheds while lubras did the work, winnowing gold at Winnecke, dry-blowing gold in their pitchis with their breath – "blowing" – or pouring one and letting the wind do it.'[24] It was difficult for European women to attain rights or to support themselves on remote minefields, but Aboriginal women were an available workforce who quickly adapted traditional implements, such as the digging stick, the pitchi (a container like a coolamon) and the yandy (used for winnowing seeds) to western mining.[25] When Hill describes alighting from the Ghan at Rumbalara to follow the Finke River on camel back in *The Great Australian Loneliness*, she only mentions that the 'quaintest mine in Australia' is nearby, giving a passing nod to its owner, Harvey, who 'employs a bevy of lubras to dig out the greasy, sulphur-coloured clay'.[26] But she doesn't expand on their working conditions, although her notes indicate she was aware these were often exploitative.

'No one has ever paused to hear the story she will never tell. She goes down into darkness inarticulate – lubra, the world's least,' Hill wrote, defending the *Loneliness*'s inclusion of a chapter about Aboriginal women.[27] Her chapter was among the earliest attempts at a sympathetic account of their predicament in frontier relations. Others such as Bleakley were aware of Aboriginal women's unsung role in northern settlement, observing: 'a lubra is one of the greatest pioneers of the Territories, for without her it would have been impossible for the white man to have carried on'.[28] The period's most extended fictional treatment of Aboriginal–settler sexual relations on the frontier was Katharine Susannah Prichard's controversial 1929 novel *Coonardoo*, about a romance between an Aboriginal 'stock-boy' and a white station owner. Xavier Herbert's

Capricornia, which covered similar themes, came out in 1938, not long after the *Loneliness*. With post-colonial hindsight, aspects of Hill's portrayal of Aboriginal women are paternalistic and denigratory, particularly the act of a white woman pausing to tell an Aboriginal everywoman's story rather than Aboriginal women speaking for themselves. Yet this chapter's attempt to alert readers to Aboriginal women's situation was unusual for an era in which they were seen as hardly human and rarely rated a positive mention in mainstream publications.

Opening *The Great Australian Loneliness*, Hill explains that while she originally journeyed to 'the Australian wilderness to study the blacks', the immensity of this subject – 'three lifetimes' worth of study' – defeated her. Instead, she found 'the whites in that vast and lonely country ... so much more "the story"'.[29] This is an honest and understandable shift in focus, given that Ernestine was a young journalist tackling intercultural themes for the first time when she set off, but it flags the issue of balance in the *Loneliness* and her ultimate allegiance to the settler narrative. Hill was strongly influenced by her first pastoralist hosts, the Duracks, forging a longtime bond with MP Durack's eldest daughter Mary. When Hill stepped off the truck at Ivanhoe Station in 1930, Mary had quit school in Perth. She acted as her father's driver on his rounds of their family's vast holdings, Ernestine accompanying them. Mary was seventeen, over a decade younger than Mrs Hill, but life in the north, its country and its people, exerted a similar magnetism over her as it did Ernestine. She also had writing aspirations and began reporting for the *Western Mail*'s women's pages to support herself when her family's fortunes foundered after the Depression in the mid-1930s and published three books, with some sentimental and romantic Aboriginal content. According to biographer Brenda Niall, Mary and her younger sister Elizabeth participated in humanitarian activities, such as concealing Aboriginal people from police during raids at Ivanhoe.[30] Mary Durack was later best known for her popular family history *Kings in Grass Castles*, published in 1959, which chronicled MP Durack's three-year trek in the mid-1880s with his father, Patsy Durack, and his uncle Michael, driving 7250 head of cattle and 200 horses from Queensland to establish their pastoral dominion in the Kimberley.[31]

Hill lionised the Duracks as the white bushmen par excellence, remnants of a fading gentry – 'the only true pioneers we have left in Australia'. Recounting their 'colonisation of virgin soil' in the *Loneliness*, she attributed any hostility to the local Aboriginal people – 'the blacks were bad indeed'.[32] In 1887 when a Durack cousin, John, was speared at Falls Creek, an angry party of police set out with black trackers to avenge his death. *Kings in Grass Castles* depicts them faltering at the limestone cliff: 'whether further more successful reprisal measures were taken for this deed can never be known. The conspiracy of silence that sealed the lips of the pioneers address colour to the rumours that spread abroad.'[33] Records set the Aboriginal death toll at seven. The pioneers' conspiracy of silence also clouded the total number of Aboriginal people killed in the East Kimberley from 1890 to 1926, a period now referred to as The Killing Times, when police and pastoralists used violence to dispossess Aboriginal people. In 1927 a royal commission was established to investigate the massacre of approximately twenty Aboriginal men, women and children the previous year at Forrest River Mission, now Oombulgurri, in a police-led raid to retaliate for the murder of a pastoralist, Frederick Hay. Lumbia, a local Aboriginal man, had speared the stockman in self-defence after Hay had raped one of his wives then bullwhipped him. Hay was from Nulla Nulla station, north-west of Wyndham, which was not part of the Duracks's holdings, but the events would have been fresh in local memory when Hill visited the Kimberley four years later.

Hill was candid in her early reporting about how brutal some encounters between settlers and Aboriginal people had been, as indeed many journalists were: colonial newspapers featured regular coverage of frontier conflict. In 'Murray – Scourge of the Myalls', a 1933 article about Constable George Murray, who was then on trial for the deaths of thirty-one Aboriginal people in the Coniston massacre, Hill stated: 'Occasional murders by the blacks in 60 years of [central Australian] history have inevitably been followed by drives of vengeance on the part of police and settlers. At Blackfellows' Bones Range, at Attack Creek, and at other places, skulls and skeletons in their hundreds have commemorated many a wholesale massacre.' She also acknowledged that white settlers had placed themselves in danger in central Australia by 'settling their cattle on the native's waterholes, confiscating his tribal hunting-grounds as pastures, and of necessity chastising him for killing a beast for food'.

Yet the disproportionate atrocities committed by the likes of Murray in response to the petty thefts and occasional murders by Aboriginal locals who'd been dispossessed from their land and resources are outweighed by her fascination with the constable himself. Hill descends into a largely glamorising portrait of Murray as a returned light horseman from Gallipoli, 'a Melbourne man, and a fine character, quiet, methodical', staking a claim with his wife and family in 'a lonely little police station ... alone amongst uncivilised blacks, and unafraid'.[34] This puff piece affects an almost bland acceptance of these killing sprees as the status quo, exonerating Murray of his monstrous culpability in taking thirty-one lives. How starstruck Hill appears by Murray suggests her susceptibility to being suckered in by the doyens of frontier life as a young reporter. No more of such troubling stories appear in the *Loneliness*; instead she soft-pedals interracial conflict, framing it as 'human dramas in a tragic country, white against black, black against white, eternal triangles, tribesmen's enmities, the grim battle of the pioneer'.[35] Hill was reliant on the hospitality of pastoralists such as the Duracks during her early reporting, and held a romantic view of their fiefdom and their nobility as the north's conquistadors. She also may have wished to present uplifting material befitting a nation-building tome in the *Loneliness*, not foreseeing the renewed life that ephemera such as newspapers would later have through digital resources such as the National Library's Trove.

In 1939 MP Durack commended Hill for her rendering of Aboriginal issues in *The Great Australian Loneliness*: 'I admire your broad humanitarian outlook so fully exemplified in your book. Your unfailing sympathy for our Native Race whose sad fate has been so clearly shown in your book.'[36] Hill gleaned her initial insights while visiting his Kimberley properties in 1930; she interested herself by 'getting information re native folk lore and dances', watching a corroboree from the 'inevitable petrol-tin seat of honour' on the sidelines to scribe what she perceived as the passing ways of a vanishing culture. Hill adhered to the early-20th-century belief that Aboriginal people were a doomed race throughout her life, although she did not maintain European culture's superiority, claiming to prefer Aboriginal people's ethic: 'here are your true Communists'.[37] Other travel writing contemporaries, such as Max Lamshed, also entertained notions of Aboriginal culture as intrinsically socialist, a notion grounded in Rousseau's noble savage, a romanticism that has long inflected European perceptions of Indigenous peoples. In keeping with this romantic view of Aboriginal people as primitive and untouched, Hill saw them as aimless, childlike nomads, incapable of adopting a western lifestyle, which was the fundamental tenet of assimilation, mooted as national policy at the first Commonwealth–State Native Welfare Conference in 1937. She also doubted their ability to be self-governing, arguing, like Bates, that making 'reserves for them on land useless to white people was valueless'. Instead, the 'wisest dispensation' was protection under the pastoralists' benevolent autocracy, in which Aboriginal people received food in exchange 'for a minimum labor' and 'the maximum freedom possible'. Of these mini-protectorates, the 'blacks of Kimberley were the happiest and best cared for of any'.[38]

Not everyone was as complimentary as MP Durack about Hill's portrayal of Aboriginal people. Predictably, other pastoralists lauded her claims that they were best placed to manage the remaining Aboriginal people in the north, but her comments drew ire from missionaries. Mary Bennett, who began teaching Aboriginal children at Mount Margaret Mission near Laverton in October 1930 while Hill was visiting the Duracks, was critical of the 'squattocracy' – pastoral feudalism – she saw at work there and in the Territory. Far from the benign, if fading, idyll that Hill depicted, the pastoral north was a punitive domain:

> where women have neither human rights nor protection if they are natives or half-castes – slavery is in operation and there is white slave traffic in black women. The destruction of the natives is caused by the white settlers dispossessing them of their land and by the settlers commercialising for their own advantage the native patriarchal system which, while exhibiting among the wild natives many good elements, has the defects of other man-made systems in that it is unjust to the women and children, treating them as property. Commercialised, it is wholly evil.[39]

While Hill might have agreed with her about the negative effects of dispossession on Aboriginal people, she thought Bennett's portrait of the feudal north was overdrawn and had 'no hesitation in saying that her allegations are not only, in the great majority of cases, utterly untrue, but a cruel injustice to the only true pioneers we have left in Australia'. Instead, Hill claimed the pastoral model gave Aboriginal people the best support in terms of food, clothing and medical attention in exchange for unwaged labour, arguing they were unable to handle money.[40]

Bennett and RS Schenk, the superintendent of Morgans Mission Station, retaliated with letters to the *West Australian*'s editor, calling out their romanticism of the pastoral industry. Schenk protested that 'more than any other industry', the pastoralists had robbed Aboriginal people of their land, been most responsible for their slaughter and 'bred most half-castes'. Pastoralists showed 'the least desire to establish the native race' because they had the most to gain; the dying race precept supported their interests. Arguing that 'where natives are cared for properly they increase and do not decrease', he cited a 50 per cent growth in the birth rate during the ten years since the mission had been established. Aware that the pastoralists benefited from 'free native labour more than any other' industry, he took issue with the idea that Aboriginal stock people didn't deserve wages in return for their hard work – 'when instructed, natives are not fools with their money' – suggesting they should be allowed to live in communities on their own land because 'if they are dispersed among whites the race will soon end'.[41] Similarly, Mary Bennett criticised Hill for underestimating Aboriginal people's ability to manage their own affairs, emphasising it was 'time that the wickedness of white men was charged to them, instead of … to their black victims'.[42]

Hill closes the *Loneliness* with a salute to the passing of the pioneer era as the introduction of the 'aeroplane, the radio and the motor-car' sweep in the 'king-tide of colonization' to the outback: 'The men who subdued the wilderness with turkey red and tobacco are quickly slipping away. I should like to be back there before the last of the conquistadors is gone.'[43] She was ultimately loyal to the pastoral model, believing it could accommodate both Aboriginal and settler interests in remote Australia by providing pastoralists with a virtually free source of casual workers and Aboriginal people the opportunity to stay on their own lands and observe cultural practices. Hill's vision was infused with romantic ideals, belying her tendency – as in much of her reporting – to overlook the more troubling practicalities on which her enthusiastic avowal of northern life hinged, in this instance the benevolent jurisdiction of individual station owners and the availability of work. Her loyalty to pioneering mythology, intertwined with mourning for loss of the Aboriginal 'story', remains throughout her published work, predicated on the view she shared with Bates and many of her era that Aboriginal people were passing.

That 'book has many imperfections that I could show you in an instant', Hill admitted to the Duracks after *The Great Australian Loneliness*'s publication, although she was glad if they thought 'it did come somewhere near' to the reality of living in remote Australia because 'you do belong to that country'.[44] The book was more widely appreciated than her understated remarks suggest: reprinted eight times by Robertson & Mullens in Australia between 1940 and 1956, *The Great Australian Loneliness* sold just under 40 000 copies, receiving warm and enthusiastic reviews in Australia and Britain. The *Sydney Morning Herald* declared Hill 'a graceful, observant and warm-hearted Australian writer', her

'Australian idyll' an '[a]dmirable Australian travel book', revealing its 'author's deep understanding and veneration of the great open spaces of Northern Australia and the people, white and black, who inhabit them.'[45] *Air Mail* endorsed it as 'a vivid and arresting page of the history of Australia … a book for all Australians to read.'[46] The *Bulletin* sardonically observed: 'A few years ago a book about Northern Australia was something of an event. Now it is a rare season that does not produce one or two,' although: 'Allowing for a certain romantic inflation, her effort is the most comprehensive northern epitome which has been written for many a year.'[47]

'A sunset to Mrs Hill is never a sunset, it is a flaming volcano', Rene Foster commented tartly. Ernestine gave the initial draft of *The Great Australian Loneliness* to Foster, her friend and fellow journalist, to read during a 120 degree Fahrenheit heatwave in Adelaide, buoying her along by lighting a fire to make a cup of tea. Rene must have stepped on her tongue many times while reading Hill's draft; she was privately horrified by its purple prose but reminded herself that 'This was E & what she had seen & how she had lived – & the wonder and the strangeness were hers also to tell about.'[48] Critical responses to *The Great Australian Loneliness* echo the polarities of Foster's comments. A British *Spectator* critic accused Hill of overstimulating the reader: 'she is so obsessed with her search for "human interest" and her job of "putting it over" that she forgets that though an article full of "punch"' may wake up a bored newspaper reader, a whole bookfull [sic] will put him to sleep'.[49] Publisher PR Stephensen cautiously described Hill as a 'high class journalist', noting her writing was marred by 'a sometimes too-obvious striving for effect', although he thought the *Loneliness* made a significant contribution to its genre and to general knowledge about the country: 'the field is so wide and the observation so careful, that readers could not fail to learn something new about Australia'.[50] Similarly, literary historian

HM Green maintained the appeal of *The Great Australian Loneliness* outshone her hyperbole: 'her stories and sketches of outback types are so good that even worn phraseology and occasional streaks of purple prose cannot spoil them.'[51]

Hill's male counterparts viewed *The Great Australian Loneliness*'s author as both asset and liability for the 'Northern School' of writing. Frank Clune criticised his fellow 'vast lousy spaces' writers for favouring story over truth-telling, singling out Hill for particular censure: 'Earnest-Tine ... certainly leaves her imagination to weave fantasies, which is all right until she imagines her furphies are fair-dinkum. Like Jack Idriess she never worries about truth.' Similarly in *Tragedy Track*, Baume railed against the excesses of Ernestine's prose, although she did offer a guarded apology for her and other journalists' contribution to the Tanami fiasco – 'our perhaps too picturesque description of dangers and privations' – in the *Loneliness*. But while 'Idriess does some weird things with history, as well as crocodiles', Clune saw Hill's lack of critical acumen – 'Poor Ernestine, she listens to all the baloney that bushmen feed her' – as a particularly female failing: 'women historians perverted history to suit their own sinister ends.' Bush writer Henry Lamond took criticism of female bush writers a step further, replying that although he liked 'old Ernestine' and enjoyed her sense of humour, it was 'Rather subtle at times. I fear, though, she's falling for the common female complaint: she's starting to preach about what should be done.'[52] Professional rivalry aside, his comments reflect the long-held male suspicion about what would happen if European women with their do-gooding ways were allowed to intrude into the traditionally white male bastion of the bush.

Other critics cast what they saw as feminine qualities of Hill's narrator, such as her empathy and unassuming stance, as advantageous in enabling others to tell their story. HM Green compared

Hill's travelogue favourably to Idriess's *Men of the Jungle*: 'Unlike Idriess, she writes like a visitor but a visitor who is sympathetic and keenly observant', noting in something of a backhand compliment that 'it is their subject that interests them, not themselves'.[53] Even the critical *Bulletin* reviewer observed that the *Loneliness* 'gains by a certain modesty of attitude in the authoress – as distinguished from her attitude to atmospheres and situations – towards her own achievement in accomplishing her journeys. They certainly could not have been either easy or comfortable to a woman bred to city life.'[54]

The curious bystander persona of Mrs Hill, ostensibly at ease among the north's panoply of exotic characters, is certainly one of *The Great Australian Loneliness*'s paradoxes. The *Bulletin* observed, 'she does not ever appear to have had cause to be lonely'; as Meaghan Morris says, 'Hill's book could have been called *The Great Australian Sociability*.'[55] Yet there was a superficial aspect to Hill's conviviality. She often stopped only long enough to be seen but not known in any place, using a reporter's stance to hide behind her notebook and turn the flashlight of inquiry onto others.

Then there's the conundrum of Hill, a lone woman, possibly a widow, dressed like a man, who left her only child to chase her journalistic ambitions, urging other European women to cultivate the outback: why didn't she take her own advice? The greatest friend of the lonely white male settler, she often held court, if FE Baume is to be believed, among admiring prospectors and miners. The old timers 'loved and admired this slim dark, dark eyed girl who appeared seemingly out of nowhere,' Rene Foster wrote, 'with practically nothing except her horse, her saddle, her typewriter and books and the makings of bully [sic] tea and some frugal food.'[56] More cynically, Miles Franklin observed to Katharine Prichard: 'She gazes at men and they think she's a siren – the asses', a line that suggests Ernestine had a strange sexual charisma, perhaps born of repression, or even an aura of untouchability post-affair.[57] Indeed, Hill doesn't appear to have had any substantial romantic liaisons after Packer. If her wandering sickness and travelling journalism were fired in the crucible of a clandestine affair and an illegitimate birth, the absent Mr Hill was in other respects a convenient fiction. Consciously or otherwise, the charade of widowhood, supported by her mother and aunt, released Ernestine from a life of child-bearing and hearth-tending, giving her the freedom to embrace the life of the New Woman, to travel and to write.

RC Packer had suffered from heart disease for years and travelled to London in September 1933 to seek treatment from a specialist. When he became seriously ill several months later, his son rushed to join him, staying until his health improved. Sailing back to Australia, Frank received news that his father had died from a cardiac arrest while cruising the Mediterranean with his wife and daughter on a P&O ship, the RMS *Maloja*, on 12 April 1934. He blamed RC's death on 'business worries', his strong sense of 'duty to the newspapers … during a most difficult period' – attempting to shore up his dynasty through Associated Newspapers – observing bitterly that his father 'undoubtedly suffered gravely as a result of the strain of this onerous work'.[58]

Hill was at sea herself, voyaging up the coast of Western Australia on the *Silver Gull*, Perth's largest yacht, which boasted luxury cabins, a crew of seven sea scouts and a woman navigator, Beatrice Grey, who impressed her by juggling 'the whole of the scientific work' while overseeing domestic arrangements and negotiating 'the navigation problems in reef-infested and unfamiliar seas'. Ernestine thrilled at 'living upon turtle-eggs and fried schnapps and 'roo-tail soup and rock oysters' while following the traces of Dirk Hartog and William Dampier in the north-west and shoring up impressions for her book about Matthew Flinders.[59]

My love must wait. Plenty of women wait for men for all manner of reasons in life and art, but waiting is the particular leitmotif of the other woman, however brave or independent a cast she puts on it. How does a mistress hear about the death of her lover when separated by great distance? Did Hill see RC's death notice published two days later in the *Sydney Morning Herald*, or receive a wire from concerned relatives when the yacht docked at Derby? Or did Mary Durack tell her the news when she joined her on the deck of the *Gull* while it moored in the Cambridge Gulf? Hill must have known how serious fears were for his health, although there's no hint about what she felt, of course, in any of her notes or letters. In 1943 she told a reporter her husband had died ten years earlier and one of her obituaries gives 1933 as his year of death – timing that roughly coincides with RC's demise.[60] Perhaps when she turned to write Flinders's story she felt she understood Ann Chappelle's psychological landscape, playing Penelope to Flinders's Ulysses, waiting for him to return. Except that for Hill, whose lover had abandoned her to roam the outback, the roles were reversed.

Without Packer's protection as protégé feature writer and sometime mistress, Hill was exposed to the interests of her rivals at Associated Newspapers – his son Frank and Eric Baume, now editor of the *Sunday Sun*. According to Louise Campbell, RC kept her on the payroll as a retired secretary after Robert's birth with a stipend of £10 a week to look after his illegitimate son, but the money stopped when Packer died. His lawful son, Frank, inherited his shareholdings; RC's estate was valued at £54 306, the equivalent of $5 million today.[61]

Hill acted swiftly. Sir Lloyd Dumas, managing director of the Adelaide *Advertiser*, owned by the rival Murdoch newspaper group, had long hoped she would join his staff as a feature writer. She finally took up his offer, shifting her home base – Madge, Kitty and ten-year-old Robert – to Adelaide in May 1934. It was a move that brought her closer to Daisy Bates, that great soak of story, on the rim of the Trans-Australian Never-Never land.

II | PASSING

4
An uneasy alliance

*'How happy shall we be working at that book together?
Cannot you realise that it must be your book?
Let me help with the presentation, because it
will be such a joy to me. That is all.'*[1]

Ooldea is much harder to visit than when Hill blithely stepped off the Trans in 1932. The *Indian Pacific* whips from Tarcoola east of the Nullarbor to Cook in the west without stopping. You can drive up from the Eyre Highway if you know where to turn off – after Nundroo Roadhouse but before Yalata – then follow the bitumen for 80 kilometres before rattling over a corrugated gravel-and-limestone road for another 60 to the railway crossing at Ooldea. No-one lives near the old siding or in the dunes or by the soak anymore. In June 1952 Anangu were abruptly removed from their country surrounding Ooldea in preparation for the British nuclear tests at Maralinga.

I'd hoped to detour to Ooldea on my drive across the Nullarbor, interested to know whether anything remained of Bates's camp. From what I'd read, a four-wheel-drive was necessary to tackle the dunes bounding the soak and even then shifting sandhills often obscured the old campsite. Nevertheless, I thought it worth trying to visit to gain some impression of what it had been like, living on the soak's banks, and whether it had really been as isolated as Bates and Hill had claimed. I knew that other Bates researchers had travelled to Ooldea several decades earlier and that they'd had guides from Yalata, the community off the Eyre Highway on the Bight where many Anangu had been relocated after atomic testing in the mid-1950s. I wondered whether there might be any Anangu who still remembered Bates, or who'd met Hill, although it seemed unlikely. Anyone who'd known Bates when she lived at Wynbring station on the East–West Line in the early 1940s would be around eighty; they'd need to be almost ninety to have memories of Hill's visit to her Ooldea camp in 1932. Remote Aboriginal people often have shorter-than-average lifespans, and I'd read that Anangu living in the area had also experienced increased rates of cancer and other illnesses from radioactive contamination after the Maralinga tests. I was curious to hear what Anangu might have to say about Bates, although I thought that if I approached Yalata Anangu Aboriginal Community, at best I might be able to speak with some descendants of people who'd known Bates. But would they even want to talk to someone researching Bates, I wondered, given how she had vilified Anangu and their culture?

I applied for a permit to visit Ooldea from the council that manages the area for its traditional owners, asking whether anyone with memories or stories about Bates would be willing to meet with me. A month later, the council's manager advised me that my permit to visit Ooldea had been approved. She told me that a couple of men from Yalata, including its chair, would take me up to the soak, 'because you won't find the camp – it won't be where you think it is'. She was right; even with a map and a four-wheel-drive, I knew I'd have no hope of locating Bates's campsite in the Ooldea sandhills.

And yes, the manager told me, some senior women with memories of Bates were willing to speak to me.

I was overwhelmed; it was beyond what I'd imagined was possible.

Except, she continued, the chair's partner had died recently, there were sorry camps in the community and her funeral was being held during the week I proposed visiting.

'Surely it will be too difficult for me to come then,' I said. Arrangements to visit an Aboriginal community might be scuppered by any number of eventualities such as people leaving to attend a local or not-so-local carnival, a rodeo or even a religious revival. But a funeral, an all-too-common event in remote community life, was definitely the worst of all possible scenarios.

The manager said the chair had approved my visit and was continuing his other activities. The older women were also expecting me.

I paused, scrambling for alternatives. It was several weeks since the chair's partner had died; it often takes longer to organise funerals in remote areas because of how far kin may have to travel from other areas. All the same, I felt uncomfortable about rocking up to an unknown community at such a time. I couldn't imagine picking my way around sorry camps and pestering a bereaved Aboriginal man to accompany me to Ooldea to research someone that he and his community have good reason to hate. And regardless of culture, who asks someone to take them on a tour during the week of his partner's funeral?

I'd deliberately left my trip across the Nullarbor open-ended because I wasn't sure how much time I'd need, so I offered to return on my way back. The manager gave me the chair's mobile number and when I rang to suggest alternative dates, he sounded relieved, saying, 'I've got a lot of visitors coming.'

Later, as I drove along a strip of the Eyre lined with dark grey gums, I passed two metal kangaroo sculptures flanking the turn-off to Yalata. The notion that the East–West Line skirted the Ooldea sandhills 200 kilometres north of the highway seemed remote and improbable, and I wondered whether I would ever visit the siding where Hill had stepped off the Trans, or battle over the dunes to Bates's old campsite.

In May 1934 the *Advertiser* featured a photograph of an insouciant Hill in Oxford bags and a stockman's hat, slouching against an upended swag propped against a giant termite mound. After three years of frequenting 'the least known corners of a sparsely inhabited continent', Mrs Ernestine Hill was mooring herself in Adelaide. But she was not so easily tethered. Being a freelance travel correspondent had been a gift to her; she hated the daily grind of newspaper reporting and being assigned routine jobs, such as writing about life in the genteel, orderly southern capital. To break the tedium, Hill had been pursuing that 'veritable Trader Horn of a woman', Daisy Bates, with what she thought was an enticing offer: to write her memoirs as a newspaper serial. Not only that, but Ernestine contemplated sending it to Spencer Curtis Brown, her agent in London, to consider publishing it as a book: 'The story, as I see it, should be a big seller, translated into many languages ... and still carry its wonder with it.'[2]

Bates had been in Adelaide to receive a CBE from the Lieutenant-Governor, Sir George Murray, for her thirty-five years' work among Aboriginal people, an honour that she cherished as 'royal recognition!'.[3] But she didn't stay long; she had pressing matters to attend to back at Ooldea. In 1933 she'd been summoned to Canberra to be considered as a government-endorsed mediator in the Caledon Bay crisis. Like Ernestine, she was unfazed by the prospect of travelling into Arnhem Land's turbulent territory, although at seventy-four she was a far cry from the soothing woman in a pretty frock, armed with sweets and an accordion with a baby in her luggage, that Hill had envisaged in this role. But the

Commonwealth government had passed over Bates in favour of Donald Thomson, who was half her age, and, disappointed, Daisy returned to Ooldea to find an even worse scenario had unfolded in her absence. An itinerant missionary had 'jumped' her camp, gathering up Aboriginal people with the help of local police and taking possession of the soak.

The following summer, drought and dust storms fanned bushfires into what seemed like perpetual being in the scrub around Ooldea soak. It was relentlessly hot, even by the Nullarbor's standards, the mercury soaring over 120 degrees Fahrenheit in the shade, making it impossible for Bates to concentrate on writing up her notes from tent life. Anangu had left the soak, shifting their camps east along the railway line to Wynbring and Cook, but Bates dug herself in. For years she'd stuffed her notes in containers around her tents; now she bundled them together, took a wana and chipped a hole in the sand inside her breakwind, and buried them in a tin trunk. Fettlers hacked firebreaks around her camp to protect her canvases from flames and airborne cinders.

Back in Adelaide, Hill regaled fellow staff with reports of Daisy's eccentric bravery, reading out extracts from Bates's letters until she came to the line: 'I am so blind that I can only smell the burning when my clothes are on fire.'[4] Ernestine demanded a meeting with Sir Lloyd Dumas, the *Advertiser*'s managing director, barging into his office saying she feared not only for the safety of 'the dearest, most difficult little one in the world' but that her notes, her lifetime observations from camping with Aboriginal people, would go up in flames.[5] Taking these inflammatory developments as her cue, Hill pitched her idea of serialising Bates's life in the *Advertiser*, stressing the significance of 'her collections of data from the now-vanished Aboriginal tribes, and the grievous loss to Australia if they should be destroyed'.

Dumas regarded her proposition thoughtfully then suggested

that the *Advertiser* bring Bates and her trunks of material to Adelaide without delay, offering a hefty advance for the rights to her life story. But although he understood the project's value and urgency, he doubted Bates's ability to write to the standard required for the *Advertiser*, observing that her recent articles had been 'diffuse, profuse, rambling, too mannered and out of date or too obscure in meaning for the present day, sometimes involved with aboriginal words and references unexplained, sometimes juvenile as in fairy tale'.[6] According to Hill, he made one stipulation: that she write the serial, not Bates.

Ernestine prevailed upon her friend again, apologising for 'straining on the leash', proposing that Bates start mailing her copy, which she would polish and type up then post back 'for your official seal of every line'.[7] Given Daisy's age, 'precious time' was going, along with the opportunity to get her memoir in print: 'you have so much of what the world is breathless to hear – you will interpret a lost people, from a lifetime's knowledge.' Besides, Hill was not without competition. Ion Idriess, her main rival, had been in contact with Bates a year earlier, proposing that he write her story.

The long-distance co-writing arrangement with Bates didn't eventuate, but Hill continued to bargain, pandering to Daisy's ego, casting the project as a joint one in which she took a back-seat role. 'How happy shall we be working at that book together?' she enthused. 'Cannot you realise that it must be your book? Let me help with the presentation, because it will be such a joy to me. That is all.'[8]

Bates swatted away Hill's requests to join her in Adelaide with polite murmurs about the difficulties of assembling her notes. Unexpected rain had soused the flames and the Spinifex people were beginning to return to the soak. Daisy was reluctant to abandon her camp, fearful of what might happen if she relinquished what control she had left at Ooldea.

The itinerant upstart who'd muscled in on her domain while she'd been hobnobbing in Canberra was Annie Lock from the United Aborigines Mission (UAM). Robust, industrious, tenacious and highly mobile, Lock spent periods working in New South Wales and Western Australia before moving to Oodnadatta in central Australia in 1924: the *History of the UAM* describes her willingness to travel as 'true to her pioneering nature'.[9] A solid, doughy, beaming presence in dowdy practical wear, Annie Lock lacked Daisy's theatrical flair and mental acuity but her stamina and relative youth – she was in her late fifties, seventeen years younger than Bates – made her a formidable rival.

Lock had been on furlough in Western Australia in late 1932 when the UAM Council directed her to investigate Aboriginal people's living circumstances along the East–West line, with Tarcoola and Ooldea as potential mission sites. She stopped at these stations on her way back to central Australia with 'my blind companion', a Miss Mary Battams, and together they trudged over the dunes from Ooldea siding to the soak. Reporting to the UAM Council in February 1933, she observed that 'The natives at Ooldea were in a destitute condition, not receiving any rations, and chiefly existing on what they received by begging from those who travelled by train and that which was thrown to them from the dining car attached to the train.'[10] Six months later she returned with another missionary friend, driving some 500 miles from Crystal Brook near Port Pirie in a buggy that had been used as a fowl's roost coupled with a retired horse she'd bought from a farmer and £2 for chaff that Constance Cooke had wired her from Adelaide. The South Australian chief protector of Aborigines had agreed to the UAM's request to open a depot if they supervised the distribution of rations – tea, sugar and flour, the less-than-nutritious European diet to which Aboriginal people had become accustomed – at the soak. Daisy had of course petitioned the protector and the commissioner of railways unsuccessfully for this role when she arrived at Ooldea, but the SA authorities looked more favourably on Lock because she was less troublesome and a member of a benevolent institution rather an unclubbable iconoclast like Bates.

Lock established herself quickly at Ooldea in 1933, enlisting Anangu in building a four-room iron cottage, a bush church, a medical dispensary and a workhouse that doubled as a ration depot and a store, with plans to open a school the following year. Along with evangelism, her missionary work focussed on practical concerns – feeding, clothing, housing and educating people. She corresponded with Constance Cooke and Mary Bennett, with whom she shared similar concerns, visiting the latter at Mount Margaret Mission at Laverton. Lock's letters lack the reach and rigour of Bates's observations in describing local Indigenous life (and her spelling is appalling), although they do reflect a humanitarian ethos. Lock proclaims that Aboriginal people are 'real socialist', and that: 'If you respect and treat a native as a human being he will treat you the same. The natives' moral laws are good and one cannot help respecting them.'[11] It was an outlook that earned her an unexpected notoriety.

In 1929 Lock was subpoenaed to give evidence to a Board of Enquiry in Alice Springs, 'concerning the killing of natives in Central Australia by Police Parties and others' – the series of raids, known as the Coniston massacre, which Constable George Murray led to avenge dingo hunter Fred Brooks's death at the hands of some Aboriginal men near Ti Tree in 1928.[12] The enquiry had been instigated in response to pressure from church and humanitarian group leaders, along with Protector Bleakley, amid continuing unease and public speculation about the treatment of remote

Aboriginal people following the Coniston massacre. Lock had been conducting mission work from a brush shelter at Harding Soak near Coniston station but had left in October 1928 as drought and hostilities mounted, taking two local Aboriginal girls to Darwin for medical treatment. En route they stayed in Katherine with another missionary Athol McGregor, where Lock met Bleakley, who telegraphed the minister for home and territories afterwards with her grim confidence that 'natives this tribe [Kaytetye] reported to her that police party including six civilians surrounded camp women making arrest and shot number of natives and several women and children were killed'.[13] McGregor also pressed for a public enquiry based on Lock's information. Local Warlpiri, Anmatyerre and Kaytetye have since estimated that 170 Aboriginal people were killed over two months.

The enquiry ultimately cleared Constable Murray, who'd led the raids in reprisal for Brooks's death, concluding each of the officially reported thirty-one Aboriginal deaths had been justified. Blame for racial tension in the area was slated instead to 'a woman Missionary living amongst naked blacks thus lowering their respect for the whites'.[14] The Adelaide *Register* dubbed Lock 'The Aboriginal Anti-Feminist', asserting she was 'performing such work that would be done more effectively, and with considerably greater safety to herself, by a man'.[15] Local station owners were loud in their complaints, but two male missionaries made the most vituperative protests. HA Heinrich from Hermannsburg mission claimed Lock had confided in him that she would be 'quite happy to marry a black', which she hotly denied to Bennett:

> Everyone knows I am dead against the white men being with the black women, but they tried to put me in the wrong ... by reporting, falsely, that I had said I would be willing to marry a black man, and that I was lowering the standard by being

among nude natives. What I said was that I do not know how any one [sic] could marry a black.[16]

This gossip, aimed at deflecting attention from the enquiry's real subject, drew on widespread moral panic about miscegenation, especially in the more unusual case of white women living alone near Aboriginal men – like Bates. The *Register* paralleled their activities at their respective soaks: '… both of whom are at least entitled to be judged heroic, [but] students of the native mind protest that the very presence of white women among black men is inimical to the maintenance of proper relationships between the two races'.[17]

Mrs Bates is 'very funny & wont [sic] speak to me or anyone here at the Siding only on any particular business [sic]', Lock told the SA protector. 'If I want to know anything she told me to write to her not to speak to her, so I dont [sic] worry her about anything.'[18]

To outside eyes, Bates and Lock may have appeared similar as lone white women camping perilously alongside Aboriginal people in remote Australia, but they had profound differences in outlook. Bates was horrified by Lock's boasts 'of her unbounded success in Christianising, civilising, educating, saving souls'.[19] As an ethnologist, she disapproved of missionaries disrupting traditional cultural practices by replacing Aboriginal names with English ones and inma with hymn-singing and Sunday School lessons. Bates was a rationalist; she'd also been sceptical about the content of *Borderland*, the spiritualist magazine to which WT Stead had assigned her as a subeditor in London. Although she professed to be an Anglican and frequently mentioned God in letters – often in the same breath as Lawrence, Havelock and Nicholson, British military statesmen and pillars of empire – it was part of a historical cultural subscription to theism as well as her performance of allegiance to Empire and all things British. Daisy was a keen observer of the natural world, habitually attracting animals to her camp, often interspersing annotations of Aboriginal vocabularies and stories in her notes with lyrical meditations on the 'shy and mystical' Australian bush:

> One is in God's own house here in the wild wide spaces … Clouds pass over sun or moon leaving soft shadows on the tender green of mallee and mulga, and the quiet hours when the wind is still and when all nature seems to rest for a moment's prayer. To watch the daily lives of bird, beast and reptile in any portion of God's great open house is to believe and be strong in faith and worship and love. One is able to enter God's house at all times, there is no need of bell or candle or book or any artificial aid to worship.[20]

If anything, Bates's passion for observing the habitat around her was more akin to Celtic nature-based spiritual traditions. After Lock's arrival, she withdrew further into her sanctuary beyond the breakwind with the birds and 'quaint little burrowing creatures of earth' for company; Lock observed the 'tittering of birds' when she passed it and the rabbit warrens beneath.[21] Visiting Anangu began gravitating to the mission with its rations rather than to Bates's 'lonely little camp'.

The two women's struggle for control over Ooldea Soak became pronounced during the Duke of Gloucester's visit to Cook on the East–West Line in 1934. Bates had something of a fetish for organising Aboriginal pageantry for the passing dignitaries; she may have imagined a reprisal of her role when she facilitated a 'native arts-spear-making and spear-throwing' demonstration for the Prince of Wales when he'd stopped at Cook in 1920 while travelling on the Trans. Even earlier, she'd been asked to stage a Bibbulmun corroboree for the Duke of York, later George V, and his wife at the Perth showground in 1901. This event had led to an encounter imbued with great significance for Bates: afterwards, while attending a garden party at Government House, she'd dropped her long black umbrella and the duke had retrieved it for her; thereafter, she fondly referred to it as her 'King George V umbrella'.

But on this occasion in 1934, the authorities turned to Annie Lock to organise a ceremonial reception for the duke. Claiming the prince had been 'terribly disgusted' by the Aboriginal performers' display of flesh in 1920, Lock clothed them in knee-length shorts, which she ran up herself, for modesty's sake, 'to be a better advertisment [sic] of the treatment & help of Australia who have taken their country & all their lively hood [sic] away from them and to show the Duke we are doing something for them in return'.[22]

Daisy refused to be sidelined, appearing at Cook, where she managed to grab a brief interview with the duke. 'Bates was in at the Siding in state with her medel [sic] on but a disappointed woman,' Lock wrote cattily to a friend.[23] But, ever the showstopper, it was Daisy who featured on the front cover of *The Sphere* magazine, a diminutive, straight-backed figure in black leaning on her umbrella, uncowed by the strapping figure of the duke in jodhpurs, toying with his crop.

Bates was aggrieved by this turn of events, pressing Hill for reassurance. Hill told her not to fret about this 'infamous' incident but to focus instead on 'the big achievements that are to come' – the proposed newspaper serial and book.[24] But Daisy continued to ignore Ernestine's overtures. It wasn't only the need to assemble her multitudinous notes or to protect her fiefdom from the missionaries that was holding her back. She'd heard that JA Lyons, the prime minister, would be passing through Ooldea on the

Trans. Status obsessed as ever, she'd requested an audience with him, hoping to discuss a position that she'd devised for herself: 'Protector-in-General', high commissioner to the Aboriginal people throughout Australia.

But when the Trans bearing the prime minister paused at Ooldea, Lyons was asleep and his secretary refused to wake him. Waiting in the afternoon heat beneath her royal umbrella, Bates was shamed again in full view of the fettlers and their wives. 'I felt such a fool standing there speechless, not knowing which way to turn, till I begged the guard to leave me the key of the lamp room, and there I hid till it was dark.'[25] Her options exhausted, in mid-1935 she packed her notes into her battered trunks and boxes and gave the contents of her tent, including her faithful set of Dickens and her tools, to 'a nice little redhaired freckled child about 10 or 11' who lived near the siding.[26] Her 'working clothes' she dispensed to Anangu at the soak, along with a 40-gallon tank of rainwater she'd kept for crisis situations. In a final tribute to the annual Empire Day celebrations she'd thrust on them, they used up the remaining water and flour to make damper for a farewell feast.

Bates left in state, like royalty, with thirteen Aboriginal men hauling seven loads of boxed manuscripts on ropes 'in a queer procession' down to the siding.[27] They also carried churinga, totem boards that she'd kept hidden for sixteen years, which she donated to the South Australian Museum.[28] Only men could accompany her to the train; the boards had to be kept away from the women, who watched from the north side of the line. 'It seemed a dream that the old life was over,' Daisy declares in the *Passing*, 'the old life of eternal wind and sand, the long, long droughts that take ten years to come and go, the so meagre yet so crowded years that I had spent in such strange company.'[29] A haunting photograph of her leave-taking shows a handful of Aboriginal men, dressed in sack-like European clothing, holding spears twice their height, clustered round the side of a passenger carriage. A turbaned Bates leans out of the window, head bowed, hands clasped as if giving a final blessing.

She had ordered that the 'warm tent and the breakwind must be kept sacred to the memory of Kabbarli', but her campsite quickly became derelict.[30] 'When Mrs Bates left, she placed a native in charge of it,' Lock reported. 'After a while the natives realised that she was not returning. They raided the camp, tore down the tent and a few days later were walking about in clothes made from the canvas. The birds were driven off and the rabbits were eaten.'[31]

Ernestine was waiting with Mrs Rymill, president of the National Council of Women, to welcome Daisy when she arrived at Adelaide Railway Station. Hill had been giving speeches to the council on topics like 'Black Australia, a Human Problem of Today' at the Adelaide Women's Club, discussing the exploitation of Aboriginal women that had occurred 'in the absence of white women in the far north'.[32] Now she could introduce its members to the woman she thought most remarkable in Australian history, whom she hoped to 'cast in immortality' through a newspaper serial and a book. She and Mrs Rymill loaded Bates with bouquets when she alighted from the Ghan; Daisy gave them to a small boy selling violets outside her hotel, paying him double for a bunch before announcing, '"Take these flowers in my arms and you can sell them" – quite oblivious of what the givers might feel.'[33] It was a gesture that reflected her propensity for random if misguided generosity and also to be emotionally tone deaf to her friends.

Bates had requested that the *Advertiser* put her up at the South Australian Hotel but she soon transferred to the Queen Adelaide Club, which had been founded by the city's 'forward-thinking women' and was, like Perth's Karrakatta Club, the most exclusive enclave of its type. This style of accommodation might seem a strange choice for someone who'd spent the past sixteen years in tents, but she preferred living at extremes – 'I never could tolerate half-measures.'[34] Daisy had a Rip Van Winkle moment in her hotel room, recoiling from the desert-worn face she hardly recognised in the mirror before distracting herself by turning on taps for the sheer delight of seeing running water.

Bates fronted up early at the *Advertiser* each day, revelling in the novelty of office life with its ambient sociality. She enjoyed pranking the staff and would 'bolt down the stairs as Mr Dumas was listening' – to her in congress with Hill – 'pretending I was going to fall – and then grinning at him'. Walking about town to preserve her hourglass figure, she enjoyed a more benign crazy dame status than she'd had at Ooldea. She was virtually a VIP, with social worthies inviting her to speak at functions and children asking for her autograph – a welcome antidote to her bruising rivalry at the soak with Lock. 'Do you remember my barging in upon you all – unable to hide my joy,' she later reminisced to Hill. 'I had been so lonely for all those lovely minds & hearts I met when I came down to write my book … you all meant a lovely South Australia to me.'[35]

What meant a lovely South Australia for her didn't necessarily equate to one for Ernestine. The pair cloistered themselves with Bates's grubby manuscripts in the *Advertiser* library – 'a glass-lined cubby of about ten by eight', the same measurements as Daisy's main tent – a young typist from the clerical department crammed in with them.[36] Hill had told Bates that the 'story of her life could be told by her alone' to entice her down to Adelaide but she took carriage of the process. She describes her 'biography without tears' approach in her memoir, *Kabbarli*: 'Method and manner of writing the newspaper serial and the book were left to me … We decided that she would talk, and I would write, and she would read for additions and amendments, and I would make "fair copy" of the work with these for her finalities.' Of a morning Daisy dictated stories from her life to Ernestine, who, ever the reporter, asked questions and took notes, which she reworked into readable prose during the afternoons. Although Bates read the resulting copy 'innumerable times, she made no amendments or corrections that I know', Hill later wrote.[37] If she is to be believed – most of the extant commentary is hers – she did the bulk of the writing of the serial that became the international bestseller *The Passing of the Aborigines*.

At an Adelaide *Advertiser* office party on Christmas Eve in 1935, Daisy lavished gifts on newspaper staff, presenting Ernestine with a diamond-encrusted watch. Hill 'sternly declined' this extravagant trinket, noting with some poignancy the dissonance between her friend's 'endless giving' and her long derelict years. In its stead, she requested 'a few brief lines acknowledging our work together' on the serialisation of Bates's life story. Hill would later claim that when they commenced their collaboration, Bates had insisted both their names appear on the title page if the serial was published as a book, 'but from all she had given in life – which I well know – and little vanities, at times, I insisted No'.[38] The *Advertiser* was to begin publishing the series under the title *My Natives and I* early in the new year and as the date drew closer, Ernestine regretted her decision. Nervous that Bates's memoir might achieve all that she'd promised in sales and acclaim, Hill volunteered that 'if the book was a success and brought in all the happiness I wished for her', Bates's affidavit on her contribution 'would mean much more to me'.

But she'd missed her moment. Bates replied several months later with a carefully worded thank you note: 'As I read through the chapters, I come upon so many evidences of your own words and sentences – the loving-kindness is a beautiful way in which you gave of your own genius to expressions – that I shall always look upon the completed work as much yours as mine.' She never gave any formal or written recognition of Hill's role, except to introduce her socially as 'my dearest friend – she wrote my book!'[39] After the *Passing*'s publication, Daisy acknowledged Ernestine's assistance transcribing her dictation but claimed that essentially they were her words and thus her book, later admonishing an interviewer: 'No, she typed it, she typed it, but every word in that manuscript is my own, every word of it.'[40] Hill was a celebrated and capable journalist, and it was diminishing and disingenuous to dismiss her contribution as merely that of a typist.

Ernestine had rescinded her rights to be recognised as co-author much earlier, when she'd bargained with Bates to coax her down from Ooldea with the promise: 'It must be your own book in every way ... A commercial association would be intolerable, an acknowledged contribution would be wrong.'[41] She'd presented this gesture as 'a gift from her to me in recognition of her patient years of devotion to her own ideals and to the people and the land we both knew and loved'.[42] But it was a gift she came to regret. 'Ernestine, with her usual damnable quixotry, allowed Daisy to claim authorship of "The Passing et [sic]" because "it gave my dear Daisy so much pleasure",' declared Barbara Polkinghorne, who knew both women and became Bates's secretary in 1945. 'Oh dearie me!'[43] Why Hill should have subordinated her interests to Bates's was indeed rooted in her own quixotic psychology.

'You know I don't think Mrs Hill was the right person to cope with Daisy Bates. She is a very fine writer, and a woman of feeling and imagination, but she did not seem to have the right feeling for Mrs. Bates.' Journalist Elizabeth Wolff, then an assistant to the Adelaide editor of the *Women's Weekly*, provided the only description that exists of Hill and Bates's working relationship in the *Advertiser* office apart from Ernestine's in *Kabbarli*. Tearing down King William Street during a downpour one day, the young reporter saw Bates 'without raincoat or umbrella, whizzing along with her head turned up to the pouring rain, and holding a disintegrating brown-paper bag', the pansies on her hat sodden, her high-necked shirt and suit streaming with rain.

Wolff rescued a couple of tomatoes that had bounced out of Bates's disintegrating paper bag onto the pavement, taking the opportunity to invite herself to the *Advertiser* office. On arrival, they 'were greeted with a mixture of concern, exasperation and horrified amusement' although the young typist 'was the concerned one', trying to rub Bates down with a table napkin before bringing a radiator to dry her soaking shoes and stockings. Mrs Hill, on the other hand, 'was more exasperated than amused and was not a bit interested in her delight in the feel of rain on her face'. She had 'the air of a nurse-maid, utterly unable to control her charge, who had almost given up trying'; so much so that Wolff queried whether she had the proper 'feeling' as well as the stamina for dealing with Bates. Daisy appeared more vigorous and youthful than Ernestine, who was then in her mid-thirties:

> Mrs Bates was at that time about 78 I think, and Mrs Hill looked to be in her late thirties or early forties. I don't know what her real age was. But she was small and very thin (no more than seven stone, or maybe less), her face was sallow and thin and her voice was a hoarse whisper, due to some ailment

in her vocal cords I guessed, and she looked simply corpse-like beside the upright and shining Daisy.

Wolff was biased and admitted as much: 'How I longed to have her job! I hadn't the brains, of course, but how I would have loved it.' A self-confessed 'very green new reporter', she was too young and inexperienced for Hill's role, and Ernestine had good reasons to be exasperated by her charge. Her glowing cameo of Bates as 'a visitant from an earlier world, but with an amazing zest for the present' shows how even a young person could be swept up in the force field of Daisy's charisma.[44]

Meaghan Morris discusses their friendship's dynamic within a more sophisticated frame, observing that Hill possessed 'an ethic of extreme personal reticence and self-effacement', so much so that her personal memoir, *Kabbarli*, 'is all about Bates'. On the other hand, Daisy's egomania and talent for self-promotion anticipates for Morris the late-20th-century era of celebrity: 'Oddly, in the age of Paris Hilton and reality TV, this makes the Edwardian Daisy Bates in some ways seem the more contemporary figure, with her flamboyantly anachronistic dress and her readiness to fashion her own legend as a public personality.'[45] Dwelling in obscurity for so many years, her ambitions thwarted by powerful men, Bates welcomed the admiration of younger women such as Hill and Wolff, eager for a screen on which to project her aspirations and inflated self-importance. Ernestine was herself quietly ambitious: at an early age, she had sent her poems to the *Bulletin* and aspired to work for a southern metropolitan newspaper, then published attention-grabbing, sometimes unreliable features to establish her profile as freelance correspondent. But unlike Bates, she wasn't born against the backdrop of an era characterised by the grand excesses of Empire and extravagant self-fashioning, and her career peaked during an economic depression between two world wars in a period marked by stoicism and austerity. Hill's pattern of habitual self-erasure also had its origins in her childhood as the obedient, convent-educated daughter of a domineering mother, making her susceptible to being swept up by older, cyclonic figures like Packer and Bates. A dance of equivocation, by turn deferential and protesting, marked her friendship with Daisy Bates.

Daisy Bates, Gauera (seated) and Balgundra (standing) while crossing the Bight by camel buggy from Eucla to Fowlers Bay, where Bates caught the steamer to Adelaide to attend the British Association for the Advancement of Science conference in 1914.
Image courtesy of the State Library of South Australia. B 70068

Daisy Bates with Aboriginal people at one of her Eucla camps, c 1914.
Image courtesy of the State Library of South Australia. B 70069

Telegraph buildings at Eucla, c 1935. Photographer: Howard Gwynn Watson.
Image courtesy of the State Library of South Australia, HG & EM Watson Collection. B47686_32

View of Ooldea siding, c 1920. Photographer: AG Bolam.
Image courtesy of the State Library of South Australia. B45287_1

Daisy Bates in 1921 after she'd begun camping at Ooldea on the East–West line.
National Library of Australia. 2628004-0

Daisy Bates (seated, centre) with a group of Aboriginal men, women
and children at Ooldea, 1920–23. Photographer: AG Bolam.
State Library Victoria. H34000

Ernestine Hill with swag, leaning against large ant hill,
Kimberley, Western Australia, c 1931.
University of Queensland. UQ:734073

Daisy Bates with Aboriginal men and her barrow, 'Augusta', at Ooldea, June 1932.
Photographer: Ernestine Hill
National Library of Australia. MS 8392 IV

Ernestine Hill's caravan in Mundrabilla country, c 1947.
Image courtesy of the State Library of South Australia, HG & EM Watson Collection. PRG 1527/3/23

Ernestine Hill and her caravan, 1949.
Photographer: Douglas Glass.
Image courtesy of the National Archives of Australia.
NAA: A1200, L12289, no 6849765

Ernestine Hill and Henrietta Drake-Brockman with dog, Jarrah, at Afghan Rocks near Balladonia, 1947. Photographer: Robert Hill.
Image courtesy of the State Library of South Australia, HG & EM Watson Collection. PRG 1527/3/35

Ernestine Hill, Daisy Bates and the Mathews family at Sunny Brae farm, Westall, 1947.
Photographer: Robert Hill.
National Library of Australia.
MS 8392 III

Daisy Bates at Sunny Brae farm, Westall, 1947.
Photographer: Robert Hill.
National Library of Australia.
MS 8392 III

Ernestine Hill, Roleystone,
Western Australia, 1949.
University of Queensland.
UQ:734074

Ernestine and Robert Hill
at Roleystone, Western
Australia, c 1950.
State Library of Western Australia
MN71 7273A/EH1/12

Eleanor Witcombe, Ernestine Hill and Beatrice Davis at Adelaide Writers' Week, 1968.
National Library of Australia. MS 7739 Box 4

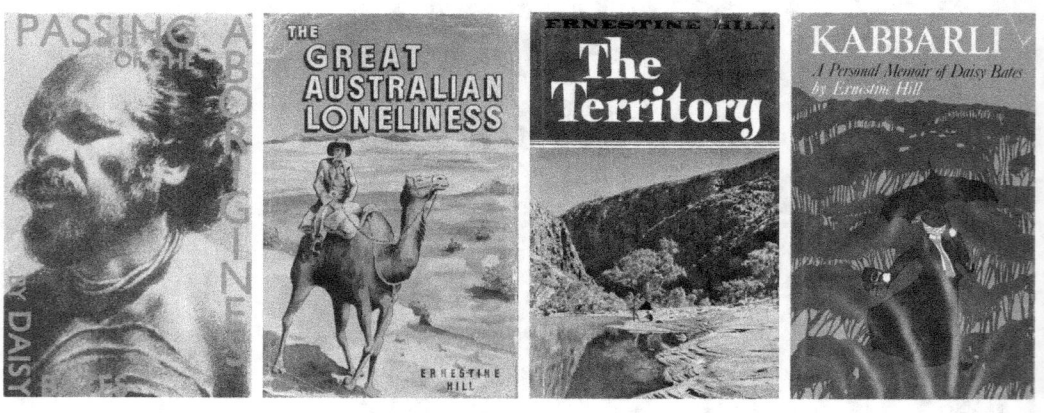

Covers of Daisy Bates's *The Passing of the Aborigines* (John Murray), Ernestine Hill's *The Great Australian Loneliness*, *The Territory* and *Kabbarli* (Angus and Robertson).

5
The Passing of the Aborigines

'The strangest, and greatest, woman in the empire.'[1]

In May 1936 Hill 'sacked herself' from the *Advertiser* after receiving a 'mysterious letter' from the Australian Dried Fruits Association, offering her a commission to write a book about the Murray River irrigation system. The *Advertiser* had published the first instalment of *My Natives and I* on 4 January 1936; in the coming months, articles from the serial would appear in other major capital dailies, including the Sydney *Sun*, the Brisbane *Courier Mail*, the Melbourne *Herald* and the Perth *Western Mail*. Hill had begun working up the articles into chapters for a book based on Bates's life, intending to send the manuscript to Spencer Curtis Brown in London. Instead, she accepted the Dried Fruits Association's offer and left for north-western Victoria. It was a crucial moment in revising the serial for book publication, when Ernestine might have been able to steer an alternative course with her agent or a publisher if she was concerned about her contribution being acknowledged. Perhaps she was so frustrated with her charge by this point that she welcomed the opportunity to make a diplomatic exit from the *Advertiser* and regain her independence from Bates.

Dumas didn't want her to go. In her place he appointed another *Advertiser* journalist, Max Lamshed to take carriage of the manuscript. Lamshed was no stranger to the vogue for descriptive journalism about exotic interior locations, having written for the

Advertiser about the 'unsophisticated Australian natives in their natural environment' while travelling throughout central Australia in the early 1930s.[2] How much of the final editing of *The Passing of the Aborigines* he undertook is unclear, but the *Advertiser* posted the book to London towards the end of 1937.[3] Rather dramatically, the plane freighting the packet crashed into the sea, but the manuscript was retrieved intact from the mailbags and sent to Spencer Curtis Brown, who forwarded it to the Scottish publisher John Murray, saying, 'You asked for a book about foreign parts and here is one', hoping the sea rescue would give it 'an added romantic quality'.[4]

John Murray had become highly influential during the 19th century through publishing the likes of Byron, Darwin, Melville and Livingstone. The publishing house had a generational dynasty stretching back to 1768; Sir John Murray V and his nephew, John Grey Murray VI, worked with Bates on the *Passing*, and continued to correspond with her afterwards, no doubt entertained by receiving missives from an elderly eccentric in a tent.[5] Once the Murrays accepted the manuscript, their initial discussions concerned the title, revisions and the thorny subject of authorial attribution. It was John Grey Murray who suggested *The Passing of the Aborigines*, which Bates declared was 'just the right title' given how she had toiled 'with my self-imposed task of making the passing easy & doing all I could for their comfort'.[6] Dumas had thought *My Natives and I* was unsuitable for a book, and Bates agreed. They had both favoured 'Kabbarli', an epithet Daisy claimed put her on a pedestal among all the Aboriginal groups she met over the years. In a sweeping egotistical statement, she said this name wouldn't need explaining to 'home readers' because it would be familiar from her articles about camping with Aboriginal people that Arthur Mee had published in *My Magazine* and *The Children's Newspaper*. Bates warmly endorsed the publisher's suggestion that Mee write the foreword, although the reader's report suggested the book be given a 'Preface by a Scientific Expert', given the author, despite her experience, 'had nother [sic] Knowledge than scholarship on the subject'.[7] The decision to align the book with a well-known journalist rather than the academic anthropological community reflects John Murray's and Bates's savvy, their recognition of the book's potential broad-based appeal, and possibly Daisy's long-time chagrin at her lack of scholarly recognition. She gave John Murray carte blanche to revise the manuscript, complimenting the publisher's efforts to bring the book into 'better sequence, & make it a connected relation which as a serial it was not'.[8] Historian Bob Reece estimates that *The Passing of the Aborigines* comprises 85 per cent of *My Natives and I*, supplemented with some other newspaper articles by Bates.[9] As for Ernestine Hill – Bates never mentioned her contribution to the Murrays, noting only the assistance of the young typist who worked with them.

When Hill read the book, she was disappointed to find it 'shorn of the earlier chapters' about Daisy's youth.[10] Material about Bates's return voyage to London and employment by Stead had also been excised. 'Murray ... strangely didn't use the personal life, or very little, which rocked me, it was very vital I thought,' Ernestine later confessed. 'Daisy was surprised too – but she never questioned anything about it.'[11] Bates may have been uncomfortable at the prospect of some 'home readers' querying its rosy portrait of her childhood among Anglo-Irish gentry. Hill was proud of her craft in this section, which she saw as substantially her own work. Daisy had in fact told her publishers that she was happy for them to scrap the original first chapter and fast forward to the catalyst for her return to Australia, her investigation of allegations of cruelty to the north-west's Indigenous people: 'that Chapter represents the "crown" of my 35 years work amongst them' and 'is unique in Australian anthropology & I saw it all from its first "degree" to its final'. Bates blindsided Hill in these negotiations, writing to John Murray: 'I would like to keep the authorship of those things it cost me so much to obtain as I am nearly approaching my seventy-ninth milestone.'[12]

There'd been another book Bates had tried to publish, one that Alfred Radcliffe-Brown had gutted. It was her sprawling leviathan of a manuscript based on her precious ethnography, assembling the vocabularies and folklore she collected from Western Australia's Indigenous peoples. She hadn't asked for Radcliffe-Brown's editorial intervention; she'd been courting the interest of folklorist Andrew Lang, proposing to the WA state government in 1910 that they fund her almost £700 to revise the manuscript under his direction in England.

Bates's language work had burgeoned out of control, and the government queried what they thought was an astronomical sum for her to work on the book with Lang. Stalling, they suggested she refer her manuscript to the Cambridge anthropological team who were planning to visit later that year to investigate Aboriginal people in the state's north-west. Alfred Radcliffe-Brown, the expedition leader, wrote to Bates, saying he might consider publishing her material in their reports from Western Australia, inviting her to join them. A lecturer in ethnology at London University, from his perspective it was a generous offer to an unschooled amateur, although it was far from the recognition Bates craved from publishing her own book. The government saw it as an excuse to shelve her funding request, despatching her instead with the visiting British academics in a new role as a 'travelling protector' on the same salary she'd received as a clerk for her language work.

Bates left Perth in September 1910 with Radcliffe-Brown, EL Grant Watson, the team's biologist and photographer, and their cook, Louis Ohlsen. However, a rift soon developed between the expedition's guide and its leader. Grant Watson, whose personality was in keeping with his Holmesian namesake, observed mildly from the sidelines that Radcliffe-Brown was modern enough not to 'repudiate the possibility of women being able to co-operate with men in the field of anthropology'. However, after working with Bates, Radcliffe-Brown declared her mind was 'somewhat similar to the contents of a well-stored sewing basket, after half a dozen kittens had been playing there undisturbed for a few days', although he hoped to 'disentangle some of that rich medley' – her wide-ranging ethnological knowledge of the north-west.[13]

Not yet thirty, Radcliffe-Brown was an anthropological wunderkind who became the first professor of the Department of Anthropology at Sydney University in 1926 and founded the prestigious journal *Oceania*. A photographic portrait shows a coldly handsome young man with an intense gaze Radcliffe-Brown had his own idiosyncrasies. Like Bates, he was given to making flamboyant statements and not averse to embroidering the truth when it suited him; consequently 'many of the erudite … looked on him with suspicion'. Arrogant, he tended to ignore people he regarded as superfluous. Even if they addressed him, he would fix his eye 'on the distance, and no reply would be forthcoming' – a strategy he used on Bates, who then 'talked into the silence'. 'She was made for his exasperation, as he for hers,' Grant Watson wrote. The problem lay in their similarities rather than their differences; it was a meeting of autocrats. Bates could not resign herself to the inferior helpmeet role Radcliffe-Brown had assigned her, if by silent pressure: 'unfortunately she considered herself capable of the leadership of the expedition'.[14] As local benefactress in the know, she saw herself nannying two British men who, with their blinkered focus on anthropological mundanities such as learning cat's-cradle-style string games from the locals, were oblivious – or chose to be – to the cultural devastation around them.

The tension reached a high point when the expedition visited Dorre and Bernier islands, offshore from Carnarvon, in November 1910. At the height of the protectionist era, when state governments legislated regimes to control their Indigenous population's lives, often segregating and containing people dispossessed from the lands, in 1904 Western Australia had established 'Tombs of the living dead' – concentration camps of sorts on these islands – where '[r]egardless of tribe and custom and country and relationship' the police 'herded together' Aboriginal people infected with western-introduced diseases such as syphilis and tuberculosis. Landing on Bernier, Bates was unnerved to find graves outnumbering men by thirty-eight to fifteen; a week later, she saw fourteen new graves. The islands were gender segregated, and Bates spent most of her time with the women on Dorre, where deaths 'were frequent – appallingly frequent, sometimes three in a day', so much so that she dared not count the graves. It was a terrifying place for Aboriginal people transported from their country, 'some of them thousands of miles, to strange and unnatural surroundings and solitude'. Some had never seen the sea before, and the medical regime was alien to them. 'They were afraid of the hospital, its ceaseless probings and dressings and injections were a daily torture,' Bates observed in the *Passing*. 'They were afraid of each other, living and dead. They were afraid of the ever-moaning sea.'

One day an old man tried 'to "walk" back over thirty miles of raging waters to the mainland' but the shores were 'infested with sharks, and he was never seen again.' The episode haunted Bates:

> The horrors of Dorre and Bernier unnerve me yet. There was no ray of brightness, no gleam of hope. In an attempt to escape them I too would roam the islands, finding them grim and

dreary. The wail of a curlew crying along the sands would startle me and set me shivering with remembrance of the dying, and the soundless wings of the giant wedge-tailed eagles, as they flew over, cast a sinister shadow on the sunny day.

Her experience led to a new high-water mark. Sitting 'in the darkness of their mias at night', Bates claimed she became the confidante of north-west people interned on the islands, learning 'much of infinite value in vocabularies and customs and pedigrees and legends', and ferrying bamburoos or letter-sticks with messages from friends and kin between Dorre, Bernier and the mainland. She slated the ease of her 'adopted kinship' to her earlier time in the north-west: 'This relationship opened the way to their confidence.' Later she capitalised on what she cast as the spiritual elements implicit in her role on the islands, alongside her practical 'little errands of mercy', to fashion a saintly identity for herself as Kabbarli:

> I had begun in Broome as kallauer, a grandmother, but a spurious and a very young one, purely legendary ... but it was at Dorre Island that I became kabbarli, Grandmother, to the sick and the dying there, and kabbarli I was to remain in all my wanderings, for the name is a generic one, and extends far among the western-central and central tribes.

She wove the various strands of her experience – linguist, social worker and shaman – into her self-mythologising as Kabbarli, a Florence Nightingale type, to legitimate her authority working among Aboriginal people.

On the islands, Bates believed her serious commitment to Aboriginal people and her growing status among them distinguished her from her male academic companions, who only 'made intermittent headway' in their anthropological endeavours. The Aboriginal internees helped Grant Watson collect shells and insects, 'and obligingly sang the songs of woggura and wallardoo-crow and eaglehawk' into Radcliffe-Brown's phonograph, then listened politely when he 'regaled them with Peer Gynt and Tannhäuser and Egmont'.[15] As this awkward cultural exchange indicates, Radcliffe-Brown was not only out of his depth in what Bates regarded as her domain but his modus operandi differed significantly to hers. His was a distant 'professorial' approach, more usually reliant on drawing on material from informants lower down the food chain to furnish his theoretical frameworks. Bates, on the other hand, employed her reporting background to pioneer a form of participant observation, immersing herself in Aboriginal culture and applying journalistic techniques of interviewing, note-taking and observation to her ethnographic work.[16]

In March 1911 the expedition party split up. Bates was riled by Radcliffe-Brown's condescension but a more serious issue was brewing beyond strong personalities vying for dominance. Before Radcliffe-Brown had left England, Lang had shown him sections of Bates's draft manuscript, commenting that 'scissors are needed for that vast and wandering work'.[17] Radcliffe-Brown set to work quite literally with scissors, pruning the manuscript, which incensed Bates, who claimed it was 'mutilated beyond repair' when it was returned to her.[18] Lang, her mentor, died in July 1912, and the project languished. Bates's magnum opus in its rambling entirety would have run to four volumes; the WA government baulked at the prospect of printing two volumes at £650 for 1000 copies.[19] Even Bates recognised it could not be 'published until it is thoroughly revised and condensed'.[20] In 1911 a Labor state government was elected, who suggested she edit and publish the manuscript herself, perceiving the project to be aligned with the previous government. The chief protector had undertaken to review her salary at the expedition's end, but her services and her stipend were terminated when Radcliffe-Brown left the state. While attending the British Association for the Advancement of Science's conference in Adelaide in 1914, Bates experienced a further blow upon the bruises she'd already received. She was horrified to hear Radcliffe-Brown recycle material from her manuscript in a public lecture without acknowledgement – it was ngar'galulla, stories that women from the Broome district had recounted to her about the spiritual conception of babies which they would not have told a man. 'It is entirely my own fault for not looking after my own interests,' she admitted to anthropologist John Mathew.[21] Daisy saw it as her anthropological scoop; the interests of the Aboriginal women who'd told her the stories didn't merit consideration, as far as she was concerned.

In 1985 the National Library published a revised version of Bates's manuscript, *The Native Tribes of Western Australia*, from her drafts that had lain dormant in their archives for several decades. The book's editor and instigator of this project, anthropologist Isobel White, confirmed that Radcliffe-Brown had taken to it with scissors – a not-unusual editing technique she also used – and that both he and Lang had made comments on copies. Indeed, Bates complained to Sir John Murray that Lang had been 'so ruthless with his queries & comments that he imposed tremendous manual labour upon me'.[22] White was 'unable to prove or disprove with certainty' Daisy's charge of plagiarism against Brown from the précis of his conference paper, which was all that remained; she thought he could have heard the stories from other sources, although he had probably been influenced by Bates's research from reading her manuscript.[23] She found Daisy's stories about Radcliffe-Brown confusing and contradictory, observing that some years after Bates had accused him of mutilating her book, she 'began to accuse him of not returning it at all. She also accused Lang of not returning the other copy though it seems to have been in her possession all the time', suggesting 'that in the second case it was because she was becoming old and forgetful'.[24]

Old, forgetful and probably demented, Bates became paranoid in her later years about theft, making further accusations about stolen material – manuscripts, diaries, photographs – along with the constant refrain that Radcliffe-Brown had stolen 'my *ngar'galulla*'. Imaginary or otherwise, this theft came to emblematise the deep ego wound she wished to remedy – her work's lack of acknowledgement, especially by male authorities – a reason why she became so proprietorial about *The Passing of the Aborigines* and reluctant to acknowledge Hill's contribution.

In 1940 Bates destroyed many of her letters, fearing in the wake of the *Passing*'s renown they might be archived and read after her death by less sympathetic eyes: 'So many fine people, both here & at home, have corresponded with me, & I must honour the great confidences placed with me.'[25] Four decades worth of diaries that she'd kept after leaving Southampton in August 1899, 'writing an entry nightly over the years as my "Monologue" to Home',[26] met a similar fate. When Grey Murray expressed concern about their destruction and how unlikely it was that, as she claimed, 'some Australian "Pepys" … would make ill use of my entries',[27] Bates replied, 'I cannot bear to think of any family being hurt through their dead people who took the wrong course through ambition of some kind.'[28] Later she explained that these people, whose 'every item & incident' she'd 'confirmed and examined' in her diaries, had been involved in the Bernier and Dorre islands' 'ghastly experiment'.[29] She also told Sir John Murray that, after investigating the allegations of pastoralists' cruelty in the north-west, she wrote a 'quiet letter' pre-approved by the archbishop of Western Australia to the *Times* – one too anaemic to elicit a response.

Bates tacitly recognised in this correspondence that some of her white contemporaries had abused Aboriginal people terribly in Western Australia, implying that what she saw on the islands was even worse than the *Passing*'s account. Her notebooks from the expedition to Dorre and Bernier make sober reading. Page upon page list names of people whose messages she volunteered to convey on bamburoos to relatives on the mainland, a testimony to those who suffered and often died on the islands. The perpetrators were long dead when Bates published her account of Dorre and Bernier's atrocities in the *Passing*.[30] There may have been damning content about other episodes in the state's history in the material she destroyed. Bates indicated to Sir John Murray that she was at pains to suppress anything that incriminated 'any white descendants of those white wrongdoers', a comment that shows her sympathies were ultimately with the Western Australian settler caste.[31]

In the lead-up to the *Passing*'s publication, John Murray sent advance copies to representatives from Aboriginal welfare organisations that the *Advertiser* had suggested might be interested in promoting *The Passing of the Aborigines*. The responses the publisher received ranged from polite misgivings to heated objections. APA Burdeu of the Aborigines Uplift Society replied that the book was more likely to appeal to 'white interest', maybe anthropologists, explaining it will not interest any members of the league to speak of, very largely due to the fact that very few of them could find the money to purchase it, as Australia has got her natives pegged on a very low economic plane, even where they are quite educated and cultured.[32]

Dr Charles Duguid, former president of the Aborigines Protection League, diplomatically wished Bates well although he thought John Murray would have difficulties selling the book because the 'references to the natives by Arthur Mee in his introduction are particularly unfortunate and clash badly with the views of those who really know the native'. Duguid was a medical practitioner who'd been instrumental in establishing a reserve area in central Australia to buffer Aboriginal people from the influence of white settlers in 1935 and provided them with annual medical services. He questioned the inevitability of Aboriginal people's passing, hinting at white settler interests in perpetuating this belief: 'If the Government and people of Australia are prepared to leave the aborigines on their own country and not take it from them for one purpose and another – chiefly gold and cattle – there is no need for them to die out.'[33]

William Morley of the Association for the Protection of Native Races refused to advertise the *Passing* because 'our work is for the welfare and uplift of our Australian Aborigines, and not for promoting the financial success of books which may be written about them'. The Association for the Protection of Native Races was committed to advocacy for Aboriginal people. Earlier in 1938, its treasurer, Yorta Yorta activist William Cooper, had campaigned for Aboriginal land rights and parliamentary representation, petitioning the federal government to remove Aboriginal affairs from the states in a move that foreshadowed the 1967 referendum. Although Bates 'undoubtedly did much good work', Morley criticised her for drawing Aboriginal people off their own country. Moreover, he found much of the book 'unconvincing in general statements apart from any supporting evidence particularly in her allegations of cannibalism among the natives of Central Australia. Nearly the whole of the allegations are based on hearsay.' Not only that but he queried why Bates did not make any further reference to her original intent in returning to Australia to investigate allegations of north-western pastoralists' cruelty to Aboriginal people, pointing out that 'during the years that followed nothing [sic] transpired of any effort made by her to appeal to governments about the injuries the natives suffered'.[34]

'File. No reply necessary.' pencilled on Morley's letter is the only clue to what John Murray may have made of these objections coming from people whose lifestyles and preoccupations must have seemed as quaint and distant as those of their author, let alone 'the natives' themselves. Australian anthropologists Herbert Basedow, Charles Mountford and Ted Strehlow and others had already objected to opinions Bates had expressed in her articles about cannibalism and other subjects, and the publisher had little hope of or interest in adjudicating between these dissenting voices. Besides, Arthur Mee's proof copy of the introduction includes a note acknowledging he'd 'added a line in case you still wish me to stress the point about cannibalism', which suggests they were aware of the book's sensationalistic potential to court sales.

Bates basked in the afterglow of *The Passing of the Aborigines*'s publication in November 1938. It sold over 4500 copies in eighteen months throughout Britain, the Commonwealth and the United States. Daisy sent the book to her usual coterie of women's guild office bearers, Anglican primates and other prominent clergy, and gave speeches to women's clubs. Lady Gowrie organised a reception for her at Adelaide Government House, and Lord Gowrie, the governor-general, requested a copy to give to the King. Daisy's royalist heart thrilled when she received a letter from Buckingham Palace saying the king had become aware of her work through her book.[35] She had at last gained the official public recognition she'd craved, that had long eluded her. Observing her friend's avidity for attention, Hill commented: 'she didn't care – she loved everything that people wrote about her.' With her desire for adulation and facility with self-promotion, Daisy was a ready-made media tart, boasting that the *Advertiser*'s advance of £500 had 'exceeded the sum paid for Haig's and Monash's books, & was, I am informed, the highest sum paid previously to any Australian author'.[36]

The Passing of the Aborigines received enthusiastic and reverent reviews in Australia, with Bates as the book's heroine becoming the subject of extravagant praise. Echoing the template Hill had set for mythologising Bates in her Ooldea articles, reviewers spoke of Daisy's 'heroic devotion' and 'remarkable story', the book presenting 'the remarkable life of a heroic woman'. While noting how her eccentricities made her the 'strangest, and greatest, woman in the empire',[37] they emphasised that she was 'of the cult of Florence Nightingale', the 'faithful friend of a vanishing race', whose 'reward has been the consciousness of easing the burdens of the lost'.[38] One reviewer hailed the book's 'epic quality, which gives it a claim to be considered great literature';[39] another thought it a wonderful romp with 'something for everyone – adventure, human interest, science, fun, horror, and tenderness, strung together on the thread of an idealist's purpose', advising some readers, such as 'the sensation seeker' to avoid the more informative chapters in favour of its more colourful content, observing that many would come away remembering little more than the stories of blood drinking.[40] The *Herald*'s reviewer commended the *Passing* as a 'valuable contribution to anthropology', while the *Sydney Morning Herald* claimed it was 'a book not only for the anthropologist and the philanthropist, but for all who acknowledge kinship in the brotherhood of man', noting that Bates's achievement was 'not the museum taxidermy of the conventional scientist' but its 'personal quality' and its 'appeal to the general reader; its vignettes of character, as many humorous as tragic, her individual contact with individuals'.[41] Similarly, the *Advertiser* reviewer commended the book as 'a human document, friendly, discursive, and entertaining' in which 'Mrs. Bates makes no academic claims, but her profound knowledge of the people with whom she has lived so long is evident upon every page'.[42]

Bates was not aspiring to write an anthropological work to gain academic kudos, as she'd attempted with her earlier, unpublished manuscript, *The Native Tribes of Western Australia*, but to communicate her opinions and experiences to the public at large. 'It is not scientific, tho' the initiation chapters look so,' she wrote to her publisher. 'It is not character drawing & it can't be said to carry plea or appeal one way or the other, & so I pray that the people who buy & read it will see my natives as I see them.'[43] Arguably, *The Passing of the Aborigines* was successful precisely because it was not an anthropological or academic study of Australian Aboriginal people but, as Raymond Firth, Reader in Anthropology at the University of London, observed, 'the first popular exposition of the matter'. The *Passing* is an early form of immersion journalism, recounting Bates's encounters with Aboriginal people in the north-west and along the Bight, the memoir strand of the narrative, the 'I' in it, being the 'eye of the needle', threading her stories like beads on a string.[44] I read *The Passing of the Aborigines* soon after *The Great Australian Loneliness*, and what I noticed was its kinship to the descriptive travelogue, Hill's forte and an excellent vehicle for generic hybridity. Beyond the *Passing*'s humanising touches, its anecdotal rather than scientific approach and gallivanting across genres, I saw the hand of Ernestine Hill.

Ernestine Hill played a crucial role in facilitating Daisy Bates's writing of her life story in the *Advertiser* office but did she have a greater share in crafting the serial that became *The Passing of the Aborigines* than Bates would admit? After pondering these issues, I approached Hugh Craig and Alexis Antonia at the University of Newcastle's Centre for Literary and Linguistic Computing, linguistic sleuths who have employed computational stylistic methods to investigate literary authorship mysteries such as whether some of Shakespeare's plays had more than one author.[45] Computational stylistics is based on the understanding that writers use certain common words in distinctive ways, and researchers in this field have developed techniques to identify specific signatures or stylistic profiles for individual authors to the extent that 'it is possible to distinguish clearly between texts according to author, genre, era, gender and even nationality'.[46]

In determining *The Passing of the Aborigines*'s authorship, Antonia and Craig thought that if distinct profiles could be identified for Bates and Hill then compared to the *Passing*'s text, one of several possibilities might emerge. If Ernestine were 'merely a typist', as Daisy claimed, the *Passing*'s text would be to all intents and purposes identical with Bates's newspaper publications predating her meeting with Hill. But if Ernestine's was, as she claimed, the only hand holding the pen, its text would be something equivalent to her own publications. In a third possible scenario, such a clear-cut result could not be expected: despite endeavouring to retain the original material's immediacy and individuality, the 'ghostwriter' would inevitably leave traces of her own signature on the text.

The researchers undertook computational linguistic testing of a collection of writing, including the complete texts of *The Passing of the Aborigines* and *The Great Australian Loneliness*, newspaper articles by Hill, and letters and articles by Bates on similar topics to those in the *Passing*, as well as the first three articles from the *Advertiser* serial. They discovered marked differences in each author's preferred use of certain words in their texts, and that distinct and separate profiles could be established for Hill and Bates. When the *Passing*'s text was analysed in relation to these profiles, an interesting pattern emerged. Some chapters showed an affinity for Hill's texts, while others had more affinity with Bates's, with nine of the book's twenty-one chapters aligning midway between the two authors. The researchers state:

> The fact that four of the chapters sit within Hill's narrative set, while another four chapters sit close by, suggests that in spite of her avowed self-effacement and intention to simply 'paraphrase' and 'arrange' Daisy's material her own writing style was not always suppressed. Equally, the fact that two chapters sit within the Bates's narrative material with another two sitting close by suggests that at times the anecdotal material of Bates was merely incorporated into the chapter without much modification.[47]

Hill's influence in the *Passing* appeared strongest in the chapters that start a story, set the scene, pick up the threads and keep the narrative going, whereas Bates's influence was stronger in the anecdotal, ethnological parts. Generally, the chapters that aligned with Bates's profile reflected the personal, informal style in her letters and articles, whereas those affiliated with Hill were descriptive but more formal in tone, suggesting her adoption of the stance of a professional journalist, suitable for addressing a wider unknown audience. The transition between the two styles was similar to the shift from an intimate storytelling mode to a more omniscient narration.

What this study demonstrated was that Hill blended her own more formal, professional journalistic style to provide a narrative framework for Bates's personal oral anecdotes, resulting in a composite ghostwritten text. It supports her assertion that her contribution to writing the newspaper serial was substantial, largely reflecting her description of their collaborative process: that Bates 'never actually wrote a line, nor did she sub-edit.' Hill explains in *Kabbarli* that while 'all material of the book was exclusively hers, only the paraphrasing, the actual writing and the arrangement mine'.[48] The computational linguistics studies reinforce Hill's claims and Reece's observation that 'she did a vast amount more than merely "help with the presentation". She was *confidante*, amanuensis, editor and typist, all in one.'[49]

Hill could justifiably feel aggrieved by her friend's disavowal of her role in facilitating *The Passing of the Aborigines*, given the book established Bates's international reputation. In addition to her 'devoted labor' on *My Natives and I*, Hill's contribution included talent-spotting Bates, as it were; her foresight in recognising the potential of a newspaper serial and book based on her friend's life, and in arranging for Daisy and her manuscripts to be ferried to the *Advertiser* office. 'Believe me,' Ernestine wrote indignantly:

> had I not met her, and seen and heard of her life and known her calibre two years before, – and during these two years she wrote to me many times while I was travelling – and then, if Lloyd Dumas had not agreed with my suggestion that she should be brought from Ooldea to write her story – or

have it written by me, – she would have been but vaguely remembered as a small pensioner of the government in more or less missionary work, giving out a few rations.⁵⁰

Bates's health limitations, especially her mental deterioration, would have prevented her from producing a coherent, major literary work without significant physical, emotional, financial and editorial support. Without Ernestine to rehabilitate her from the sandy margins, at best Daisy would have been remembered as an obscure, do-gooding crank. But if Hill's role was more than that of amanuensis and ad hoc agent, then not only could she lay claim to a stake in *The Passing of the Aborigines*'s popular success, but she must bear some responsibility along with Bates for its effect on Aboriginal people.

The Passing of the Aborigines was hugely influential for several decades after its publication, becoming an international bestseller and a staple of Australian school curricula during the 1940s and 1950s. John Murray reprinted *The Passing of the Aborigines* four times within four years following its initial publication, and Oxford University Press published the first Australian edition in 1944, which was reprinted twice. Bates's success with *The Passing of the Aborigines* riled anthropologists because, as Bob Reece points out, it 'had both elevated her to the status of a world expert on Aborigines, and given further authority to the popular assumption that their extinction was unavoidable', implying the ultimate obsolescence of their own endeavours.⁵¹

Yet although Bates's anthropological counterparts were mostly men, it would be overly simplistic, a cheap equality-feminist crack, to suggest they were merely critical of the *Passing* because they were jealous of her achievement as a woman. Raymond Firth warned against viewing the *Passing* as a serious scientific ethnographic work. He challenged the London *Sunday Times* reviewer's claim that Aborigines were vanishing 'because no one, except Mrs. Bates, has ever managed to enter with sympathy into their fearful and fluttering minds', pointing out that they'd been the subject of anthropological study for many decades. Instead, he observed the socio-economic origins and self-justificatory nature of Bates's and white settlers' claims that Aboriginal people were doomed to die out, writing: 'The issue lies far deeper, in a radical conflict between the values and way of life of the tribal aborigines on the one hand, and those of the Europeans who wish to develop the natural resources of the land on the other.'[52] Other anthropologists shared his concern about her assertions that Aboriginal people were a dying race, along with her obsession with cannibalism and her demonisation of mixed-descent people. These views were commonplace in the early 20th century.

In 1956 Oxford University Press contacted John Murray, saying their stock of the *Passing* was dwindling and they were reluctant for it to go out of print: 'It is still the best book on its subject.'[53] It took John Murray a decade to reissue another edition, which featured a foreword by writer and journalist Alan Moorehead, himself a great populariser of Australian experience, like Hill. The book was reprinted in 1972 in response to the 'current surge of interest in Australia in the study of the Aborigines' accompanying the 1967 referendum on Commonwealth recognition of Aboriginal people and the rise of race-related civil rights movements.[54] But as Aboriginal people gained greater control over the public narratives about their lives and culture during this period, the primacy of *The Passing of the Aborigines*, and Bates as its ideologue, as 'the best one dealing with the natives of Australia', was fiercely interrogated. The book has since been widely condemned as an inaccurate, insensitive and destructive source of information about Aboriginal culture. Nevertheless, it has occasional resurgences of notoriety: as recently as 2007, Pauline Hanson cited Bates's beliefs about cannibalism from *The Passing of the Aborigines* in defence of One Nation's platform disbanding government policy supporting Indigenous people.

Bates and *The Passing of the Aborigines* did well in an era in which urban white Australians were curious about Aboriginal people but not necessarily sympathetic to their circumstances because, with Ernestine's assistance, she framed her ethnographic observations through a personal lens. Why Bates, beyond her eccentric chutzpah and essential narcissism, as a white woman living on the Nullarbor's edge should become a cipher for her time's complex attitudes is a whole other question to which I'll return.

You 'couldn't cage Daisy Bates, even if her cage was pleasantly padded and had all the mod cons they could produce,' journalist Elizabeth Wolff observed. After eighteen months in Adelaide Bates absconded to Pyap, confessing to John Murray, who continued the editorial wrangling with her, that there'd 'been so much delay, confusion, postponement, alteration, and worry that I have had to run away from it all and pitch my tent on the banks of Australia's one big river – the Murray'.[55] Pyap is a nick on an elbow bend of the river just over the South Australian border, just under 200 kilometres from Adelaide: distance was never a deterrent to Bates. Loxton, at the elbow's crook, the nearest town, is a lush Riverland hub with a chequerboard of wide streets hemmed by citrus farms. Isabell Tindall, who remembered Daisy camping near her family's fruit block when she was a child, described how they used to ferry her to Loxton for shopping and how Bates once spoke at their primary school. The local children visited her camp, listened to her stories, ate her freshly baked damper and boiled lollies. Ever the child whisperer, photographs show Daisy enlisting local schoolkids in the inevitable game of 'Here we go round the mulberry bush' and dandling a toddler on her knee in the midst of a height-ordered, school class–style shot outside her tent by the river at Pyap.

Driving up to Alice Springs from Melbourne one time, I parked overnight among a cathedral of gums on the Murray's broad banks near Loxton, planning to search for Bates's old campsite. In the morning I continued past orchards and wineries, then turned off a discreetly signposted road to Pyap. It led to a boatshed and a launching ramp on a quieter inlet with smaller, scruffier gums on banks with pink-yellow sand. I rummaged about a tussocky slope facing the river until I found a stubby brick monument with a plaque stating that Daisy Bates had 'lived hereabouts in a tent 1936–1940' having 'laboured nearly 40 years at Ooldea Soak, S.A. and other W.A. Parts'.

'She came there hoping to find aborigines … but there were not any about (unless the settlers looked a bit that way!!!)' Tindall wrote, reflecting the era's attitude about Aboriginal people of mixed ethnicity.[56] Bates expressed her prejudice in harsher terms, telling John Grey Murray that only 'derelicts', collected by the government and missions, lived in the area because the 'fertile river banks & valleys & uplands were amongst our first White Settled areas, & the intrusion of every pioneer family meant the extinction of its native group'. She hadn't seen one Murray River native since she'd begun camping there in January 1937: 'And so The Passing of the Aborigines is a true title for my book'.[57]

Bates's choice of Pyap for her latest camp seemed curious to me. It was closer to Adelaide and a more hospitable place to live than the Nullarbor but very different to anywhere else she'd camped, with much more fresh water and fruit available. Compared to the larger, wealthier agricultural centres of Renmark and Loxton, Pyap was a decidedly down-market if small and unremarkable enough pocket over which to attempt staking another claim to dominion unimpeded. It was also somewhere relatively low budget to live.

Despite Bates's boast about the *Advertiser*'s generous advance, she'd found it difficult to sustain her upper-crust existence at the Queen Adelaide Club. She offered to assemble her manuscripts for deposit at the National Library over two years at £400 per annum, but when the Commonwealth government vetted her proposal, Professors Cleland and Fitzherbert gave their support but AP Elkin, who'd seen her living conditions at Ooldea, put the kybosh on this sum, suggesting instead she be given the modest stipend of £2 a week. In April 1936 the minister of the interior granted Bates an allowance following Elkin's advice and provided her a secretary, Edith Watts, with an annual salary of £214, and office space at £50 per annum in Adelaide. That Watts's salary was just over Bates's indicates how academic and government authorities valued the latter's expertise, although the transcription and assemblage of Daisy's notes for archival storage was itself no mean feat. The 23-year-old secretary was confronted with eight tin trunks full of pencil jottings on scraps of paper from various camps, and was subject to constant interruptions from Bates herself, wanting to regale her with anecdotes from tent life. It took Watts four years to work her way through Bates's notes; Daisy was 'a little bit displeased' with her secretary for daring to visit her fiancé's parents in New Zealand in the middle, although Watts delayed marrying until the project was finished.[58]

Bates relocated to Pyap early in 1937 after calculating she could live there on £26 per annum as opposed to £37 a week in Adelaide, and continued to post back and forth instalments of her notes with Watts. Bill Garner speculates that Pyap's history as the last utopian socialist campsite on the Murray in the 1890s made it 'probably a good spot' for her 'where people were sympathetic to those who chose to live this way'.[59] She did mention to Grey Murray that people in the area were in the employ of the Dried Fruits Association, Hill's sponsor for *Water into Gold*, so it's not inconceivable that Ernestine may have drawn Daisy's attention to the river's hospitable banks.

Hill travelled up and down the Murray for several months collecting material for *Water into Gold*, which she wrote in another three, working from 9 am to 2 am each day.[60] A travel book extolling the industry of fruit growers in north-western Victoria, it was published by Robertson & Mullens, Angus & Robertson's forerunner, in 1937. *Water into Gold* ran to almost a dozen editions over the next two decades, selling just under 34 000 copies, which highlights the popularity of Hill, the genre and her subject matter for mid-20th-century Australian readers. The book was reprinted in 1958 with a foreword by then prime minister Robert Menzies: 'This book deserves many more editions not only as a piece of Australian literature but as a true epic of human endeavour' – a comment underscoring its perceived value in nation-building.[61] It was *The Great Australian Loneliness*, published several months later in 1937 by Jarrold & Sons in London, which established her as the travel genre's frontrunner and consolidated her significance as a writer whose publications contributed to shaping national identity.

Such was Hill's loyalty to Australia as her nation of origin and the wellspring for her creativity that she never felt the lure of the 'Old World' or the urge to return 'home' to Britain, despite being offered a paid opportunity to travel internationally. After the *Passing*'s publication, the Commonwealth government proposed sending Bates on a lecture tour to England, the United States and possibly Europe, inviting Hill to shepherd her – 'as "lieutenant", as lady's companion, convenor, public relations, as buffer against the world for her seventy-seven years'[62] – as well as to write the lectures. 'Oh I would have had to do all that. D.B. would have loved the glamour of it,' she later confessed, although the 'vulture-shadows' of war made her nervous about travelling overseas. Besides, '"I was captain of my own soul" – young & foolish' and would not have been 'any good at all [with] the business acumen etc required' and 'I had neither the talent nor the temperament for public life.'[63] Instead, Charles Mountford delivered the lectures in what sounds like a public relations exercise for the Australian government, to assure the world that it was treating its Aboriginal people well.

Hill may have declined this extension of her previous Boswellian role to concentrate on her own work rather than Bates's. She'd long nurtured a passion for navigator Matthew Flinders, another relentless wanderer, and made the Mitchell Library in Sydney her next port of call, planning to research a book about him. She'd become interested in this national historical icon while sailing to Arnhem Land when she realised her lugger's skipper was using the original maps Flinders had made to chart the Gulf in 1802 because they were still considered reliable enough to use. Hill's fierce loyalty to Australia, its history and topography, as the main focus of her writing would be accompanied during the war years with a growing conviction that her work was of national significance.

A few days shy of her eightieth birthday Bates made her will, after some prodding by John Grey Murray, who was concerned about where to direct future royalties from the sale of the *Passing*. She was still 'manual-labouring' on the Murray's banks, cooking in a kerosene bucket, upending logs, practising her physical jerks, sometimes with local children, and dealing with the occasional flash flood. An awkwardness had set in among her 'kindly German friends', who'd been happy to see her return from eye treatment at the district hospital but were holding their breath at rumours of impending war in Europe. Daisy had been egomaniacal enough to try and intervene, writing to Hitler to let him know about the sense of community in Loxton – 'I think I wanted him to see the tragedy of these fine settlers if anything dreadful came to a head.'[64] There'd been no reply, of course. It's a measure of her capriciousness and paranoia that on other occasions she protested about government support for the conspiracy of 'German-controlled' missions in SA.

Bates felt she was 'oddly becoming aloof from my own world', birds and possums being her most regular visitors, close enough for her to see 'their quaint, sharp little faces & noses & ears' as they roosted in the trees near her tent at night, eating meals from 'tables' she'd set up for them.[65] Jack Bates had died at Mullewa Hospital in Western Australia on 13 April 1935. It was Hill who'd told her; the hospital had contacted Ernestine several years after his death when the *Passing* came out, asking her to let Bates know. But Jack had long been dead to Daisy; she'd referred to him as 'late' for the past two decades. As for Arnold, she wasn't sure where he was – maybe Sydney, maybe New Zealand. He'd trained as an engineer then married a young music teacher named Lola in Moree in 1913, and they'd had two children, Jean and Ronald. Daisy had written to Arnold from her camps on the Bight, toying with the idea that she might visit Lola and help out with the grandchildren, although really she had no intention of leaving her natives. During the war Arnold had joined up – he was in the infantry then the flying corps – and her letters to him had been returned unanswered. Bates had plagued the authorities for a response but it seemed he'd taken refuge in military service as a reason not to reply. She consoled herself by saying he had shell shock; that his memory was shot.

Above all, Daisy missed the true worthy recipients of her care, 'my dear Aborigines'. Sometimes she heard rumours about people she'd known at Ooldea, wandering about the Nullarbor 'with no abiding home or friend'. She was restless at night, thronged with 'memories of their "homing" to my little tent' and was longing to return.[66]

III | GHOSTING

6

A wraith, flitting by

'I think I am growing a lonely queer little one – "funny".'[1]

After the telegraph line was laid in the late 1870s but before there was a road or a rail, an Aboriginal man people called Jimmie became the first postie to ferry mail across the Bight's span from Fowlers Bay to Eucla. Navigating 'by his own waters' with a bit of tucker and tobacco in his shirt, he rested a week between journeys in what was a month's circuit. In 1914 when Bates was preparing to attend the British Association for the Advancement of Science Conference in Adelaide, she estimated the trip would take twelve days one-way by camel buggy. I drove the distance between the two old repeater stations in a day, skirting the treeless plain to which Bates longed to return in her later years. The Eyre itself was an uncompromising slash across the Nullarbor, bounded by monochromatic chewed-out farmland and densely wooded grey-green jarrah forests. Occasionally I pulled over after catching glimpses of the coast's startling beauty from the highway, walking out to the edge to gaze at the Bunda Cliffs' sharp limestone flanks plunging into the Bight's sapphire water. The headland's vegetation had its own unexpected subtleties; I strolled through low springy bushes dotted with wattle and tiny wildflowers. 'The welcome of the west,' Ernestine wrote in her travel notes, 'in the delicate and lovely little legumes running along the barren ground and leagues and leagues of paper daisies and wildflowers even in this far "desert" country.'[2]

As the day lengthened, the west's welcome took a more ominous turn with clouds darkening over the Bight. I arrived at Eucla on the plain's western end before dusk in time to secure what I thought was prime real estate in the local caravan park: a spot about 200 metres from the cliff face. My eyrie overlooked the hazy olive-brown plains below girded by foaming sea, a blunt dog's leg of road visible in the scrub leading down to the telegraph station not far from where Bates camped in 1912. My only neighbours were a young European backpacker couple in a Kombi; motorhomes were parked in a phalanx of sensible rows away from the clifftop. Terrible gales blew up during the night, rocking my van from side to side as if it were a boat on choppy seas. I rolled over, lay on my back and listened to the elements – the whining wind, the rain's staccato on the roof, the distant churn of waves lulled me to sleep. Sudden noise woke me at two in the morning, and I pulled back the van's curtains and saw the backpackers hopping out of the Kombi to bring in their washing from a line they'd suspended between trees. Worried my campervan might capsize or be crunched by a widow-maker, I consoled myself by saying it surely wouldn't flip over unless there was a cyclone.

The next day I drove down to the beach to see the remnants of the old repeater station. A roofless, boxy sandstone shell nestled behind a tree-covered dune not far from the road, sand banked up over the original floor, the archways of doors still intact. Photographs from one of Hill's journeys on the Eyre show the telegraph station with a corrugated iron roof in 1947. I scuffed through the sandhills to the beach in hope of seeing the jetty where Bates stepped off a cargo steamer on the verge of her 22-year camping odyssey in the Never-Never lands. It was a good kilometre's walk to the shore: the tide was high, and only a short strand of sand festooned with wind-whipped hanks of maroon seaweed between the surf and the dunes was dry. About ten struts of the jetty remained, with a swag of shags and seagulls clinging on for dear life in the squall. The jetty stopped abruptly, as if it had forgotten its purpose.

It wasn't what I'd expected. My mental image of Eucla had been of a bustling, 19th-century port, although by the time Bates narrated her life story to Hill, it was 'nothing but a name on a map ... a street of ruined houses almost completely engulfed in the sand'. Its glory days were in the late 19th century, after the gold discoveries in Coolgardie and Kalgoorlie. Hill recalled a very old man, EJ Stretton, visiting her caravan in 1949 on the Eyre Highway. He told her that there'd once been thirty-two telegraph operators and their families living at Eucla, and kangaroo hunters camping around the inland cliffs. That the township had once had a social life of dances, debating societies, a billiard room, a tennis court and horseracing was hard to believe, looking at what was left of the jetty and telegraph station.

The town was in decline when Bates arrived in 1912, but even so she was careful not to settle near other whitefellas, pitching her tent 2 miles away from the telegraph station in the dunes to be closer to the Aboriginal people camping in the area. The night before, when gales tore at my van on the clifftop, I'd thought of Daisy, peering out at the ocean's 'sweeping billows', from her canvas nook in the sandhills, wondering how boisterous the winds would become. She had a brief interlude on a sheep station two-and-a-half days' travel away on the Nullarbor after a friend, Beatrice Raine, asked her to help her brother manage the place, but this farmstay confirmed she was no longer suited to settled life and a year later she pitched her tents again at Eucla.

Storms buffeted my van as I drove further west. It was gruelling work, ploughing the campervan with its moulded hi-top roof into blinding rain and headwinds. I felt like a skipper, trying to steer a small, unwieldy galleon during a tempest. Perhaps it's the ghost of Daisy, I joked to myself, a restless, disconsolate queen in search of a dominion to rule, thundering out her wrath at not being appointed paid protector. I pulled off the Eyre several times for a break, too tired to concentrate on the road anymore, fearful of the semi-trailers that thundered down the highway, refusing to drop their speed.

Mid-afternoon, I crawled into the roadhouse at Cocklebiddy, tired of battling with the elements. The man behind the desk told me a few people had berthed already for the night rather than continue. A cyclone was brewing off the Bight; it wasn't worth dying to get to the next destination. I parked my camper in a paddock set up for caravans and took my laptop into the roadhouse, which I did when I wanted a break from the van's cubicle-like interior, which was suddenly more claustrophobic in wet weather. The bar inside had a *Northern Exposure*-style ambience, with an ugg-booted Aboriginal woman pulling beers and making wisecracks with white locals and passing bikies. I propped up my fancy-pants MacBook Air on the counter and wrote notes over a couple of reds, occasionally swapping words with my fellow barflies, more comfortable in this setting than I often felt among other tourists.

On the road I was very much an anomaly as a lone fifty-ish woman in a van, lost between the travel generations – the younger, often European, millennial backpackers in retrofitted vintage Kombis and the roaming retirees in glittering mini-mansions on wheels. Occasionally I would see gen X parents taking their kids in a motorhome round the country, but they were in the minority. My contemporaries were mostly at home, I imagined, sandwiched between caring for ageing parents and school-age children. I was usually the youngest person at a campsite, which surprised me. Retirees were the most numerous, circling their folding chairs and slapping down plastic tables for a happy hour at dusk, raucously swapping travel tales and tips like flocks of loud tropical birds. At caravan parks, especially the larger ones, there was often a man, not always the same one, whom I dubbed 'the Rooster'. The self-appointed fulcrum of caravan social life, he would talk loudly on his phone, give unsolicited travel advice – derived from his experience of crossing the Nullarbor eleven times, and so forth – direct large rigs out of narrow sites, explain the best place to get a satellite signal or which way to point your solar panels. Back in Melbourne, I'd joked to friends that I was a grey nomad in training, although it'll be another two decades before I can afford to retire, but I didn't identify much with these travellers and their lifestyle. I had an occasional polite chat with an older couple at a fireplace or a road stop, but retirees usually ignored me, not knowing how to place me, I suspect, an obscure woman researching other obscure women.

'Is that for two?' caravan park staff would ask when I went to pay for a site, the assumption being that I was travelling with a man, a partner or maybe a friend. Regardless of age, a certain stigma attaches to being a solo female traveller, not only because of the perceived risks, but because you're a woman who cannot be immediately identified by her relationship to others. It was a stigma I was used to as a single, childless woman, along with the increasing invisibility that had accompanied entering my forties. Once the pressure of the biological clock had subsided, and it became clear that I was not going to have children or a conventional family life, I experienced a fade-out. It's a truism for middle-aged women to complain – or be expected to – that they have become invisible, no longer valued for their youthful looks or promise of fertility, but to be a single, childless woman in your forties is to experience the sting of social irrelevance earlier than you might otherwise. If forty-something women feature as a subject in social policy discussion and public platforms, it's usually as working mums. Negotiating work and parenthood is undeniably a valid topic of social debate – for fathers as well as mothers –

yet this focus on women as ever in terms of reproduction sidelines other dimensions of their experience, other passages through midlife, other acts of juggling, other ways of contributing socially and living well. When middle-aged single and childless women occasionally appear as a blip in the public eye, they are framed negatively, as subjects of pity, such as news stories about older women being catfished online. Or as figures who inspire hostility and reproach, like Australia's first female prime minister, Julia Gillard, whose childlessness was treated with suspicion: 'ditch the witch'. All this fear and condemnation, despite studies reporting for decades that single women experience a higher quality of life than their married counterparts.[3]

After turning forty, I felt freer to embrace the substance of what these studies have long shown about the quality of single women's lives. I didn't mind being 'out of the game', as it were, feeling the fetters of obligation loosening; not having to worry about pairing up with someone or becoming pregnant before it was *too late*. The social invisibility of the no-longer-fertile woman is challenging but it is not without advantages. Somewhat dauntingly, you are no-one's priority; you are no-one's partner, no-one's parent, no-one's dependent child. No-one is beholden to you, and you are beholden to no-one. With this comes a terrible yet wonderful lightness of being. Sometimes the failure to register socially can seem more damning than invisibility, a state almost of non-existence. Women often rely on the web of female friendship for support, but the lack of obligation underpinning these networks means that as a single woman, you can also tumble quickly to the bottom of others' priorities (and I guiltily acknowledge that I have been less available to my friends at times while writing this book). Middle-aged, single, childless women are, as vanning poet Beth Spencer observes, 'Low on the priority list, out of necessity … Able to disappear (no-one really notices).'[4]

Yet being able to pull a disappearing act allows you the freedom to pursue your own interests, as Daisy did in her mid-forties, turning her sights to linguistic and ethnographic work, the memory of husbands and son retreating far into the distance. It also gave her more licence to travel, quite literally, not just intellectually and psychologically. This impulse, to kick away the jesses and take off, is something I recognise within myself. After I announced my plans to drive across the Nullarbor, a couple of friends expressed an interest in accompanying me but when our schedules and commitments did not align, part of me took a sneaking delight in vanning it alone as a way of embracing the eccentricity of my position. On the road, I welcomed, even encouraged, invisibility rather than draw attention to myself as a lone woman traveller. It was not just a matter of feeling safe, but being comfortable with my solitariness. Travelling further, I found the upside of invisibility was a sense of weightlessness, the freedom to roam about and observe other people, other places.

'I think I am growing a lonely queer little one – "funny"', Ernestine Hill wrote not long before she bought a caravan, and I wondered the same thing about myself.[5] Was my behaviour becoming distinctly odd? How was it that I had ended up at the age of fifty alone in a campervan? I asked myself. And no place is more apposite than that portable hermit's cell on wheels, life pared back to essentials – a bed, a fridge, a water tank, some cupboards, solar panels, a table and camping chairs, tools and a thunder bucket – to contemplate your fundamental solitariness. Was I a loner drawn to the study of two women like myself?

'Loner' often refers loosely to someone not in a conventional relationship or family situation, although it more properly denotes an intrinsic aversion to social connection. 'Someone who dislikes company,' the *Macquarie Dictionary* definition states baldly, (then qualifies with a bizarre example: 'he was a loner who lived a sheltered life with his elderly parents and had wanted to go into the desert in an attempt to gain self-confidence' – something of a steep learning curve for a sheltered loner), or 'someone who takes often unpopular independent action, without outside assistance'.

Ambivalence about social connection is threaded throughout Bates's and Hill's lives. Although both took unusual independent action for women of their era, they were often thirsty for company. They telegraphed their presence by mailing articles to papers and letters to friends and family, sometimes daily – behaviour that doesn't suggest that of absolute loners. During my travels in the van, I posted updates and photos every day on social media. I did this not only as a safety precaution, so people would know my whereabouts, but from a desire to communicate my experiences, as Hill and Bates did through their copious letter writing. Social media possesses a satisfying immediacy, with friends able to witness episodes from your daily life, and its digital camaraderie buoyed me on the road, as it has done whenever I've worked alone from home.

Although Hill and her newspaper editors wove a mythology about her as a lone woman wanderer in the outback, she frequently relied on the hospitality of others, hitching lifts from posties, eliciting the patronage of pastoralists and dossing down at homesteads. Her son Bob accompanied her during the 1940s and 1950s, as did writers and journalists such as Henrietta Drake-Brockman, Eleanor Smith and Vera Hamilton on stages of her trips. Hill's writing was also preoccupied with alleviating the isolation of those in remote Australia. Louise Campbell told me her greatest concern was lonely women in the outback; that she was aware of the fraternity that existed between men and was keen to foster connection between women.[6]

'I might be solitary,' Bates says in the *Passing*, 'but I was never lonely.'[7] As a 'confirmed wanderer, a nomad even as the aborigines', she possessed a sense of resoluteness, jettisoning social connections as she sailed off to Eucla to commence camping on the Bight. 'I do not think they quite approve of my work amongst the natives, but that is a mere detail,' she wrote in 1910 to a fellow amateur anthropologist, Georgina King, of others' responses to her tent life. 'I have given up all social life to my work. I am as happy as Larry over the "sacrifice".'[8] If anything, Bates was more of an autocrat than a loner, her high-handed personal style making it difficult for others to work with her, attempting to control her surroundings with rigid prescriptions for engaging with Anangu at her camps and by using the fantasy of class distinction to protect herself from contact with low whites. For all her desire to retreat from urban settler life to white civilisation's periphery, her letters sometimes display a demanding neediness for human contact. Often she was content with her own company: 'I am quite happy in my Solitude. I see my kindly hostess at meals & I try to do chores & keep my own room.' Yet the pall of loneliness could descend: 'I've got my little teapot & tea cups & oh oh what would I not give to make Ernestine a cup of tea ... I am very lonely – spiritually, mentally.'[9] Solitude implies choice, but loneliness is a reluctant condition. One state can easily slide into the other, as Bates was acutely aware, sometimes content with being alone, at other times longing for company.

'I am but a wraith, flitting by,' Hill wrote in her mid-forties to a friend.[10] Her life as a travelling correspondent had become that of a water-skater, gliding across the surfaces of large expanse, her peripatetic curiosity about other people offset by her reticence and social withdrawal, especially in cities. Bob Hill later accused her of 'not ever mixing with people', saying that 'a mad pursuit of writing drove her all over the countryside'. To which Ernestine replied 'in a bemused way' that it was more about 'a passion for more people, their lives, land, experiences, etc, than for writing'.[11] Bob thought his mother was 'out of place in Australia'; that she 'wrote about Australia in the way that Shakespeare wrote about Verona' and was detached from the exotic types she described in the curio sketches from her travels.[12] As Hill entered her fifth decade, her wanderer status became more entrenched as she continued her mobile lifestyle of scattered social contact without attaching herself to any particular place.

In 1938 Dame Mary Gilmore mooted Hill as a possible office-bearer for the Fellowship of Australian Writers (FAW), then quickly discarded this idea because she was 'one of the wanderers', rightly intuiting that Ernestine, with her New Woman–style penchant for knocking about remote Australia in Oxford bags was not suited to conventional office-bearing roles or to organisational life. Hill had begun renting 'a neat, sunny highly modern but moderate flat' in Kings Cross to be close to Sydney's Mitchell Library while she was researching *My Love Must Wait* and also 'just for the joy of being in Bohemia – a different sort of wilderness to the last one'.[13] But she remained very much a satellite to southern literary life and coalitions such as the FAW, the first organisation dedicated to supporting Australian writers and promoting their work. On one occasion, she apologised to Henrietta Drake-Brockman, the Perth branch FAW president, for backing out of a public speaking invitation because it was 'a physical and mental ordeal that in a big gathering I cannot face'.[14] Drake-Brockman was Perth-born but had lived in the Kimberley during the 1920s, publishing novels, stories and sketches for the *Bulletin* and *Walkabout* based on her experience, and Hill felt comfortable sharing her reservations about the FAW and southern urban literary life with her. It wasn't the first time she'd baulked at a social engagement; she also turned down an invitation to speak at the SA Women's Lunch: 'They want a Presence, and I do hate to disappoint them, and feel apologetic from the start. The written word is such a barricade, but meeting people in the large always gives me a sense of loss.'[15] Shyness is too simple a word to describe Hill's reticence, her habitual abnegation of self and tendency to withdraw: it was a form of social anxiety that had become enmeshed with her dislike of the urban south. She described cutting and running from a Sydney literary lunch – 'social life in cities sears me somehow' – preferring to be '[w]andering around in the Great Vague, with just an old bearded josser in the landscape or a camp of blacks'.[16] The extent of Hill's social avoidance was such that when Margriet Bonnin contacted some of her literary contemporaries, Marjorie Barnard, Eleanor Dark and Kylie Tennant, after Hill's death, they reported only fleeting sightings of Ernestine among the Mitchell Library's stacks or on the fringes of a FAW party in Perth.[17]

If Hill avoided the FAW and southern literary circles, she sympathised with their local struggles with 'the capitalists, as represented by the editors of little "pages" roundabout in the magazines'. She'd been doing it tough as a freelancer after she left the *Advertiser* in 1936 and was certainly aware of how precarious writers' livelihoods were in Australia: how dependent they were on editors who 'keep their stuff for months without acknowledging it, lose it with stamps, snavel the idea if it is a good one, ignore it if it isn't – a heart-breaking business. I wonder there was not a revolution long ago.' Writing ironically to Drake-Brockman about 'the way Australia encourages her writers', she confided: 'I have to wait weeks, sometimes months, for money for work done … This has been a shocking year for me.' She hadn't received any royalties since the previous year and she was worried that her British publisher, Jarrold & Sons, had 'pretty well killed the "Loneliness"' with amendments to the second edition.[18]

Although Gilmore passed over Hill as a potential FAW office-bearer because of her wandering ways and lack of literary clubbishness, she became a strong advocate for Ernestine as a writer while she was living in Sydney during the early 1940s. Dame Mary, who could lay claim to being her day's leading Australian woman of letters, was a powerful ally to have. A formidable literary figure who'd participated in radical labour movements, such as William Lane's attempt at establishing a working man's paradise in Paraguay, and edited the women's page for the *Australian Worker*, she was a prime mover in establishing the FAW in 1928. Ernestine had first met Gilmore when she was fifteen during a school holiday visit to Sydney and once she'd established her household in the Cross, Dame Mary, who had a flat nearby on Darlinghurst Road, enlisted Hill in recording her memoirs. Gilmore was certain that these, along with her diaries, needed to be preserved because it was in the national interest, and revelled in having a personal scribe – 'A treat to have my own manner of expression preserved … The matter shows that, with a good shorthand writer, I can dictate'.[19] But Hill was not entirely comfortable with this arrangement. Once when Gilmore asked whether she'd typed up her shorthand notes yet, she 'evaded and said it was not very good; that it had no fire'. 'I am afraid her style, which is non-philosophical, and descriptive of facts only, and mine, will not coalesce,'[20] Dame Mary declared. She slated the problem to her being a thinker, whereas Hill was merely a writer, and engaged professional stenographers to type up her diaries, which were later archived at the National and Mitchell libraries. Hill's reluctance to act as recording angel was understandable, given the part she'd already played – to her own detriment – in ghostwriting Bates's memoirs. Her friendship with the older, domineering Gilmore in some respects reflected her relationship with Bates and, beyond her, Madge Hemmings.

Dame Mary did, however, provide Ernestine with wholehearted and useful support during the 1940s. In 1939 she introduced Hill to George Mackaness, an English teacher, lecturer, historian and past Sydney FAW president, suggesting she ask him to provide a reference for her application to the Commonwealth Literary Fund (CLF). Although the fund had been established in 1908, it had only recently adopted a grant-based system to subsidise practising writers, offering five literary fellowships for work to be undertaken in 1940. Hill had been amassing 'extraordinary stuff of the Territory' from her Mitchell Library research and applied for a fellowship to write 'an unusual historical work of the Territory'.[21] Approaching Mackaness, she emphasised that the outbreak of war had 'so accentuated the difficulties of obtaining a living by free-lancing' that, as her family's breadwinner, she was seeking the fellowship as 'the best thing that offers for a livelihood' and to produce 'a life's work for a very much beloved country'.[22] Both Mackaness and Gilmore supported her application, and in 1940 she became one of the first recipients of a CLF fellowship, which she used for further research for *My Love Must Wait* and *The Territory*.

In making a case for Hill, Gilmore stressed to Mackaness that her situation was 'really urgent, worse indeed than I thought it was, owing to the war cutting down space and roster of free-lancing work, and to her mother being so aged and her boy at school'.[23] Madge Hemmings was seventy-eight and, according to Gilmore, 'Full of enthusiasms and high blood pressure. But senility is at the door.'[24] Bob Hill later claimed his grandmother 'ended up life living in Sydney in very reduced circumstances … senile, ranting & raving' before making a side-swipe at the avoidant Ernestine – 'but still more "normal" than mother because she was involved in things didn't cut herself off from the world'.[25] Turning fifteen in November 1939, Bob may have been unaware of how money worries crowded Hill, some of which concerned him. He'd been attending the prestigious Sydney private boys' school Cranbrook, where she'd enrolled him 'never dreaming that money would be short', although she contemplated sending him to work in the new year.²⁶ Admitting she found 'the actual living of life very, very difficult – if only we could just dream it away with a clear run for the things we love to do', Ernestine asked the ever-forbearing Aunt Kit down from Brisbane 'to take Bob and mother off my hands' and manage their household in Sydney.²⁷

'I would be so much happier doing a Bagman's Stamping Ground for them than women's pages,' Hill confessed to Drake-Brockman, 'but they think it sells the paper, so that is the main thing.'²⁸ In 1940 she found employment with the *ABC Weekly*. Her *Advertiser* colleague, Rene Foster, had contacted the editor, Sydney Deamer, suggesting if there was 'any loophole for outside recommendations' that he consider Ernestine Hill on the basis of her versatility in terms of material and genre, adding 'privately, she is desperately hard up'.²⁹ Deamer offered Hill the editorship of the *ABC Weekly*'s women's page, which she accepted although ambivalent about the role. Indeed, she was 'sturdily against knitting' and the other traditional feminine fare that featured in women's pages, but knew that while newspapers were rationing their space and budget for freelancers 'we must be glad of the job in hand according to its lights'.³⁰

Still, a regular gig for the *ABC Weekly* was not to be sneezed at. A serial that accompanied the Australian Broadcasting Commission's radio programming schedule, the *Weekly* became a significant source of middle-brow literary and social commentary over the next two decades, publishing reviews by John Hinde, Vance and Nettie Palmer, stories by Florence James, Beatrice Grimshaw, Ruth Park and Henrietta Drake-Brockman, and journalism by fellow 'great wide space' writers Frank Clune and William Hatfield. Hill had initially pitched a travel service to Deamer, in which she'd write a small article in response to inquiries from motorists each week, claiming it would boost the new serial's circulation. She was aware of how Australia was – or had been, before the war – opening up for tourism, writing, 'I know this country extraordinarily well, and could be of infinite help', but Deamer offered her the women's page instead.[31] Knowing that she could not be easily contained, he gave her scope to roam, acknowledging that 'she will write as she likes, because we have a feeling that what she likes is what the reader, whether in the city or outback, likes also'.[32]

Hill opened her first *ABC Weekly* editorial addressing 'the women of Australia, from Cape York … to the Darling Ranges' as 'one who has wandered and lived among you … I feel we are none of us strangers' assuring them that 'Week by week, you will be my story.' She used the despised craft of knitting to link women making socks for soldiers across generations and the country's expanses – 'Far away on the last border fences the women are knitting against time.'[33] Historian Jeannine Baker observes that 'Society saw women's primary duty in wartime as serving the national cause. Their role was largely supportive; their responsibility was to maintain the "unseen battalions" in the background and allow men to get on with the real business of the war.'[34] But if wartime officially tightened traditional prescriptions of women's roles, it also provided opportunities for loosening them, as Hill was aware. She quickly turned from domestic pursuits as subject matter to championing the contribution Australia's 'land girls' were making to the war effort by taking on traditionally masculine tasks. 'What can she not do? She can drive a truck and mend a plane, and till a field, and telegraph, and canteen-cook, and scrub out a ward, and knit.'[35] Hill's wasn't the only dissenting voice about what was considered appropriate material for women. Listeners such as Eva Linn complained about the typical content of women's radio programming;

that she was sick of being told how to scramble an egg – 'Any man in the world feels competent to say What Women Want, of course, and it not unexpectedly turns out to be Instruction in Work He Wants Done for Him.'[36]

The *ABC Weekly* job provided Hill and her family with some financial stability after the 'breathtakingly haphazard' way she had been receiving cheques for freelancing, but it wasn't her first love and tethered her again to the City of Everlasting No.[37] Deamer joked about her professional restlessness in one editorial, entreating readers who wrote to her: 'please do not paint too alluring a picture of sunrises and sunsets over the wide spaces. We want to keep her with us as long as we can without having to resort to padlocks.'[38] Women were still carrying their swags out in the great wide spaces, Hill noted wistfully in an editorial titled 'Long trail of romance'.[39] She wanted to join them. 'I was weary to death of Sydney,' she wrote after receiving an invitation to Broken Hill, 'and longing to see some stars instead of neon lights.' She began using the *ABC Weekly* as a springboard for travel writing, which she found re-energising: 'in health and in spirit it has been my salvation – a little of the old out-door work.'[40] Soon enough, she had shifted the focus of *ABC Weekly* women's page to her more usual, geographically wide-ranging preoccupations, from Australian Inland Mission nursing sisters at Fitzroy Crossing to female factory hands in Melbourne's Flinders Lane. As in the *Loneliness*, she assembled stories mainly about European women's experience, with occasional nods towards that of Asian women, such as Madame Chiang Kai-Shek, the political leader of Darwin's Chinatown, and Aboriginal women's tough predicament in the pastoral industry. Her content also prefigured a book she began drafting (but ultimately never finished) in the 1950s, 'Women of Australia: Story without End', in which she intended to celebrate women's history since white settlement.

One of Hill's more ambitious feature ideas for the *ABC Weekly* was coverage of the refugee crisis in Darwin precipitated by Australia's entry into the Pacific War after the Pearl Harbor attack in December 1941. Unprepared for military strikes, the bulk of Darwin's population was quickly evacuated, including 2000 women and children, before the first Japanese air raids in February 1942. Most left by ship, but some travelled south by road and rail, passing through the Barossa Valley, where Hill was staying. The North Road was itself 'strange news', she told Deamer. 'Men in the know' had strongly advised her 'to go up the road for great stories … Darwin evacuees coming down … Myaladharra blacks and desert rats mining the gypsum deserts for strontium and other war minerals … crowded camps and foot-walkers of strange persuasion … unending good stories that would interest the whole world'. Rail travel north of Quorn in South Australia was prohibited and temperatures were over 105 degrees Fahrenheit, but Hill was undeterred, hoping that she and Deamer might persuade the military authorities to let her head further up the highway if she promised to focus only on human interest stories about women and child refugees, with 'not a word of camps and troops'.[41]

Ernestine found the army less than amenable to her requests to hitch on their lorries, which were strictly for transporting fuel and stores: 'They were very nice to me, but asked me to wait … I offered to take my own swag and food, and sleep out. They still said no.'[42] Jeannine Baker observes that the Australian military 'treated women journalists with suspicion, even at times hostility', during the Second World War; female reporters were 'not permitted to be officially accredited as war correspondents or to report from operational areas'. The perceived need to provide them with separate accommodation and transport was a further deterrent.[43] Hill did well to get as far as she did and to receive some relatively civil pushback. She posted Deamer a story and photographs about the Darwin refugee crisis and promised more was to come, pressing him for more money. The cost of travel and accommodation in wartime to research these articles had absorbed most of her salary and her royalty payments – so much so, she was 'practically unable to give friends Christmas presents', let alone family at home.[44] She requested a raise of £1 per week to cover these additional expenses, arguing that she was contributing to the *ABC Weekly*'s prestige by reporting on the North Road exodus. She also hinted at her own rising literary stakes: Doubleday was planning to publish the first American edition of *The Great Australian Loneliness* the following year, and *My Love Must Wait* had been sent to them for consideration.

If Hill's livelihood as a writer had been precarious at the start of the decade, her editorship of the *ABC Weekly* women's page consolidated her public profile. According to Kylie Tennant, the *Weekly* soon 'became a very widely read and influential journal' after it commenced in 1939 and 'the influence on the reading public at this time of the opinions of Ernestine Hill could not be underestimated'.[45] She also delivered publicity talks for the *Weekly* on ABC radio on topics such as the Australian pearling industry, 'the first white women in Australia' and 'before the white man came'. Her reputation surged with the publication of *My Love Must Wait* in Australia in late 1941, which leader-page articles heralded in major Melbourne, Adelaide and Brisbane newspapers. The first edition sold out in mid-December 1941, two months after publication; in spite of wartime paper shortages, six Australian print runs were sold in four years, and the book was published in England in 1944 and America in 1946.[46] Literary academic Anna Johnson states that 'By 1948, Hill's publisher Angus & Robertson had sold almost 100,000 copies of her only novel, *My Love Must Wait* (1941), based on the life of Matthew Flinders, setting a sales record at the time for a novel written by an Australian author and printed in Australia.'⁴⁷ Filmmaker Charles Chauvel bought the world film rights to *My Love Must Wait* for a then-record price – 'which ran into four figures' – for any Australian novel.⁴⁸ The film was never made, but the book was read as a radio serial during 1946 and again in 1968–69.

Hill originally titled her Flinders book *He Named Australia*, but Walter Cousins, the managing director of Angus & Robertson, thought it was too evocative of school history textbooks, so he suggested *My Love Must Wait*. Cousins also rebadged it as fiction, although Hill concurred with Mackaness's description of it as 'a new type of biography' – 'fundamentally, it is fact – dialogue from log, descriptions built up from his own letters' – an insight anticipating the genre of literary nonfiction.⁴⁹ Hill envisaged different mediums and markets for *My Love Must Wait*, writing the manuscript with film, theatre and radio play adaptations in mind, 'without losing its value as a standard work on Flinders'. Two composers were even inspired to write a song based on the book's account of Flinders first hearing that his wife could not accompany him on his voyage, which had been given fresh significance during wartime when 'so many must "wait their loves"'.⁵⁰ Hill readily assented to their right to use the same title as her book. It was all grist to her Australianist mill: 'I want this remarkable life story to reach the people of Australia, because they ought to know it.'⁵¹

My Love Must Wait was widely acclaimed, apart from jibes about its stylistic flummery – 'From the first page of her introduction, Ernestine Hill makes it clear that she is going to offer Romance with a capital "R," something larger and fluffier than life' – and stylistic sleights of hand such as set 'stage scenes'. The *Bulletin*'s Red Page reviewer provided the most substantial critique of *My Love Must Wait*, in conjunction with Eleanor Dark's *The Timeless Land*, which was published in the same year. While a 'staggering difference' existed between the two novelists' approaches –

Dark's realism versus Hill's romanticism – he observed they shared a common cause: 'Behind all Australian fiction of this kind there seems to lie a patriotic impulse as well as an artistic. The novelists are trying to create a nation as well as a novel.' Despite some misjudged poetic effusion, the reviewer thought Hill's 'floral clock' of Australian history was warmer and more 'truly an instrument of art' than Dark's 'cold, rarely chiming timepiece'. He concludes: 'These are outstanding books, and the writing and publication of them in war-time is the sign of true vigour in the Australian culture.'[52] His mention of wartime in the context of nation-building is significant: these bestselling novels provided consolation and a sense of pride, in a time of war, that Australia was worth fighting for. Hill consciously catered to a popular market with *My Love Must Wait*. She and Cousins had 'both agreed that history must be sugar-coated in a work of this kind, and for Flinders's sake, to reach the multitude'.[53] Creating uplifting, nation-building material during wartime cannot have been far from their intentions.

In *The Art of Time Travel*, historian Tom Griffiths frames Dark 'as probably Australia's most influential historical writer of the twentieth century', based on *The Timeless Land*'s inclusion for many years on the Victorian school curriculum and translation into other languages, as well as her serious dedication to historical research.[54] Hill enjoyed a similarly high profile in the mid-20th century through the popularity of *My Love Must Wait* as a wartime bestseller which was translated into other languages and reprinted as a paperback during the 1960s, along with her other standout works such as the *Loneliness* and the *Territory*. She protested that 'every fact can be verified' in her account of Flinders but, as in her portrayal of Bates, she romanticised him, downplaying more negative aspects of his personality and exploits. The *Bulletin* reviewer may have found Hill's floral clock warmer than Dark's 'cold, rarely chiming timepiece' but through its attempt to 'tell a story of the white settlement partly from the black man's view', *The Timeless Land* offered a more serious and philosophical excursion into Australian history.[55] Dark's novel continues to attract critical interest for its contribution to historiography, most recently from Tom Griffiths and journalist Stan Grant.[56]

My Love Must Wait, with its fanciful and sentimental prose, fell out of favour with the postwar emphasis on literary realism. Moreover, its romantic and populist nation-building portrayal of Flinders quickly dated with the emergence of postcolonial rewritings of Australian history, following the civil rights and Aboriginal self-determination movements in the 1960s and 1970s, which toppled white settler icons and gave voice to marginalised perspectives.

Hill was resolute about her spin on Australian history in *My Love Must Wait*, defending it as an antidote to the cultural cringe: 'if we did dramatise our country a little more for the million, it would do us much good. That inferiority complex that seems to be a hang-over from the colonial and convict days and makes us ape the English in super-sophistication and boredom won't do.'[57] Fellow writers expressed private chagrin about her populist rendering of Flinders: Franklin complained to Prichard that Ernestine 'had made too much of a mush of my beloved Flinders' for her to be 'dazzled by her'.[58] Criticism notwithstanding, Hill was excited by the book's success although she'd found completing the manuscript intensely stressful, writing to Drake-Brockman in September 1940, 'I am in most horrible throes. My book on Flinders has to be finished in 19 days! – acres and acres to do. And another one to be finished by December.'[59] The other book was *The Territory*, which would not be published for a decade.

For Hill, the circumstances behind the writing of *My Love Must Wait* were 'very heart-breaking, a tragedy just as poignant, with my mother's death before she could see it, as those of Flinders' own story'.[60] Margaret Hemmings was suffering from cardiovascular disease and sliding deeper into dementia, but her death from a stroke on 15 June 1941 winded Ernestine. Hill's correspondence from this time is veiled on the subject, as if she's retreated behind the façade of wartime stoicism and her responsibilities as a reporter. 'In a very sad period of life I have had the heart to seek no one,' she wrote to Mackaness while travelling for the *ABC Weekly* several months later.[61] It was over a year before she began to reflect more openly on how this loss affected her, in letters to friends.

Although Madge Hemmings had often been a volatile and overwhelming presence in her daughter's life, Ernestine felt her loss keenly as that of a best friend and confidante as well as a mother. Madge had remained interested in her daughter's creative and professional endeavours, supporting her throughout the writing of *My Love Must Wait* – 'my mother was the only true self-sacrificing and perceiving friend in my struggle to finish that book' – which Hill dedicated to her.[62] Wartime Sydney took on a menacing, nightmarish quality for Ernestine, becoming again a canvas for the projection of loss and anxiety. 'I have just come home from Mary Gilmore's through the black streets of Kings' Cross and the city where everything is sinister now – a City of Dreadful Night – men on the trams and ferries with their heads in shadows and their spectacles horribly gleaming,' she wrote to her cousin, Coy. 'I love the great darkness of the lonely fields, but this gets me down.'[63]

Early in 1942 Deamer told Hill and Max Afford, another *ABC Weekly* special writer, that their jobs were unsustainable, given 'the new newsprint cuts and war conditions', and gave them two months' notice. They had both been expecting to be laid off, and Hill saw it as an opportunity to resume roaming the outback's 'lonely fields':

'I trust he has mistaken the flush of delight that overspread my chops as one of shame and regret.' Deamer suggested she take leave straightaway but continue to send articles, nudging her towards the ABC's Information Shortwave headquarters, who wanted 'Australian "background" writing to the "hot news" being sent by their American weekly broadcasters'.[64]

The arrival of US troops in 1942 to support Australia in fighting the Pacific War fostered American curiosity about all things Australian. 'Little America' – aircrew squadrons camping in north-western Australia to defend its coastline – was 'pounding the frontline and rear bases of the Japanese', although at night 'there are card games in the mess, and gin squashes at 1/6 each, and in the tents a floatable interest in books. There is a genuine interest in Australian literature.'[65] Xavier Herbert's *Capricornia* was the camp's bestseller, with *The Great Australian Loneliness* – the first Australian book to be distributed to the US troops, reframed by Doubleday for American readers as *Australian Frontier* in 1943 – running a close second. Doubleday's edition of the *Loneliness* greatly pleased Hill – 'they are making Australia, through my little book – a wonderful story'. Along with *My Love Must Wait*, the Australian and American reprints of the *Loneliness* launched Hill from well-known journalist to one of the country's bestselling authors. As Anna Johnson observes, her outreach became international during the war:

> Hill's vision for writing as critical in securing the nation's geopolitical future confirms her commitment to the pivotal role of accessible, educational, and informative literature, not only for her fellow Australians but for an international reading public. Her perspective from within journalism and the publishing industry reveals another side to the USA's entry into the Pacific War – the demand for Australian writing.[66]

Influence aside, Hill hoped she was on the verge of a financial windfall from the American sales of *Australian Frontier*.

Once her *ABC Weekly* job had been axed, Hill moved her domestic headquarters to Adelaide, which she found less stressful than the noise and climate of Sydney as well as closer to the outback. Bob had finished school and taken up an internship as a 'sub-cub' reporter for £1 per week at the *Advertiser*; Hill wished to channel him into supporting her research for *The Territory*. Aunt Kit accompanied them as housekeeper – she was 'a dear little cook some of the times, but she wilts a good bit, and can't live on without the round of the bargain basements and her cronies three or four days a week. 'Twas ever thus.'[67] Her aunt might have been a dedicated if idiosyncratic housekeeper, but her 'wilting' was of significant concern.

In June 1942 Hill was struck by 'a bright bolt from the blue sky' when Prime Minister John Curtin offered her a two-year appointment as an ABC commissioner, saying 'he knew of no woman who had as wide a knowledge of Australia and its people as she (Mrs Hill)'.[68] With her customary humility, she first thought the nomination had come to her by mistake; in fact, the three men on the selection committee were unanimous in their support for Mrs Hill because she was not 'a political woman, nor tied to any special movement, and she must know Australia and its people'.[69] It was a seemingly nonpartisan decision, aimed at building national spirit in a time of war. A romantic rather than a materialist, Hill thought the creation of a tradition of letters, grounded in bush mythology, should ground Australian identity. She was both entertained and dismayed by the socialist and internationalist sympathies expressed by a sizeable swathe of the Australian literary community, writing to Drake-Brockman after attending a couple of FAW meetings in 1940, 'each time that Red element you mentioned amused me'. She thought the focus of the 'Bellowship of Australian Skiters' – as PR Stephensen dubbed the FAW before he became their vice-president – should be more local: on Australia itself.[70]

Romanticising her modus operandi as usual, Ernestine described receiving the news of her appointment while 'sitting by the fire … droving a mob of cattle overland – on the typewriter, not of course in actual fact … writing the story of the great cattle migrations to and from the North of Australia'. She took on 'this vital national work' as an ABC commissioner with vision and energy, as a practical opportunity to improve the circumstances of those in remote areas. Recalling how 'when I first set my course, by a lonely star … it was a very silent country' twelve years earlier, she knew 'what radio means to the outback people' because it had filled the silence of the loneliness – for non-Indigenous people – with European music. She vowed to bring literature to remote readers as well; plays and serialised books were now being broadcast through metropolitan stations. The ABC 'will always be a bond between the men – and women – of Australia', she stated, although its commitment to meeting the 'needs of a woman's everyday life' could be strengthened, especially since they 'need each other more than ever before' in wartime.[71]

Hill's role expanded to travelling commissioner early in 1943 and she soon embarked on a gruelling itinerary – 'Adelaide to Canberra, Yass, and all round to Kosciusko, back to Adelaide, thence North to Birdsville, through Queensland to Broken Hill, White Cliffs, Wilcannia. Marooned by enormous floods at Cooper's Creek, 80 miles wide of water, and thence to Sydney' – canvassing hundreds of 'keen listeners' about their requirements and requests for radio programming.[72] A year later, she made a first recommendation to put the ABC's racing broadcast over the national network on shortwave on Saturday afternoons. This request might sound insular and mundane, but it highlighted problems with reception for outback people. Most stations had 'woreless-cum-pedal-wireless' but relied on shortwave for unbroken reception, although there was little opportunity 'of hearing either National or commercial stations during the heat of the day, nor, indeed, in the hot nights'. She followed this recommendation with others reflecting her real passions, women's and children's programming, suggesting the ABC provide 'serials of a lively nature' – school broadcasting linked in with correspondence lessons – plus a 'woman's session of wider and brisker general interest'. More than anything else, she thought 'a first-rate editor of long experience in journalistic work, and of proved ability in selecting "stories" and speakers' to broadcast a woman's hour each morning would be 'a great benefit in very lonely lives'.[73] As commissioner, she extended her previous advocacy for women in the bush through the reporting that informed *The Great Australian Loneliness* and her women's page for the *ABC Weekly*. A decade later, she observed to Anne Tully, a Durack cousin:

> God moved in a mysterious way to bring me out among the real Australian people all over just in time – radios and radio-activity and aeroplanes and highways have made such an immense change that it seems all such sameness and and [sic] commonplace compared with the past when the world <u>was</u> wide.[74]

It was a modest statement, downplaying her perspicacity as a journalist and later as ABC commissioner in understanding the difference that expanding infrastructure networks – transport and communications – would make to those in remote Australia.

Hill also continued to impart an awareness of the diversity of outback life to urban audiences through her ABC radio talks. In a fascinating broadcast, 'Before the white man came', she described meeting with a group of Aboriginal people in the Flinders Ranges who explained to her how Australia was demarcated according to tribal boundaries and 'divided into five times as many provinces as Europe, all more or less Communist in the true ideal of the word'. Prior to colonisation, Aboriginal people had established a 'commerce as continent-wide as ours, a religion as firm in faith, and in picture, song and drama an art that expressed his race. More than that no nation can achieve.'[75] These were stirring, yet potentially provocative words during wartime, when Australia was concerned with shoring up a unified identity and defending its borders. The only other Europeans who shared this perception of country were anthropologists such as Bates and Norman Tindale, whose 'Map showing the distribution of the Aboriginal Tribes of Australia' was published in 1940. This idea of an alternative Aboriginal domain was a theme to which Hill would return after the war in *The Territory* and her vision for other works.

'Many Australians imagine her a tall, gaunt, authoritative woman,' a profile about Hill's appointment as ABC commissioner enthused.

> Five feet five inches, she weighs about 100 lb., can endure driving 400 rough miles in a battered truck and still smile, can camp under the skin in rain for a week, and has never been really ill in her life. No trail, or lack of a trail, daunts her.[76]

Ernestine had arrived as a public figure, although she retained a residual social awkwardness. Yvonne Palmer, a childhood friend, remarked 'how amusing it was to see "Society" falling over Ernestine … the same people who used to say "she was so different" and impliedly uninteresting – now want to entertain her – and probably ask if "the mosquitoes at Darwin are as bad as at Double Bay"!'[77]

However, the fissure between Hill's romantic persona as vagabond correspondent and her stressful lifestyle was widening, the wear of constant wandering and writing taking its toll as she entered her forties. Not long after *My Love Must Wait* came out, Gilmore reported that Ernestine had visited, bringing oysters to celebrate: 'But I ate them all. She is too thin and eats almost nothing. Her nerves on "Flinders" have worked her stomach dry.' Hill's appetite did not rival Dame Mary's, and she complained of a gastric ulcer, but these comments highlight her overtaxed state. 'This story can all the guest-houses of our troubled little pilgrimage tell,' she wrote to Alice Mackaness, George's wife, describing how she'd written *My Love Must Wait* 'over a long period of plain anguish', often working until 3 am after putting in 9.30 am to 6 pm days for the *ABC Weekly*.[78] She told Curtin she had put in '12 years of 15 hours a day service to my country, writing always for Australia'.[79] She continued to be plagued with financial uncertainty. By the end of 1943, she'd received £300 in income from her ABC commissioner position and £500 from book sales over the previous two years.[80] She had expected to reap £6000 from US sales of *Australian Frontier* after its publication in 1943, but although the book sold 62 488 copies, her royalties (US$624.88 at one cent a copy) were diminished by taxation.[81]

After moving to Adelaide, Hill still made sporadic 'astonishing' appearances at Gilmore's Kings Cross flat while on ABC business in Sydney, bearing flowers and fruit which she rarely ate herself. Dame Mary arrived home one day to find Ernestine waiting on her doorstep before her first commission meeting the next day in Canberra with 'such dreams of making the work not only Australian, but widely and embracingly Australian.'[82] But Hill's 'burning flame' died out quickly. The tedium of commission board meetings was such, she confessed, that when someone mentioned 'paralysis' towards the end of one, 'she felt she had to say "I don't know how you feel, but I have paralysis of the posterior with sitting so long!"' 'She is so thin the bones are on the muscles,' Gilmore reported, 'and she is so virginal to look at, and in mind, the expression was simply intellectual daring. It came from the top storey and not from the bottom!'[83]

After Madge Hemming's death, Dame Mary cast her role in Ernestine's life as a maternal one: 'The dear girl told me she felt toward me as though I were her mother; that she always had me at her back.'[84] But it was Aunt Kit, who'd been as much of a mother as Madge to her and Bob, whom Hill relied upon to anchor their family unit. Then one evening late in May 1943, as she, Bob and Kitty gathered round the wireless to hear Henrietta Drake-Brockman read her 'very delightful part in "Over to Youth"', the unthinkable happened: her beloved aunt had a stroke. Kit was rushed to hospital but did not regain consciousness and died that night. Her aunt had high blood pressure and had been seriously ill several years earlier, but Ernestine struggled to reconcile her death with the fact that she'd been talking and laughing only moments beforehand. She guiltily observed that Kit had been 'doing far too much all the time, and for everyone in the world she met'. For the first time, Hill was wholly responsible for managing Bob's and her own affairs without her older female relatives' support. Kit's death also was a terrible echo of Madge's passing from a stroke two years earlier, amplifying Ernestine's sense of being cast adrift: 'It was all dreadfully like Mother's leaving me, and these two were so much from babyhood in my life that nothing will be the same again. There's just Bob and me.'[85]

Compounding Hill's emotional fragility and grief at the sudden loss of these strong maternal figures from her life was her son's impending conscription. She and Bob were 'both anti-killing' – self-declared pacifists horrified by the thought of either killing or being trained to kill fellow human beings, but it was her state of mind that was at stake.[86] A week after his eighteenth birthday, Ernestine wrote to Alice Mackaness that if he 'should be taken into this war, before he is 20, I will not have the heart to go on'.[87] Hill began lobbying Curtin to defer her son's conscription until he turned twenty because he was invaluable to her as a research assistant on 'work of outstanding value to Australia'. Her writing, she reminded the prime minister, had been hailed by British reviewers as 'of great value to Empire' and also 'awakening lively interest' from the US in Australia.[88]

Robert Hill was a 'no-show' on 1 January 1943, the first morning of his military service at Keswick Barracks in Adelaide. His mother rang the National Service Office an hour and a half after he was supposed to arrive, explaining they were applying to the military court for exemption. The magistrate, RJ Coombe, heard Bob's case in early March and granted him six months' leave on the basis that separating him from Ernestine would have a deleterious effect on her health and 'also upon her ability to continue her literary work'.[89] Bob had left his *Advertiser* internship the year before to assist her. Hill claimed he was essential to her both as a companion and a research assistant; that when she was not engaged in ABC responsibilities, she worked on the book from 10 am until midnight each day. She sent the prime minister a desperate telegram requesting that Bob's conscription be stayed, ending 'regret approach but position urgent as cannot comply regardless of action to be taken'.[90] After seeking the military authorities' advice, Curtin told Hill politely but firmly that 'unfortunately the enemy is at the gates and he is not greatly concerned at the moment with literary work, unless it contained instructions for the armed forces in the art of war'.[91] In response, she gave him an advance copy of *Australian Frontier* – a token of her work, advancing knowledge of Australia to an international audience.

Once Bob's six months' leave ran out, the Hills submitted another application. After a hearing on 5 October 1943 at the Adelaide Police Court, Robert Hill was granted another two months' leave to help his mother research her Territory book, all 200 000 words of which she'd promised to deliver to her publisher the following January.[92] During the hearing, a medical doctor, Leon Opit, was asked to assess Hill's psychological state and consider the effect of her son's conscription on her wellbeing. After examining her, Opit declared 'he had seen few women quite so neurotic or unbalanced as Mrs Hill',[93] that she 'seemed to think he "was against her" and was involved in a conspiracy to deprive her of her son'.[94] Hill was so fraught that he had been unable to complete his examination, and Opit admitted that if Bob were called up, it might 'make her mental equilibrium more disturbed than it is at present'.[95] Hill later complained that the second hearing had been particularly cruel and unfair, rendering her incapable of focussing on her work; that she had been subjected to a barrage of 'belittling questions' by solicitors and that Dr Opit had not made a proper attempt to examine her and his evidence was therefore 'most harmful and untrue'. However, the scornful tone of newspaper reports on the hearing indicate that public sympathy for the 'well-known author' with her requests for special treatment for her son was ebbing low.

The Hills's solicitor wrote to HV Evatt, who was then attorney-general, asking him to intervene, but he demurred on the grounds that it would be wrong for him to interfere because 'Mrs. Hill's case is actually only one of many other similar cases.'[96]

Hill wrote to Curtin a month after Bob's second hearing, appealing for clemency, requesting her son be allowed to assist her for another few months. She even managed to meet with Curtin in November 1943 while she was on commission business in Canberra; he advised her to consider enlisting her son in the merchant navy. Curtin deferred to the advice of the minister for labour and national service, who informed him that since Robert Hill had already appealed to the magistrate, who'd granted him an extra two months' exemption from service, a further extension would not be made.

On 6 December 1943 Robert D Hill was the only member of AAF Mob 30 not to report for duty. The area provost sergeant was despatched to the Hills's listed place of residence in North Adelaide, only to find they had left a month earlier without notifying the National Service Office, which Bob was required to do so within seven days of relocation. Instead they left 'c/- Broadcasting Commission Sydney' as their forwarding address. Hill had in fact contacted the ABC in early November, saying she did not feel well enough to attend a commission meeting in Sydney the following week. After two days' holiday in Mildura, she rang an ABC official on a Sunday morning, saying she could travel there if accompanied by her son, proposing that they catch the Murray Valley bus service to Albury, where they could pick up tickets from the stationmaster and continue by express to Sydney in time for the commission meeting on Wednesday. The ABC agreed to these arrangements in view of her fragile health; it's not clear whether they were aware of supporting the Hills's subterfuge. Ernestine might rage that 'injurious and untrue publicity has driven us from our home'[97] but failure to notify the army of Bob's change of address was itself a punishable offence 'in both civil and military categories', and they faced possible imprisonment if they continued to obstruct his conscription.[98] Indeed, Bob's absence 'might be proved to be a more serious offence', Kidd, his area captain, warned, 'due to Mrs Hill having stated that neither she nor Robert could see that their obligations, nationally, went further than the writing of books in which [the] early history of Australia was portrayed along the lines of historical novels'.[99]

'Captain Kidd doesn't know anything about our world of the Bright Historic Shades', Ernestine told Alice Mackaness, and she and Bob appeared to have slipped off into them.[100] Gilmore, who'd last seen Hill in September 1943, wrote to George Mackaness early in the new year, 'Am worried over Ernestine. No reply to my letters, and no one sees her. She is nearly frantic over Bob, and his call up.'[101] A month later she still hadn't heard any word of Hill – nor had Rene Foster in Adelaide, and one of Mackaness's letters had been returned to sender. In January, Coy received a pencilled note from 'Roadside – Innamincka', asking her to wire £50 to Tibooburra which Ernestine would pick up a fortnight later, saying her publishers owed her £100. Hill had taken matters into her own hands and found a position for Bob as a jackaroo at Cordillo Downs Station in Sturt's Stony Desert in the north-east corner of South Australia. In the process, she sent CJA Moses, the ABC's general manager, her travelling commissioner's recommendations for radio programming in remote Australia after clocking up some 6000 miles in two months. 'The past three months have been a mad and broken-hearted wandering,' she told Coy.[102] She also struggled with 'very tangled thoughts ... This long appalling mental strain is badly affecting my mental health.' She had not recovered from her mother's and aunt's deaths, and Bob was her 'only reason for living on, the joy of my work and life'.[103]

'I shall not attempt to tell you where I have been or where I am going at the moment – we must leave it to the near, I hope, future. Regarding my being lost – on the contrary, my dear, I was found,' she wrote enigmatically to Drake-Brockman from Adelaide in March 1944. 'Escape? I'll say so! ... I'm off for the G.W.Spaces as soon as I can make it, for a breath of clean thought and fresh air, and to live a life that matters.'[104] In fact, a hearing had been scheduled for Bob the following month in Broken Hill, and Ernestine was hoping to make a case for his essential work as a jackaroo. Gilmore, who'd protested against conscription of only children during the Great War, arguing it was 'a crime to cut off the whole ancestral inheritance at the root', swung into defence of the Hills's cause.[105] Echoing Hill's argument that her writing – and her teenage son's assistance – was 'national work', Gilmore sought the Mackanesses' aid: 'Bob might be good manure in a trench, but her books are Australia, and we can replace life (curious as it might seem) where we cannot replace the lost historical, without which we cannot build the spiritual and actually, the directive to some extent.' Moreover, she knew that Hill relied on Bob for practical and psychological support: 'Also she is a lonely creature, very dependent on the one to whom she clings ... I feel that her very life is at stake ... The sight of her tragic face would melt a stone.'[106]

Both Hill's literary mentors petitioned Captain Kidd to reconsider Bob's case on the grounds of his mother's health and his contribution to her writing. They received acid responses from Kidd. 'Does she really think that the writing of books,' he stormed, 'is more important than the securing of Peace and safety for the future generations of Australians? If so I am afraid she does not realise just how serious War really is.' Kidd held strong opinions about Hill's influence on her son – that 'he was being trained along lines which, in a man's world, were decidedly effeminate and false' – asserting that, 'if properly handled', 'psychologically ... association with male elements as against his past mode of life, would be the making of Robert'.[107] His parting volley was to suggest the publicity surrounding Bob's trial would affect public opinion of Mrs Hill and dint sales of her work.

Ernestine met Bob in Broken Hill, where he attended court on 24 April 1944, but the case was adjourned until 11 May. She found his hearing a 'dreadful ordeal'; it was 'gaol or submit'.[108] Rumour was that Captain Kidd 'had it in for Bob, and was determined he would not be beaten: the tyranny of the autocrat to whom nothing matters but the rule of his own ego'.[109] Hill feared that, given her high profile, the military authorities intended to make an example of her to deter other cases. Her efforts to find her son essential work were vetoed by regulations stating that 'no change of employment, subject to the issue of such notice [i.e. call-up], will be considered'.[110] Bob was directed to Cowra recruit camp in New South Wales, where he was left in a kind of military limbo. Ernestine planned to follow him, although she didn't have the slightest idea of where she'd stay. There'd been an outbreak of scarlet fever in Cowra, so she was looking to board at a farm outside town. It was 'rather a harrowing thing to have to be a camp-follower of the Army', she told Coy, but she was 'fighting to keep the only link to life – Bob'.[111]

At the end of October 1944 Hill wrote: 'Bob is going back to Cordillo Downs – they have let him go.'[112] Robert Hill had been discharged as 'mentally unfit' for service, after three psychologists had made a 'long study of his case' and decided that 'Bob would be much more use to the world outside … So he was released to return to pastoral work on psychological grounds.'[113] But Ernestine was gutted. 'I can't write these days,' she told Coy. 'My world has gone. I often try to write to you, and can't.' During the six months between Bob's court hearing and his release, she all but disappeared from public view and was only contactable 'c/- ABC'. She resigned from her position as commissioner in September 1944, pleading ill health, although she had to tender her notice of resignation three times – the ABC wasn't keen to see her go – protesting she 'knew how horrified they would be to find me dead on their doorstep one morning'.[114] After Curtin refused to extend Bob's exemption in December 1943, she'd told him somewhat churlishly that she had 'no other course but to resign' in the absence of support from her son, her health and spirit being 'so much impaired, and my mind so distracted, that I can do no more'.[115] She recommended other female journalists – Constance Robertson, women's editor of the *Sydney Morning Herald*, and Vera Hamilton, the editor of *Woman* – in her stead to run the ABC Women's Hour she'd proposed.

Hill confided in Mary Durack that she had other reasons for leaving:

> had I understood the regime I could never have accepted the appointment. I thought I could help in the creative and developmental sphere – and it was purely administrative as I discovered ... I was hoping to penetrate somehow to the programmes and the creative, ideas for writers, encouragement of the young, and so on, but I was a very small voice in a big departmental wilderness.[116]

Being an ABC commissioner was not the visionary post she'd imagined; Ernestine was not a natural bureaucrat and she was frustrated at not being able to implement her proposed changes to programming for women, children, writers and outback listeners. Nor did the commissioner's salary compensate for 'the burden of being on the ABC' and its drain on her literary work, especially since the books she had planned were 'piling up undone or hindered'.[117]

By New Year's Eve 1945, Ernestine was rhapsodising about Bob's return to Cordillo and his enthusiasm for the interior: 'he wanted so much to go back to that weird old world of Sturt's Stony Desert in the Vanished Inland Sea.'[118] She'd always hoped that Bob would join the bush tradition by becoming a cattleman in his youth 'and "go obsarvin' matters till he dies"'; a more cynical interpretation of her wish might be that she was transferring her own prescription for mental health issues to him.[119] Released from her bureaucratic role, free to wander where she willed, she felt reinvigorated by travelling inland, describing Birdsville and its environs as 'an incredible wilderness, all this country – a blend of hell and fairyland'. This might sound as though Ernestine was back to her old hyperbolic, romantic self, but she and Bob were scrambling for a psychological toehold on their lives. A week later Bob suddenly appeared in Birdsville, '160 miles of desert away' from Cordillo, because he was concerned about how she was faring in the heat and the fate of the manuscripts she'd been working on for years. Hill was afraid he'd done 'a very foolish thing' by breaching the conditions of his exemption from military service, 'but he seems so worried about me after all our trouble that he is really not himself. I don't think we either of us have been for years. We seem born to sorrow as the sparks fly upward. I don't know what will happen now.'[120]

Bob posted his mother a concrete symbol of their enmeshed relationship from Cordillo: two links 'from an old bobble-chain I found at Brady's waterhole on Innamincka … they are forged iron linked eternally, bound up invisibly by fundamental laws. They symbolize you and me. Though free to move, we are inseparable at heart, bound together under fire, through stress, and when, as I found them, resting by the still waters.'[121] He would have been around twenty when he sent this token seeking to cement their relationship, an age when most children are individuating from their parents. Not only had Hill become more reliant on him as her sole close family member, but Bob was indebted to his mother for her dedication to fighting against his conscription. As a child, he had found her a somewhat distant, almost mythical figure, most familiar from her travel letters which Aunt Kitty read to him, but he grew closer to her through their shared wartime ordeal. Their relationship was the reverse of Bates's relationship with her son, Arnold, who used his military service in the First World War as a convenient excuse to ignore his mother, reflecting back her behaviour towards him for most of his life by putting distance between them permanently. Although Bates was extroverted, seeking praise and admiration from her fan base, as it were, she imposed strong boundaries and distance between herself and others, using distance as a way of controlling her relationships. More of an introvert, Hill tended to gather a few intimates around her, subjugating herself to them as a way of eliciting their support, a pattern that was reflected in her relationships with Packer and Bates. After the war, she became increasingly dependent on Bob, as her closest remaining family member.

Hill had dreamed of 'when Bob and I would be free to get some little trundling thing that went, and go back through Australia in his youth' and, once he was free from his responsibilities at Cordillo, they travelled to Darwin and purchased a 'blitz buggy' from army disposals.[122] She had just finished her 'little Flying Doctor book of 50,000 words', which she'd been inspired to write after summoning the Royal Flying Doctor Service to Cordillo Downs to ferry her to Broken Hill in January 1944. The Flying Doctor had been due to visit the Diamantina district in south-west Queensland, bordering the Simpson Desert, and the pilot agreed to meet Ernestine en route from Tibooburra in Innamincka. Hill needed to fly from Broken Hill to Sydney for an ABC meeting. No-one's time was wasted, however, as she gathered writing material from observing patients besieging the doctor on his remote rounds.[123] *Flying Doctor Calling* was published in 1947; Hill returned to *The Territory*, the manuscript of which she'd promised to submit to Angus & Robertson by the end of 1945. She would continue to do so each year until its publication in 1951, in what became a pattern of writerly procrastination over the following decades. She was, Bob observed, 'all the while working at her literary projects, though at times seeming strangely listless about their fruition'.[124] 'I have quite lost heart …' Ernestine admitted to Mary Durack. 'To tell you the truth I am often weary of waking, and the prospect of waking for the next 20 years.'[125] But she also felt the imperative to write, to make the most of the time left to her: 'I must try to get ahead with the real purpose, the work … The Old Australia is fading away out there, and my little job is to help to keep it … when you hear I am off with a swag, be sure I am happy.'[126]

7
Derelict on the Nullarbor

'... one pernickety old hum-bug, Daisy Bates'.[1]

After several years' silence, Daisy Bates was back in the news. Early in 1945 the Adelaide papers expressed concern that the 84-year-old grandmother of 'three generations of wild and near-wild aborigines' might not be able to carry on her legendary work after she'd been transported to Port Augusta Hospital for medical treatment.[2] She'd been camping since 1941 at Wynbring Siding, a remote outpost on the Nullarbor, but in January 1945 a bush nurse visiting from Tarcoola had reported Bates's deteriorating health, especially her eyesight, to the authorities. Her vision had been fading for years; she had 'sandy blight', the popular name for trachoma, a blinding, contagious inflammation of the eyelids common among impoverished desert dwellers. More alarmingly, the South Australian police had heard rumours that Daisy was preparing 'to take off for Streaky Bay in the company of an elderly native, travelling on foot over a road that had been overgrown by scrub for some years'.[3] The department had conspired with the police to transport her to Port Augusta, which she'd resisted until she'd been 'compelled to dress in city garb and compelled bodily into a vile car' by two 'gangsters' after midnight and deposited at the hospital.

Indignant and aggrieved by this 'frightful manhandling' but still 'full of fire, and of spiritual fight', Bates returned to Adelaide in March 1945 to wrangle her remaining manuscripts into order at her office with her latest secretary, Barbara Polkinghorne.[4] When she opened the battered tin trunk Daisy brought with her, Polkinghorne saw 'Packets and packets of tea, split and spilt over everything'. Bates had been hoarding tea coupons that Ernestine Hill had mailed to her at Wynbring in a 'gesture of great friendship from one tea addict to another'.[5]

Although an article in the Adelaide *News* describing Kabbarli's return to civilisation had been credited to a 'Special Reporter', Mary Gilmore thought she recognised Hill's cadences when she read it.[6] Was it possible that Ernestine was back in Adelaide visiting her friend? On the publication of the *Passing*, Hill had wished 'the old one lots of success with it' but Gilmore detected resentment beneath her diplomatic veneer.[7] When Bates's name came up in conversation during one of Hill's visits to Gilmore's flat, Ernestine had claimed she'd written the book. Not only that, but her name 'was to have gone on the book with Mrs. Bates's name, in recognition of her work in making the material shapely and readable. In the publication Mrs. Bates put only her own name.' Lloyd Dumas, who'd given Hill leave from the *Advertiser* to facilitate 'Mrs. Bates's wandering recollections', had also endorsed Hill's CLF application 'because she had written Mrs. Bates's book for her'.[8]

'I could never understand the Daisy Bates I knew – tight little waist, tight little mind – writing that deeply warm book until Ernestine told me she had done it,' Gilmore remarked in her diary. Incensed, she went in to bat for her diffident younger friend. Once when she visited Tyrrell's Bookshop and asked whether they stocked any of Hill's books, she received the answer no writer wants to hear – 'They said "Unheard of!"' – and told them that 'Ernestine had been the writer (as collector, interviewer, editor and shorthander) of Daisy Bates's book.'[9] Several years later Gilmore rang Miles Franklin to expound at length about how 'Ernestine

Hill had ghosted Daisy's book, and Daisy took her name off during the proofreading.' Franklin had 'chuckled in the whiskers I haven't got'; she still hadn't forgiven Hill for her saccharine treatment of Flinders. Nor did she care much for Bates or her book because of how she 'went about out-ginning the gins without picking up anything deeply knowledgeable'.[10]

Gilmore refused to pander to the popular mythologising of Daisy as a saint. 'The stories Ernestine has of Mrs. Bates as she knew her would make a book on its own, while as a character in a drama only Marie Tempest could do her justice. She has play-acted all her life.'[11] Everything she'd heard from Ernestine confirmed her worst suspicions about Daisy. But where was that girl now? Gilmore had thought she was still out Birdsville way with Bob; she'd been hoping Ernestine might visit Sydney now her son's ordeal was over, although perhaps she was further south. Maybe Bates had summoned her, and they were together in her Adelaide office, Daisy talking blarney to Ernestine, listening with her reporter's notebook in hand.

Lush and abundant as the banks of the Murray were, Bates had been an alien in a foreign land at Pyap. After hearing that derelict Aṉangu were roaming the Nullarbor, she begged the Commonwealth government to help her return, pleading that her natives 'had lost the tranquility of my presence' – but to no avail.[12] In February 1941 she announced her intention to resume her ministrations to them, telling ABC interviewer Russell Henderson it was 'my duty, and my work' because her poor eyesight barred her from making a more conventional contribution – 'I can't knit and sew, and do the necessary work that is required for the Red Cross' – to the war effort.[13]

In May 1940 Bates travelled down to Adelaide to put her affairs in order and assist Edith Watts in assembling her manuscripts for archiving by the National Library. She also set aside a 'big deed box in the Adelaide Bank of Australasia's Vaults, full of all my typed chapters, Legends, etc', addressed to Sir John Murray, which he could apply to access in the event of her death.[14] She was wearing her King George V badge, she informed him, 'for duty borne' – in honour of having given 'my only son in the service of our beloved King's Father George V' – the son from whom she'd been estranged since the last war, although she probably wished to impress her publishers with her patriotism: John Grey Murray had received a commission as a captain.[15] She continued work on her manuscripts in Adelaide for almost a year, but her congenial arrangement with her secretary had ended when Edith Watts left to get married several months after Bates arrived. It was a considerable loss for Bates, who would later complain about the difficulties of getting Watts's replacements up to speed, although she was hardly easy to work with herself. In February 1941 she departed for Canberra to attend a ceremony in honour of the National Library's acquisition of ninety folio boxes of her material. Once back in Adelaide, without Hill or Watts to help her negotiate the intricacies of modern urban life or to muster her wayward words into sense, she floundered, resolving to return to where she truly felt at home.

On the eve of Bates's departure to Wynbring, the *Advertiser* reported that she planned 'to write a story of native "spirit babies" and publish it as 'legends especially for the children of Empire', dedicated to the royal princesses and their family.[16] The manuscript was 'Ngar'galulla Law: The Country of the Spirit Babies', based on stories that women in Broome had told her during her early visits to the north-west. According to ngar'galulla lore, babies live in a spiritual country playing with each other's totems before they are born. Conception occurs when they travel under the sea from the land of the unborn and appear in their fathers' dreams before entering a woman as a spirit through her mouth or her navel to be born. Bates was eager to publish this material as an integral part of what she considered was her life's work; she also wished to assuage her long-lasting grievance with Radcliffe-Brown, whom she had accused of having stolen 'my ngar'galulla' during the 1910 Cambridge expedition. But she did not acknowledge the Broome women's ownership of these stories; she considered them too primitive and socially inferior to merit consideration or consultation. Instead she used her era's 'doomed race' precept to justify her appropriation of the women's intellectual and cultural property, underscoring the value of preserving their stories for the future 'when the Australian aborigines have become a memory'.[17]

While visiting London in 1938, Max Lamshed had dropped off another Bates manuscript, 'The Passing of a Race: Australia's Stone-Age Nomads' to Curtis Brown. When John Murray Publishing received 'Stone-Age Nomads', as they referred to it, they noted internally it was 'of a character different from Daisy's "Aborigines"' and commissioned a reader's report. The manuscript consisted of stories Bates had assembled at Dumas's prompting, and the reviewer found the material failed to hold his attention after a few chapters – 'the whole business becomes very heavy going'. He observed it did not possess the *Passing*'s autobiographical drive: 'But in spite of all the love and care she has lavished on collecting the myths of her beloved Aborigines, she lacks the inspiration which we find in her earlier book when she is telling the story of her life sacrifice to these primitive people.' This comment indicates that Bates was not capable of shaping a narrative and how much she'd relied on others, especially Hill, who'd left the *Advertiser* before the drafting of 'Stone-Age Nomads', to craft the *Passing* into a readable form. 'This book would not stand a chance of success on its own,' the reviewer concluded, recommending that some stories be reworked into the *Passing*'s next edition, but John Murray thought it was too difficult to do without removing necessary content.[18] The publisher warned Bates that the 'acute paper famine' – the wartime paper shortage – had made serious inroads on their capacity to reprint the *Passing*, and discussion of the manuscript's potential publication ceased.[19] At 1942's close, John Murray estimated they could publish a further print run of 1000 copies of the *Passing* with a reasonable profit margin, but they baulked at such an undertaking with wartime restrictions and recommended Australian publication instead. Oxford University Press (OUP), John Murray's subsidiary in Melbourne, printed the first Australian edition in 1944, much to Bates's chagrin; with her usual imperialist snobbery, she wanted it published solely by John Murray. The Australian edition was reprinted twice, and ER Bartholomew, a travelling book salesman who represented OUP in Australia, suggested a further Australian print run of around 5000 or 7500 under John Murray's imprint because 'There is still a much larger demand for this splendid book than you are able to fill from your limited London stocks.'[20]

After the war, Spencer Curtis Brown stumbled across a copy of 'Stone-Age Nomads' in his London cellar and wrote to John Murray, asking whether they might reconsider publishing it, given the paper shortage was easing. Grey Murray replied diplomatically: 'We went through it very carefully at the time, and have thought about it again, but I am afraid that under present circumstances we cannot take it on, however much we would like to do so for reasons of friendship with and admiration for Daisy Bates.'[21] He mooted whether OUP might consider 'Stone-Age Nomads', or whether Bartholomew might find it another Australian publisher, but these suggestions came to naught. However much esteem and affection the Murrays had for Bates, their continued reluctance to take on 'Stone-Age Nomads' suggests they were dubious about her capacity to deliver a publishable manuscript.

Nevertheless, Bates continued to lobby them with proposals, including the ngar'galulla project. She blamed her limitations on her circumstances rather than her personal failings, complaining that 'I can't write a line here & I can't live in town under £400 a year', although she'd chosen to live at Wynbring Siding.[22] She requested the same amount from the government to finish 'Ngar'galulla Law', and in September 1944 the Commonwealth granted her a literary fellowship of £250. Whether there were any hospitable circumstances, in town or on the Nullarbor, in which Bates might complete a manuscript was another matter.

'After all these years that you have lived under canvas,' John Murray mused after receiving a couple of snapshots of Bates posing with a fettler's family at Wynbring Siding, 'I wonder whether you could ever settle down to an ordinary house existence?'[23]

It was a good question, but this extraordinary existence had become second nature to her. Wynbring was smaller, even more isolated, than Ooldea; the Trans shot through without stopping. Daisy erected her two tents – now fragile from exposure to the desert winds and patched with calico a friend had sent her – in the scrub about half a kilometre's walk from the siding. A small fortress, it was girded with a brushwood fence and a corrugated iron gate supported by two upright railway sleepers; as at Ooldea, it was '"Out of Bounds" to the Siding, & I place myself out of bounds to the people, & houses there'. Except for children, who had always been her delight. She inducted some of the fettlers' kids into 'here we go round the mulberry bush' and allowed them to play inside the breakwind. Later, when they left Wynbring, she looked to 'God's wee creatures' for company: 'Some lovely little Blue Wren families have adopted me & fully take the place of my absent children & adult friends.'

Bates gathered firewood, drew water from a nearby 400-gallon tank and collected her private mailbag from the goods train when it made a set-down every two or three weeks. All by herself, or so she claimed. Subsisting on as little as possible, she refused to use ration books – too much trouble with her failing sight – which meant she couldn't buy butter, meat or clothing throughout the war. Fruit, vegetables, even potatoes and onions were scarce, although a 'relief train' later brought oranges and tomatoes from Port Augusta. Whenever she had a cabbage, she would take four or five weeks to eat it, leaf by leaf: 'my "wants" have always been very primitive.'[24] A fettler's wife gave her a couple of loaves of bread and butter each week and the occasional bacon rasher, although Bates couldn't stomach meat if she had seen it raw so she relied on eggs for protein. Fearing that tea 'might suddenly fail to reach Australian shores should the fortunes of war turn against us', she used Ernestine's coupons to shore up a private supply.[25]

'Tea is my "meal & drink",' she professed, making three daily 'tea meals' of an egg beaten and mixed with tea and Sunshine milk.[26] Alvis Brooks, one of the few white adults to make it past the breakwind, described sampling one of Daisy's 'tea meals'. Brooks perched on the end of a canvas stretcher inside the main tent, holding a cup into which:

> Mrs Bates poured a dash of powdered milk that had been made so long ago that the tin had rusted and the milk was now muddy orange in colour. Into her own cup she broke an egg and gave it a couple of quick turns with a spoon in the

hot tea. By this time the heat and the flies were really turned on and the sight of the partly cooked egg floating around in the green transparent cup was almost too much for me. The bilious-looking fluid in my cup was quite beyond me but the problem was solved without causing offence to Daisy by pouring small amounts on the sand which was the tent floor behind the stretcher each time she looked away from me.[27]

Sugar wasn't available, so Bates didn't bake scones or cake except when she conspired to make a pudding one Christmas. There wasn't 'a "plum" within cooee, but there will be thousands of things', she promised, and ground up some cereal, crushed the contents of a friend's food parcel 'indiscriminately with a rail bolt' and mixed them together with condensed milk, stewed peaches and boiled currants in a two-gallon tin dish, then topped it off with squashed cooked apples and Sunshine milk. She served the 'pudding' to the 'nice children' who visited her camp on Christmas Day, giving them pennies wrapped in paper as she had done with their mothers and grandmothers at Ooldea, inducting them into the ways of Home and Empire.

Bates boasted that her 'old native friends, male & female, come & camp with me, & I fed them daily'; that they'd begun jumping the train to visit her as soon as they'd heard she was at Wynbring.[28] Rather than revive her old campsite and compete with the missionaries near the soak, she'd established her camp at Wynbring because it was 'still a part of the old travelling & barter routes of my Ooldea friends'.[29] But many Aṉangu she'd known, young and old, had died in the six years she'd been away, a sign, she believed, they were 'steadily passing ... because of the present corruption of their contact with XXth Cent. & its horrible "white" vices'. She was disturbed to hear that missionaries had taught English to people at Ooldea in her absence, which she had never done, believing it would encourage contact with white settlers because the 'fringes of civilisation hold much that is not-good in humanity'. Nor had the mission observed kinship and age-based cultural practices in the time since she'd left Ooldea; she thought the older men were losing their authority over the young people – to her, yet another sign of cultural deterioration. Some of the younger ones helped her 'reinforce my breakwind around my camp', and in turn she rewarded them with 'special bacca, hat, etc.', but it was merely play-acting at reciprocal relations.[30] Young men, who'd passed through initiation while she was at Ooldea, had formed marauding gangs and rode the trains, spearing livestock, begging and stealing food from fettlers, soldiers, and the mailman at Tarcoola. They were 'Police mobs': 'a rabble the police hunted from Kalgoorlie to Port Augusta, and back again, boarding every train & unhappily picking up the worst low white vices'.[31]

The police were as much a rival to her authority as ever, and their visits to Wynbring Siding when there was 'trouble among the natives' were often distressing.[32] Sergeant Groverman, who was stationed at Tarcoola, once took a fire stick and burned out the Aboriginal camps around Bates's breakwind because he thought the people gathering there were lazy and needed to be moved on. Another time, she told Sir John Murray she'd 'heard gunshots fired & moaning women running – the shots were evidently fired over their heads' in what sounds like an account of police dispersal. A week later she 'saw to my increasing sorrow two large trucks of men & women, collected by Police for some misdemeanor elsewhere' pull into the siding. Bates's own behaviour towards these people was fairly punitive: she stood by the train for a moment, offering 'to take them again when their poor hearts & minds & spirit were "cleansed" ... just a few words & the train passed on'.[33] 'Unclean' was her euphemism for suffering from venereal disease, and early in her stay at Wynbring Bates tried asserting her powers as Kabbarli, 'dismiss[ing] every man, woman & child from my camp' for two winters, telling them to go back to Ooldea 'until they had become "clean inside"' because she 'found conditions existing which I could not allow'. Banishment was harsh, especially in the desert where you might be isolated from potential food and water sources, your people and your country, and Bates knew it. She told Sir John Murray it had been a last resort: 'the old ones cried but they had to accompany the young people.'[34] But she'd lost whatever hold she'd had over young and old.

'I am wholly cut off from the Siding nowadays,' Bates wrote in June 1944.

Drought winds tore at her tents, dust storms blotted out her 'old star companions' and there was 'no rain for 8 or 9 moons! No rain at all!' She struggled to sleep, sometimes rising after midnight because she found 'such night walks send me back tranquilly to bed'.[35] She wore dark glasses but it was hard to escape grit, living in a tent, and her eyes took over a month to heal once they became inflamed.

Temperatures rocketed to 126 degrees Fahrenheit, and she retreated to bed to escape the heat, feeling 'more greatly handicapped at this camp site than I have ever been'.[36] She only let the fettlers assist with physical tasks that were beyond her, although she once accepted a meal from one of their wives when a 116 degree Fahrenheit day got the better of her. Such offers were an imposition, not only because she didn't want to admit to frailty but because their type was 'so much beneath her socially she would not consider eating with them or even talking to them'.[37]

When troop trains stopped at Wynbring, soldiers would run down to see Mrs Daisy Bates at her camp. She was lonely enough to capitalise on this attention from a more welcome strata of people: 'I have been glad to see the new faces & to hope the same dogged & jolly Australian Courage that so animated those fine soldiers of 1914–18 will carry each & all of these to victory.'[38] Perhaps these boys reminded her of Arnold; once she fancied she caught sight of him on the train.

Her isolation from the siding reached murkier depths when the contents of the tank near her camp subsided, leaving 'but a small & rather grubby few inches in it'. She decided it was the result of a Communist plot, 'some Labour boss from somewhere' having 'told fettlers they must not give the natives water'.[39] She'd always risen before dawn, but she began trudging up to the siding tank and ferrying several gallons of water to her enclosure each day by 6 am to escape the rising heat rather than ask those Communists, the fettlers, to help her. One day after capsizing under the burden of her 4-gallon load, she braved the idiosyncrasies of the siding's tiny communications hut to send an 'S.O.S. wire' to the prime minister. Next morning, after seeing her carrying two buckets of water from the siding, the fettlers followed her back to the breakwind and filled the nearby tank. Bates thought the PM might have prompted their actions, although she was yet to receive acknowledgement from him of her telegram. Her behaviour had long had a paranoid edge, but this kind of magical thinking, along with claims of a Communist plot, suggest her mind was drifting like the sand around her tents.

'Huh, she windmills,' an Aboriginal man said, putting a thumb in his ear and waving his fingers in a rotating manner when Constable Alvis Brooks told him she'd come to Wynbring to 'take 'em Kabbarli long time walkabout to Port Augusta'. After receiving the Tarcoola nurse's report about Daisy's need for medical treatment, the Department of the Interior had issued her a first-class rail pass to travel to Port Augusta, which she'd refused to accept. Before the war she'd been allowed to ride for free 'up and down the railway track like Lady Bountiful', handing out flour, sugar and tea to Aboriginal people, a right that had been revoked in favour of the rail's use by the military. She now eschewed trains, 'consider[ing] her importance was far greater than mere troops and their stores'.

Fearing they would have to mount a search for her, Inspector Burke of the South Australian police had despatched Constable Brooks to 'bring back to Port Augusta without fail, one pernickety old humbug, Daisy Bates'.[40] Brooks caught the overnight train, 'a little matter of 300 miles', to Wynbring, where Bates received her cordially, inviting her inside the breakwind, although it soon became apparent that she had no intention of taking her allotted seat on the 4 pm return train. Brooks rang Burke from the communications hut, and they devised an alternative scheme in which Sergeant Groverman from Tarcoola would drive to Wynbring at 10 pm, then ferry Bates well over 300 kilometres to Pimba, where an ambulance would be waiting.

Bates continued to stall inside the breakwind, drafting a telegram to the prime minister on the back of an envelope – 'Urgent, private. Prime Minister. Arrangements already in hand to take me West Coast. Cannot consider any other route. Daisy Bates'. Brooks pretended to send it and, when no answer was forthcoming, persuaded Bates to accompany her by car. Daisy procrastinated about dressing, inadvertently mooning Brooks while fighting her way into a whalebone corset – 'all I could see of her was a pearly, bare behind' – refusing to leave until the policewoman had found the right gloves. Wearing her '"going to town" outfit', accompanied by her black umbrella, her meat safe and a tin trunk of personal effects, Daisy was finally bundled into the waiting police car at 12.45 am.

The journey was nightmarish for all concerned. Groverman, the police officer who'd torched Aboriginal camps around Bates's breakwind, avoided speaking to her because he thought her a 'dangerous old bird'. Daisy developed carsickness, blacking out at one point, but they managed to deliver her safely to the Church of England hostel at Tarcoola by noon. Brooks was yet to tell Daisy she would be travelling by rail rather than car to Port Augusta the following day and fretted overnight about how she'd coax her onto the train without using physical force. Next morning when they arrived at the station, the constable spied a bargaining tool – the 'sacred umbrella' that the Duke had retrieved for Bates. Brooks grabbed it and leapt into the carriage crying, 'The umbrella and I are going to Port Augusta, and if you want it, you must come too.'

Groverman, who'd stealthily offloaded Bates's luggage into the guard's van, gave her a heave and she followed the umbrella onto the train. At every stop along the way, people brought Daisy tea and biscuits; 'like Queen Victoria receiving VIPs, she received it as her due'. By the journey's end, Brooks was thoroughly sick of Daisy, whose conversation 'consisted of self-praise for her good work with the natives and a desire to impress upon us that she was indeed quite a superior person and her friends all influential people'. At Port Augusta, there was 'another kerfuffle on the platform, because there were no photographers or reporters to meet her'. Brooks couldn't help reflecting on the gap between myth and reality, recalling how she'd attended a church fete as a child to raise money for 'brave Mrs Daisy Bates who lived alone with the natives in the desert, and fed and cared for them … That was the impression I grew up with, as did many others.'

After the police officers deposited Bates at Port Augusta Hospital, the matron found that Daisy was undernourished and that her eyes needed urgent treatment – 'she could barely see in daylight' – but that she was otherwise fit. Indeed, Brooks observed that 'despite her 85 years, she was as active as I was at then 35 years and could certainly outsmart [me] in stamina, both mentally and physically'. The SA police congratulated Brooks after her 'ordeal with Mrs Bates', suggesting that her story be cited as an example for women police of a 'constructive method of handling'. The constable was granted two days' extra annual leave to compensate for her two-and-a-half days without sleep.

Bates lapped up the nurses' attention on the ward – 'Royalty could not have done a better job' – although many staff were, like Brooks, cynical about her high-and-mighty behaviour. Laurel E Randell, one of the nursing sisters, wrote: 'we never heard anything that made us feel she was doing anything practical to help the aborigines ... We were rather resentful of her reputation of being the Saviour of the Aborigines because we knew of the work being done by two selfless women at the local mission.' Alarmed by Bates's skiting about her culinary prowess and the puddings she had inflicted on Aboriginal people at her camps, Randell concluded there was little substance in Daisy's reports of her own welfare activities: 'Rightly or wrongly we nurses formed the opinion that she was an old fraud.'[41]

The power of Batesian mythology was still so strong several decades after Daisy's death that Brooks's story about pinching the sacred umbrella to lure her onto the train was not included in a 1987 history of SA policewomen: 'the Editors refused to put in such things about such a "wonderful woman".'[42] Eleanor Witcombe, who wrote the screenplay for *My Brilliant Career* and began researching a biopic of Bates during the 1980s, observed there was 'quite a lot of subdued antagonism towards her – a lot of it, no doubt, suppressed because of the "legend"', and that Inspector Burke had told Brooks not to 'spread around all she knew about Daisy because people liked to have their legends'. Witcombe heard similar tales to Laurel Randell's one: that a fettler's wife, rather than Bates as she boasted, had run up dresses for Aboriginal women at Wynbring Siding. That Daisy would have died from pneumonia and malnutrition in her tent at Wynbring if two fettlers' wives hadn't looked after her. That Bates didn't carry water from the siding by herself: Aboriginal women collected it for her. They also dug a hole to bury her trunk to protect her precious notes from bushfires.

Witcombe was part of a group called the Daisy Chain, which included Ernestine Hill, Elizabeth Riddell, Barbara Polkinghorne and Isobel White, who corresponded about 'Batesiana' from 1968 to 1988 as Bates became subject to more rigorous historical research and cracks emerged in the mythology surrounding her. After Isobel White had taken stock of Bates's manuscripts at the NLA while editing *The Native Tribes of Western Australia*, she commented that Daisy 'wasn't always truthful. Moreover she sometimes contradicited [sic] herself, with different stories that didn't fit.'[43] This observation might seem like an understatement, but White was feeling her way in regard to Bates's psychology, uncertain whether Daisy was merely becoming 'old and forgetful' in some instances or other factors were at play in her 'contradictions'. Barbara Polkinghorne, Bates's secretary in the mid-1940s, remarked that it was difficult to keep Daisy's 'attention on the job in hand'. There was a word people were reluctant to use publicly in reference to Bates, although Anangu, nurses, missionaries and others hinted at it and, after her death, Daisy Chain members and other researchers mooted it. 'Re the "senile". I KNOW it is a contentious adjective,' Witcombe wrote to Polkinghorne. 'She was, at the time, mad as a hatter ... but this admittedly could simply have been her eccentricities accentuated by starvation.' She speculated that Bates was 'probably a bit senile' by the time she was evacuated from Wynbring, although she'd been 'pretty loopy when Ernestine brought her in to the *Advertiser* office a decade earlier in ways that could be explained, if necessary, as "eccentricities"'.[44]

Hill described Bates as having 'a way of suddenly mistrusting and dismissing her friends',[45] which Polkinghorne more bluntly called an 'Increasingly strong persecution complex', elaborating on how for 'no apparent reason she would turn against people – not only again wellmeaning [sic] strangers but sometimes she became fearful of her most affectionate friends'. Polkinghorne was alarmed one morning when she arrived at the Adelaide office and realised that Bates didn't recognise her:

> She sat rigidly erect (as always) but very pale and with her hands clenched in her lap so that I wouldn't notice they were trembling. It was indescribably painful to see her calling on every ounce of courage to face someone whom she now imagined to be threatening her, determined not to flinch.[46]

Daisy's idiosyncrasies became pronounced during her ninth decade. She made more paranoid accusations of theft, wrote worthless cheques willy-nilly and wandered incessantly, behaviours indicative of dementia.

While researching *Desert Queen: The Many Lives and Loves of Daisy Bates*, biographer Susanna de Vries sought a retrospective diagnosis of Bates's mental health status from Dr Lilian Cameron, who concluded that she 'was not suffering from Alzheimer's disease but from the much slower onset of vascular dementia'.[47] Echoing Witcombe's insight, de Vries attributed this development to Bates's poor diet, which was high in starch and saturated fat but low in fresh fruit and vegetables, and consequently lacking in essential vitamins and minerals such as thiamine, niacin and iron. Although physically fit, Bates would have been malnourished and dehydrated after two decades subsisting on this diet while roughing it on the Bight, a lifestyle that would 'harden her arteries and slow down the flow of blood to her brain ... resulting in aberrations of thought processes and obsessions'.[48]

This hypothesis concurs with reports of Bates's paranoid behaviour, such as her suspicion of 'low whites' and conflicting complaints about lost or stolen manuscripts, and photographs from her mental health break in 1918 and relocation to Ooldea onwards. Similarly, Witcombe suggests that 'around 1923 Bates went "around the twist" because of undernourishment and heat exhaustion, and dug into her early work to write articles for money without carefully checking the truth of what she wrote'.[49] As Bates's mental state deteriorated, the quality of her journalism also declined, becoming simplistic and repetitive. According to Hill, Dumas assigned her as a ghostwriter to Bates in 1934 because he doubted her ability to write readable copy, a misgiving other newspaper editors shared.

Where does wilful fabrication slide into the vagaries and delusional thinking of dementia, and how responsible was Bates for her own deceptions? If Daisy's mind gravitated towards cannibalism and mixed-descent people as fodder for delusional beliefs in her later years, she had personal motivations for amplifying frontier prejudices and mythology such as her desire for acknowledgement and a revenue stream. Bates may have been old and absent-minded, she may have suffered from deteriorating mental health – including the onset of dementia – for some time when Hill met her at Ooldea, but she definitely had a track record as a fabulist from her early days in Australia.

A period of idealisation of Bates followed her death in 1951, much of which was grounded in Hill's fond portraiture of Daisy in her journalism and 1973 memoir, *Kabbarli*, and Elizabeth Salter's 1971 biography, *Daisy Bates: The Great White Queen of the Never-Never*. More creative works celebrating Bates appeared during the 1970s and early 1980s, such as James Tulip's 1974 documentary *Daisy Bates: Invocation to Earth*, and the opera of the same name by David Malouf with music by Diana Blom; and Allan Curtis's play *Kabbarli*, performed at Studio Sydney in 1983. Sir Robert Helpmann also enlisted Hill and later Eleanor Witcombe to write screenplays for a Bates biopic, but a film was never made. As the suppression of Alvis Brooks's innocuous anecdote about stealing Daisy's umbrella suggests, there was a strong pull, even an imperative, to protect Bates as a national treasure for several decades after the *Passing*'s publication.

'My own explanation of the kind of person Daisy Bates was is possibly one that Ernestine Hill would reject,' Barbara Polkinghorne declared. 'But I don't think it is possible for her to be objective about Daisy because of her (mostly) uncritical affection for her.'[50] Outside private comments to friends and fellow Daisy Chain members, Ernestine was reticent about the contradictory and paranoid aspects of Bates's behaviour, tending to gloss over them as folksy idiosyncrasies or endearing vanities. A decade after Hill's death, Bates's mythology and contradictions began to unravel as startling revelations about her early life in Ireland and Australia emerged, following the publication of Margaret Carnegie and Frank Shields's *In Search of Breaker Morant: Balladist and Bushveldt Carbineer* in 1979. While researching the Breaker, Carnegie became aware of evidence that a Daisy May O'Dwyer, of Glencurra, Tipperary, had married Edwin Henry Murrant at Charters Towers on 13 March 1884, just shy of a year before her marriage to Jack Bates in February 1885.[51] In 2008 Susanna de Vries revealed details of Bates's marriage to a third husband, Ernest Baglehole, on 10 June 1885, at St Stephen's Anglican church in Newtown. Baglehole was fourth mate on the *Zealandia*, which had docked in Sydney, and he was still married to a Jessie Rose back in London.[52]

Further shade was cast on Daisy's claims to be a Protestant descended from Anglo-Irish gentry. Much of Bates's fanciful juvenilia had originally appeared in *My Natives and I*; Hill had mourned its omission from the *Passing*. Salter also drew on this material in opening her 1971 biography of Bates: 'She was born in Ashberry [sic] House, a rambling old building on the wide wet slope of Caraig Hill in County Tipperary, Ireland.' Salter embellished Daisy's origins, describing her as 'a daughter of privilege', with a family tree dating back to William O'Dwyer, who was created a baron by Edward III. During the 1980s when Witcombe researched Daisy's childhood in Ireland for her screenplay, she discovered that Bates's family were neither distinguished nor the owners of Ashbury House, which was in the hands of the Bridge and Smyth families between 1813–80, a period including Bates's youth. Witcombe thought Daisy had claimed a connection to this stately home because her maternal relatives, the Hunts, possessed land adjoining a large holding rented by Timothy Bridge – 'the tenant of Ashbury!' The Hunts had owned a significant holding of 77 acres in the 1850s, an acquisition that lifted them 'into the realm of solid citizens. Not exactly gentry, but sort of respectable middle class.' By 1862 when Daisy was three, most of their land had passed into other hands: 'So how she can have clear memories of Grandma Hunt presiding over the domain in Ballycrine, is beyond me.'[53]

Ballycrine House was tiny compared to Ashbury, as was the family home where Daisy spent her childhood years: her father James Dwyer's bootmakers' shop, a four-room tenement on the main street of Roscrea in Tipperary. The Dwyers and the Hunts were Catholics: Bates's mother, Bridget, was buried in the Catholic section of the local cemetery after she died from tuberculosis in 1864. It wasn't she who'd passed tragically after the wail of a banshee at Daisy's birth, but a twin brother, Francis, who died not long after they were both baptised at St Cronan's Church on 21 October 1859.⁵⁴ Daisy was christened 'Margaret': Bob Reece suggests that 'Daisy' may have been a nickname punning on the French name for the flower, marguerite – 'an everlasting Daisy, and indeed there is something of the perennial about her'.⁵⁵ She had more siblings than she'd acknowledged, including an older sister, Mary Ann, who became a nun, then another named Catherine or Kate; her brother James and another set of twins, Joseph and Anne, were born after her. James and Joseph O'Dwyer later became the first Catholic magistrates in the North Riding of Tipperary. Kate O'Dwyer improved her social status in more conventional ways for a woman than Daisy by marrying a Captain Robert Brownrigg in 1882 and becoming a London socialite. Rather than genteel or privileged, the Dwyers were modestly middle class. They were thoroughly aspirational, and possessed the smarts and drive to claw their way out of hardship to attain social status.

Within a year of Bridget Hunt's death, James Dwyer had married Mary Dillon, a local farmer's daughter. Like many 19th-century Irish who'd lived through the turmoil of the Great Famine and the rise of the Home Rule movement, James and Mary sailed to North America in hope of building a new life for their family, but James died during the sea passage. Afterwards, the Dwyer children were probably farmed out to relatives, including Grandma Hunt, who died several years later in 1868.⁵⁶ Daisy was listed as an orphan enrolled at the Sacred Heart Convent's school in Roscrea from 1872 until 1876. If she travelled with a family like the Outrams across Europe during her teens before she left for Australia, it's more likely she did so as a governess, as befitted her class.⁵⁷

The dazzling tapestry Bates embroidered of her youth and its messier underside reflect the fortunes of the Victorian orphan, who rises above misfortune or has their noble origins recognised, a staple of Daisy's favourite author, Dickens. Having lost her parents and her beloved grandmother by the age of ten, then given free schooling by the nuns, did the bright, high-minded charity girl smart at her exclusion from the life of privilege of which she caught glimmers at nearby Ashbury House? By the time she regaled Ernestine with her overblown origin stories, so iconic in their pretensions to Victorian notability they bordered on cliché, they were probably so deeply engrained in her psyche she believed them, loving to 'dwell upon the beauty of long ago' as she did in her tent in the sandhills. She dropped genteel names to blot out her Irish Catholic origins, to rubberstamp her credentials as a devoted daughter of Empire to mainstream Anglo Protestant society in Australia.

For the Becky Sharp–like governess making her way in the new colony, marriage was a must, a way of locating herself socially and ensuring her respectability, especially as a woman. Beyond a shared passion for horses, the dashing, poetry-reading Edwin Murrant, then Jack Bates, with his outback empire-building prospects, both suggested opportunity to Daisy. Her third marriage to Ernest Baglehole, an old flame of hers from back home according to de Vries, may have been a distraction from her disillusionment with Jack Bates, an attempt at curing her 'nostalgia' while in Sydney. None of these marriages were ever formally ended. Jack Bates was the only husband about whom Daisy recorded her thoughts and then in a fragment of memoir written in the third person, as if to distance herself from the whole disappointing matter. She was probably wary of leaving any evidence of other marriages; a charge of bigamy could result in several years' imprisonment.[58] On the other hand, 'divorce in colonial Australia was costly, rare, difficult': men could only divorce on the grounds of adultery, but women had the harder task of proving pretexts such as cruelty and bestiality.[59] Consequently, bigamy, a form of 'poor man's divorce', was not uncommon in 19th-century Australia. The lack of centralised public state records, the rudimentary infrastructure and challenges of communicating across long distances in a sparsely populated land mass made it possible to obfuscate the existence of other spouses. This was particularly the case if you wanted to start afresh with someone new halfway round the globe; wives and husbands 'back home' could be conveniently forgotten or their death falsely proclaimed.[60]

Nevertheless, to paraphrase Oscar Wilde, to 'lose' one husband seems like misfortune, but two looks like carelessness. What was behind Daisy's rapid succession of marriages within fifteen months – an adventurous, flirtatious, highly sexed nature or an underlying unhappiness and instability, or a combination of these? Bates was renowned for her coquetry and for using flirtation as currency. 'She had a way with men,' Edith Sinclair – her former secretary, the excellent Miss Watts – said. 'I'm sure they really were captivated by her. I don't mean she was brash or anything. She really did it very well indeed ... [She expected them] to be gallant, and a lot of them were in response.'

Sinclair mild-manneredly commented that Daisy flirted with men and had married several times because 'she'd like attention'; Eleanor Witcombe, a more hard-nosed character, called Bates a cockteaser.[61] Isobel White suspected she 'didn't think she was committing bigamy, not at least by her own standards' although she doubted whether she was 'a model of propriety' in her youth: 'Actually I admire her rather than condemn her for it. It is another example of her extreme bravery and defiance of convention. She did many things that most of us would not dare to do.'[62] It would seem something of a stretch, however, to project post-sexual-liberation-era ideals onto Daisy's trigamous situation and suggest that polyamory or open marriage would have appealed to her. Those close to her detected an innocence beneath her coquettish façade. Sinclair was 'really quite convinced' that 'once she would be confronted with sex in real life she probably shrank away like anything. I can never see anything of her being – you know, she might have committed bigamy and all that, but it was not for the sex side of it so much.'[63]

She recalled how 'amazed' Daisy had been 'that a girl of your age should know what contraception is' prior to marriage – Sinclair was in her mid-twenties and engaged to be married when she was Bates's secretary. Daisy's response here may have reflected her naïvety and lack of experience at the same age: White questioned whether her marriage to the Breaker was consummated.[64] As mentioned earlier, after Arnold was born, Bates was so horrified by childbirth – an experience for which she was wholly unprepared – that she reputedly swore off sex for life, another strain on her marriage to Jack.[65] Although she corresponded with male anthropologists such as RH Mathews about sexual practices and sub-incision in the north-west – the margins of some of his letters are decorated with drawings of sub-incised penises like schoolboy graffiti in a textbook – their discussion possessed a degree of scientific abstraction. Sinclair commented on how anomalous Daisy's surprise at her knowledge of contraception seemed, given their daily work included

> all this outspoken stuff about the initiation and how, you know, the cutting off of the foreskin and all sorts of things like that. You know it was all right for me to know about that, but the other thing was not allowed. It was very Victorian, wasn't it, don't you think?[66]

Bates's propriety drew as much comment as her coquetry: both 'weapons' of the Victorian lady's armoury. 'Mrs Bates had neat features completely controlled, and a neat little body, slim and straight-backed,' Violetta Woods, who met Daisy in her later years, wrote. 'She was too well-bred in the Victorian style to show any violent emotion I'm sure, but she had a delightful sense of fun.'[67] Her sense of propriety, so often recalled by people who knew her as an older woman, may also have been a cover for her youthful indiscretions.

Daisy might have been more daring in her youth but she would have been sensitive to the implications of breaching convention and may have rationalised her concurrent marriages to herself. Crossing state boundaries several times and spending five years in London gave her the opportunity to distance herself from uncomfortable memories and persuade herself that she had only ever married Jack Bates. The father of her sole child, she had to settle for Jack for the sake of propriety and she needed marriage to amount to anything in colonial society. Attention was one thing; recognition quite another. If there is a common thread throughout Bates's life, it's her Becky Sharp–like aspirationalism and drive for success. When marriage proved disappointing, she adopted a new love – anthropology – although yet again she found herself courting admiration and respect from men.

Bates observed a split within her personality: 'I am two people, one I like and the other I do not know. A thing of patches am I – here an exultation of duty, there a love of fun and frolic and again of melancholy.'[68] She was duplicitous, often deliberately, in her dealings with others and in how she presented herself, but the notion of duality is inadequate to encompass all the Daisies and her many contradictions. As Witcombe observed, 'Indeed, the most consistant [sic] thing about Daisy is her inconsistency.'[69] Bates's psychology possessed a double-sidedness insofar as she concealed aspects of her identity while drawing a sense of self by defining herself in relation to others, often as a social superior. She had a great capacity for compartmentalising, for splitting off past selves – the others she did not know – and presenting grandiose projections of herself – the 'one I like' – to the world.

My musings about Bates often echoed this idea of her duality during my early research, as I pondered whether there'd been two Daisies, an outer one and an inner one. The outer Daisy was the curio, the eccentric reject, fighting for recognition by white men as a woman of science, protecting herself with a carapace of lies. The inner Daisy was the reclusive observer, camping among the dunes with Aboriginal people, delighting in the Nullarbor's beauty, wanting to know the local names for plants, animals and stars. But the more I read of Daisy's letters and notes, the more perturbed I became by her 'inconsistency', particularly in her relationship with Aboriginal people; her attitudes to them were contrary in ways that couldn't always be attributed to the conflicting mores of her era or her desire to transgress them. A conversation recorded by Ellen Louttit, who met Bates in Adelaide the year before she died, reflects these contradictory impulses. When she asked Daisy whether she knew any Aborigines 'of outstanding character', she said, 'No, they were just black people to me', a comment which floored Louttit. Attempting to qualify why Bates said such a thing, she wrote, 'but whether she did not wish to hurt any of her protégés, or she pitied and loved them all equally, I do not know ... She was a very old lady then and perhaps her mind travelled back to when she first saw them in their camps.'[70]

Perhaps Daisy was playing to the gallery here by attempting to assert her 'superiority' as a white woman in polite society in

Adelaide. Dementia might account for a degree of contrariness; conversely, it might have disinhibited her enough to betray her real attitude to Aboriginal people. Yet in the letters she wrote to Hill while she was in exile at Streaky Bay in the mid-1940s, her mind certainly did travel back to her early camps. She remembered her days with Joobaitch and Fanny Balbuk at Ma'amba Reserve fondly and professed to be aching 'to get back to my poor old natives', as if drawn by an inexorable ocean current.[71] Again, her repetitiveness and desire to wander could be interpreted as symptoms of dementia, but did she have any genuine concern for Aboriginal people's welfare?

Or did Daisy protest too much in her love for them? Fired by her desire for acknowledgement, had her intense focus come to settle on Anangu because they were marginal people whom she thought she could control? Barbara Polkinghorne believed this prospect motivated Bates: at her camps, she was 'Queen of the "blacks". No interference, because no-one cared enough about them … she was left in control of what she wanted to control.'[72] Had she manipulated their good will, having observed how Aboriginal people incorporate others into their kinship networks, to present herself as Kabbarli, their protector, to the white mainstream world? Or did a more fundamental bond compel Daisy to try to return to her old life with Anangu on the Nullarbor?

8
The lady living over the hill

'Yet during all my years, months & days amongst them, I have been safe, & "cared for" in their own way by the elders of every group in every one of my camps.'[1]

Two weeks after I'd crossed the Nullarbor I was back on the Eyre, willing myself into alertness. I'd risen at 4 am to catch the redeye from Adelaide to Ceduna, and the relentless similitude of the parched grazing lands lining the highway weren't conducive to concentration. I'd returned the campervan to the rental company in Perth; I was now driving a four-wheel-drive I'd picked up at Ceduna's tin-shed airport. Winds buffeted the SUV's white armadillo sides, although not as fiercely as on my previous trip. But I wasn't as worried about enduring the elements as I was about the prospect of gatecrashing a basket-weaving workshop at Fowlers Bay.

While I was in Perth, I'd touched base with Yalata's manager, who'd been away when I'd made arrangements with Russell Bryant, the community's Aboriginal chairperson, to visit Ooldea. The manager hadn't heard about my proposed visit. The sorry camps were winding down at Yalata, she told me, but half the community was travelling to another funeral at Kalgoorlie, although Russell was still around. He'd had a lot of social obligations to meet and, understandably, he just wanted to take off now.

I paused; how was Russell? I felt awkward about imposing on him.

He was all right, the manager said, but he was very sad. His wife had died from diabetes complications unexpectedly during her sleep. She was forty.

Only forty! I'd automatically assumed that she and Russell were an older couple when I'd heard about her death – one of those kneejerk reactions born on my part of privilege and having high living standards. However familiar I was with the sobering statistics about remote Aboriginal life, their realities still caught me off-guard.

I asked whether there was anyone else who could take me to Ooldea, mentioning the name of another senior man from Yalata who'd been suggested to me as a possible escort.

'He's a sick man,' the manager said. 'He can't drive.'

I wondered whether any of these men should be coming with me if they were seriously ill and grieving.

'You can't go there by yourself!' she said sharply. 'Women can't go there alone. Haven't you been told that?'

I hadn't, although I'd suspected that was the case from what I'd read about Ooldea Soak's proximity to male cultural sites.

'What happens if a woman goes there by herself?' I asked, curious as to whether she was concerned about me visiting a place associated with men's business, my need to be accompanied by bush mechanics, or both.

'All sorts of things. Punctures, broken axles, accidents! Take three Aboriginal men with you – take as many as you can!'

I blanched inwardly at the thought of traipsing around an unknown remote community, trying to drum up male tour guides, not to mention sick and grieving ones. Strict gender protocols operated in the communities where I'd worked in central Australia, which meant that women worked mainly with women, rarely with men.

'What about the senior women?' I asked. The ones who'd

agreed to speak with me about Bates. 'Are they at Yalata or heading for Kalgoorlie?'

They weren't at Yalata now, the manager told me. Nor were they travelling to Kalgoorlie or would they be in the community during the dates I'd proposed. If I wanted to catch them, I would need to detour to Fowlers Bay, where they were attending a basket-weaving workshop that week. And no, she didn't know where the workshop was being held, but she seemed to think I'd find it easily enough.

I was used to receiving such nebulous directions while working in the Territory. You can arrange to meet with some people in a community but if they're not there, you might be told to look for them at an outstation 50 kilometres down the road or at a town another couple of hundred kilometres away. Even then, you might only chance upon them fuelling up at a bowser on the main drag or after swinging by the local town camps to see if they're staying in relatives' houses. But given that I didn't know whom I was looking for and I'd only passed through the area once before, the prospect of chasing basket-weaving women at Fowlers Bay was disconcerting. Where would I find them? Would they be sitting along the sea front, engulfed by swirls of raffia? What if they'd taken off bush somewhere to weave?

I recognised the turn-off to Fowlers Bay from my previous trip along the Eyre. The tarmac soon became a ribbon of firmly packed orange dirt slicing through low, scrubby maroon-tinged olive bushes and saucer-shaped salt pans. My spirits lifted when I saw what looked like a ripple of vanilla ice cream cresting the grey blur of saltbushes. True to my Sydney origins, I thought, they must have great surf here. Drawing closer, I realised that white-yellow sand dunes embraced the township, swooping along the curve of the bay, overhanging the cluster of original sandstone and more recent prefab buildings. Great mounds of purplish seaweed lined the shore. The ubiquitous coastal town jetty stretched out through turquoise waters, a vantage point for watching whales, although they'd recently left the area and were only to be seen up at Head of Bight.

On her 1947 trip across the Bight, Hill described Fowlers Bay as 'a very remote corner of the dreamy old west coast of South Australia', declared that it 'could be one of the most beautiful tourists [sic] resorts, but of course the same might be said of nearly the whole coast of Australia'.[2] It was still a picturesque, if isolated, hamlet, whose main attractions, apart from its beauty and historical significance, are whale-watching and fishing. It doesn't receive reticulated power or water; I could only access fleeting 3G by standing on a picnic table and holding a Telstra dongle aloft on the foreshore, an indication of how remote it still is a century after Bates camped in the area. In 1914 she bush-bashed her way into thick scrub half a mile from town, shifting her tents over the next five years between Wirilya, Yuria Waters and Yulbari, the furthest of which was 70 kilometres from Fowlers Bay. 'Wirilia' is signposted on the Eyre but the other sites are only accessible off dirt tracks, expansions of Aboriginal tracks, places you'd need to be taken by someone in the know.

I wheeled cautiously around the township, looking for any signs or clues about the whereabouts of the women's basket-weaving workshop. Despite the vague instructions I'd been given, Fowlers Bay was compact enough for it not to be an impossible task. I scanned the buildings, wondering whether the workshop might be at an Aboriginal organisation, an old scout or church hall, or some other public place. Then, turning onto a street away from the foreshore, I saw a handsome white-stuccoed sandstone hall: the Fowlers Bay Institute. A bunch of Aboriginal women were having a smoko out the front. That's it, I thought, that's where the workshop's being held.

Easing to a stop, I wound down the window and stuck my head out, saying I'd come to meet with the Yalata mob: did they know where I could find them?

They gestured towards an old shed behind the hall. I parked the vehicle and walked down towards it, a smaller, sandstone box with glassless frames for windows. The manager had told me I would recognise Mima, the Yalata women's spokesperson, easily when I met her. Peering through a window frame, I saw a solid-looking woman with white shoulder-length hair, exactly as described, sitting in the midst of some women warming themselves round a small burner.

I edged my way awkwardly inside and asked, was she Mima, the go-to person for Yalata?

She nodded, and I explained why I was there. Mima rose slowly, saying she would take me to the women I needed to see. Stately and purposeful, she moved with an unruffled calm that accompanied all her interactions. She was about a decade older than me, but she possessed a gravitas that made me feel like a gawky teenager beside her.

I followed Mima inside the hall, where lunch was winding up. The workshop participants were scattered about, some still eating, others sitting cross-legged on the floor, weaving. Mima showed me a felt artwork with a circle of blue like a waterhole at its centre and four slabs of colour marked with black semi-circles to indicate women sitting. Pressing the edge of the artwork thoughtfully, she told me it represented women coming from Yalata, Oak Valley, Ceduna and Cundeelee to weave and be strong in their culture. The workshop had involved a cultural exchange between women from these four south-west areas and some Finnish delegates, wearing distinctively patterned fez-style hats and clothing, who sat at their own table in one corner, solemnly weaving.

Mima led me to two older women, Rita Bryant and Margaret

May, who were fiddling pinwheels of raffia and rushes into basket bases. Dressed entirely in pastel hues with a fetching crocheted tam-o'-shanter clamped over her grey curls, Rita had small, dark dancing eyes that immediately drew you in. Seventy-ish, she looked younger than Margaret, a woman with a kind gaze, whose face was framed with white desert hair sticking out like sunrays.

I chatted with the women, saying I was interested in hearing any stories or memories they had of Daisy Bates, and they nodded knowingly: they'd been expecting me. I suggested we talk outside somewhere, maybe in the shed. The hall had been renovated recently and its interior was pleasantly bright and airy, with high ceilings and exposed beams, but the acoustics weren't ideal. I'm softly spoken and I was worried they wouldn't be able to hear me above the background noise.

Two more women sidled up and sat at one corner of the table, saying they had some Daisy Bates stories. One announced that her great-great-grandfather was Bates's lover.

'That man was walking around Ooldea,' she said. 'He saw that woman and he sang her, and she fell in love with him.'

I started. This was news to me. I knew about Daisy's bigamy with white husbands but I hadn't heard of any Aboriginal lovers. In photographs of the Bates memorial at Ooldea, its plaque features a naked Aboriginal man facing Daisy and brandishing a shield; Salter identifies him as 'King Billy' – one of the western renamings Bates decried – although she doesn't discuss him at all in her biography. I'd presumed he was a significant local elder rather than a paramour of Daisy's.

'She was walking all over Australia, even over to Victoria,' the other woman continued. The mention of Victoria surprised me; had they heard I'd come from Melbourne? Were they dropping it in as a landmark for my benefit? Or was it a reference to Bates's camp at Pyap, near the Victorian border? 'She went many places.

She went everywhere; she was working welfare. When she came back to Ooldea, she found he – her Aboriginal lover – had died.'

They paused, then the first woman asked, 'Shall we tell you another Daisy Bates story?'

I felt uncomfortable. These women were much younger than the senior women, maybe mid-forties at most, so they would not have had direct contact with Bates. Although my research was in its early stages, I reckoned I would have read about such a sensational piece of gossip: that if it had any teeth, the old people would have told this story to Isobel White and other anthropologists at Yalata. The narrative about a woman being sung by a man is also fairly ubiquitous, like a stock rom-com meet-cute. And given Bates's active contempt for mixed-race unions and children, it seemed unlikely that she would have had an Aboriginal lover. I feared they were telling me gammon stories.

The conversation petered out. The women with whom I wanted to speak, the ones whom I'd been told had childhood stories about Bates, had lost interest and wandered off: possibly a reflection on the veracity of the Aboriginal lover story. I politely sidestepped the two women and ducked outside to see where the others were. Goodness knows what I'd do if they'd taken off.

I found Margaret May smoking with another woman in the sun, and Rita perched on her walking frame's seat. I joined them, leaning awkwardly against the wall. Everyone was a bit taciturn; not only, I suspected, because I was a strange white woman but because English wasn't their first language. They knew why I was there, so I didn't repeat my request but waited for them to respond.

All of a sudden, Mima bowled up, saying, 'Let's go off in your car and find somewhere quiet to talk.'

A rush of activity followed. I walked over to the hire vehicle, opened its doors, and the ladies bundled inside. Rita ordered me to fold up her 'pusher' – the walking frame – and stow it in the boot.

These women were adept at handling white do-gooders.

Just as we were about to drive off the lot, the workshop leader, an authoritative white Australian woman in a patterned fez, steamed out of the hall, running down to the car.

'Where are you going?' she asked, an edge to her voice. 'You can't go. There are activities planned for this afternoon.'

'This lady wrote to us, and we said we'd talk to her,' Mima said emphatically.

I shrugged apologetically. 'We'll only be half an hour or so.'

Mima directed me to head back along the coast road. It was slightly hilly, saltbush interspersed with jarrah on either side, dotted with houses on stilts peering over the vegetation towards the sea. She motioned for me to pull off at the mouth of a dirt track that ran up into a small clearing, where we parked, and the women piled out of the van. I unfolded Rita's walking frame for her from the boot, and we joined the others, who were sitting cross-legged with enviable flexibility on a patch of firm sandy ground. Mima gathered up some bark fragments for kindling; I screwed up a post-it for her to use as a lighter. Always the fire: a symbol of warmth and coming together.

The women faced me in a semi-circle, speaking in rapid Pitjantjatjara, which Mima translated. Margaret May was the oldest and did most of the talking, Rita Bryant adding details. Margaret was born in 1937, and she knew Daisy Bates when she was up on the railway line, chasing Anangu. Rita's stories were from older relatives who'd known Daisy from Ooldea Soak and Wynbring Siding; Bates had been living her final years in Adelaide when Rita was born in 1949. The other woman, Joy West, was another couple of years younger. A calm, watchful presence, she listened with interest, saying little.

One day Margaret May settled at Ooldea mission with other kids from the desert. The Spinifex people knew there was a place where their family went and didn't come back from: it was Ooldea mission. They were put in there, boys and girls, at Ooldea. They used to take off to see the lady living over the hill.

Daisy Bates was living both ways: the ways of the Spinifex people, the Pila Nguru, from the north-west of the Nullarbor, who visited Ooldea Soak, and of the white people. The Spinifex people were learning from a white woman. They loved her because she was teaching and doing things for them. She was looking after all of them, Anangu, giving them food, blankets, clothes, tobacco, flour and tea leaves – *not tea bags*.

True to the spirit of Bates, they were adamant about her tea-drinking habits.

She called the Aboriginal kids to her. She only wanted the black ones to come and visit. She would make tea, give them fruit and have treats for them. She would speak in English to all the kids from the desert, use their English and Pitjantjatjara names. She would say, 'Don't cross the railway line' to the kids, and 'That's the Tea and Sugar train', and look after the kids at the campsite, stop them from going by themselves on the train tracks. She'd buy drinks and treats from the train, keep them for the kids, feed them, let them stay. Treat the kids good way, teach them all the songs to sing.

She loved to sit down with the old people. When the old people had ceremonies, she'd always dance with the ladies. They'd call out to her, and she'd join them. She knew all the cultural business. She was doing inma with them at Ooldea. The old people can sing her song.

Margaret and Rita rubbed a figure of eight in the sand.

The number eight was one song she always used to get up for and dance with the other ladies because it's a women's song. She'd always go with the minymas. The women always took her out; she'd do anything for the Spinifex ladies.

'Did she get painted up to dance?' I asked.

'Paint wiya, no,' Margaret said.

'But she was still in all her white clothes?' I persisted. 'She never took off those clothes?'

'Uwa, yes.'

The commentary's tempo changed.

Friend – she always had a friend – an old Aboriginal man.

My heart raced slightly; was the story about the Aboriginal lover true after all?

Daisy Bates was walking round at Ooldea. He was always walking with her on the sandhills; he was only a friend, not a husband, just helping her round, being a protector, looking after her – making a fire, a breakwind.

'They were living in the same tent?' I asked.

'Separate, looking after,' Rita said. 'Husband wiya.'

That old man would go and camp near her tent. She would give him food. Others thought he was a boyfriend or a husband. But still others said he was her friend, leading her in the right direction, telling her where to go, not to touch things with her hand. That old man used to tell her not to go to sacred sites.

'Were there male cultural sites near Ooldea Soak?' I asked.

Uwa, the women said. He was keeping her away from business, inma. She'd keep her eyes down. He would teach her about insects, trees, animals, give her the names in Pitjantjatjara on the sandhills. They were learning both ways.

One day, Daisy Bates went to Wynbring; she had had enough of Ooldea. The Ooldea kids were all worried about her; they were singing for her to come back. They would jump on the train to see her at Wynbring and sit down with her there. She was still working at the station. They'd visit her campsite, and she'd play games and sing songs.

I asked where her camp was.

'On the train side of the railway,' Margaret and Rita told me, drawing a diagram in the dirt. 'On the other side, there were rock holes, sacred rock holes. On this side there were houses. There were white people and Anangu.'

'And where was Daisy Bates?' I asked.

'Anangu,' Rita said.

'She was staying with Anangu?' They nodded. 'She was up there at Wynbring, and you used to go and visit her. What happened when she was at Wynbring?'

'She went old when she was at Wynbring. She would get sick. She would say, "I'm going." When she was ready to go, she would come and tell Margaret she had problems with her heart. She told a lot of people there. There was crying, crying. She was looking after all of Anangu, giving them blanket, clothes, food to eat.'

Margaret and Rita lapsed into Pitjantjatjara, occasionally punctuated by the word 'umbrella'.

'Hide herself,' Rita explained. 'She put up the umbrella to go on the train. She was hiding her face.'

Margaret cowered slightly, shielding her face to demonstrate.

'Them cry. They were all crying, "Don't go. You know we want you."'

I was a bit confused about whether they were describing Bates's departure from Wynbring, as it had been by car with two 'gangsters' in the dead of night, although maybe other kin had witnessed the pantomime at Tarcoola station with Alvis Brooks luring Bates onto the train with her George V umbrella, that portable shelter and emblem of Daisy's tenuous, sycophantic connection with royalty. If it was her leave-taking from Ooldea, it was probably a story that older family members had told them. Bates gives a saccharine, melodramatic evocation of leaving Ooldea in the *Passing*: 'Crooning and crying, they gathered round me on the slope of the sandhill ... The last I saw was the soft strained farewell in my natives' eyes.'[3]

I prodded the women for more details. 'Daisy Bates was up at the railway,' they said simply. 'She went on the train to Port Augusta; she went to Adelaide.'

But whichever of Bates's leave-takings it was, what this anecdote highlighted was that the memory of an outpouring of affection on her departure wasn't only on her side. Indeed, I was surprised by how favourable their memories of Bates had been so far, although maybe they were telling me what they thought I wanted to hear as a white woman, a sanitised version. Somewhat tentatively, I asked whether they'd heard some of the tougher stories about Daisy Bates – about how she'd excluded people of mixed descent from her camp and spread rumours about Aboriginal cannibalism.

There was a moment's silence. The women looked nonplussed, as if they didn't know what I was talking about, then began speaking in short bursts, Mima translating.

'Only a few people didn't like her – the half-castes and quarter-castes. She'd turn around and say, "You go away. You're half-caste mob." She would chase them away.'

I found the women's expressions hard to read. Maybe they thought I was repeating slander from other people about Daisy Bates for them to refute. Perhaps they were deflecting my queries about Bates's cannibalism stories because they were understandably uncomfortable engaging with this subject. Maybe I was asking too many questions about difficult issues too soon. I was reluctant to press them further, given the content's sensitivity. Besides, their attention was waning. I sensed that things were winding down.

'*Finished!*' they said in the perfunctory way remote people often end social exchanges, then scrambled to their feet, dusting down their clothes and snuffing out the fire.

Driving away from Fowlers Bay after I'd returned the women to the institute hall, I mused about the conundrum of Bates. I'd expected the women to be more negative about her, ambivalent at best, but, rather than conjuring up the sinister figure of 'Daidj Bate mamu', they seemed genuinely fond of Bates. I wondered whether their stories about Daisy were happy and fairly trusting because they'd been kids when they'd met her or first heard about her. Margaret had known Bates at Wynbring, when she'd been at her frailest, most vulnerable and in need of care from others, perhaps making her a more sympathetic figure than at any other time. Nevertheless, hearing these memories from an older woman who'd visited Daisy's camp as a child gave them the texture of authenticity.

'Yet during all my years, months & days amongst them,' Bates wrote in 1940, 'I have been safe, & "cared for" in their own way by the elders of every group in every one of my camps, & have been assisted in my world of recording their customs, dialects, legends, by each & every group.'[4]

As for the notion that she'd had an Aboriginal lover – if Daisy was guided by an Aṉangu male elder at Ooldea as she was by Joobaitch at Ma'amba Reserve, she may not have wanted to mention her reliance on him publicly in her articles and lectures because of the stigma attached to white women consorting with Aboriginal men, like the censure directed at Annie Lock as 'a woman Missionary living amongst naked blacks'. That Daisy had been looked after – by elders, by women who called out for her to dance with them, by the cheeky children who jumped the train to see where she'd gone – explained how she'd managed to survive for so long, especially when she became old and frail while camping on the Nullarbor's rim. The women's stories also suggested Bates possessed a core of affection for Aṉangu, caring for them by providing food and blankets, giving the children treats, dancing with the minymas, walking on the dunes with her protector, learning the local ways. Yet there was, as always, that fundamental element of inconsistency in accounts of Bates. How could these more positive stories be reconciled with those of her more damaging activities? Had she really been living 'both ways', as the women said, protecting Anangu as they protected her?

IV | HOMING

9
Gypsying to windward

'So the thought of caravan. And the future of caravans in Australia, the perfect continent for them – awakening to our heritage of sun.'[1]

Late in 1945 Bates found herself marooned among the starch and clatter of an Adelaide ward, sans Dickens and her hatboxes full of notes. She'd shifted from Port Augusta to her old city haunt, the Queen Adelaide Club, but she'd been packed off to Trent Hospital after she wounded herself, tripping while alighting from a tram. Hospital was no place for her; she fretted about the adipose tissue settling on her sparrow-boned frame, skipping when she could to keep the process at bay. She still kept regular work hours from 10 am to 4 pm, walking two-and-a-half miles (4 kilometres) and back every day from the hospital in Unley to her office in the Exchange Building on Pirie Street, where she worked with the latest 'useless' secretary on her manuscripts. Bored and restless, she plotted to get back to her tent life, writing: 'I think my sheer loneliness for my natives arises from my many years with them alone.' Wynbring was not an option; equipment from her tents lay rotting about the siding where the 'gangsters' had uprooted her.[2]

Escape, 'crude but effective', presented itself in the form of the Birdseye bus service to Streaky Bay. It was the perfect ruse; no-one would expect an 86-year-old to make the onerous 700-kilometre journey there by bus. 'I think the matron must be gasping over my departure,' she told a friend. Hardly pausing for breath herself at Streaky Bay, she paid Mrs Nieass, a storekeeper who was travelling back to Penong, £10 to drive her 220 kilometres to Bookabie – 'bad water' – a waterhole just before Fowlers Bay, near where she'd camped three decades earlier.[3]

As the car neared Bookabie, Bates claimed her natives 'ran and ran to get round the car their eyes streaming with joy', having travelled some 80 miles from Ooldea after they'd heard she was coming. With her usual braggadocio, she described handing out food to them while Mrs Nieass shrank back in the car.[4]

'Darling Hill,' she wrote, 'if you had seen their poor faces well with tears of joy at seeing Kabbarli filling umpteen mouths with quivering exciting joy.'[5]

'Joy comes in happy tears.' But was it their joy or her own? Daisy dropped the phrase 'my natives' joy' into her letters to friends, as if trying to persuade herself. She'd hoped to resume camping in the area, but some local farmers – the Nieasses among them – had taken over her old site 'so I could not rest any more there. I must have an area free from any kind of white people'.[6]

It had been a fruitless effort. She told her 'poor natives' to look for another place with a permanent water supply, left food gifts with the storekeeper, instructing her to stock flour and sugar for 'Kabbarli's people', then returned to Streaky Bay.[7] Mild-mannered Mrs Nieass continued to update Bates, saying she'd allowed Aboriginal people to stay on her farms because they were 'so homeless and hunted by the police. It is so sad for them.' Daisy was in limbo herself, shuttling between the Criterion and Flinders hotels at Streaky Bay, nibbling away at her Commonwealth Literary Fellowship of £250 per annum. The local housing situation was acute, with many workers staying at hotels. Later in the year Mrs Mudge, who ran the Flinders, nudged some relatives, the Thompsons, to take her in as a boarder.[8]

Bates was 'persuaded to come in to this farm at Streaky', although she wasn't entirely comfortable living with members of the third generation of white farmers rather than Aboriginal people in the area. She rotated between the Thompsons' two properties – Pantoulbie, on the road to Port Lincoln, and Westall, 16 kilometres out of town – and the sleepout behind their relatives the Mathews's farm, Sunny Brae.[9]

She stayed aloof from her keepers, living 'as she would in a whirly', surfacing for meals but otherwise subsisting on tea, cheese and biscuits in her room, doing 'everything herself, eating less than a sparrow'. Vida Thompson never entered her room or washed her clothes or saw her washing them, either, although Bates always looked neat and tidy. Daisy did light chores such as making her own bed and kindling the fire, although she could 'do no more skipping rope business or running up stairs & down'.[10]

Sometimes she'd hitch up her skirts around her waist and run or stride about the fields. A photo taken at Pantoulbie shows her straight-backed, darkly clad Mary Poppins figure, complete with straw boater, on a rope swing suspended from a branch's arc before an admiring Mr Cyril Thompson, no doubt impressed by her vigour. Always more at home with children than adults, she spent more time with the Thompson kids. In another photo, she hangs off a fence with Beverley and Natalie Thompson, drawing them close in a shepherding gesture. The little girls – blonde dumplings of children – wear flowers Daisy pinned to their frocks.

Bates's gaze is not quite focussed in these photographs. Her sight, ruined by years of infection by desert grit, was a constant source of irritation, especially for someone who took great joy in writing letters and reading Dickens. But there's something else in her eyes, as though she's looking out from a long way within or surfacing from a deep well. It's the eerie gaze of a sleepwalker, of a wanderer cut adrift from her moorings. Her body still cracked with a whip-like strength after years of skipping rope and hauling her barrow of supplies over the Ooldea dunes, but her mind had eroded like stone whittled away by hot desert winds – a sobering loss for a self-styled scientist who'd lived by her wits, compiling compendia of Aboriginal lore and language.

Of an afternoon, Daisy would take her stick – a long, stout mallee branch – and roam about Westall. One night when Cyril Thompson was herding his sheep, he saw Bates up in the hills above the beach, digging a hole, somewhere she could 'put her hip of a night' to sleep like local Aboriginal people. Another time when Daisy hadn't returned by dusk, Vida sent out a search party to look for her. They followed her tracks through a barley crop down to the beach, where they found Bates at around eight or nine at night. She'd clawed her way to the top of giant boulders, where she looked out and saw big stones on the water which she mistook for a boat 'and she was waving and yelling and screeching to them to come and pick her up'. A young policeman scrambled up a steep cliff to collect her at half-past two in the morning. She was stiff and sore for days afterwards, having 'walked up among the big Boulder granite Rocks tumbling about & bruising her face & body with falls on those granites'.[11]

In these Lear-like ramblings, waving her mallee stick against the elements, raging against unknown ghosts and age's leaching of mind and vitality, Daisy traced out lines of flight to take her back, a sovereign in exile, to her people. 'You remember Joobaitch's death?' she asked Hill, recalling his last words when he lay dying at Ma'amba Reserve. "Don't let me be taken to hospital. Don't let me past the Koonya tree on which my spirit must rest before I pass on thro the sea …" And I thank God because his spirit rested on his father's & grand-father's spirit tree.'[12]

But what had become of dear Ernestine Hill? Bates had been pleading with her to visit: 'How I wish you could fly here & share camp with me & let me tell you all those old native things that will be so emblematic of those W.A. old natives & their lives – I have written to try & get back to my old life there.' She wasn't sure where Ernestine was – maybe somewhere in the Northern Territory. She'd been in contact with ER Bartholomew, John Murray's Australian agent at Oxford University Press, telling him 'Ngar'galulla Law' was in progress, but her eyes were troubling her: did he know Hill's whereabouts? Daisy was keen for her old friend to join her and 'be my other self with my MSS', explaining that Ernestine had been her 'fidus Achates' while she was writing *The Passing of the Aborigines*. Bates impressed on Bartholomew and the Murrays what a well-published and knowledgeable author Hill was; how she'd discussed with her 'all my natives MS. especially this last series that I can't get into the right mood for'. There was no-one else who could help her write the final draft. 'Ernestine is so receptive & so hypersensitive in these things,' Daisy wrote, 'that I long to have her near to me.'[13]

Was there another dimension to Hill and Bates's partnership? The desert eccentric was renowned for her strange charisma; thirty-five years after her brief rainswept encounter with Daisy in Adelaide, journalist Elizabeth Wolff declared that Bates was 'the most fascinating person I've ever had the privilege of meeting'.[14] But did Daisy inspire something more than youthful admiration in Ernestine while they worked together in the *Advertiser* office? When Bates wrote to Hill from Streaky Bay in the mid-1940s trying to entice her to collaborate on 'Ngar'galulla Law', she prevailed upon Ernestine's affections in no uncertain terms, closing her first letter: 'My love for you is unalterable, but I think my youth is going. Let me know what <u>you</u> think.'[15]

Daisy was in her mid-eighties, her mind and eyesight were fading – she boasts she can't see her own scrawl on the page – but her words possess an undeniable intensity. When I first read this letter in a sheaf of Bates's correspondence in the Fryer Library, I was struck by her parting words to Ernestine. What love was this, I wondered, so strong that she described it as unalterable? And how could Bates only be aware at the age of eighty-six that her youth was fading, and what did she want her youthful energy for – merely to work with Ernestine again? Curious about the crumbs of subtext Bates had thrown out about their friendship's dynamics, I ploughed on through the rest of Daisy's letters to Hill, not caring whether I strained my eyes trying to decipher her deteriorating script.

'Darling Ernestine,' the next begins, 'I am reading your letter with tears of joy and sorrow, sorrow that I cannot see you or be near you, or talk to you & show you my love for you. I do <u>want</u> you so badly, but respect <u>you</u> have your special work up there.' (Up there being the Top End where Hill had been researching *The Territory*.)[16] Imploring Hill to whip her off west in a caravan in May 1947, Daisy writes:

> You & I could go together, I wouldn't worry you, but I love to be with you ... so that we can go & come where we chose – I am so keen to be near you – & to have your dear face before me, but I won't thrust myself upon you darling, only if we could be near by I should love it ... I so long for your nearness.[17]

She imagines not only seeing Hill, but touching her again:

When I <u>do</u> see you, and please God I do see you before I pass out, it will be to look at your kind dear stoical & honest face Ernestine & to love the <u>strength</u> in it – that <u>quiet</u> strength that is yours.

Affectionately yours, I want to see you & touch your fine straight hair. I have a fat Imperial Typewriter which I can't use & there's no one to use it.[18]

While staying in a Dickensian boarding house in Adelaide in 1947, Bates describes the 'lovely furniture' in her room with the thrill of someone who's been without luxury for a good while. She delights in the 'cool feel of the ancient & priceless mahogany (or is it cedar)' of the bed, which she explains, in what seem like unmistakably homoerotic overtones, is 'a large double bed. What would I not give to lie with you there for once'.[19] Daisy's letters to Ernestine are sprinkled with endearments like 'Darling Pal' and 'my best & dearest friend'. She closes one with 'I love you so dearly & long for you', ending another with an enigmatic flourish, 'How I long to see you Ernestine, & hear your dear voice, & beg your pardon if I have offended your lovely sensibilities by my Crude Gaieties – but it was intoxicating <u>all the time</u>.'[20]

Letters are among the rawest of material, especially personal correspondence, where a writer may express her thoughts and feelings unguardedly, believing her words will only be read by the intended recipient. Reading other people's letters can have the effect of eavesdropping, of hearing words not intended for your ears, even when the correspondents are long dead. Rifling through Bates's correspondence to Hill decades later in the Fryer Library, I felt disoriented by the immediacy of her voice and the pull of her plaintive, repetitive, circuitous tropes. Daisy was by then very old, and her letters, with their crazy offers of tokens from her shared history with Ernestine – Imperial typewriters, camping trips west – were the product of an age-fractured, probably disintegrating mind. But were they merely the entreaties of an isolated woman, longing to have intelligent conversation and company with another? Or had I stumbled on the vestiges of something else? What had gone on in the Adelaide office and, more to the point, what happened behind the breakwind at Ooldea?

It was my first encounter, up close and personal, with Bates, and on reflection I wondered whether I was misinterpreting the flamboyant flourishes of another era's sensibilities. Daisy was a Victorian; perhaps she wrote to others in a similar florid style. In his Bates biography, Bob Reece speculates that Daisy nurtured a secret passion for William Hurst, her long-time correspondent and editor at the *Argus*, who published many of her articles. After corresponding with Hurst for over a decade, Bates finally 'barged in' at the *Argus* and *Australasian* offices in Melbourne, en route to Canberra, in 1933. She 'had been so longing to meet you face to face' and hoped that he and the other newspaper staff weren't overwhelmed by the rather Irish way in which 'I let myself give vent to the joy of meeting you all'.[21] On her way to set up camp at Wynbring in 1941, Daisy invited Hurst to take tea at the Quamby Club in Melbourne, prodding him to greet her at the station: 'I should like to see your clearly remembered face on the platform there.'[22] The following letter politely acknowledges their meeting: 'We had such a lovely time, didn't we?, at the Quamby Club? & I was so glad to see you & talk to you & tell you all about my hopes & fears.'[23] Bates was in her early eighties, Hurst was in his late sixties, and her description of this meeting is more sedate than their previous one. She was also a habitual flirt who'd been much admired by men when she was younger; perhaps she was embarrassed by her faded beauty when she finally met Hurst face to face and shrank back from the encounter. Corresponding with another person over a long period can also convey an emotional proximity that might not be matched in real life. In a letter, she could unburden her hopes and fears, describe her experiences at length, have her own soapbox in a way that might not happen in a polite and incidental tête-à-tête at the Quamby Club. Bates was candid about the challenges of her life and work with Aboriginal people in her correspondence with Hurst, but did she ever imagine romance or anything else flourishing between them, especially much later in life?

Bates later destroyed all except two of Hurst's letters, so how he expressed himself in corresponding to her is unknown. When he resigned from editorship of the *Argus* in 1937, Daisy commended him for his 'never failing courtesy, kindness, chivalry, towards me and my natives in those arduous years at Ooldea' which earned her 'most respectful regard & affection', so that when she finally met him 'it was, to me, the meeting with a friend of years'.[24] It's a warm and polite acknowledgement of his editorial support that does not stray beyond the respectable bounds of friendship. Generally, I found Bates's correspondence to Hurst lacked the heightened emotion of hers to Hill; that she did not write to him or anyone else with such overblown protestations of love and friendship. Yet as much as she pleads and cajoles in her letters to Ernestine, Daisy can also flip a jarring 'back to business' switch, shifting quickly from vulnerable to imperious, which made me question whether her intentions were affectionate, romantic or even benevolent. The roles in their original alliance were reversed; Daisy wanted something from Ernestine. She was chasing after her desperately in the way that Hill had once pleaded with her to come down from Ooldea to Adelaide and collaborate with her.

'Letters – at least the kind that writers write – are journals addressed to someone else,' biographer James Atlas writes. 'However self-conscious, however contrived in tone, they are addressed to a recipient – an Other. The monologue becomes a dialogue. Even in his silence, the addressee influences the tone of the letter's author.'[25] Only Bates's side of her correspondence with Hill during the mid-1940s exists. Monologic at the best of times, Daisy appears confounded by Ernestine's initial lack of response. She ponders Hill's 'long silence' out loud, as it were, in her letters, although she is contrite when Ernestine finally replies in late 1945: 'Your dear letter came to me and fills me with sorrow because I am sure you are not well and I can realize what you must have gone through in that torrid zone', presumably a reference to the deaths of Hill's mother and aunt, and Bob's conscription battle.

Bates apologises for being a poor friend – 'I look back & see myself with you & feel that I have been unworthy of your dear friendship in many ways and shortcomings dear friend & ask you pardon.'[26] She hints at remorse over her treatment of Hill during their previous collaboration: 'I look back on our contact with each other in those "Passing" Days – & I reproach myself greatly for my own shortcomings, but you saw my old camp life & would see (mentally) how I had to live up on my own to it as things happened.'[27] Daisy sugar-coats her own guilt-ridden agenda here; she never apologises directly for failing to acknowledge Hill's contribution to 'my book'.

'Burn these letters of mine, Ernestine,' she writes in one of her last letters, 'my honour is in your hands & my good name.'[28]

Ernestine didn't burn them, although in 1970 she told Barbara Polkinghorne that she once 'had stacks of Daisy's long letters, but I've never been one to keep and use the letters of friends, now such a racket'.[29] Why she preserved this particular batch of correspondence may relate to their historical significance, documenting the last years of Daisy's life. The desire to prove Bates's guilt in failing to acknowledge her contribution to the *Passing* – the implication behind Daisy's confessions of being an unworthy friend – may also have been a compelling motivation.

Ernestine's preoccupation with Daisy waxed and waned throughout her life, for decades after Bates's death. In corresponding with other friends while she was fielding Daisy's entreaties from Streaky Bay in the mid-1940s, Hill describes her in affectionate, if sometimes dismissive, terms and her missives as 'pathetic little letters'. Hill had plenty of reasons to be annoyed by her old friend by this time, as well as having experienced her own 'torrid zone' during the war, but had she ever entertained anything more than starstruck admiration for Bates, that Daisy was appealing to in her letters from Streaky Bay? When Ernestine brought Bates to the *Advertiser* office, she was free to develop a new romantic focus since RC was dead. She also had a tendency to idealise people, especially older ones capable of assuming an iconic status, such as Packer, Gilmore and Bates. When she first met Daisy – a woman indulging her passion for ethnographic observation while living in a highly remote location, ostensibly without support – she embodied many aspects of a lifestyle Ernestine esteemed. As a bluestocking living on the Nullarbor's rim, Bates epitomised the civilising role Hill envisaged European women playing in the 'loneliness'.

Both women shared a psychological and social loneliness as a result of their past relationships. They had effectively defected from traditional family and domestic life, having put marriage behind them and their sons into other people's care. While the clandestine nature of Bates's bigamy and Hill's affair might suggest an openness to other forms of love, the secretive nature of their relationships was born of the need to avoid social censure by appearing to uphold their era's mores. In falling outside the marriage contract, Ernestine and Daisy had lost the cornerstone of economic security for women in the early 20th century. They instead supported themselves independently by writing about remote Australia, bringing a further precarious dimension to their lives that made other bonds and networks – especially their friendship – all the more vital.

'It seemed that we had an understanding and an interest that was different from the kind you have with lovers ...', author and academic Julienne van Loon writes in *The Thinking Woman*, pondering the influence of a friend on her life long after her death. 'Such stability as there was, was imagined, and eros is never entirely absent from any vital friendship.'[30] There was a vital energy to Daisy and Ernestine's collaborative partnership, grounded in their common journalistic and ethnological interests. Intense intimacy often infuses female friendship; it can also ebb and flow over time, in response to changing circumstances or shifts in dynamics, as Bates's remaining correspondence to Hill suggests. To fix an intense female friendship such as theirs on a sexual continuum, or collapse it into an echo of marital coupledom, is potentially to underestimate the power of women's alliances, the solidarity and solace they provide beyond work and social structures defined by male interests. Female friendships possess a sinuousness beyond conventional heterosexual relationships; they are freely chosen, not grounded in obligation like family relationships, which gives them their strength and flexibility. Often enduring longer than marriages, they are the webbing, the net, that women rely on to bounce back from a bruised heart or a relationship breakdown. They also provide an essential source of support for solitary women without the traditional ballasts of partner and family.

For Daisy to be so high-handed in her treatment of Ernestine at the *Advertiser* office made her betrayal of her friend all the more brutal. Yet a twitch upon the thread of longstanding loyalties, shared experiences and confidences can stir up the embers of friendship, and Hill was kind enough, susceptible enough, to be drawn once again into Bates's manipulative web. Ernestine's personal motives in allowing herself to be swept up again in this dynamic were also questionable, at which Daisy herself later hinted darkly. Hill's obsession with Bates continued until her own death, like that with a lover you know you should – but never quite – give up.

In late 1945, when Hill finally responded to Bates's letters, she was in Western Australia, where she was revising her own manuscripts. Although Daisy might have '10 books waiting your publication of them', Ernestine parried back, saying she had '9 or 10 books to be typed' with 'so many publishers at Home & in Australia waiting impatiently for them'.[31] Hill was reluctant to be drawn into the editorial vortex of working with Bates, although she paid her a flying visit at a Streaky Bay hotel while 'passing by' on her way back from Perth in September 1946. Walter Cousins at Angus & Robertson had been pressuring her for another book, saying that 'a book a year is better for an author than a special book every two years'.[32] Ernestine was still promising to finish *The Territory*, but she felt piqued by this request, given that *My Love Must Wait* continued to sell strongly.

The following year, she finally succumbed to Bates's pleas to whip her off west in a caravan and, using royalties from sales of *My Love Must Wait*, she bought 'a great little pilgrim van' in Melbourne to hitch behind the blitz buggy that she and Bob had driven down from Darwin.[33] Rescuing Bates wasn't the only mandate for her mission. Hill had received sponsorship from the Fuel Board, an allowance of 20 gallons a month, to support her travel and research on the trip for a book provisionally titled 'Australia's Home', to describe the country's unseen beauty and riches. 'So the thought of caravan,' she wrote on leaving Melbourne in June 1947. 'And the future of caravans in Australia, the perfect continent for them – awakening to our heritage of sun.' Caravans had been marketed since the mid-1930s as an option for holidaymakers wishing to traverse the continent without relying on train or boat timetables and as a cheap alternative to the variable standards of outback motel accommodation. 'Carefree, no schedule to adhere to, no timetables to watch, and an absence of the orthodox routine of the holiday guesthouse,' a 1936 RACV *Radiator* article extolled the caravan's virtues. 'I can visualize our magnificent highways teeming with this class of transport.'[34] Hill had anticipated this development with her proposal to Deamer in 1940 of a travel service page for the *ABC Weekly*. By 1950 she observed there were 'no end of the pilgrims rushing around Australia by air, land and sea – they come in on every ship and place, hitch-hiking the g.w.spaces, working their way or booking with Thomas Cook'.[35] As Australia opened up for tourism during the post-war era, caravanning proved ideal for her own purposes.

'Her present mode of caravan travel is pure luxury to Ernestine Hill,' 'Joan Pilgrim' observed when she caught up with the Hills on the Bight in 1947, comparing it to some of her previous conveyances.[36] Pilgrim was an alias for Vera Hamilton, one of the journalists whom Hill had recommended as a host for an ABC women's hour. 'Moty-car catchum house,' an Aboriginal woman commented on seeing the buggy towing the van, and indeed the caravan provided a portable shelter and home for the Hills at large in Australia over the next two years. It also doubled as an office of sorts – Ernestine kitted it out with a small desk up one end and a strip of carpet down the middle – where she could write while on the road. She delighted in the ease the caravan gave her to roam the country, occasionally dipping into southern cities, musing that 'I travel south and east only so that I can go north and west again.'[37]

Like Bates, she harboured romantic ideas about the remote northwest as a remnant of traditional Aboriginal life, as well as being the last bastion of white pioneering mythology associated with 'old Australia'.

The Hills moored their caravan behind a boxthorn hedge near Sunny Brae, the Mathews's farm, at Westall, where Bates was boarding in winter 1947. Life at Sunny Brae, they observed, was fairly austere. It was 'a primitive little family farm, where Mother milks 15 cows, but the family is kind and bright though the place is primitive and rather helter-skelter' and there were 'more bags than blankets on the beds'.[38] Bob took a photo of the farming family, their lodger and her guests during the Hills's stay at Sunny Brae. In this portrait, he cast the Mathews as 'Australian Gothic', with Mrs Mathews and her older daughter wearing pinnies over floral frocks, while a lanky, raw-boned Mr Mathews, complete with hat and tie, dandles a well-nourished youngster on his knees. A slight but palpable gap exists between the family, and Hill and Bates, who look like visitors from another era. Ernestine appears, to use her own words, 'skinny and sinister': there's an abrupt transition from the glamorous shots of her as an ingénue reporter, still used to accompany her articles in the early 1940s, and her stern and watchful figure in later photos.[39] Elizabeth Durack, who knew her during the 1950s, described her somewhat uncharitably as 'a little dried up leaf'.[40] Dressed in a tailored suit as if on a journalistic assignment, Hill leans proprietorially against the back of Daisy's chair, her dark helmet of hair accentuating the shadows on her gaunt face. Black-clad and immaculate, a waxwork effigy stiffening into posterity, Bates stares straight ahead.

Ernestine was characteristically more worried about Daisy, closeted away in a shed behind the Mathews's farmhouse, than her own rustic circumstances behind the boxthorn hedge at Sunny Brae. It was late August, and cold grey rain swept in from the Bight, dripping between the shed's sheet iron walls. Bates had hardly stirred from bed over the winter, and Hill found her very frail, if 'wonderful', for eighty-seven. She was still wearing the clothes she'd had French tailors run up for her in Perth in 1899: they fit, no doubt because of her exercise regime, although they were 'an epic of tatters, her two blouses both grey with age and in a thousand pieces and one pair of antediluvian "coms" [long undergarments unstitched at the crotch] that she washes at night and hangs in her room to dry'.[41] The habits of decades of tent life were hard to break. Ernestine wrote to her cousin Coy, asking her to send 13 yards of silk, which Vida Thompson later ran up into a 'beautiful pair of – I forget what they call them: not pants, anyway … One with no middles.'[42] Bates had wanted to pay her hosts the £4 weekly stipend from her Commonwealth Literary Fellowship, although Mrs Mathews would only take £1: Bob Hill thought they 'were looking after her partly from a sense of duty to Australia'.[43]

Bates was despondent, talking of 'quitting this world'. Although she'd pleaded with Ernestine to sweep her off in a heavy-duty vehicle for camping, she was quite defeated by the Hills's 'furnished caravan' and its gadgets, each 'having a knob or some such which I ran into', claiming that she 'would not have been able to dodge the thousand & one comforts' if she travelled with them. No doubt the caravan lacked the simplicity of Gauera's camel buggy, and Bates would certainly 'have worn the life out of dear Ernestine', but Hill soon realised that Daisy's complaints about the vehicle's cushiness were a cover for her deteriorating health and inability to embark on a major camping venture.[44] Yet whenever Ernestine hinted that she and Bob 'must be getting on soon', Daisy would develop hypochondria: 'the most frightful and extraordinary symptoms that never were, I am perfectly sure, medically known before'.[45]

Ernestine spent two weeks with her old friend, the only person allowed in the inner sanctum of Bates's shed-like room, listening and taking notes while Daisy recounted more stories from camping with Aboriginal people. Apparently they were so deep in congress one day, they failed to notice when a bed-warmer – a house brick heated in the oven and wrapped in a piece of blanket – began to smoke the blankets: 'mother thought it was a miasma but it became plain enough what it was in time to save Daisy.'[46] Bates lumbered her with 'volumes of notes to write another book for her' – the ngar'galulla story – along with a bamburoo similar to the ones she'd ferried between Aboriginal people on Dorre and Bernier Islands and the mainland during the Cambridge expedition.[47] She claimed that while she was working in Western Australia, a dying Aboriginal doctor in Gascoyne had bequeathed her this particular bamburoo, along with the rights to cross country anywhere.[48] It also symbolised communication – 'invitation to the big Jalgoo – circle – corroborees' and had sexual connotations, as its shape suggests – 'orgy corroborees, phallic, of young men and women'. Bates presented the bamburoo to Hill with a dramatic flourish: "'Yanda noggin inyillee!" … "Sun sitting down inside. I've kept that for you, because you're my spiritual child, don't you know?"'[49] Frustrating as the imposition of a further manuscript must have been when Hill had her own pressing deadlines to meet, her exchange with Bates at Streaky Bay appears to have strengthened her ethnographic resolve – that Bates was quite literally handing on the baton to her.

The Hills lingered at the Mathews's farm for a fortnight before moving on to Ceduna and Fowlers Bay. They still had 60 gallons of fuel from the Fuel Board they needed to use by the end of September. Others were clamouring to join their entourage. Doreen Aldred, a Perth friend who wanted to play secretary by typing up Hill's chaotic notes, met them at Fowlers Bay, and Vera Hamilton, then a young reporter and 'a very vigorous and bright-minded soul', joined their cavalcade at Ceduna. Her behaviour amused Ernestine, perhaps reminding her of her younger self: 'the Sydney journalist in the quietness, dashing about and asking tempestuous questions, writing for dear life – you learn you don't have to do that.' Decades of outback flânerie had mellowed her own journalistic practice: 'The mind absorbs the best quite easily in a leisurely way in the outback, and it is surprising how good the memory becomes even for passing names and facts.'[50] But the whole caper was getting out of hand. They already had a flock of tents – one for Bob as well as Ernestine, another for ablutions, and a library, recalling Bates's camp behind the breakwind – and Hill thought they might need another double tent to accommodate everyone, delighting in the idea that they would 'finish up like the Sheikh of Araby'.[51]

Yet none of this conviviality compensated for Daisy's absence. Ernestine had held out hope until the end of their stay on the Mathews's farm that Bates would still join them on their trip west. In 'Australia's Home', she makes only a couple of scant references – 'Daisy's rain tree totem story' – to Bates, a silence that Bob later interpreted as a sign of her disappointment that her old friend was not coming with them in the caravan, caravanning west being a trope from Daisy's letters which had come to represent their continued friendship.[52]

The Hills ran aground at Coolgardie on their voyage west after the Juggernaut Buggy's 'raggy tyres' wouldn't inflate.[53] Ernestine didn't mind this turn of events; she loved this 'very dreamy little town of long-ago gold', and they camped there until December 1947, Hill welcoming the opportunity to work on *The Territory*, 'my old man of the Arafura Sea – 145,000 words done and "still little bit long way."'[54] Katharine Susannah Prichard, who was researching the final book in her 'Trilogy of Gold' nearby in Kalgoorlie, visited the Hills in their caravan on her way back to Perth. Ernestine enthused about their meeting – it was 'an unexpected pleasure' and 'a very happy night'[55] – although Prichard was more circumspect, especially about their location's charms: 'in the hot weather, I do appreciate the mod cons – baths & decent sanitary arrangements. Afraid I'm not so fond of the simple life as I used to be. Particularly when it includes flies & red-backed spiders galore. Ernestine seems to take them in her stride.'[56]

Prichard invited the Hills to park their caravan in the orchard at her Greenmount house when they arrived in Perth so Ernestine could work on her much-delayed Territory book, an offer she took up before spending several months at a guesthouse on a farm in Toodyay near Northam. Finding the guesthouse too noisy, she soon moved back into the caravan, although her hosts gave her a study of sorts in the 'brown house', a ruin of a cottage on the farm, where she typed away, sunlight slanting through the curtains, the 'usual chaos of old notes around'.

'Tranquil Toodyay is a gift after all our fevered wandering hither and yon,' she wrote, but Bates soon disrupted her writerly reverie, badgering her to polish up the ngar'galulla book for publication.[57] Hill divided her time equally between her own book and Bates's manuscript in view of what she called their 'gentleman's agreement', underscoring that, as with their previous collaboration, she 'had no thought of asking either an acknowledgment, a share in royalties or an editor's fee, and Daisy well knew this'.[58] Earlier in the year Bates had asked her bank manager to write a note stating 'my wish is that all the future books of mine ... Ernestine Hill may edit and publish', which may have been the gentleman's agreement. But she fretted about 'Ernestine's silence' in response to her letters, speculating that Hill might be devoting her energies to Robert's future rather than revising the ngar'galulla manuscript.[59]

Bates had stopped requesting a caravan after the Hills's visit to Streaky Bay, although she still dreamed of escaping to Alice Springs or Ernabella Mission to 'nurse the natives', despite being in need of care herself. She made it as far as Penong, where she sipped tea on the verandah of Mrs Nieass's store, hoping to find some of her old Ooldea friends 'homing' in the area. Her sight was so bad she could only feel the sunlight's heat; she could no longer see the sky: 'I miss my stars; miss them greatly.'[60]

'I am in such a sunny corner and longing to have you somewhere in the vicinity,' she wrote, encouraging Ernestine to join her for a cup of tea on Mrs Nieass's verandah.[61] After receiving 'many sad letters regretting the high-handedness about the other book' from Bates, Hill relented and made a desperate canter, travelling 1000 miles by road in June 1948, to visit her in Penong. She felt for her old friend; Daisy's health was deteriorating, she was desperately lonely and longed for companionship. Ernestine also thought it was imperative that they continue revising Bates's manuscripts, which contained:

> remarkable legends, sometimes in a sentence, and in this age of so many spurious aboriginal legends, they must be written soon. She loves all the drama and excitement and big yacki so dearly that, after her long, hard and remarkable life and for the rare little character she is, it would be good if they can be published before she dies.[62]

Hill described her contribution to working on this material as 'fitting the jigsaw together, tracking up Aboriginal words in her glossaries, enhancing the simple stories with just a touch of drama or poetry for appeal both to children and as general literature with anthropological verifications and value – a link in the world's mythologies that delighted me'. Her role was mainly editorial, although she enjoyed the project's ethnographic underpinnings.[63]

Although this collaborative episode appears to have been harmonious, Ernestine received a 'brusque note' from Bates later in 1948, demanding she return the ngar'galulla to John Preece, an Adelaide-based bookseller and literary agent, for him to deliver to John Murray on his next trip to London. Preece's bookshop was then a staple of Adelaide cultural life, publishing works about South Australian history and Aboriginal matters by Basedow as well as Rex Ingamells's infamous Jindyworobak anthology. Bates, who was no longer able to live at a distance from medical treatment, was living in the Adelaide Hills with Beatrice Raine, her old friend whose brother she'd helped out in establishing his homestead on the Nullarbor in 1912. Daisy often travelled into the city, where she frequented Preece's bookshop on King William Street, along with old haunts such as the Queen Adelaide Club. Preece found Bates still 'so full of life', yet 'a little vague about things and hark[ing] back to years of long ago', observing that 'at eighty-nine the old lady, after a lifetime with her aborigines, does not find it easy to adjust herself'. She lived on a pittance – her CLF stipend plus a pension of £3.3 per week bestowed on her 'by a "grateful" Government – a recognition so small that it was an insult', which she supplemented with royalties. Bates felt the *Passing* had been neglected and wanted to boost its sales, whereas Preece thought it had done well in Australia. John Grey Murray agreed with Preece that the book had had a good run, although it had gone out of print in Britain during the war. Whatever its sales were in Australia, he hoped Bates didn't try to rely on royalties as her main source of income, although he promised to send £20 to her bank account against future earnings.

Preece was concerned about the chances of retrieving the ngar'galulla manuscript from Hill: 'that lady in search of characters,' he wrote to Grey Murray, 'is caravanning in Central Australia which, unlike an English county excursion, probably means a couple of thousand miles "out bush". So we must wait until she returns to civilisation.'[64] Bates had told him she'd left her papers with Hill merely 'for safekeeping'; there was no hint in her correspondence with the Murrays that Ernestine had them for any other purpose, such as revision, or that she might be disappointed about having to relinquish the manuscripts, given her work on them.

Hill was aggrieved by the request for the material's return, and asked Bates for three weeks' grace to complete the manuscript, 'all as a labour of love to appear with my own book simultaneously', an attempt at placation that a paranoid Bates may have read as self-aggrandising.[65] A short, sharp telegram from Preece followed, asking for all Bates's material, which Hill bundled up and posted to him in Adelaide.

John Murray Publishing's interest in another Bates book was tentative at best. Until he saw the manuscript, it was impossible to know whether it was suitable for publication or better off in a museum, Grey Murray told Preece, joking that Bates had once offered to send him a collection of artefacts, 'but we felt that calling authors might get hold of a boomerang and use it against their publisher, and it seemed more suitable that her collection should be of benefit to some museum in Australia'.[66] Joke or not, his references to museums and artefacts suggest how he categorised her material – as obsolete curio pieces. He had road-tested an earlier version of the ngar'galulla book in 1945 with his son – yet another John Murray – at her suggestion. Although Bates had assured him she had captivated some 100 students from a girls' college in Adelaide with its stories and accompanying sketches, Murray was:

> very distressed to report that his [son's] interest wandered. I daresay the fault was entirely his – or perhaps was mine in the reading of it – but I do not think that he is an exceptional fellow and other opinions that we have obtained agreed that this account of the aboriginals is a little difficult.[67]

He advised Bartholomew to seek Australian publication of the manuscript, saying he might try to sell some copies if OUP took it on, warning that 'We do not honestly feel that the story is treated in a way that will hold children's attention. It is hard enough for grown-ups to understand the beliefs and taboos of the aboriginals.'[68] Bartholomew informed him that while Bates had been hoping the book might be ready for the Christmas sales, OUP was still behind schedule because of post-war restrictions, and that he too was 'personally inclined to think that some of it is somewhat difficult for young readers'.[69]

John Preece received five parcels of Bates's manuscripts and one of photographs, accompanied by a long letter, from that 'caravanning lady', Ernestine Hill, at his Adelaide bookshop. Hill had been affronted by his request. She described the nature of her working relationship with Daisy over many years and how she'd recently persuaded the Department of the Interior to increase Bates's stipend from £4 to £5.5 a week – of none of which Preece was aware. 'Obviously she (Mrs. Hill) was very hurt to think that she had been "turned down" in a rather ruthless manner by an old friend,' he told Grey Murray:

> and by the intervention of one, to her, a stranger. Moreover she stated in her letter to me that the reason Mrs. Bates gave (i.e. that she handed over the manuscripts in the first place for safe-keeping at the time of her serious illness) was not true but they were intended for Mrs. Hill's future work. How far this is true or not I cannot say but I feel there may be some element of truth in it – for the old lady at about that time was indeed seriously ill, and I hesitate to suggest that Mrs. Hill, from her attitude, may have had some other interest in the papers.[70]

Somewhat regretful at having stumbled, if unwittingly, into this quagmire, Preece thought it wise to hold onto the manuscripts. Although he'd observed Bates's degree of incapacitation, he never contemplated Hill as a 'suitable person' to draw out a 'story' from her wayward notes. Instead, he warned Murray against allowing the material to fall into her hands:

> (I am not sure that I should mention this) but it is better you should be forewarned, if a Mrs. Ernestine Hill should write to you and claim some interest or rights in these manuscripts, it would be better to defer any action until you know the facts. There was during recent years some bitterness on Mrs. Hill's part.[71]

Nor was Ernestine a party to any of the conversations about valuing the manuscripts. He understood that Hill felt hard done by, but he remained loyal in his support of Bates as the material's author, rather than attempting to unravel the wrongs and rights of the situation. Daisy's earlier lack of recognition of Hill's work on the *Passing* probably amplified her chagrin on returning this work-in-progress after labouring to make it publishable. Beyond revising the ngar'galulla manuscript, what Hill planned to do with Bates's material is unclear; she may have hoped to incorporate elements of it within her own writing, such as her 'Australia's Home' book. Or perhaps she was beginning to contemplate the grander mapping projects of Aboriginal and settler mythology she later envisaged preserving as her 'sixty years of fragments' in national archives and imagined that possession of Bates's notes would legitimate her position as a folk ethnographer.

A tale about a stormy encounter between Daisy and Ernestine, which may have been their last meeting, passed into Batesian lore at Streaky Bay. Daisy was on the main ward of the town's hospital but, according to Margaret Kelsh, who was then its matron, she didn't speak much to anyone: 'when she wasn't writing she'd lie down with her face to the window and rest.' Hill spent a week with her 'compiling something they were going to publish later on', but the pair had 'a bit of a row'. They were so noisy that Matron Kelsh had to ask – 'whether she was called Mrs or Miss or what she was called, Ernestine Hill' – to leave, because she was upsetting Bates and the other patients.

'Get that woman out of here!' Daisy roared.

Kelsh wasn't sure why the two women argued; she thought it was about 'some of Daisy's diaries that she sort of didn't seem to be able to find' and that 'Ernestine Hill might have them, but Ernestine Hill declared she didn't have them'. Bates destroyed her diaries in 1941; unless she'd forgotten this, it's more likely they fought over the manuscript material she'd given Hill to revise, but which in her fractured mental state she thought her friend had stolen.

The day after Bates's quarrel with Hill at the hospital, she told the matron 'she didn't want to see Ernestine Hill again: she didn't want to see that woman again, don't let her in.'

'But I didn't have to worry,' Kelsh concluded pragmatically, 'because she left town that night.'

In fact, Ernestine and her son had marched into the matron's room at two in the morning, turned on the light and told her they were leaving Streaky Bay. As you do – an incident that at best suggests a last-ditch attempt to maintain contact with Bates; at worst, the Hills's sense of their own importance. The whole episode has a melodramatic tone, conjuring up for me a high camp, Hollywood Gothic scenario, with a saturnine Hill looming at the foot of various hospital beds. It was startling enough to be remembered long afterwards by locals: Kelsh told Aileen Treagus this story in 1999 as part of an oral history project, and Rae Brewster recounted it to me when I first spoke to her on the phone and later at the museum.[72]

Hill never mentions this encounter with Bates in *Kabbarli* or anywhere else. Admittedly, she doesn't come off well in the Streaky Bay accounts, but her silence about the episode suggests she was stung by her friend's accusations, even if she thought they stemmed from dementia. *Get that woman out of here … don't let her in …* As if Hill were a vampire who might return after dark, when it was Bates who'd refused to officially acknowledge her contribution to *The Passing of the Aborigines*. The episode sounds like a case of projection, with Daisy's fear about material being taken morphing into a fantasy about Ernestine stealing and taking the kudos for her manuscripts.

Bates had been making accusations about missing material as far back as the *Advertiser* office days, but she wasn't only paranoid about misplaced photos and manuscripts. Several months after their visit to Sunny Brae, Mrs Mathews wrote to the Hills that Bates's 'memory has got very bad, indeed and she accuses us of this that & the other. This is missing & thats [sic] missing, some of you must have taken it. She seems to have a feeling still that we keep her mail' – observations which, along with Kelsh's accounts of Bates's behaviour on the ward, support the theory that she was suffering from vascular dementia in her last decade.[73]

I found the timing of this story difficult to place – had Hill stayed on in the Streaky Bay area after she left Sunny Brae farm in August 1947, or had she brought Daisy in to the hospital after the Penong visit in mid-1948? – but in any case Bates continued to accuse Hill of stealing the manuscripts, even after Ernestine had mailed them to Preece. Although she wrote to Hill at the end of 1948, thanking her for returning the manuscripts, she was still obsessing about the fate of her ngar'galulla project – 'a booklet of the first thing and the only thing that was never gathered before – legends of these aborigines and these were the most fairy-like – don't you know – fariy [sic] -like and most lovely' – in the last recorded interview with her. She still blamed Hill for its disappearance, claiming she'd given it to her 'two Christmases ago', but although Hill had written back each Christmas, saying she'd returned them, they had 'never turned up … and what can you do? I wouldn't have done it to Ernestine myself. No, and it was the bulk of my manuscripts.'[74]

'Daisy May has turned up again,' Hill observed to Drake-Brockman in 1950. 'She'll be 90 [sic] on October 16, and wants me to have her Legends back for her.(!) Preece and the English publishers had them two years and can do nothing at all.'[75] In corresponding with friends, Hill did not appear to – or she was careful not to – take offence at Bates's contradictory and demanding behaviour; her comments about her difficult and confused friend are almost blithe, despite the grief Daisy had caused her. 'As you say, she was up-stage and difficult at times,' she wrote to Polkinghorne, 'and at times a little wearing – or contrary – pride and prejudice and all – but one learns in life to love people as they are and not as we think they ought to be, when we mightn't love them at all.'[76]

'Come back, dear Ernestine', Bates implored. But Hill did not return. If the tenor of their reported exchange at Streaky Bay Hospital is anything to go by, Daisy's paranoid recriminations are reason enough for Ernestine to have kept her distance. She may not have wanted to be reminded of the loss of her mother or her aunt, either, by watching the decline of another older woman she'd admired. Besides, she was worn out by her own wandering ethic: 'My own life was wearing and exacting, with endless writing in Sydney and Melbourne, seven thousand miles of travelling' throughout northern Australia'.[77]

Bates spent the last two years of her life derelict, although she roamed Adelaide's prim chequerboard of streets rather than the Nullarbor Plains. She left Raine's place in the hills and shifted between the Torrens Park residence of a nurse she'd befriended, a convalescent home in Semaphore, a granny flat in Brighton and a private hospital in Prospect. Preece's bookshop was her central port of call; she often ended up there 'with an assistant from another shop, or a policeman in tow'. The bookseller felt sorry for her: 'It would have been so much kinder had she passed out quietly during her last illness, than to have reached this stage when no one wants her.'[78] Daisy's connections to her 'mysterious son', as Preece called him, and her grandchildren were distant and nebulous. The year before her death, Arnold and his son Ronald surfaced in Adelaide, hovering perhaps in anticipation of her death and a potential inheritance. 'Both stayed a few days,' Preece told Murray, 'asked if she needed anything, did little and departed. They have not been here since, but presumably at the end will come into the picture again.'[79]

Preece played a de facto son role, trying to sort out Bates's finances to ensure she had enough to live on. He warned Murray against letting Bates know about any further royalties paid into her account because she would only spend them. Grey Murray took stock of the situation, and told Preece and Bartholomew that John Murray Publishing would pay her £12 a month. She was unlikely to live more than a year, so he didn't envisage paying more than £144, which is how much he anticipated OUP's next print run of 4000 copies of the *Passing* would earn. 'One can only hope that she will not live long,' he wrote, 'because it is really rather a pathetic winding up of what was, in its way, a distinguished and certainly a useful career.'[80]

Daisy told Preece she didn't have a will, as 'she had nothing to leave anyone' – she'd forgotten the one she'd made at Pyap – but she wrote a formal note 'instructing that in the event of her death all her manuscripts were to be handed to me to be dealt with as I felt fit' – a development that may have aggrieved Hill, if she knew about it. What Preece's motivations might have been in taking custody of Bates's manuscripts, as a bookseller who'd published material on Aboriginal themes, is another consideration altogether. 'When she speaks of the manuscripts returning to her possession,' he informed Grey Murray, 'I stall her by saying that she must get a room first where they will be safe – especially as she is "being robbed" – and until she can do that they are safer in my possession.' He even suggested the Scottish publisher visit Adelaide, 'talk to the lady while she is still with us and grab those manuscripts', although if Murray were to give Bates an advance of some kind to rework her ngar'galulla book, 'quite frankly it would be in the nature of a gift for, from what I have seen of the manuscripts in her possession, though they should be preserved, they are unpublishable in their present state and would require a great deal of editing with the necessary entailed expense' – a task that Hill had been doing pro bono.[81]

After Bates's death, Preece discovered the will that Murray had advised her to make at Pyap, which set out 'quite plainly her wish that her manuscripts should be published if possible, or disposed of by sale, but if sold must first be offered within the Commonwealth', stipulating that her trustees must consult first with her publishers. Preece told the Murrays that he had eight or nine folders of Bates's notes and one of her photographs in his possession and offered to sift through them for publishable material, warning that Elders, Bates's solicitors, 'know nothing about publishing, the value of manuscripts or how to handle them'.[82] Grey Murray agreed with this proposal, and Preece prepared a 'fairly comprehensive' report 'as an act of friendship', without requesting any remuneration. After 'plodding through' some 10 000 typed foolscap sheets of Bates's notes, Preece informed John Murray they had no commercial value: 'The upshot is as briefly as possible there is nothing in the whole box I can recommend to you.'[83] He sadly concluded that:

> in all this material there is no consecutive story or attempt to plan one. Except for her one book, 'The Passing of the Aborigines', Mrs. Bates never got beyond the making of notes or writing short articles, and she kept on making notes (and losing them) until almost the end of her life. When she came back from 'the bush' her life's work was finished. Her sight was failing and her health undermined; for several years she was ill, in one hospital or another. It was too late for her to write.[84]

He speculated that Bates's manuscripts might be of interest to researchers, although he knew Bates had been 'at variance with a number of scientists and most professional anthropologists' and thought it was unlikely that any of them would want to compile her notes in book form. Preece didn't recommend Hill, the person who'd assisted Bates in writing her 'one book', no doubt deterred by Daisy's accusations about that caravanning lady who'd stolen her notes and intended to use them in her future work.

As for the ngar'galulla manuscript – Ernestine reported rather snippily in *Kabbarli* that she'd heard it had languished in the back of Preece's bookshop after Bates's death. In the late 1960s, Elizabeth Salter retrieved some manuscripts from one of Daisy's tin trunks in the Barr-Smith Library's basement, which had been donated to Adelaide University, and Barbara Ker Wilson assembled a collection of children's stories from this material. *Tales Told to Kabbarli: Aboriginal Legends Collected by Daisy Bates* was published in 1972 by Angus & Robertson with illustrations by Harold Thomas, the Luritja man who designed the Aboriginal flag.[85]

Adelaide had been unexpectedly hot over Easter in 1951, and Bates took to her bed at Prospect Hospital. Before the heatwave descended, she had been lapping the hospital's 4-acre grounds every day, still warding off layers of adipose tissue and searching for her natives. On 17 April she asked the matron to kiss her goodnight, sank into sleep and did not wake.

Daisy had wanted to be buried on country, as it were, 'with her *wanna*, digging-stick, and *pitchi*, wooden scoop, as a Woman of the Dreaming in her own home ground at Yooldil-gabbi [Ooldea] or at Eucla, where she became the Keeper of the Totems in the Australian desert lands'.[86] Instead, she was interred at North Road

Cemetery in Adelaide: 'a lovely peaceful spot, green lawns & flowers, & nicely kept,' Beatrice Raine told Ernestine.[87] One hundred people attended, including Bates's grandson, Ronald Hamilton – Hill thought it 'strange, when they preserved such a long silence while she was living'.[88] His father, the mysterious Arnold, did not make an appearance. Daisy had wished 'that some of her "children" would be there': the true recipients of her attention and care. Strangely enough, 'the very morning of her passing', a 'very well educated' Aboriginal man came to the door of one of Bates's friends. The friend asked him to 'get some natives to go to the Cemetery', but only an Aboriginal woman with no connections to the people from Ooldea or to the south-west turned up.

Hill didn't attend the funeral. She had avoided Adelaide for the past few years, but in the days leading up to Bates's death, she telegraphed Raine frantically then wired her £2 for a wreath – behaviour infused with guilt and regret. Her brilliant, prickly, quixotic friend – 'the dearest, most difficult little one in the world' – had died nursed by strangers, without family or anyone close at her bedside, her affairs managed by a local bookseller.

Beatrice placed Ernestine's wreath at the graveside, encouraging her to visit if ever she were passing through Adelaide. Hill didn't take up the offer, although she was a great frequenter of cemeteries; instead, she revisited Daisy's grave in words and imagination. Raine had told her the ceremony for Bates was disappointing, believing that she 'should have had a military funeral, or state, with all honors'.[89] Ernestine gave Daisy such an affair in her memoir of Bates, *Kabbarli*: 'It was virtually a State funeral in Adelaide, attended by leading parliamentarians, university professors, officers of societies geographical, historian, ethnological, and of all benefit societies, education authorities, missionary circles.' In an even more elaborate embroidering of the truth, she imagined a 'quiet and solemn little crowd of Aboriginal Australians gathered at the graveside, saying good-bye in the name of their antique race to a lifelong friend'.[90] She was aware of the facts of the situation from Raine's letter, which remained in her possession until her own death. Ever the romantic idealist, Hill depicted the funeral she wanted for her friend, one befitting 'the most remarkable woman in Australia's first two centuries'.

10

The great-great-grandmother of that welfare mob

'I had begun in Broome as kallauer, a grandmother, but a spurious and a very young one, purely legendary.'[1]

In 1952, the year after Bates's death, Aṉangu were forced to leave Ooldea and the land surrounding the soak. The UAM mission was closed down and people were dispersed; soldiers shunted them onto trucks and trains, despatching them to country not their own in South and Western Australia, and the Northern Territory. Others walked with the missionaries over a couple of hundred kilometres of dirt tracks to the 'Big Camp', a new Lutheran mission that had been built at Yalata on the remains of an old sheep station near the Eyre Highway. Unknown to them, South Australia had brokered a deal with the British government to permit atomic testing 55 kilometres north of Ooldea at Maralinga. No-one had thought to consult with Aṉangu about this decision, one that would have devastating impacts on them and their traditional lands.

Walter MacDougall, a native patrol officer, was in charge of this operation, directing people away from Maralinga and Woomera Rocket Range. In an article titled 'The politics of space and mobility', anthropologist Maggie Brady describes how he controlled Aṉangu's movements in often physically and psychologically coercive ways. One technique he used was 'shoving them off': installing a checkpoint at the Tarcoola railhead and refusing travel without authorised passes, as well as closing ration depots at Ooldea and later at Coober Pedy for anyone heading north of Yalata. He reinforced this approach with the more insidious strategy of 'easing them off' by manipulating elements of traditional stories to scare people away from the testing zones. MacDougall played on the Spinifex people's beliefs that 'Waṉampi' – 'a dangerous water serpent or rainbow snake', a mythological being who 'travelled over and under the ground' creating land formations – inhabited the caves and blowholes that honeycomb the limestone underlying the Nullarbor to ward them away from the test sites. Brady reported in the late 1990s that 'waṉampi stories have now become enmeshed with the warnings, rumours and half-understood facts of contamination associated with the Maralinga tests'.[2]

The Spinifex people were never comfortable about being resettled at Yalata on another Aboriginal mob's country, with poor soil that local white farmers had rejected. They said the land was 'paṉa tjilpi'; that it made them feel old and they longed to return to their homelands.[3] For centuries they had been walking the expanse that is now Nullarbor Regional Reserve to wherever food and water were plentiful, visiting Ooldea Soak. Once the East–West Line was laid, they had quickly adapted the train into their lifestyle, travelling to Tarcoola in the east and Cundeelee in the west and beyond to attend ceremony. Even after they'd been officially resettled at Yalata, Aṉangu continued jumping the rattler to travel to other places for ceremonial purposes, despite the danger of contamination by what they referred to as 'poison' – radioactivity – so strong was their connection to country.

The light still pale on the saltbushes, I struck out on a back road behind Yalata the day after my meeting with the senior women at Fowlers Bay. I was heading north towards Ooldea with a carload of people from the community, my guide Russell Bryant, the community's chair and pastor, in the passenger seat beside me. He pointed out where Aṉangu had camped before 'walypala' came, near a rockhole or a soak – barely discernible creases in the landscape to my eye. We turned off the dirt road onto a stretch of bitumen where semi-trailers lumbered past, hauling explosives to and minerals from the nearby Iluka mine. Aṉangu were none too happy about mining in the area, Russell told me, although they couldn't do much about it because of previous agreements. They had been involved, however, in protests against the SA government's proposed nuclear waste dump on Maralinga lands and in consultations with BP about plans to drill in the Bight.

Veering off the bitumen onto another dirt road, we ground past salt lakes, the terrain becoming grittier and the corrugations sharper. Water tanks were dotted here and there, left by the army as an alternative to the soak: we stopped at one and filled our bottles with rainwater. About an hour into our journey, Russell motioned for me to pause, winding down his window. A red-orange mound shimmered in the heat haze above the plain's silvery-grey sweep in the distance.

'Ooldea,' he said.

I'd arrived at Yalata just before dusk the previous day, where I'd met Russell Bryant. In his mid-forties, dressed in black, wearing a cloth cap and accompanied by two little dogs, he had the same round face and bright, lively eyes as his mother Rita, but he looked sad. He'd been planning to take off now that sorry business for his wife was over, he said, but yes, he'd enjoy a bush trip to show me the remains of Bates's old campsite.

The community was undergoing redevelopment, and Russell

was camping on a not-so-vacant lot beside a house belonging to his family. Rita was living inside with her grandkids, while the middle generation of adults was in small tents on the lot – a way of dealing with cramped space and overcrowding within the house, and also the equivalent of having your own room and a morsel of privacy. Russell told me he preferred sleeping outside; it was too noisy and crowded inside the house. But he'd rather sleep under the stars in the bush, in any case.

Mainly men – brothers, uncles, nephews – and Russell's older sister Sharon were outside their tents, sitting around a campfire, heating meat and cans of food over its embers. I squatted alongside Russell, who explained to them in Pitjantjatjara why I was visiting. I pulled out a map of the Nullarbor that was jammed permanently in my back jeans pocket and unfolded it on the ground. Russell pointed out the remote WA community his grandmother was from and his grandfather's birthplace near another station on the Trans line, explaining his authority to speak for the area's history. His family had come from the desert with other Spinifex people, and lived up on the railway line and camped by the soak.

More explanations and translations of Pitjantjatjara words followed. My mind reeled with detail; usually I'd be hungry for this type of information but I was tired after belting along the Eyre after four hours' sleep. I made my apologies, saying I needed to find my accommodation; Yalata's manager had told me I could stay in one of the dongas for visitors in the old caravan park on the community's edge.

I drove back towards the highway, where I found a row of boxy demountables fringed by gum trees. The boarded-up shell of a roadhouse was nearby; Russell later told me it had been abandoned because it was full of asbestos. The area was slightly creepy in the way that semi-derelict accommodation often is in the outback, like a deserted amusement park.

I was happy to retreat inside my allotted donga; I like sleeping in a small, plain room. When Russell had said he'd rather sleep in a tent, I felt I understood something of what he meant. I'd found the capsule-like space of the campervan with its lack of distractions far more conducive to sleep than most upmarket motel rooms. But despite my fatigue, I struggled to still my racing mind. I sat on the donga's camp bed, eating a can of tuna and flipping through some academic articles about Daisy Bates at Ooldea I'd brought with me. Ever the girly swot, I invariably overprepare for any research-related activity, although it usually turns out to be a waste of time. I hadn't had anything to drink – like many Aboriginal communities, Yalata is dry – but I felt lightheaded, skimming over the familiar names of Pierre Bourdieu, Nick Couldry and other male luminaries quoted so earnestly in these papers and the intellectual circles I'd frequented in Melbourne, and stifled a laugh.

I was used to entering remote Aboriginal communities as a member of a team from a government or an academic institution, accompanied – shielded, even – by research paraphernalia: iPads loaded with surveys, PowerPoint displays explaining legislation, agreements and consent forms for community members to sign. Indeed, there's little about the research consultation process, with its time-consuming paperwork, hierarchical institutional rubberstamping, its laboured attempts at mutual comprehension and requirements for careful documentation, which is not stilted and contrived. Which is ironic, given that one of this process's antecedents is Bates's participant observation technique, which she believed was more responsive and empathetic to its subjects than the authoritarian practices of academic anthropologists like Radcliffe-Brown.

As an independent writer, I'd welcomed the opportunity to strike out on my own and, like Hill, follow the story in anything that came along. All the same, I had requested permission to visit

Yalata and Ooldea through the appropriate channels beforehand. Around the campfire, I'd explained to community members what I was doing and its implications, as you would in a research project. I used props like my notebook and recording devices (often my phone) as unobtrusively as possible. I knew our communication wouldn't be without barriers – that of language, at the most basic level, let alone of different cultural understandings and historical damage. But acting in my own capacity rather than as a government or a university researcher, I found it easier to sit back and let community members take control on the bush trip the next day.

Did this make me foolishly naïve, perhaps like the women whose stories I was tracing – like Bates, kicking idiosyncratically against the goads of recognised authority by taking off by herself to talk to Aboriginal people? Or like Eric Baume's caricature of Ernestine Hill as the crazy woman journalist chasing after 'wild Myall blacks', eating damper and drinking bad well water, 'deliriously happy, with adventure running through her veins like fire', eagerly clutching at the romantic fantasy of 'going native'? Certainly, I felt an affinity with Bates and Hill in following my own compass outside of official structures and without the conventional supports afforded by working with a team. Like them, I was pursuing a story about cultural origins, although I did not share their belief that Aboriginal people and their cultures were primitive and doomed to die out. I was travelling to Ooldea in a turn on Hill's quest, trying to unravel that 'surprise in the primeval scene, a question mark' – the influence of the Kabbarli mythology over settler women's relationship to Aboriginal people and country. Which was in essence reflected in the question I asked myself that night about the research orthodoxies I'd inherited: how was it that simple exchanges between both parties had become so vexed and complicated? Sitting on the camp bed, listening to the breath-like breeze rattling the dongas' walls, the dogs riffling through the rubbish outside, the ghostly remains of the asbestos-riddled roadhouse nearby, knowing that the people up the road had cycled through this area for years, so much of this legacy seemed like vanity, like chasing after the wind.

The next morning I left Yalata with Russell, Sharon and her husband Sean, and David, an old fella from Pipalyatjara with a rheumy cough who rarely spoke. We reached the railway crossing at Ooldea around noon and, as if on cue, the Transcontinental's successor, the *Indian Pacific*, hurtled past. I'd always imagined the Trans ploughing phallically through the landscape as a symbol of western contamination and corruption, but the train looked old and tatty, towing more freight containers than passenger carriages in its wake. Here, as elsewhere in remote Australia, it had been replaced as a symbol of connection and modernity by a Telstra tower, which loomed skeletally from the plain, its outline firming, as we drove towards the old siding.

Ooldea itself was stark and exposed, all gravel and flat blanched land scored by the rail track like a horizon's infinity line. The siding itself no longer existed; the desert winds had whittled away the platforms and fettlers' huts to the barest of bones, any fireworthy wood having been harvested long ago. A modest fragment of tools, utensils, bolts and hinges sluiced across the rusty earth. Even in Daisy's time, when the siding had a platform surrounded by a scatter of huts, where the Trans stopped and the Tea and Sugar train made regular set-downs with supplies, any outsider who washed up here must have felt desolate and marooned, especially with the sun blazing down on a 45 degree Celsius day.

Russell paced across the orange gravel towards the railway line, then halted. With a preacher's sense of performance, he laid his hand on top of a small white obelisk protruding from the sand like a molar tooth. I followed, recognising the silhouette of a familiar figure in a beekeeper's hat and an Aboriginal man with a sword and shield garlanding a bronze plaque with the inscription: '1859–1951 Mrs Daisy Bates C.B.E. Devoted her life here & elsewhere to the welfare of the Australian "Aborigines".'

'She was the great-great-grandmother of that welfare mob,' Russell said. 'I call this lady ...' He paused as though hunting for a derogatory enough term then broke off apologetically. 'I'm a little bit wild about that lady.'

'It's okay to feel wild.' I was worried he was scared of offending me. 'I don't mind what you say about Daisy Bates – good or bad. I want to hear what you think.'

'People were living in the sandhills all around Ooldea,' Russell continued. 'They were bush boys; they didn't speak English. Daisy Bates would go looking for half-caste kids in the sandhills. She would take the half-caste kids to Koonibba mission. She was doing the wrong thing, taking kids from them. The government, Daisy Bates, welfare – were bad people, taking kids from their families.'

He turned and headed for the vehicle, but I hung back for a few minutes, absorbing the scene and his words. I'd expected to hear Anangu express grief and anger about the damage Bates had inflicted on their people and culture, but some of Russell's commentary surprised me. I'd read about Daisy's contempt for half-castes and her practice of banishing Aboriginal women who associated with white men from her camps, although I couldn't remember anything in her correspondence from Ooldea and Wynbring to suggest she'd been actively involved in child removal. Admittedly, my research was in its early stages; I might yet come across records of her involvement elsewhere.

Bates's spat-out tooth of a monument merged into the eroded plains behind me as I walked back to the car. Did I really want to breathe life into the rusty remnants of European occupation washing around my feet in the orange dirt? I asked myself. I knew that some people believed Bates's activities were so reprehensible her story should not be retold. Feminist historian Ann Standish thought it might be better if she were allowed, witch-like, to sink like a stone. I certainly didn't intend to lionise Daisy as Ernestine had done, although I'd been surprised the day before by how fondly the women had remembered Bates. There was always another layer to her story to consider as it unfolded; it was this that drew me in, suggesting it was worth unravelling for what it revealed about the complexity of her relationship with Aboriginal people.

I rejoined the others in the SUV, climbing back into the driver's seat. Russell was keen to move on to Ooldea Soak for lunch and, despite what I'd been told about the difficulties in finding Bates's campsite, I didn't imagine the terrain would be too hard to negotiate. The road leading up to the railway crossing had been pocked with potholes and serrated with limestone shards, but it wasn't rougher than anything I'd encountered before in remote Australia. I was still wondering what all the fuss was about; whether the imperative to take several Aboriginal men with me was just an offshoot of the general hysteria about a white woman being alone in the Australian bush.

The vehicle I was driving was a Mitsubishi Pajero I'd hired from a local rental company specialising in four-wheel-drives. I'd wanted a Toyota – often the brand of choice in the desert, because of their robustness and high clearance – but I'd delayed booking a vehicle until a week before I left Perth, still unsure whether the trip would go ahead. When I rang the hire company, they only had two vehicles available: an old Toyota land cruiser and a newish Pajero. I'd asked for the Toyota, but they assured me I'd find the Pajero 'more comfortable'. I gave in, despite a nagging suspicion that a 'lady vehicle' was being foisted on me and I'd be better off on the kitchen-table-hard seats of an old LandCruiser. An alarm had been ringing in my brain ever since – 'See if you can swap the car' – although I'd blocked out the voice of intuition, or more likely of commonsense, with rationalisations about needing not to catastrophise. But I should have listened.

We crossed the rail tracks, turned onto a dirt road and began ploughing up a sandy incline. I've always found sand the toughest to negotiate – it's where I've had most mountain biking accidents – and feared we wouldn't make it.

'Faster! Harder!' Russell yelled.

The vehicle swerved, almost fishtailing – it would have been fun if I didn't have a cargo of four people and the undercarriage of a hire vehicle to worry about. After the Pajero had blustered and gasped over the hill's crest, I pulled up, handing the keys to Russell. He plunged the car down the slope, riding its undulations as if it were a big dipper.

I'd imagined the dunes at Ooldea to be like the flour-white hills at Fowlers Bay, except rolling for miles without a skerrick of vegetation like the siding's plains. In the photographs that Hill took of Bates's camp, the soak had looked bleak, strewn with harsh scrub and the occasional windswept bush. The images were also black-and-white, which added a dimension of sombreness. I wasn't prepared for how vivid the soak would be: a literal transition into technicolour. The dunes themselves were deep orange, netted with white pin daisies and purple, yellow and red bush flowers after the prolonged spring rains, a striking contrast to the grey flats of the treeless plain. While intellectually I understand Aboriginal people's connection to the land where they're born, its cycles and stories as a concept, I doubt I'll ever completely fathom the depth of that attachment. But on seeing Ooldea Soak with its sheltered beauty and its faithful spring of water, I caught a glimmer of why Anangu would have felt so bereft at being forced to leave this country they had cherished for so long for the alien pana tjilpi of Yalata's Big Camp.

The dunes dipped down into a saucer-like plateau where we parked. Russell led me to an orange hillock staked with a stark sun-blackened mast of a tree, denuded of leaves, like a Viking galleon's burial barrow. The corrugated curve of a water tank, now lying flat on its side, was visible near its base. I asked whether it had been there in Bates's time, wondering if it was the one she'd stored her library inside, but they told me the missionaries had used it for baptisms. A tangle of half-dead bushes and striplings were twisted into a windbreak nearby – similar but too recent to have been a vestige of the mulga-stick fence enclosing Bates's camp and barred with a prickle-bush at night.[4]

When Bates's first biographer, Elizabeth Salter, visited the campsite in the late 1960s, she observed it was 'overgrown now, but marked by the outline of what was once her windbreak'. Her two Aboriginal guides handed her an iron peg and a corroded pannikin that had belonged to Bates. In 1988 an archaeological survey team found that little was visible of Bates's camp except for the tops of some petrol tins she used to mark its border and the base of three thin posts, which probably marked the base of her observatory platform. They thought the mound marked a remnant of the original windbreak. SA historian Tom Gara, one of the survey's co-writers, told me that when he'd visited Ooldea a decade ago, the dunes had blown across Bates's campsite and there'd been little to see; he doubted they'd eroded since then. My interest was more in Ooldea as a cultural and historical place, but part of me wanted to drop to my knees with a biographer's avidity for clues from the past and fossick for relics in the sand.

My guide seemed uncomfortable about spending too much time at the campsite and much keener to show me the remains of the old UAM mission, in part, I thought, because of his church affiliations but also because of what Bates represented. There was definitely more bric-a-brac from the mission to see: an old feed trough, iron supports from old dwellings, a rusted BP petrol can, an old washer turned into a burner with holes punctured round the base. Peppercorn trees lined a seam in the sandhills; the missionaries planted them as a windbreak and a source of shade. Russell showed me a small wooden frame in the seam where mission staff used to drop a bucket to get water from the soak.

'Anangu were living in the sandhills – there were people all around,' he said. 'They came to get water, a feed, a hair cut, clothes, church from the missionaries. They give them flour, tea-leaf – not tea bag – give them everything. Plenty with food, with clothes, were going to school at the mission.'

Bates had also fed people at Ooldea, although her means were limited and she relied on good-will donations from southern friends. Her camp was an easy walk from the mission buildings – maybe 200 metres. Initially she kept her distance from the missionaries but Russell suggested that her Aboriginal protector, whom he identified as 'Mr Windlass's father's father', had persuaded her to camp closer to the mission for her own safety. When I'd broached the issue of Bates's possible paramour at Ooldea around the campfire the night before, Russell and the others had insisted, like the senior women, that he 'just a friend, not a boyfriend, the first Aboriginal man that Daisy Bates met who came in from the bush. He had been learning English with Daisy Bates. Maybe he was an interpreter, talking to Daisy Bates.'

'Aboriginal people knew this place before the missionaries and the bomb test at Maralinga,' Russell continued. 'Missionaries saw people walking around naked, and built a camp. They were doing good for my people, bringing them out from the bush to water. Plenty school, learning bush ways. Missionaries buy them clothes, just wanted to look after them.

'Daisy Bates – she was like a spy, spying for welfare about those half-caste children. That's why she gave them tea-leaves and blankets. She put about a lot of lie stories because she was looking for half-castes. She would put them on the train and send them away to Riverland and Adelaide.

'Later, when some came back to Yalata, they found their family were dead. They tried to learn language but they had no culture. They were still in sorrow, still grieving, asking why people took them from their family. They only had one or two family members left – only two, three or four are left. They were slowly learning but grieving in sorrow. But they couldn't make it and they died.

'That lady who was here was hateful to our people.'

Given the turn the story had taken, I asked Russell whether he'd heard what Daisy Bates had written about Aboriginal cannibalism.

Russell looked stormy. He leaned closer, dropping his voice. 'Daisy Bates started putting about stories about people eating their children. Anangu don't eat their children; they eat kangaroo, bush meat.'

I suggested that Bates's obsession with cannibalism had been a smokescreen for what was happening at the siding – mixed-descent children being born after the railway workers had forced themselves on Anangu women or pressed them for sexual favours – and he said the women had had sex with fettlers because they were hungry and wanted a free feed.

'When I spoke to those ladies at Fowlers Bay yesterday,' I said, 'they looked as if they didn't know what I was talking about when I mentioned those cannibal stories. Do people still talk about those stories?'

When the women hadn't engaged with that line of questioning, I'd been worried that I'd committed some fundamental breach by raising the subject at all.

'We don't tell those stories because children will get depressed

The great-great-grandmother of that welfare mob

and leave the community,' Russell said. 'This place is making me sad now, thinking about the things that have happened here.'

Saying he wanted to 'go walkabout for a bit', he peeled off, wandering across the dunes. Grief hung around him, and I imagined he needed time apart to recharge.

I returned to the vehicle to find the others had eaten most of the sandwiches I'd bought that morning from the community store. The sun was still high, although it lacked the bite of midday heat; the consensus was that we should start driving back. Not game to take on the dunes again, I handed Russell the car keys when he reappeared. It was definitely tougher grinding back up the sides of the soak's bowl. The Pajero stalled twice, wheels spinning redundantly in the sand. Everyone clambered out. Sean and Russell lay on their fronts in the baking orange dirt, digging out the wheels. The hire company had promised me tools so I looked in the boot for a shovel but there wasn't one, just a rather useless hazard flag, a jack and a crowbar. I hunted around in the shrubs on the side of the dune and found a mallee stick bent like an elbow that I used as a trowel.

Sean climbed into the cab. A well-built man in his fifties with boofy grey hair shaved up the sides and a black shirt with ripped-off sleeves exposing clearly defined biceps, he'd told me earlier that he was 'the camel man', that he used to drive camels and horses across the dunes. Russell and I braced ourselves against the back of the vehicle and pushed. The Pajero sputtered forward another 50 metres before the wheels began spinning again. The vehicle's undercarriage and its wheels were half-buried in orange sand. I was now in no doubt why I'd been told to take as many Aboriginal men with me as possible to Ooldea.

The men took stock of the situation, and I heard the word 'lady' rising above the staccato of Pitjantjatjara. Too right, the rental company had given me a lady vehicle lacking in mechanical oomph, like a pink power drill set or a woman's bike with a fat-bottomed seat, floral basket and streamers dangling from the handles. Yet despite my unsuitable vehicle I had faith, maybe from watching too many episodes of *Bush Mechanics*, that they could work out how to get us out of there.

They directed me to tear switches from bushes and lay them on the tracks on the dune. Most of the branches I ripped off seemed pretty puny; the camel man produced small trees. The idea was that the surface would be firmer to drive over: 'in the old days, people put down railway sleepers for the Land Rovers.' If we had an air pump, we could have let down the tyres to cross the sand, but my toy lady car did not contain this useful tool.

'Next time, when you come, bring that troop car,' they said to me, referring to the troop carriers often used as people movers in remote communities. 'Next time, bring that Toyota!'

The camel man and I did most of the hard yards, sliding about in the dirt on our fronts, cupping our hands to scoop out sand from around the wheels. Russell disappeared from time to time, either to go 'a bit walkabout' again or to have a smoke. Sharon and the old fella sat in whatever shade they could find. Occasionally she would call out, 'You right, kungka?', then start singing, 'Oh what a feeling! Toyota.'

Finally, when we'd hollowed out the sand round the wheels and laid down two tracks of branches leading up to the dune's crown, Russell took the driver's seat. Sean and I removed the spare tyre to reduce the vehicle's weight, and positioned ourselves behind the back of the cab for the initial push.

Russell ploughed over the switches and saplings, then catapulted up the hill, the vehicle ricocheting over the crest as if it were in a pinball machine. The camel man and I rolled the spare tyre up to the SUV, then hoisted it into the boot while the others climbed into the car.

The great-great-grandmother of that welfare mob

'Daisy Bates, see you Daisy Bates!' Sharon sang as we drove down towards the railway line. 'That Daisy Bates was always a troublemaker!'

It was getting late. My hands were orange-red on the wheel in the early evening light. Over a quarter of a tank of fuel was left, enough to get everyone back to the community before dark, although Russell was keener for me to drive to the nearest bowser at Nundroo roadhouse, about 30 kilometres from Yalata. When we turned into the servo, the penny dropped. It was seven-thirty; they wanted to stop for dinner.

Later, as we devoured fish and chips inside the vehicle, Russell and I talked about why Daisy Bates told the 'liar stories' she did about Aboriginal people. He thought Bates knew the truth but had begun to believe what was in her head.

'Yes, I've wondered whether she started to believe her own lies, too,' I said, remembering the repetitive tropes of her letters, where she seems to be trying to persuade herself as well as her reader. 'I don't want to let her off the hook, but I've thought that perhaps she was demented. I'm not quite sure how to say that in your language, but when she came to Ooldea she was getting old, she was going in the head, she was kata kura …' I reached for the only Pitjantjatjara word for poor mental health I knew.

'Ah yes, kata kura,' Russell said. 'Yes, she was kata kura.'

I told him that Bates had had a loose relationship with the truth even when she was young: about how she pretended she only had one husband but probably had another two at the same time. Russell and the others hadn't heard these stories, although they seemed pretty nonplussed about the husbands.

'Did she have any children?' Russell asked.

'Yes, she had a son, Arnold, to Jack Bates,' I said. 'Daisy went to England and left Arnold in Australia when he was a little boy, then came back later. She was never that close to him. When she was old and dying, she tried to get her friend Ernestine to bring him to visit her, but he wouldn't come.'

'You see, God punished her because she did the wrong thing,' Russell said, pounding his fist on the dashboard. 'That Daisy Bates was a naughty girl. She lied about Anangu. They called her grandmother, Kabbarli, but if I see one of Daisy Bates's great-great-grandchildren, I'm going to punch her!'

'Some white people say the same thing about Daisy Bates as Anangu do – that she was a liar,' I said, 'but I came here because I wanted to hear what Anangu have to say about her now.'

'We want the story that Daisy Bates was a liar to go out into the world,' Russell said. 'My people have two big stories – Maralinga and Daisy Bates – that people want to hear.

'But we have a lot of stories. People should start thinking about Yalata people instead of Daisy Bates, because they are still Ooldea people. If they want a story, they can get a good story from us.'

The long shadows these 'two big stories' cast continue to affect Anangu people – quite directly, in the case of Maralinga. The Maralinga test area extended across 3300 square kilometres, and the atomic testing has had long-term effects on Anangu's health and capacity to live sustainably on country. Russell Bryant told me that people remained undetected in the bush as far west as Warburton during the test period, many later suffering illnesses and physical deformities from the bombs' fallout. Some men from Yalata were exposed needlessly to radioactive contamination by being engaged to work in clean-up operations at Maralinga after the bomb tests, without shoes or protective clothing, unlike the white staff. Many developed skin irritations and breathing problems; a considerable number died of cancer in their forties and even younger. 'All

The great-great-grandmother of that welfare mob

Anangu mens who worked at Maralinga finished now,' community leader Yvonne Edwards told author Christobel Mattingley. 'Used to have a lot of old people when we first came from Ooldea. But only a few now ... All our people end up in cemetery because of that bomb.'[5]

Bates's impact on Anangu and other Aboriginal people is less intangible, although no less insidious than the radioactive black mist that hung over the lands. Russell indicated that the 'liar stories' she spread about cannibalism still had the power to affect Anangu psychologically, to the extent that they protected their young people from hearing them. The morning after the trip to Ooldea, Rita Bryant took me aside, saying there'd been talk in the camp the previous evening about some of the questions I'd asked about Daisy Bates. She told me about several mixed-descent children who'd been sent away to Riverland on the train. When they came back to Yalata, they didn't know anyone and they couldn't find their mothers. She wanted me to hear this story so that I would understand that not all of the community members' memories of Daisy Bates were good ones.

I'd been surprised when Russell had told me that Bates had been spying for the welfare authorities, chasing children and putting them on the train to be taken into care in Adelaide and the South Australian Riverland. I knew that she had shunned mixed-descent children, banishing them and their parents from her Nullarbor camps, but I found it hard to believe she would collaborate with state officials and the police, given her antipathy towards them. Privately, I wondered whether Annie Lock, or missionaries such as Harry and Marion Green, who ran the UAM Mission at Ooldea from 1936 until it was forced to close in 1952, might have been involved in child removal. When I asked Russell whether he'd heard of Annie Lock, he shook his head; later when I showed the older women in the community a picture of Lock, none of them knew who she was, although they identified the A*n*angu children with her in the photograph. Given the eldest of the senior women had been born in 1937, after Lock had left Ooldea in 1936, this wasn't surprising. They did, however, remember the Greens' time supervising the mission; Mr Green had given Rita her English name. When I asked the women for the birth years of the children they suggested Bates had sent into care, they gave me dates from 1950 onwards, which meant they were too young to have been removed by her, as she was in Adelaide by that time and died in 1951. Unless there were other children from earlier generations who'd been taken from Ooldea in the 1920s and early 1930s, and from Wynbring during the 1940s, I suspected that the missionaries rather than Bates were strongly implicated in the removal of children from camps along the East–West Line.

Back in Melbourne, I searched for historical traces of both Bates's and the missionaries' participation in child removal at Ooldea and the surrounding area. One story I found was that of Lorna Graham, the daughter of a Pitjantjatjara/Yankunytjatjara woman and a European railway labourer who'd lived near the soak during the early 1930s. She recalls her mother saying how Bates would come round and say, when she saw her, 'Oh! watjilyitja', meaning 'half-caste'. She and the other kids were 'too frightened of Daisy Bates – all in white – shoes, socks white, dress white, umbrella white with netting on the top'. They hid from her in the bushes: '"Daisy Bates" we singing out all the time – "Daisy Bates". Teasing, she was looking around everywhere – can't find us – we're under the trees hiding. Gets the police and all.' Graham describes the policeman giving them rations and telling them to stay at Ooldea, because a mission was to be built there. When she got 'bigger and bigger, Miss Lock take me to Quorn. (To Colebrook Children's Home.)' Daisy, she comments, 'Wouldn't stay then at Ooldea – old people follow Bates again to Wynbring.'[6]

The great-great-grandmother of that welfare mob

On 1 June 1936 in a letter about UAM business, Annie Lock mentions getting a pass from the Department of the Interior for Lorna, 'a quarter caste girl of ten years' who was 'always afraid of bush life, and always clung to me', to take her to Port Augusta Hospital to treat an ear and nose infection.[7] Afterwards, Lock took her to Colebrook Home, where Lorna stayed for some years, returning to Ooldea when Bates was at Wynbring. Lock was affiliated with Colebrook Children's Home near Quorn, where Aranda, Arabana, Antakarinja and Pitjantjatjara children from central Australia were sent from 1927 to 1944. She established the first UAM home in an iron shed at Oodnadatta in 1924; a few years later, Matron Ruby Hyde moved its residents to Colebrook to take them away from 'harmful' influences within their immediate environment so it would be easier for them to assimilate into white society. While Lorna's story describes how Bates chased mixed-descent children away from her camp, it was Lock who facilitated Lorna's relocation to an institution.

There is some evidence that Bates took an interest in potential government intervention into mixed-descent children's lives before she camped at Ooldea. In July 1914 she appeared before the SA government's Royal Commission on the Aborigines, two years after her appointment as honorary protector on the Bight. Responding to a question about the presence of mixed-descent children in the Eucla district where she'd been camping, Bates stated:

> There are two children that I now want to get away from their mother, because she is rather a drunken woman; but the Western Australian Government sent a letter saying that it hesitated about taking away children from their mother. In the meantime I am afraid of what will happen to the little ones while I am away.[8]

In *Queen of Deception*, biographer Brian Lomas cites several examples of how Bates drew the chief protector's attention to mixed-descent children, in one instance assisting the police directly in a child's removal. She made these recommendations in passing as part of her remit as a travelling protector in Western Australia, a position she wanted the government to validate with paid recognition.[9] By the time she was at Ooldea, her relationship with the SA authorities was frequently antagonistic, and they never seriously entertained her petitions to become a paid protector; at Wynbring, she appears to have had a hostile relationship with the police, who purged Aboriginal people from her camp. However, a policeman who'd known Daisy at Wynbring told scriptwriter Eleanor Witcombe when she visited Yalata during the 1980s that Bates 'used to send him down girls sometimes': 'Now what girls these were – were they detribalised girls who needed jobs or homes or whether they were half-castes she was sending down to be sent to somewhere, I don't know. But she kept in contact with the police about things like this.'[10]

This rather sinister statement recalls Lock's and Bennett's concerns about the police being inappropriate as protectors of Aboriginal people, especially young women, as well as suggesting what Bates euphemistically termed sending people 'to Coventry' might have entailed. If the policeman's story is true, Bates's role in bringing young women to his attention also lends support to the idea that she was 'spying' for the police, or at least particular police with whom she was on friendly terms.

The 'concern' that Bates expressed about the fate of mixed-race children she encountered while travelling as a protector in Western Australia, the 'half-castes' she chased from her camps on the East–West Line and the young women who'd had sex with white men in exchange for food reflected her preoccupation, and that of her era, with racial purity. She exercised this concern in relation to miscegenation in order to elevate her status, to set herself apart from the Aboriginal women and children who visited her camps as a civilising influence, whitewashing aspects of her past that did not conform with the moral standards of the day. This power dynamic was always present in her activities. While Bates showed some compassion in distributing food and clothing from her own modest means to Anangu when their access to resources were diminished through the building of the East–West line, in doing so she set herself up as a saviour figure, modelling an early form of welfare dependency and white paternalism towards Aboriginal people. The evidence that Bates was a prime mover in widespread institutional child removal while she was at Ooldea and Wynbring is patchy and inconclusive; if she tipped off authorities about the presence of mixed-descent children near her camps, she appears to have done so informally. However, it is the damaging beliefs she spread through her journalism about the threat miscegenation posed to racial purity, and notions about Aboriginal women killing their children, that contributed significantly to a public ethos sanctioning Aboriginal child removal.

Why Bates, rather than others such as Annie Lock, Ruby Hyde and the Greens, is remembered in relation to the stolen generations reflects how she, in setting herself up as a white kabbarli figure, became a cipher for white women's welfare activities in the Ooldea area and beyond. In a children's book published in 2000, *Down the Hole, Up the Tree, Across the Sandhill: Running from the State and Daisy Bates*, central Australian women Edna Tantjingu Williams and Eileen Wani Wingfield recall how Anangu parents would warn their children not to jump the train near Ooldea for fear of being caught by 'that whitefella ... old Daisy Bates': 'Wala, walariwa! Oh tjitji apakatja tjuta – wala! Walariwa!' – 'Run away, run right away, you fair kids and keep running! That kungka is getting off the train there!' The concern was that 'if they catch us fair kids, they put us in a home then – in Ooldea' – the UAM mission – although who 'they' refers to – Bates, the missionaries or someone else – isn't clear in this sentence.[11] The book also describes how the old people used to hide children down rabbit holes and tunnels near Coober Pedy, although Bates never visited or lived in that area.[12] These stories, along with the book's title, indicate that Bates had become incorporated into local lore as a sinister, witch-like figure, a mythology that may have been mapped over those of the missionaries and others involved in state-sanctioned child removal as 'Daidj Bate mamu', the playground bogeywoman taunt that Isobel White heard while working at Yalata. Tom Gara drew similar conclusions after working with Aṉangu at Yalata and Oak Valley: 'So it seems that Daisy Bates has just become a general ogre to the people almost, or what she represents, when it wasn't really her who was doing it ... Daisy has come to symbolise white women in general possibly, or something like that.'[13]

How much influence Bates's legacy has had over Aboriginal people's lives is difficult to gauge. Her conflicted relationship with the people whom she claimed to serve is reflected in the differing opinions that Aṉangu still express about her. As far as Bates was concerned, Aboriginal people were her true 'children': in her will, she directed her estate to 'the relief of poverty and distress and the improvement of the conditions of life in such manner as my trustee may think fit among the Australian aborigines residing in or resorting to the district of Ooldea and its vicinity in the State of Western Australia'.[14] The fortunes of those who camped with Bates at Ooldea Soak present a microcosm of the effects of her legacy, and of other successive regimes of mission and government policy, over generations of Aboriginal people in her breakwind's vicinity and elsewhere across the country.

The great-great-grandmother of that welfare mob

The symbolic role that Bates manufactured as 'great-great-grandmother of that welfare mob' legitimated certain imperialist public policy approaches and popular perceptions of Aboriginal people in the mid-20th century. Communications academic Lisa Waller argues persuasively that in casting Bates as the 'voice of reason' during the 1930s and 1940, the news media masked their role in promoting these policies:

> Bates was, first and foremost, a journalist and a news media celebrity; but ... her highly influential book and legend have not always been recognised as news media products, resulting in her 'singular influence' often being mistaken for individual influence. This provides a smoke screen for the news media's power and responsibility for shaping public understanding and the policy environment.[15]

Why Bates's outlook and opinions about Aboriginal people should have been consecrated by the media of her day – through the efforts of Hill and Dumas at the *Advertiser*, then later Curtis Brown and John Murray in publishing *The Passing of the Aborigines* – lies in the fact that she gave messages that policymakers and the general public wanted to hear: that Aboriginal people were passing, that their culture was brutal and primitive, in order to justify white colonial possession of their land. For all the male anthropologists' chagrin at the public stature Daisy was given, her gender was essential to her being consecrated as the 'voice of reason' during this period. This doesn't relate to her historical primacy as the 'first in her field' as a woman anthropologist; other female contemporaries, such as Mary Bennett, may have been too challenging in what they had to say about humanitarian abuses on the frontier to have been allowed to assume this mantle as a public figure. Daisy herself alluded to what she saw as her singular suitability to this role as a white saviour and purifying force while prevailing on Hurst to lobby the Commonwealth government to give her £1000 a year 'to stop the halfcaste menace': 'No use sending Prof. Spencer – the subject wants a woman – wants me in fact. I'm the only woman that can deal with it on mission institution [sic] and elsewhere and it's worth 10,000 a year to the Commonwealth.'[16] Against the backdrop of reports about European men's violence towards Aboriginal people and coercive relations with women in the Australian interior, it was highly palatable for the white urban mainstream to believe a white kabbarli was 'smoothing the pillow' of a race assumed to be dying out.

Bates's story became influential because it was associated with a seemingly benevolent white female figure – in Hill's flamboyant words, a potential Australian icon, a 'Joan of Arc with visions and voices, or a Boadicea holding besieged tribal realms, or a Gertrude Bell of imperialist politics and policies, or a stained-glass missionary Mary Kingsley'.[17] It was of course Daisy's friend, Ernestine Hill, who had kickstarted the media's mythologisation of Bates by identifying her life and character as a sensational scoop for an article then for a newspaper serial and a book, and as such must bear some of the blame for the promotion of Bates's distorted views about Aboriginal people and culture.

Ernestine Hill continued to memorialise Bates after her death. Although she had missed Daisy's funeral in Adelaide, she later attended a brief remembrance ceremony for her friend at Ooldea. That 'incorrigible wanderer' was riding the Trans from Perth after collecting material in Western Australia in November 1954 when a railway official told her the governor-general, Paul Hasluck, had unveiled a memorial to Bates earlier that day at Ooldea.[18] Nearing the siding, Ernestine insisted on alighting as she had first done two decades before. There she encountered the remnants of a party of 100-odd dignitaries who'd attended the ceremony earlier that day, including Professor Cleland, to whom Bates had sent boxes of bones and artefacts: 'they wouldn't have a bar of Daisy once, but they think the world of her now,' Hill observed caustically.[19] She crossed the tracks to see the cairn 'to the memory of her terrible years alone' in what she later described as a romantic atmosphere in an article fittingly subtitled 'Woman into stone'. 'There in the desert moonlight I looked upon the memorial in the leafy shadow of a small tree, so prim, so trim, so erect it might have been the little lady herself waiting to welcome me, for we first met under that tree.'[20] The monumentalisation of Bates that Hill began in her 'Woman of Ooldea' article twenty-two years earlier had culminated literally in the erection of a physical memorial, an event she and Lloyd Dumas foresaw in their original discussion about bringing Bates to the *Advertiser*. Ernestine continued to mythologise Daisy, intent on her friend being 'cast in immortality' despite the awkward dynamics and accusations of theft that had characterised their relationship. Daisy had always been easier to idealise from afar; death conveniently put her at a permanent distance, and over the next two decades Hill would seek to gain greater ownership over Bates's story than she had been able to secure while her friend was alive.

V | DREAMING

11

A surrealist's madness

*'I must try to get ahead with the real purpose, the work …
The Old Australia is fading away out there, and my little job
is to help to keep it … when you hear I am off with a swag,
be sure I am happy.'*[1]

After returning to Melbourne from the Nullarbor, I began conspiring to buy my own campervan, having been impressed by van life's convenience and opportunities. Travel has always been one of my greatest research expenses and having a mobile room of one's own would help defray accommodation and meal costs – or so I justified the purchase to myself. Several months later I sold my old runabout, replacing it with an affordable mid-1990s Toyota HiAce commuter van I found on Gumtree that was kitted out to suit my purposes. Its previous owner had been a woman in her early thirties who'd driven up and down the east coast to do sound and lighting for events. My bid wasn't the highest – a couple planning to tour the country outbid me – but she accepted my offer because she wanted the van to go to another solo woman in the arts.

Once I had my own campervan, women – usually lone travellers or single mothers – began approaching me at service stations and in car parks, enthusing about their vans or their plans to purchase one, wanting to see the fit-out inside mine. Why I hadn't encountered them on the Nullarbor I put down to having travelled a well-patronised tourist route in a clearly marked hire vehicle, speculating that having my own idiosyncratic, slightly the worse for wear van marked me as a genuine, more approachable fellow traveller. I also discovered a Facebook group with over 5000 female members dedicated to solo caravanning, camping and travelling. Vanning it alone as a woman wasn't unusual, as I'd thought. Instead, a quiet legion of solo women travellers was weaving across the country's highways and through its back roads. Safety concerns were an inevitable topic of online discussion among fellow solo female van-lifers: old-timers urged newcomers to project confidence at campsites and to remember that most violence against women occurred at home and from people they already knew. How to support yourself with housesitting and itinerant work along the way was another frequent topic of conversation; many of the group members were over forty-five but, rather than being well-heeled retirees, they'd sold up and purchased a van because it was cheaper than paying off a mortgage. I wasn't surprised, considering increasing reports that women fifty-five years and over are the fastest-growing group of homeless people in Australia – a reflection of facing challenges such as buying a house after decades spent in the gig economy or out of the workforce supporting a family, and a general bias against older workers.

I'd seen signs of an older underclass on my journey through the south-west, some docked in humbler recreational vehicles in country town caravan parks. I woke one morning in Kalgoorlie at a memorial park where you could free camp to see a bus opposite my van with a sign up for business in its back window. I watched as a couple, maybe in their sixties, wearing old football jerseys and trackie daks, scrambled out to start their morning rituals, and speculated whether they'd been small business owners who'd lost out in the recession or older workers who hadn't been re-employed after taking redundancy packages. In *Nomadland*, American journalist Jessica Bruder documents the burgeoning of an older group of people, out of work with no longer recognised skills, living out of 'workampers' across the United States, supporting themselves with seasonal and casual work, following the 2008 worldwide recession. They are members of a new cohort emerging within the contemporary precariat, a social underclass characterised by chronic insecurity and instability. Economist Guy Standing distinguishes this group from the 'lumpen-precariat consisting of sad people lingering in the streets, dying miserably' who don't participate in formal economic activity, although 'their labour is insecure and unstable … associated with casualization, informalisation, agency labour, part-time labour, phoney self-employment and the new mass phenomenon of crowd-labour'.[2] Creative practitioners form another subset of the precariat. Despite often being highly skilled and educated, they generally experience a lack of appropriate remuneration in exchange for their labour and survive on cobbling together irregular sources of income. The precariat is also a 'dangerous' new class because it rejects 'old mainstream political traditions, rejecting labourism as much as neoliberalism', although these traditions equally marginalise workers such as older people, those with no longer relevant skills and those in the arts.

After I purchased a campervan, I realised how many women, at a similar age to Ernestine Hill and me, had gravitated towards using a van-like vehicle to support their writing practices – Sian Prior, Kim Mahood, Mary Anne Butler, Claire G. Coleman among them. In *Vagabondage*, poet Beth Spencer relates how she bought a hi-top camper for herself when she couldn't afford a flat in Melbourne. After being diagnosed with multiple sclerosis, the late Gillian Mears retrofitted an ex-ambulance van, which she named 'Ant and Bee' after the children's series, as a portable home and writing studio. Aboriginal writer Ali Cobby Eckermann was living in a caravan when she learned she'd won a major US literary prize. Janet Frame stayed in a caravan in her sister's backyard when she returned from Europe to New Zealand. But the ultimate spectre of where this lifestyle can lead is Eve Langley, the author of *The Pea Pickers,* a 1942 book about two sisters who cross-dress to pick fruit in Gippsland, which Hill declared was the great Australian novel. Langley lived her last years in a shack in the Blue Mountains bush, where her body was found several weeks after her death.

For Ernestine Hill, the caravan represented a vehicle of autonomy and escape from 'the complication of life from the multiplication of life in the big cities of Australia' in a further evolution of her hobohemian protest against the encroaching urbanisation of regional areas. It accommodated her twin desires for spontaneous wandering and writing about the country, the freelance lifestyle she preferred. In this respect she is a forerunner of the bohemian precariat rather than the roaming retirees. The ABS currently defines 'grey nomads' as 'reporting "no usual address", where all people were aged 55 years or over, were not in the labour force and were staying in a caravan, cabin or houseboat on Census Night'.[3] Hill was in her late forties when she purchased her caravan – close but not quite close enough age-wise to this definition (not to mention Bob, her travelling companion, then in his early twenties). She was still working as a professional writer, surviving on dribs and drabs of royalties and advances for proposed books, and payment for freelance articles published in magazines like *Walkabout.*

But after spending a couple of years on the road in the caravan, the line between hobo and bohemian, between the wilful wanderer and the tramp, began to wear thin for Ernestine. 'You may think the raggle-taggle gypsy life is carefree and joyous – tra-la – it is just about double the work from morning to night', she wrote to the Mackanesses in 1948 after 'zig-zagging all over the south west'.[4] Wandering had become 'a dreadful addiction, away beyond the railway lines with petrol at 5/- a gallon, squandering all the writing months on buying more miles, those blank and dusty miles'.[5] At Coolgardie, 'one of the old journalists marooned before the shores of time' said to her – '"Do you mind if I tell you what's the matter with you?" – and when I said no, I didn't mind, he said "You can't stop."'[6] Her weary compulsiveness spread to scooping out the relentless dust seeping into the caravan; so much so that she sold it at the end of 1948, 'bidding good-bye to the gypsy trails of grinding along through the dust storms and house-keeping on the way. There has been too much house-keeping and I cannot write.'[7] Retyping manuscripts became part of Ernestine's repertoire of obsessive, procrastinatory behaviours: 'through dust-storms and bog and flood on the big trail of Australia, about nine times it has been typed',[8] she wrote of *The Territory*, the last of Hill's travelogues and her penultimate book. Indeed, it was the only one of the many works she began over the next two decades that she would publish before her death.

'What a story, this north! Like a surrealist's madness,' Hill enthused of *The Territory, her tribute to a place epitomising a former way of life in northern Australia*. A rambling, epic historiography, complete with illustrations by Elizabeth Durack, it is her most substantial and comprehensive work. Hill frames *The Territory* as an investigation of why this last frontier bastion – this 'problem child of empire, land of an ever-shadowed past and an ever-shining future, of eternal promise that never comes true' – did not deliver on the riches imagined for northern expansion.[9] But, as in the *Loneliness*, she seeks to upend the national bias towards citified southern identity, and the book's appeal lies in her wholehearted embrace of the complex and quixotic nature of Territorian existence, the heroism and humour of those who live there.

The Territory received positive and enthusiastic national and international reviews when it was released in late 1951. Much of the critical commentary reflected the balance Hill aims to strike in this book between stories that celebrate the joys and idiosyncrasies of life in this rogue territory and those relating the more challenging aspects of its history. The *Times Literary Supplement* (TLS) pronounced *The Territory* 'a treasure house of the most beautiful lies – gay and macabre, tender and boisterous, fantastic and tragic', its reviewer displaying a touristic fascination with its description of macabre episodes from the formation of Australia's 'wild west'. Ken McConagher of the *Age*'s literary pages declared the book to be 'authentic and true' after establishing his credentials as a reviewer 'who knows the Territory from a saddle', although he thought it sometimes failed to convey 'characters adequately or ... the heat and eerie stillness of the north'. In contrast to the *TLS* reviewer, he was tellingly subdued in his acknowledgement of the 'many ghastly stories' Hill recounts from the Territory's past. Closer to home, Katharine Susannah Prichard deemed *The Territory* 'a splendid piece of work ... A well-written, & straight hard-hitting story'.[10]

Prichard may have been instrumental in encouraging Hill to give fuller, more even-handed and less idealised treatment of northern life than she had done in *The Great Australian Loneliness*. According to Bob Hill, Prichard 'tried to influence [the] tone of the Territory' during her visit to the Hills's caravan at Coolgardie to make his mother 'expose social ills & the evils of the present govt & administration'. She took issue with Hill's romantic idealism, privately describing her as 'a strange, otherwhereish creature with big, beautiful eyes, a hoarse voice & curious incapacity to argue logically about anything'.[11] For her part, Ernestine criticised Prichard for letting 'Communism colour her outlook so much.' Although Hill was not opposed to Communist ideals and believed them to be inherent within Aboriginal culture, she thought that Prichard and other FAW members had lost their bearings in protesting the rise of fascism during the war, and that their focus should have been on creating a national literature rather than on international politics.

Bob Hill later claimed the two women reached a '[f]inal tacit agreement not to discuss communism' and that the placatory Ernestine found Prichard too hard-line in her 'tragic political views – [she] couldn't be impartial … [which] upset E.H.'[12] Whether or not prompted by her heated discussions with Prichard in the caravan, Hill's treatment of race relations and frontier conflict in the north is far more searching and comprehensive in *The Territory* than in her other books. Indeed, what I find most striking about *The Territory* compared to the *Loneliness* is her bracing frankness in portraying episodes of white hostility to Aboriginal people and other cultural minorities.

One story Hill tells is that of Rodney Spencer, a prospector during the Territory gold rush days, 'known for his savage vendettas against the Asiatic', such as burning their accommodation. He later became the first man in Territorian history to be sentenced to death for murdering an Aboriginal man, whom he accused of stealing rice. Outside the court, Hill reports, 'there was uproar. The Territory was outraged. You couldn't shoot a nigger any more!' Spencer's sentence was commuted to life imprisonment and he was later released in response to protests from northerners that mercy was required because Aboriginal people had killed his relatives. Aware of the antipathy between northerners and southerners, especially in relation to racial issues, Hill uses an arch tone to convey her criticism of the response to Spencer's case: he was 'an unfortunate choice' for a martyr. No records were kept of white murders of blacks in the Northern Territory until 1911, she observes, 'and after that the verdict "Not Guilty" is so monotonous that it seems a matter of course', emphasising that: *'No white man has been hanged in the north or north-west for murder of a native.'*[13]

When I first read *The Territory*, I was surprised by how much more candid Hill is prepared to be in recounting massacres than she was in the *Loneliness*, such as that at Skull Creek in central Australia. She describes how in 1874, not long after the opening of the Overland Telegraph repeater station at Barrow Creek, a mob of Kaytetye people attacked its occupants in retaliation for local settlers' theft of their land and mistreatment of Kaytetye women. A linesman and an Aboriginal labourer were fatally speared, and the stationmaster was mortally wounded. Before he died, he managed to tap out a message in Morse code to his wife at Alice Springs Telegraph Station. The message alerted a trooper named Erwein Wurmbrand, who assembled a 'punitive expedition' of police and bushmen. Unable to save the stationmaster in time they swept across the countryside 100 miles east of Barrow Creek, 'herding all blacks before them' into a range which, Hill states, 'for grim and sufficient reason, is on the map for ever with the name of Blackfellows' Bones'.[14]

The phrase 'Blackfellows' Bones' pricked my memory. I recalled reading it in 'Murray – Scourge of the Myalls', Hill's 1933 article about Constable George Murray's part in the Coniston massacre half a century later at 'Blackfellows' Bones Range', also near Barrow Creek.[15] I also remembered it from a fragment titled 'The old woman's eye' in the Hill Collection, which described 'the old-time punitive raids' in her home state of Queensland:

THE OLD WOMAN'S EYE.

Aboriginal skeletons and skulls, with broken shards and widows' caps, unearthed by oil searchers in Bedourie sands of the Queensland Far West, are relics and remembrance of the 'Tintapperty' punitive raid and the infamous Black Police camps of Queensland's earlier days.

'A Stone Age graveyard,' somebody suggests. So it is – with a vengeance – a graveyard that covers over a thousand square miles of 'blackfellows' bones,' one of the many in Australia, marking the famous victories of the oldtime punitive raids, the battles so easily won, with guns.

A white man believed killed by blacks could be avenged a thousand to one.[16]

Hill is much less guarded and unqualified in this fragment than she is in *The Territory*, where she treads cautiously in critiquing its history. In line with her avowed impartiality as a journalist who knows no 'colour-line, nor bias, nor loyalty, save to the story' in the *Loneliness*, she is careful to highlight the human drama on both sides of tragic events, such as the Barrow Creek stationmaster's poignant last moments telegraphing his wife. But she is far more direct in *The Territory* in condemning what she referred to more obliquely as 'human dramas in a tragic country' fifteen years earlier in the *Loneliness*, and less biased towards police and bushmen than she was in earlier articles such as her profile of George Murray. In these respects, I find *The Territory* remarkably forward-looking, pre-empting the 'other side of the frontier' critique of Australian settler history that emerged during the Aboriginal rights and self-determination era of the 1970s and 1980s.

But above all, *The Territory* is infused with a melancholic nostalgia for a way of life that Hill had glimpsed during her early travels in remote Australia. She continues to write from the perspective that Aboriginal people were fast disappearing, portraying herself as a campfire scribe scrabbling about in bower-bird-like activities, gleaning shards of their culture before they were forever lost. She also seeks to record the ways of the jaunty bushman, whose type was disappearing in the wake of the Second World War. 'You'll meet the last of him' in northern Australia – the Territory, the Kimberleys or Far North Queensland – she writes, casting him in *The Territory*'s last chapter as a noble 'conquistadore', embodied for her by pastoral families like the Duracks, 'the cattle pioneers of the north'.[17] Although she was aware of pioneering culture's excesses, she accorded this cohort a natural nobility and mourned their era's waning, writing: 'Future Australians will see him in tapestry or mosaic, antediluvian as King Arthur's knights. He is a knightly figure. Red-brown as the country.' He – and it is only a 'he', and a white one at that – has grafted himself onto the landscape, acquiring some Aboriginal skills along the way – he can 'track like a blackfellow' and so forth.[18] Hill interprets the white bushman's vigour in adapting to the Australian outback as a sign that he is this country's most appropriate successor in the wake of what she perceives as Aboriginal people's inevitable passing.

Travelling throughout remote Australia after the war, Ernestine observed how Aboriginal people's circumstances were changing. She left Melbourne optimistically in 1947, 'bound out for the Australia where the happy aboriginal, at the other end of the scale before the racket civilisation began, is content with the warmth of the wood fire and sun, no clothing coupons'.[19] Instead, she was confronted by a post-war diaspora of Aboriginal people disenfranchised from their country on the road. 'Blacks. "Nowhere sit down, allabout finish." Won't go to mission – "they finishem all my friend. We want to go to our own country, nutting here. That Blackfella finish my boy, little young-fella".'[20] At Mundrabilla in the south-west, she met several Aboriginal women who'd been working on outlying stations. One of these was Nellie: 'She belonged to W.A. but was across with Ooldea mob … she was among strange natives on the other side of [the] Nullarbor. "All-time me sit down one woman, me all-time cry. I never knockabout big mob corroboree."' Two of her male relatives had been sent to Koonibba, the Lutheran mission on the Bight near Ceduna, where they'd died: Nellie thought they'd been poisoned and sung by 'the stranger blacks' so she was trying to return to her own country. She was destitute: 'Policeman give you clothes nutting. Never gottem blanket. Policeman won't give him.' She'd 'been walkin about naked' until a stationer's wife had given her a dress. She asked Hill for some man's boots – she had '"big jinna" – for walking in the needle-bush'.[21] Ernestine wrote to her cousin Coy, asking her to post clothing, as she often did for Aboriginal women she'd met while travelling. She took notes wherever she could of Aboriginal language and stories, describing her practice 'as a writer, my method of making friends with the dark people everywhere was a little impromptu wongi with them by the creek or the wurly'.[22]

Hill later described in *Kabbarli* the impact of the shift that occurred during the Second World War when Aboriginal people 'all over the continent … were mustered and moved to the nearest missions and compounds', some to the armed services, many thousands of miles from their country, 'to be employed in priority industries and factories, the children at native schools, and all under control and curfew rules'. The demise of what she perceived as a mutually beneficial relationship between pioneers and Aboriginal people in an informal, northern white protectorate was accelerated by massive social changes wrought through civil rights activism during the 1960s. 'In a spectacular success of education and adaptability they have asked and received the liberty to vote and to drink alcohol,' she writes, with an arch nod towards

Aboriginal people's achievement of full voting rights by 1965. The same period saw strikes and protests by Aboriginal pastoral workers in response to poor labour and living conditions, most famously in Vincent Lingiari's Wave Hill walk-off, the catalyst being the Conciliation and Arbitration Commission's decision in 1966 to establish equal wages for Aboriginal labourers in the cattle industry. As WA writer Steve Hawke observes, the cultural winds of change in remote Australia 'blew down an industry, a regime, a culture that for the best part of a century had thrived on a semi-feudal system of co-dependence between the all-powerful station bosses, and large communities of unpaid Aboriginal workers and their families'.[23] Hill didn't begrudge Aboriginal people these reforms, noting they had been delivered 'equality instead of slavery in the award wage, the conditions of employment and the State their good provider in youth and age'. But she believed they had 'lost their country and their Dreaming': that they had experienced irreparable cultural loss through a 'blending of all the tribes, languages mixed together and forgotten in favour of English, the children brought up with no knowledge of Aboriginal crafts, laws, customs' and that 'those who returned to their own countries would not revert to the nomad life of fathers and mothers'.[24]

Recharting the highways and waterways of her youth over the next two decades, Hill was only too aware that her own cultural milieu was fading. She eschewed the creep of suburbia into rural areas, declaring that while she had 'loved the miles and the Loneliness when its people were real. Now it seems they're much of a kind in slices of cities with Neon signs and washing machines, high schools, supermarkets, aeroplanes daily and bitumen roads of cars nose to tail, making Australia small.'[25] Nor did she relate to the newer, more commercialised breed of tourist, declaring that the 'people of the Alice and Stuart Highway to Darwin, and the N.T. are all changed and strange since I was last there'.[26] Far from her youthful self-portrait as a carefree copyboy travelling light with a swag and a typewriter, Hill became weighed down by her ever-accumulating trunks of notes and unfinished manuscripts to which she whimsically referred as 'a weatherworn swag of all kinds and conditions of so-called work'.[27] She became a literary bag lady, in thrall to her own baggage yet questioning the relevance of her vision. 'I still tote around a back-breaking weight of ever-growing piles of "material" of what I still might think is of worth to Australia,' she wrote to Mary Durack, 'but I am no longer sure – the world has changed.'[28]

Ernestine also became burdened by personal freight, as Bob began to strain at their bond of 'forged iron linked eternally, bound up invisibly': his indebtedness to his mother and her reliance on him. After the war, mother and son were never too far away from each other for long, often travelling and sharing accommodation together, becoming such a close-knit dyad that the constant mentions of 'Ernestine and Bob' in friends' letters from this period make them sound like a couple. Bob's attachment to his mother became a constant emotional undercurrent throughout his adult life, one he came to despise but on which he also capitalised. They wrote regularly to each when they were apart – as Hill did with other relatives and friends — although Bob detected a distinct dynamic in their correspondence, later commenting: 'All these letters reflect the same thing, a sort of alternating wail between me and mother. She once now and again – I all the time.' According to him, Ernestine burned many of his letters from the mid-1950s because 'she was worried that they might demonstrate too much material influence and mutual dependence. – too sensitive!'[29] But the 'alternating wail' may well have issued from events involving Bob that rent the fabric of Ernestine's personal literary universe.

Mother and son had ostensibly parted when they sold the caravan at the end of their travels in the late 1940s. But unable to resist the lure of travel for long, Hill replaced the caravan with an old Dodge utility truck on the back of *Territory* royalties and a publishing advance in early 1952. She set out again on the 'pilgrim path' with Bob and WA writer Eleanor Smith, driving 1000 miles following the 'trans-continental tracks of the explorers' up to Murchison and across to Wiluna to join the Canning Stock Route, making notes for more manuscripts.

Perth had been the natural conclusion of the Hills's journey across the Bight in 1948, and they continued to dock there, Hill often staying on its outskirts at '*Darjeeling* – a typically Ernestinian lodging house in the Darling Ranges'.[30] Bob, who'd had lessons at the Meldrum School of Painting in Melbourne in 1946, was seeking to develop an artistic career and, when he wasn't on the road with his mother, worked in Perth as a house painter and later as a general dogsbody at the Busselton Underwater Observatory. They often socialised with the Duracks in their family home at Nedlands, including Bess, the recently widowed matriarch of the family, her daughters Elizabeth (the artist who'd illustrated *The Territory*) and Mary, and her five children, affectionately known as 'the bunnies'. The Duracks remembered these convivial occasions with the Hills fondly. A photograph from this time shows Bob and Ernestine, in shorts and sandals, frolicking like a pair of woodland satyrs outside Darjeeling.

Once when Bob stayed with Ernestine at a small country town hotel in Western Australia, he described hearing other guests, 'the bank boy and the schoolteacher [have] very noisy sex just outside my door on the verandah. I was feeling pretty depressed. These Henry Miller sides of life seemed to miss mother entirely.'[31] She also appeared to miss the Miller-esque aspects of her son's life. Bob was renting a small cottage at Dalkeith 'not very far from Mary's down on the river', and Durack, who was writing her epic family history *Kings in Grass Castles*, began working at 'his little shebeen' to have some peace and quiet from the kids and the phone. Bob also visited her at Nedlands, telegramming his mother on one occasion that 'all was "extremely bright at Mary's"'.[32] She'd married Horrie Miller, a pilot, in 1938 but they were living virtually separate lives, with Horrie managing a family property in Broome while Mary supervised the children's schooling in Perth.[33] When Mary became pregnant with her sixth and last child, Ernestine wrote offering comforting advice a couple of weeks before his birth on 21 May 1955, observing to Anne Tully, a Durack cousin, that 'a new small Miller, probably John' was about to take up residence with the 'bunnies', apparently blithely unaware of the child's likely paternity.[34]

Several months later Bob left Perth for Kalgoorlie to work as an ABC trainee reporter, intending to set up 'a workable HQ' for himself and for his mother to finish 'Wise-cap'. Ernestine had berthed at Sydney, and was thinking of heading to Far North Queensland.[35] Bob's reporting gig was short-lived, and in October 1955 they moved into a guesthouse in Cairns together. The affair was over; Bob was crashing. He'd taken to wearing a Holy Mary medal – his ex-lover's namesake – around his neck and attending confession, all of which Hill approved, entertaining the idea that if she returned to the fold, sales of 'Johnnie Wise-cap', the novel she was writing, might soar given that one-quarter of Queensland's population was Catholic. She thought it was good that Bob had been 'bumped right out of that little western nest', sensing that something had happened in Perth, but feigned disinterest, thinking it best not to pry – 'I don't want to know, I want him to move on!' The dam wall of denial had burst by the new year. Ernestine confided to Coy that she had been through 'a real little Valley of Humiliation', referring enigmatically to 'grief and complications over someone else', and Bob having been in 'a maddening tangle for two years' and 'the domination of his mind by Mary Durack'.[36]

The psychological drama peaked when Hill tried to throw herself into the sea, although she 'was rescued by a "kind policeman" who Bob says shouldn't have rescued her'.[37] Bob was in his early thirties when the affair started: that his first significant relationship was with an older married woman who was also one of his mother's best friends made it all the more challenging and transgressive for Hill. Mary Durack was fourteen years younger than Ernestine but eleven years older than Bob – old enough to be a rival mother figure. Her own marriage to Horrie Miller, a much older man and a divorcee, and thus 'married' as far as the Catholic church was concerned, had been viewed as controversial and rebellious at the time. Hill stopped asking after John Miller once she realised who his father was; the Duracks subsequently referred jokingly to him as 'the unspeakable one'. If Hill's refusal to acknowledge Bob's affair and her grandson's existence seems hypocritical, she probably did not want to be reminded of the clandestine circumstances of her son's birth, which she had long sought to suppress. No correspondence between Hill and Mary Durack exists from mid-1955 onwards, and Ernestine only occasionally mentions Mary in letters. Their friendship may have faded over time and distance as other of Hill's connections did, but the affair seems to have unsettled the affectionate bond between the two families.

In the wake of the affair, Bob blamed his mother for stymieing his emotional development. He blamed her for what he had or hadn't become, and the unstable, wandering lifestyle she'd modelled for him: 'It was she who had preached "romance" of the Australian outback to me when a prudent influence would have more objective.'[38] He blamed her for wanting him to continue in the 'old Ernestine Hill firm', painting and photographing the landscape while she wrote, never taking responsibility for failing to establish himself as an independent artist. 'I am believed to be despotic, neurotic, hawk-eyed and dominating, as a result of my own "queer life",' Hill wrote in bewilderment to Coy. 'I never knew it was queer.' His other complaint was more typically Freudian. 'Bob says the trouble is I love him too much. Maybe I do. But we both are too emotional nowadays.'[39] Hill observed they both had depressive, obsessive tendencies; Bob reported that he was suffering from mental fatigue while his mother was battling melancholia: their 'alternating wail'. Rene Foster later speculated that the psychological roots of Hill's enmeshed relationship with her son were in her affair with RC Packer: that it was an echo, all that Ernestine had left, of her original love. Their bond was, Rene considered, 'something more than that of mother and son. It is the aftermath of what must have been a passionate love, and then, only a dream that could never be realised.'[40]

But if his mother had substituted him 'for a husband and lived for him', as Bob claimed, conversely when he 'became involved with women she could no longer write – dried up in a way creatively': an egotistical interpretation as to why Hill didn't finish 'Johnnie Wise-cap' and the other works she had planned. However, it wasn't only her conflicted dynamic with Bob that destabilised Hill, but the cumulation of '[l]ittle humiliations and lack of money and feelings of helplessness' she experienced as her profile as a writer was declining. She was also beginning to display symptoms of emphysema, suffering bouts of pleurisy in the early 1950s. By the end of the decade, she was 'on the beginning of her downward trend, the strain had been too much'.[41]

During the mid-1950s, Hill drifted alone up the 'coast of the holy ghost' of her home state, planning to 'write all the way' as she cocked at the ports of her childhood – Mackay, Townsville, Brampton Island, Cairns, Cooktown, Thursday Island. She lugged her typewriter and trunks of notes with her, travelling by train or boat – 'I have too much impedimenta, alas, to fly' – joking that she'd rather 'take a camel or a lugger any time'.[42] She sometimes sojourned in southern cities, although her dislike of the urban south had if anything intensified with age. Sydney was 'the most painful patch of Australian life there's no doubt whatever' where 'the money just goes', whereas Melbourne was 'a bit of a grey monotony,' a 'smoke city at its worst', and she bridled at 'Adelaide's regimented righteousness and Rightness that can't go wrong'.[43]

But life in Far North Queensland could be kind to a penniless author: 'The best thing about Brampton is that you can wear old clothes and go barefoot, which is quite a boon.' Local shops and hotels let you run a tab and didn't keep too close an eye on whether you'd paid it. Hill frequented the ubiquitous cheap guesthouse, bedsit or room above a pub, subsisting 'on tea and biscuits, the occasional nourishing meal, and Codral and Craven A'. Debts gnawed at the dwindling royalties from reprints of her old titles and advances for promised books, although she claimed never to spend anything, shillings going mouldy in her purse. She became run-down, worrying about her health in letters to friends as though it were an unruly child, a distressing predicament for someone who'd been 'so quick through life, blessed with that "iron constitution" like a bit of wire'. Sometimes she thought she might have a blood deficiency and be in need of a tonic; at other times she was so nobbled by depression 'that life was a grieving and a long hill to climb, that I couldn't surmount'. She was treading water, struggling to write.[44]

Hill had plans for more creative works – a 'quick slant' of eighteen books, short stories, twelve plays and a 'novel musical'. In 1959 she visited Cooktown to research a script about the arrival of its namesake to be re-enacted at the foot of the Cook Memorial Monument. It was a brief reconnaissance mission, which she spent browsing through old births, deaths and marriage registers. The wife of local magistrate Alan Queale invited Ernestine over for afternoon tea; they found her 'rather vague at this stage but, nevertheless, interesting to talk to'. The owners of the hotel where Hill stayed later told Queale that she 'spent a good deal of time writing in bed and smoked cigarettes incessantly as is evidenced by the large number of cigarette burns on blankets, pillows, etc., in the room she occupied'. He'd heard she was working on a book that she never published, although he understood that 'her main, or one of her main, reasons for coming to Cooktown was the hope that she might experience a cyclone'.[45] Her wish wasn't granted, so she tacked further north to Thursday Island to work on the script.

A year later she washed up in hospital on Thursday Island, for a while the 'only whitefella' on the ward. Her stay was like a tropical retreat, 'the ships slanting by and the Islanders singing … they haven't lost their love of their own language and island race'. She'd burnt her arm seriously on an oil lamp flame, but she also suffered from bouts of pleurisy and a nervous head, which she attributed to failing sinuses 'that necessitate the Codral and digestion impaired causing lack of weight, and concentration, and sensitivity and all'. She was emaciated, her weight occasionally peaking at 6 stone (38 kilograms); it seemed her 'posterior has worn through from years of sitting down', but the doctors were 're-upholstering' her. She didn't recognise herself in the mirror. Her face had shrunk beyond recall; it was 'as long ago and far away, faded and gone in the most painful and puzzled time of all my life'. Two years later, staying at Arcadia Hotel on Magnetic Island eating pub meals she could afford on the off-season tariff, she was 'yet only five stone ten', although her face was rounding out, becoming recognisable again.[46]

In July 1960, a month before her hospitalisation on Thursday Island, Hill had received a Commonwealth Literary Fund pension of £7 per week for life, which was granted to those who'd made a significant contribution to Australian literature. She smarted at the honour; it was the writers' equivalent of an age pension. She was sixty-one, but its award marked a milestone when she realised she was an age she'd once thought of as elderly: 'Mary's [Gilmore] had one for years, and Daisy Bates. I feel OLD.'[47]

It was Beatrice Davis, her longtime editor at Angus & Robertson, who'd precipitated this development. The publisher was losing hope that Hill would deliver on her list of proposed books, but remembering how 'brilliantly successful' Hill had been with a Commonwealth Literary Fellowship to write *My Love Must Wait*, Davis suggested that Ernestine apply for one 'stating Wise-cap as the work begun but not completed, because of lack of financial security'.[48]

Hill had been promising Angus & Robertson 'Johnnie Wise-cap', which she described as 'a history, a novel, of the Aboriginal race', since the mid-1950s when she started it.[49] Excited by her description of this 'rich and strange' story, 'vividly different from anything else we have ever seen', Davis had deposited an advance of £100 in Ernestine's account in 1955 so she could write without 'financial harassments'.[50] But Hill began to find A&R's contracts 'less reasonable and more exacting than that of 18 years ago' and refused to be cowed by their demands for a new book. Indeed, the publisher's attempts to slot 'Wise-cap' into their printing roster for their 1955 Christmas trade program and Anthony Hordern's catalogue was antithetical to Johnnie's – and her – anti-capitalist, nomadic ethos. It was 'against the very spirit of the book, the Johnnie Wise-cap wisdom that I am trying to preach. The treadmill of human slavery for coins is what puzzles him most of all, and from which he retreats.'[51] She was irked by, if maybe fearful of missing out on, the commercialisation of Aboriginality, commenting after Melbourne's Moomba Festival in 1951 on how Aboriginal people were 'in every paper, and shop windows advertising everything they're the rage, a crazy craze over there'. 'It's going to be a ferocious vogue, this Christmas aboriginal stuff,' she declared when Charles Chauvel's *Jedda* was released in 1955.[52]

She still published articles in journals like *Walkabout*, and did so up until 1968. Indeed, she would have supported herself with freelancing, if it were not for 'Johnnie all the time'. By 1960 her former bestsellers were viewed as 'semi-classics' requiring smaller print-runs of 3000 – a reflection of her dwindling popularity and topicality as a writer since *The Territory*'s publication. Davis thought that 'Wise-cap' would be 'very good, but it will not, I feel sure, be in the bestselling class at all' and offered Hill a small advance based on royalties at 10 per cent – the same rate for any titles reprinted. In 1963 she sent Ernestine a cheque for £450 – 'since you appear to need it so urgently' – although her account was in the red by £311. Angus and Robertson advanced £250 against royalties for the ongoing sales from *My Love Must Wait* as well as the reprint of *The Great Australian Loneliness* and *The Territory* that year. *Flying Doctor Calling* had sold out in late 1958, but its sales had been so slow they were not reprinting it. The remaining £200 was an advance on Hill's new manuscript, as long as she submitted it before the end of the year. Otherwise it would be deducted from future royalties on reprints.

Davis knew Hill's situation was precarious, but she also thought Ernestine had contributed to her own fortunes, or lack of them. She listed Angus & Robertson's stipulations in a letter accompanying the cheque of £450, ending with a parting volley of tough love: 'The fact remains, as you know so well, that the only solution for your comfort and peace of mind is the delivery of a new book to us'.⁵³

Ernestine was relieved when Bob became engaged in January 1961 to Jackie Scrivener, an artist he'd met on Magnetic Island. He was thirty-seven years old, and Hill believed he'd delayed having his own family for too long. She thought Jackie was an excellent choice – or at least put a diplomatic face on their engagement – describing her rather generically as 'a little nice Magnetic Island girl … small, fair, 25, gentle-mannered and quiet – blue jeans and blue eyes sort of thing but can be very pretty'. She was aware too that Jackie's appearance as a 'little person of simple needs and tranquil mien' was misleading; that she 'knew her own mind and will not be "put upon"' – qualities she thought made her a good match for the significantly older if unruly Bob.⁵⁴ But neither Bob nor Jackie had much earning capacity as artists, and the tranquillity and simplicity Hill had first seen soon evaporated. The couple also had to contend with the psychic 'bobble-chain' yoking mother and son together. Bob saw his marriage to Jackie as a significant turning point in his relationship with Ernestine, although he later reflected that 'in many ways the picture was unchanged by marriage and the consequent removal of mother to a lower position in kinship'.⁵⁵

Although mother and son were separated for periods of time, they were inevitably drawn back into each other's orbit even after Bob married. Hill's friends queried the healthiness of her relationship with her son. Rene Foster was sceptical about his closeness to his mother, fearing he manipulated her for his own gain – 'Bob just lived upon her (and I told him once).'⁵⁶ After staying with the Hills for several days, Eleanor Smith reported to Beatrice Davis that 'the atmosphere created by Bob is anything but helpful'.

In an unusual step that blurred professional as well as personal boundaries, Bob once asked Davis whether Angus & Robertson would provide a loan of £2000 for a deposit on a house for them, to which she replied tartly in the negative. It was a reflection of what Bob described as the dynamic of 'material influence and mutual dependence' that characterised his relationship with Ernestine.

Of Hill's friends, Rene Foster was the most openly critical of Bob, which was fuelled by a power play for custodianship of Ernestine in which she became engaged with him. In 1966 Foster suggested that Hill stay with her in Adelaide to ease her financial distress and bring her closer to her family and the grandson she was yet to meet. Ernestine had been renting a small flat in Roleystone, on the fringe of Perth's jarrah forests, an area she loved, although it chewed up two-thirds of her CLF pension. Nevertheless, she was trying to entice Bob and his young family to join her. Jackie had given birth to their first child, Luke or 'Lui', in February 1966, and the family was living in Queensland. Shortly afterwards Bob found a job at Iron Knob on the Eyre Peninsula – half a continent closer to, yet still far away from, his mother – and Jackie moved with Lui to Adelaide where she had relatives.

Rene offered Ernestine free board: 'nothing but in-and-out love and companionship and light and fire bills in winter'. A frugal literary aesthete accustomed, like Hill, to a precariat lifestyle, Foster had once received a similar request from Gilmore who, at age ninety-four, had invited her to stay to write her memoir: 'She said I am to sleep on her settee and live on tea and toast with her and wonder at it all ' Ernestine was tempted by Foster's Boston-marriage-style proposal, although she wasn't keen on the thought of wintering in Adelaide – 'the sun and sea are not so radiant there for growing old', especially for someone suffering from chronic bronchitis. Bob was alarmed by this development, observing that 'Rene's taste in comestibles was extremely austere – she lived a life of thought and needed very little fuel – mother on the other hand, had to be almost tempted to eat a little of very, as she would call it "tasty" food' – a reference to Hill's longstanding gastric ulcer. Early in 1966 she reported weighing '6 stone but much better to look at', although at a height of five foot four she was severely underweight.[57]

Bob's lampoonery of Rene as a well-meaning, eccentric, elderly spinster who was too unworldly to provide Hill the practical support she required might sound like misplaced filial concern, but he had his own agendas. He and Jackie had been fighting, and she was threatening to leave. When his mother arrived in Adelaide in 1967, he supposed Ernestine did not want to 'add tension to an already terrible atmosphere', although she was contributing to their rent from her CLF pension. Hill took up Foster's offer of free meals, accommodation and literary solace, but the promised flat turned out to be 'a sort of furnished gazebo in a damp and sunless garden'. She quickly became depressed by these dank and cheerless conditions after living in Perth's heat and light. When Jackie later left with Lui to stay with her sister, threatening to file for divorce on the grounds of mental cruelty, Bob invited his mother to live in their Adelaide home, a proposal she gladly accepted to escape Rene's gloomy gazebo, although she suspected he wanted her to protect him from the wrath of Jackie's relatives.

Mother and son's reunion was temporary. Jackie returned after six months, announcing she was pregnant, and Hill moved into another flat to focus on writing. Her granddaughter Celeste was born in March 1968, and Bob began teaching at the SA School of Arts. The job was more in keeping with his interests and talents but the pay was meagre, and he persuaded his mother and his wife that it would be in their best interests if Ernestine rented a small room at their place. While this somewhat claustrophobic domestic arrangement was grounded in Bob's financial and emotional dependence on his mother, it was not without benefits for Hill. With overtones of the old Ernestine Hill firm, the family discussed establishing a press dedicated to publishing Australian titles. Ernestine wrote a chapbook, *About Lasseter*, based on the account Paul Johns had given her of the explorer's last days, which Jackie illustrated and printed under their imprint, the Scrivener Press, in 1968.[58] But the creative domicile was straining at the seams, and 'Mother did not like such a suburban hidey-hole', so the family relocated to a larger house near Mount Lofty in the Adelaide Hills in 1969.[59] Hill enthused about being able to catch a glimpse of the Nullarbor from her new eyrie, but she was soon complaining about the cold and saying she had to leave the south altogether, rather than endure another winter there. Early in 1970 Bob bought a large truck, bundled Ernestine and the rest of the family on board and drove to the Sunshine Coast.

12

This little breathlessness

'It is so hard to hope for the future – everything changes, peters out. So we just keep on for the love of it.'[1]

Summer 1971: A dense fog swaddled Buderim Mountain, where Hill was cooped up in a plantation house overlooking the Sunshine Coast. There'd been no sunlight at all for thirteen days; it had been like living through a biblical plague. Sheets of rain had fallen across the state, 100 inches (over 250 centimetres) since Christmas. Mangoes and pawpaws became waterlogged, vegetables were washed out of the garden patch. Windows and drawers warped shut, matches would not strike, paper clagged like a blotter in the typewriter; everything was covered in whiskers and mould. Like her lungs. She was perpetually breathless, as if inhaling fine spores. Early in the new year, Bob had taken his family to live in Perth while he chased work. He'd left Ernestine in the plantation house which Stella, Jackie's mother, owned, and she felt her peculiarity among her suburban hinterland neighbours.

'So old are nearly all the people of Buderim they have retired like hermit crabs into the innermost deeps of their shells,' she wrote to Bob. 'Nothing whatever but bowls. Octogenarians.'[2]

She was seventy-two, which she didn't care to admit if she could help it, and overshadowed by a creeping obsolescence. Her correspondence with like-minded friends in the west such as the Duracks and Henrietta Drake-Brockman had dwindled over the past two decades. When she attended Writers' Week at the Adelaide Festival in 1968 along with literary contemporaries such as Rene Foster, Mary Durack and Beatrice Davis, Henrietta Drake-Brockman's passing had been announced. There'd been other deaths, too – MP Durack, Katharine Susannah Prichard, Connie Robertson – and most devastatingly of all, her cousin and loyal correspondent for many years, Coy Bateson, had died in 1962. Hill might have brought this loneliness upon herself, with her constant travel and habitual withdrawal, but she longed for close companionship, as Bates had done during her last decade. 'I never seem to have a kindred spirit near except in ecstatic rushes of ten minutes.'[3]

'Sam rings up now and again between benders –' Ernestine wrote to Bob from her eyrie, 'whatever is there for a man alone?'

Sam Fullbrook, a painter and a neighbour in Buderim, suggested a kindred spirit of sorts to Hill. He was, like her, a hobohemian dwelling on the fringes of urban artistic circles. Over two decades younger than Ernestine, he looked up at her as embodying 'old Australia' as she had once done of pioneering types like MP Durack. He was struck by her enthusiasm for Australia, perceiving it as a hallmark of her milieu: 'it is something lacking in succeeding generations – yes I think we have lost something.'[4] Fullbrook had been a knockabout lad who'd left his childhood inner-city suburb, Chippendale, in 1952 to develop his painting technique while travelling as a manual labourer across the country. He'd worked at Marble Bar in the Pilbara, where he painted Aboriginal stockmen, sympathising with their struggle for better wages and conditions, declaring that 'spiritually, they all had top hats'.[5]

Fullbrook began visiting Hill, ostensibly to chat 'about her west', although he had designs on her as a potential subject for an Archibald Prize portrait entry. With her characteristic modesty, Ernestine at first resisted his entreaties to sit for him, doubting the painting's subject would stir the slightest ripple of interest; when she sat for him, she regretted she could not be 'a more dazzling personality'. The image she saw emerging on the canvas was 'a simple picture of the listening kind, hands a bit vague, hair neat as an apple pie, spots from a frock I had floating around … nothing to set the Fountain on fire'.[6]

Sam was a heavy drinker who'd been in treatment, and it's rumoured they both had more than a tipple during the sittings at his old plantation house.[7] When he later sent her a tiny, 10-cent slide of the painting, Hill may have been tempted to attribute the final portrait to inebriation. She was aghast at seeing her image reflected back with 'criss-cross eyes in a heavily-plastered face with spike smears of raging red lipstick and dyed-looking hair and thick long white wrinkled gloves'.

'It's like a rag doll out in the rain or an old harpy actress making up in the dark,' she wrote to Bob. 'It was undistinguished when we saw it, but fairly mild – like me – quite gentle, and kind, considering years and years too late. I wouldn't like the children to see it, even.' She thought Sam had tinkered with the painting since their last sitting, but he denied ever putting 'a brush near it' and blamed the slide's quality.

She had been 'a woefully dim bulb'. 'The Sam picture is indeed a poor trick,' she declared when it was to her surprise and dismay shortlisted for the 1970 Archibald Prize, 'friends are writing it is appalling, that I should sue him, I should have known.' Hill thought she would become a public laughing stock, an apprehension corroborated by early reviews: 'I was the joke but even so! I was the "frothiest, spottiest … literary lady Ernestine Hill with a Coco Chanel hair-do and Mary Gilmore gloves" and Sam that "wittiest of all." No hair-do or gloves but there you are!'[8]

When the portrait was hung in the Art Gallery of New South Wales with the other shortlisted Archibald entries, she relented, clinging proudly to Melbourne *Herald* critic Allan McCulloch's comments that he preferred it to Eric John Smith's winning portrait of architect Neville Gruzman, describing it as 'evanescent … a lyrical work in which the slanting figure with its yellow spotted dress and the delicate features seem to swim in a sea of pale refulgent green.'

Money became an issue with the portrait, as it was on other fronts for Hill. Originally Fullbrook offered her the portrait as payment in kind, saying he only wanted the Archibald Prize, if he won it. Hill 'wasn't keen', but courteous as ever, didn't knock him back because it 'would have been rude'. When Fullbrook began negotiations with the Art Gallery of New South Wales about the painting's sale, he offered Hill 'half the swag of it'. Although touched by the gesture, privately she 'was appalled and certainly said I didn't want that', not wanting 'them to get the idea I was after the chips'. But she regretted ceding her rights to potential revenue when the gallery bought the painting for $4000 and it featured on the cover of *Art International*. 'My face can't be sold down river regardless of me? I wonder what the copyright is.' Her remorse echoed her anxieties from her creative partnership with Bates – who owned the artwork, the creator or the subject? – except the roles were reversed here, and she was the subject, protesting against the artist's co-option of her. Although Fullbrook had seemingly bowled her over with a gust of male hubris, Hill's dynamic with him reflected hers with Bates years earlier: once again, she had been too polite, kind and deferential, and had equivocated for too long, failing to assert herself, which left her feeling as though she'd been erased rather than acknowledged through the portraiture. Sam didn't 'even say "Thank you" to me until he was told to,' she protested to Bob. 'And never even a carrot out of the garden, or anything but discussions about <u>him</u>. I will do it, against better judgment. I'm not going to be silent all my life. One must be alive.'[9]

Was this living, this time in the shadow of rain with this 'little breathlessness of emphysema'? Anything that involved exertion – 'walking, talking, hurry, worry, bending' – she found painful and, with winter coming, living at Buderim was not sustainable with its 'withering cold and bronky foggy dew' that made breathing difficult. Like Bates in her final decade, Ernestine hankered for the west, certain that a warm, dry climate like Perth's would relieve the pressure on her lungs. Stella was planning to sell the plantation house, and they discussed leaving Queensland together to join Bob and Jackie in Western Australia.[10] But before winter set in, Hill left the mist-trapping gullies of Buderim for Brisbane's warmer air.

She needed to be closer to medical treatment, now the fog of emphysema had settled over her lungs. She hoped the medicos might 'buoy me on', but their prognosis was far from cheering. They ordered her to swap 'the reflective and philosophic cigarette' for the constant companionship of an oxygen cylinder, and within a year she'd spent time on a two-bed ward at Chermside Chest Hospital. Three women asthma sufferers cycled through the other bed during her stay; all of them died. 'It was a new and un-literary view of Death – not our grim Reaper, nor cold dark Gulf,' Hill wrote with detached curiosity. 'The medical acceptance of mortality is much more natural, not awesome.' A doctor told her she only had another year or two to live. But she still planned to finish her life's work.[11]

'(Easy when talking to her to completely forget she is old. – Leans on elbows on table – leans forward with excited eager face),' Margriet Bonnin wrote on a spare page in her notebook. 'Voice husky well modulated beautiful'.[12] A young postgraduate student at the University of Queensland, she began visiting Hill regularly in Brisbane to interview her as part of her masters and later doctoral research. Bonnin's family had migrated to Australia when she was seven and, with her outsider perspective, she'd always been 'fascinated by the ways in which Australians related to their country'.[13] Her mother, Nancy, a senior librarian at the Fryer Library, had suggested that Ernestine Hill's travel writing might provide an interesting avenue into this area, and Bonnin contemplated making it the subject of a PhD.

Nancy Bonnin had met Hill at Lloyds Bookshop, which Louise Campbell ran, in Brisbane. She was keen to build up the Fryer's Australiana collection, and had acquired papers from Oodgeroo Noonuccal (Kath Walker) and Judith Wright. Derek Fielding, the university librarian, had suggested Bonnin contact Ernestine after Rene Foster had indicated that Hill might have some Queensland material among her copious notes. In fact, a vice-chancellor's luncheon had been held in Hill's honour when the University of Queensland learned that she was living in Brisbane, but Ernestine was a no-show: her deteriorating health and reclusiveness counted against her appearance. She hadn't been out socially since she'd left hospital eight months earlier, becoming 'as shy as a wisp of ghost, faded away from everyone'. Nor was she comfortable with academia, despite corresponding with Professors AC Cawley and AG Mitchell about aspects of Aboriginal and Australian English language and culture. She saw herself as a pilgrim outside the 'walled city' of university English departments, more at home with 'the Bedouins of the Birdsville Track – or the anthems and elegies of gold' than with Jane Austen.[14]

Nancy Bonnin was undeterred, and immediately won Hill's confidence when she visited her at Lloyds Bookshop: Ernestine found her 'a very natural nice Queenslander'. Bonnin was 'extremely keen' about the Queensland notes and tried to persuade her to work on them in the Fryer Library – there was even talk of putting her up in a flat on campus – but Hill demurred: 'but oh, you should see them and all the creative work that's nearly done with them. They've taken my whole life. These Australian travels or knowledge, all I had.'

While being treated for emphysema as an outpatient at Chermside Chest Hospital, Ernestine leased a house across the river from the University of Queensland's St Lucia campus. Bob moved in with her; he'd returned to Brisbane in mid-1971 after failing to find sufficient work in Western Australia and had been pottering about Lloyds bookshop, helping out Louise. Jackie and the children were staying at Buderim with her mother. Once Bob was reunited with his own mother, his marriage entered its final tailspin, and he and Jackie did not reconcile again.

'Believes in telepathy, etc,' Margriet Bonnin wrote in the margins of her memo pad. 'That at certain times people are "meant" to meet each other at fortuitous moments – like now we can "help one another". Destined to be a "wonderful association".'[15]

Hill enjoyed Margriet's company but Bonnin found her 'very chary & diffident about talking about herself & what she has done'. She'd shrug off Bonnin's proposed PhD topic by suggesting that other *Walkabout* writers, such as Henrietta Drake-Brockman, would be a more worthwhile subject of a critical biography: 'she's the author you should be doing.' Margriet suspected 'that the biographical information I will obtain from Mrs Hill will be more about other people than about herself'. While working with Bates, Ernestine revealed she'd promised to 'never ask her anything of her personal life' – a dictum she carried into her own writing. She commented that 'her work didn't contain enough "personal" information', Bonnin noting 'said with pointedness' in an aside, which suggests Hill was aware that it was a criticism. Defeated by Ernestine's notorious reluctance to talk about herself, Margriet broadened the focus of her thesis topic to Australian descriptive travel writing during the 1930s and 1940s.[16]

Ernestine welcomed the young woman's visits as an opportunity for exchange, an echo of her earlier working relationship with Bates, albeit with a potential role reversal. She'd been struggling to 'package up' her notes for years; stacks of them, often several feet deep, lined the floors and walls of her Brisbane home, so much so that there wasn't a spare patch where she could spread out – 'we desperately live round them and hop them to go to the telephone or bed'. These were Hill's 'sixty years of fragments' from her travels, observing life across the Australian interior, and her unfinished manuscripts. Convinced of their ethnographic value, she told AC Cawley, chair of English at Queensland University, that she was 'finishing up a life-time's collecting of Australiana, to express it so, at our ghost of a national shrine'.[17] She envisaged despatching her manuscripts to state libraries across the country, if not the NLA, and had engaged a typist for that purpose several years earlier, planning to clear the 'decks of a great deal of copy'.[18] But they hadn't made much headway, even with two typewriters firing at the same time, and Hill couldn't afford any more 'sorting, filing and compiling help' on her CLF stipend. In mid-1971 Rene Foster suggested to Beatrice Davis that what Hill needed was some financial assistance and a trained research officer to organise her papers – that the job was really beyond 'frail little Ernestine'. Davis wrote to the National Library requesting that they appraise Hill's manuscripts and the situation at hand. Ernestine really needed a Miss Watts, someone with a more orderly mind, and Margriet Bonnin appeared to be such a person. Mrs Hill 'seems to feel that I will be able to help her finish some of her unfinished work,' Bonnin wrote to Foster. 'I would of course be very grateful for such an opportunity and hope that the notion of having someone here who is enthusiastic will encourage her in reconsidering some of the projects she has ignored of late.'[19]

If Hill couldn't rally herself to finish 'Johnnie Wise-cap' or to organise her notes, another project galvanised her into action: she had 'Daisy beside me, all mixed up' when she arrived at the Sunshine Coast in 1970.[20] She had begun writing a memoir based on her personal experience of her friend, only too aware that others were mining the Bates seam.

The previous year, Elizabeth Salter, an expatriate Australian writer living in London, had received a Commonwealth Literary Fellowship to write a biography of Bates. Salter had published a memoir of her time as secretary to Edith Sitwell, and she was later commissioned to write Robert Helpmann's biography. She had put out a call for people with memories of Bates in Australian newspapers and magazines, then travelled 'home' to interview them and to visit some of Daisy's old haunts. Hill was polite upfront about Salter's project – 'Good luck to Miss Elizabeth Salter – she seems very enthusiastic, and it's all grist to Daisy's Mill' – although she privately expressed disappointment that her rival should be given $9000 to write 'from her "fashionable Hampstead flat"' the life story of 'a quaint and lonely little woman who gave everything in fifty years for what was then a crazy ideal'.[21] Polkinghorne remarked to Foster that Salter had a nerve, thinking she could write Bates's biography: 'For almost five years, I've been asking people, periodically, "Where is Ernestine Hill these days?"'[22]

Prompted by Foster, Sir Robert Helpmann contacted Hill

while she was still living at Mount Lofty in early 1970 about a Bates biopic he was planning with Katharine Hepburn in the lead role. Helpmann was dashing between the opening of the Adelaide Festival, meeting with Nureyev in Sydney and rehearsing with the ballet in Melbourne for the festival opening, and he wanted to ring, if not meet with, Hill. 'I will be eternally grateful to be able to discuss with you the character of this great woman,' he wrote, adding apologetically she may have heard that he'd bought the rights to Elizabeth Salter's Bates biography, but it wasn't true. He thought Salter's book might be 'perhaps a second-hand knowledge of a great woman', whereas he – and indeed, Miss Hepburn – wanted first-hand knowledge, so he was turning to Hill. She didn't have a phone so they corresponded, initially with lashings of mutual admiration. Ernestine was of course ecstatic, ostensibly on Bates's behalf, about Helpmann's filmic interest in her old friend's life: 'dreams come true for Daisy's immortality! – that of Miss Katharine Hepburn, genius to portray the most remarkable woman in Australia's 200 years of history. Daisy's ghost would be dancing in glee.'[23]

Communication between them continued in this vein. Helpmann was 'flattered' by the epistolary Hill, finding her letters 'thrilling' and 'charming', even taking the liberty of forwarding one to Miss Hepburn. He was most anxious to see her before he left for London in mid-1970 to tie up any loose ends about the film. Despite a strike impeding telegrams and phone calls, and Helpmann being detained by 'urgent ballet matters', they finally met up during the Adelaide Festival, where he and Hill spent an afternoon discussing the project.[24]

Over the next two months, Hill worked quickly, undeterred by a dose of the Asiatic flu, to assemble a treatment for a screenplay based on her 'Daisy book'. But Helpmann's flirtation with her soon flamed out, and negotiations became more distant and nebulous the following year. Charles 'Harry' Bateson, Coy's husband and Louise's father, stepped into a de facto agent role, negotiating with Helpmann and his solicitor, and later with Angus & Robertson, on Ernestine's behalf. He despatched Hill's 'enlarged synopsis' of her Daisy book to Helpmann, who thought it was of little use, because she 'had dramatised it too much with the film in mind', with Hepburn in the lead role.[25] Moreover, it included too much detail about Bates's early years, based on the material from *My Natives and I* excised from the *Passing*, which would result in too long and too costly a film. Instead, he wanted to focus solely on 'Bates in Australia' (a hint, perhaps, that Bates's childhood tales strained others' credulity). Helpmann resolved that Hill should be retained instead as an adviser, and consequently his solicitor proposed a lower offer for the relevant chapters and any additional assistance, rather than an option for her book.

In June 1971 Hill wrote to Helpmann to recall her Bates manuscript, saying she was willing to consult on the film for free and that she'd 'never estimated my work in terms of money' and 'couldn't bear him to think I was angling for his money'. It was a generous, if self-abnegating, face-saving gesture. 'The reason of this is that he has dropped me out, without a word – rudely and completely,' she told Bateson. 'I think you will understand that I will not be slighted – health is such I could not be involved with script writers or film stars on location, even this year.'[26] Helpmann, like Hill, suffered serious health problems, resulting in him being hospitalised in London, and communication from afar had been difficult, dwindling over the past six months. But Ernestine was under no illusion that he had dumped her and had done so without explanation. By late 1970, there were announcements in the press that Helpmann had purchased the film rights to Salter's as yet unpublished Bates biography. She'd heard that he'd been consulting on the project with Mary Durack, her erstwhile friend, who'd never even met Daisy, although in 1969 she'd published *The Rock and the Sand*, a history of Catholic missions in the north-west which included research into Bates's activities at Beagle Bay.

Then, in news that stung more deeply than the prospect of Helpmann using Salter and Durack as the key sources for the screenplay, she learned he'd purchased the rights to *The Passing of the Aborigines* – the book that would not have been published without her own unacknowledged literary midwifery. Louise Campbell later reflected to Eleanor Witcombe:

> Nor is it very gratifying that at no time we know of did he personally write Aunty Ernie himself to tell of the concluding moves he was making, the acquiring of the rights in The Passing. Against that, we have to realise that he was probably just anxious to have the Rights to anything which gave him potential if the film did come off – and naturally as cheaply as possible.[27]

The film was never made. In 1976 Helpmann engaged Witcombe to write the screenplay after two failed attempts by other writers based on Salter's book, which Hepburn had rejected. But the collaboration faltered, according to Witcombe, because 'Helpmann kept disappearing and wouldn't come up with any money'. In 1983 Witcombe set up a company, Ooldea Films, determined to produce her own biopic as revelations about Bates's marriage and her humbler Irish Catholic origins were surfacing, but she ultimately failed to secure funding. Besides, the cultural tide was turning against Daisy. The revelation of Bates's lies about her personal history had not only attracted curiosity – they'd detracted from her saintly reputation and the reliability of her ethnological work. Bates had also become, Witcombe observed, the 'bête noir' of the current generation of Aboriginal activists, especially those of mixed descent, who 'violently opposed' perpetuating her name in any way.[28]

If the Helpmann venture had become an agonising series of negotiations and betrayals for Hill, it firmed her resolve to finish her own Bates memoir, although Bateson warned her the Australian publishing situation was 'pretty grim'. British publishers were reducing their Australian print runs, and bookstores in Australia were downsizing.[29] Yet despite this bleak outlook and although A&R was already committed to publishing Salter's Bates book, Davis thought there might be room for Ernestine's Bates memoir because it was 'vignette' not biography.

Hill typed on. 'It is so hard to hope for the future – everything changes, peters out. So we just keep on for the love of it.'[30] It wasn't only the love of writing or the faint prospect of income that motivated her to continue the screenplay project as a book, but ownership of her friend and her story. 'Her possessiveness about DB always puzzled me,' Davis wrote after Hill's death:

> for Ernestine was such a generous creature and would surely
> have forgiven the old lady her excessive vanity and pride
> and failure to give Ernestine her due. I know little about
> Helpmann's treachery; but I do know how disturbed Ernestine
> was at Elizabeth Salter's undertaking the biography; and I'm
> sure she didn't really intend to write one herself even if she had
> been capable of it in those later years.[31]

But Helpmann's treachery had inflamed an old wound. Originally Ernestine had only confided Bates's betrayal of her – 'Daisy's book was written by me, as you know, and many know' – to family and close literary friends, such as Mary Gilmore. Ernestine began to make bolder, more public claims over the years after Bates's death.

In 1971 journalist Max Brown aired this piece of literary gossip in an exposé of 'that starched and corseted saint', anticipating the publication of Salter's biography. 'But look again charming reader …' he asked, 'if Daisy didn't write it. Who did?' Back in 1963 'the ablest and most travelled of Australia's writers and a top-class journalist', Ernestine Hill, had told him she'd 'ghosted' *The Passing of the Aborigines*. Her confession explained the book's 'extraordinary contradictions', combining 'the field notes and misanthropy of a savage old lady (Daisy) with the high skill, poetry and certain quirks of a younger, more brilliant woman torn between a genius as a writer and her opportunism as a journalist (Ernestine)'.[32] Mary Durack wrote in a more circumspect 1967 *Age* retrospective on the *Passing*:

> There seems no reason why it should not now be told that we owe 'The Passing of the Aborigines' to the devoted labor and the skilled editing of Ernestine Hill, who was never given and never claimed any credit for this task. Nor did she allow any hint of another voice to blur that of Daisy Bates whose story, full of warm humor, pathos and kindly perception did much to awaken Australians to the Aborigine as a human being.[33]

Back in 1935, Ernestine had claimed she only wanted recognition as a co-author to reflect her own literary prowess but, after several decades of financial hardship, she'd become anxious about her potential loss of earnings from Bates's bestseller. She was concerned about who had the rights to the early chapters of *My Natives and I*, which she saw as substantially her own work and 'the most interesting part' – and also the most fictitious, as it transpired. She was worried that Elizabeth Salter might 'lift' some of this material without acknowledgement, and wrote to her solicitor, inquiring whether she had any claim to 'copyright of my work in the writing and preparation of serial and so protect – not the material but the writing of the chapters and passages devoted to the life story, and the writing throughout?' Enclosing a copy of Bates's thankyou note, she reinforced her request's seriousness with 'I have never made public the credit of writing this book until now – when strangers intervene', although she had gone public by proxy through Mary Gilmore, Mary Durack and Max Brown's claims.[34] Asserting 'I wrote the Life and I wrote the Book – from Daisy's material in a full-time series of interviews daily in the library of *Adelaide Advertiser*' to Charles Bateson, who edited *Kabbarli*, she offered this letter to him and Beatrice Davis to reproduce in that book as evidence of her authorship of the *Passing*.

Both Hill's solicitor and her publisher advised her she did not hold copyright – Ernestine complained that Davis was quite 'lofty' about the matter – to the *Advertiser* material not included in the *Passing*. But rivalry with Salter, along with Helpmann's 'treachery' and Bates's dissembling over her contribution to the *Passing*, drove her on. Hill believed she had the mandate to write the memoir she called *The Real Kabbarli*: 'From twenty years of friendship and infinite knowledge of power, I am the one to do it, and Daisy would almost tearfully ask me to.'[35]

'Too breathless to talk at all. Result of spending all of yesterday sorting etc with Mrs Campbell esp. Johnnie Wise-cap.'

By mid-1972 Hill couldn't walk far at all. Movement made her breathless; her strength was ebbing a little every day. In July she took to her bed and stopped writing, only asking once for her notes. She moved into a nursing home, ostensibly to free Bob to look for work, but she didn't like it, so Bob brought her back to his place and organised regular visits from a nurse. Hill's doctor 'made it very definite that she was entering a terminal phase of emphysema, and that she could not expect to live more than a few weeks'. Ernestine agreed to enter hospital, where she was placed on a six-bed ward, her struggles being made quite public in that new and unliterary view of Death. She cried out for air 'in a really terrible tone', Bob wrote in a harrowing letter to Rene afterwards, although 'her heart, being very strong, virtually carried on without oxygen'. He agreed with the nursing staff that she should be given a sedative, and three hours later she died, her 'heart finally accepting defeat'.[36]

Hill was buried 'just under a tree', as she'd wished, at Mount Gravatt Cemetery in Brisbane. In a fitting gesture to Ernestine's love of the diverse north, a Torres Strait Islander pastor conducted a service for a knot of family and friends by her graveside a few days after her death on 21 August 1972. The mainstream newspapers published obituaries drawing on the iconography of her youth, celebrating her as a woman of courage. Alan Queale was disappointed there'd been so little acknowledgement of Hill's death in Brisbane, where he was now a magistrate: the *Catholic Leader*, who'd published some of her early writing, didn't post a funeral notice or mention her death. It was churlish, given her national profile: 'the Church can be a bit uncharitable towards her children who stray from it … yet as a good Australian and a good writer the matter of Faith should not have been taken into account.' Those close to her expressed their grief privately. 'You must know that I feel her passing deeply,' Charles Bateson told Bob. Not only had he worked closely with Hill in her final years, but she was a reminder of past happiness, of his first marriage to Ernestine's cousin Coy. 'Anyhow, my affection for poor, tragic Ernestine and my admiration for what she contributed in illuminating the Australian background at a time when so little was known of it made me more willing to do anything possible to help her work be properly appreciated by her fellow Australians,' Beatrice Davis declared.[37]

Hill's debts at her death totalled $712.92. She had royalties of $306.43 owing from Angus & Robertson, but these and personal effects did not quite bridge the gap: her Olivetti typewriter and Minolta camera were valued together at $70, and her household goods at a total of $100. Relatives mooted whether Ernestine had lodged a tax return for years, although her income was possibly too negligible to be taxable. A year later, her solicitor mailed a cheque of $26.18 for half-year royalties, commenting: 'This demonstrates how Mrs. Hill's royalties have been declining over the years and could be important in establishing this fact.'[38]

Then there were her trunks, with their motherlode of notes. Foster and Davis contacted the National Library about valuing Hill's papers, which Rene hoped might provide the basis of a legacy for Hill's grandchildren. But when an NLA official appraised the material, 'the decision was that on the whole, it was worthless'. Instead, the Fryer Library acquired Hill's papers as part of its local Australiana collection.[39] As for the rumours of an unpublished manuscript that was her real legacy: Davis told *The Australian* to expect news of a posthumous Hill book, excited by the prospect of unearthing 'Johnnie Wise-cap'. But when 'Wise-cap' was found, Bateson could only assemble six complete chapters although it comprised sixteen draft chapters with plans for a further two. 'She seems to have spent her last few years looking very busy,' he told Davis, 'but in fact doing no more than retyping, almost without alteration, a chapter or short story she had written several years before. I had, of course, suspected this and now know that I was correct.' Davis thought Ernestine had had a mental block for fifteen years, stopping her from completing anything: 'I believe her incessant nervous typing, which she called working, was merely retyping: she was, as you know, a superb typist, and I think this activity must have soothed her in her despairs.' There'd also been hints about another near-complete manuscript, a personal memoir, but, true to form, her papers yielded only some biographical snatches about other high-profile figures Hill had known, such as Archibald. The memoir was the one Ernestine had been writing about Daisy, a telling slippage, continuing their friendship's blurred boundaries and lopsided dynamic. Hill had finished *Kabbarli*, Davis thought, because 'the Salter biography, the prospective film, and her conviction that Daisy belonged to her, spurred her on'.[40]

13

A fleeting project

*'I am no anthropologist, and these stray notes of mine ...
are no attempt to set a figure in mosaic, but only a
bower-bird's playground of shining bits and pieces ...'*[1]

On Australia Day in 1965, Ernestine Hill recorded 'setting my own judgment of 66 years of three generations of memories in Australia – of my own and others, the last of the first of the invaders – and, in other words, a bangtail muster of a "big mob"': a big mob of stories.[2] Reading this gloss some fifty years later in her archival material in the Fryer Library, I was intrigued by how she'd framed her lineage – not in the triumphalist rhetoric of pioneering or the cautious phrasing of white settler history, but the provocative language of invasion. Stumbling across snippets like this in Hill's appropriately named '66 years of fragments' gave me pause for thought: when did white Australians with a family history similar to Hill's – and for that matter, my own Anglo-Celtic antecedents – start referring to themselves as invaders? It seemed more than a coincidence that she should be making this 'judgment' on 26 January – a day whose celebration as the anniversary of the First Fleet Landing, that landmark of white colonisation, Aboriginal activists had protested against as early as 1938, recasting it as a Day of Mourning. I'd originally heard of proposals to change Australia Day's name to Invasion or Survival Day as an undergraduate student during the anti-Bicentennial protests of

1988. With youthful arrogance, I'd presumed my generation was among the first of the invaders to entertain this shift in semantics and outlook following the political activism accompanying the push for Aboriginal self-determination in the 1970s. But how aware had Hill – and others from previous generations of settler Australians – been of the unsettling, race-related aspects of our history?

Questions like this compelled me to keep scouring Hill's archives to understand her personal history and how she had come to these realisations. At the same time I knew that while some of her observations were progressive, others would be considered ethically suspect from a 21st-century, postcolonial perspective. In another snippet titled 'Wirra' I came across in her manuscripts, Ernestine imagines she shares an affinity with the Aboriginal women she'd seen, uprooted from their country, wandering the back roads, carrying a coolibah or wirra of goods, in her case lugging 'this wirra of mine [that] now holds over sixty years of memories, travel, research, within Australia and our generations'.[3] She assumes she has a right, even a mandate, to collect and tell their stories as she did in the second-last chapter of the *Loneliness*, believing that Aboriginal people, as the victims of white invasion, were dying out.

Given some of the outmoded cultural baggage accompanying Hill's legacy, what is the significance of her vast published and unpublished corpus? Although she aspired to document the disappearing ways and language of Aboriginal and pioneering cultures like Bates, her notes lack the systematic rigour of trained anthropologists, who'd secured a place in the Australian academic landscape by the mid-20th century when she shouldered this ethnographic burden. She acknowledges as much in *The Territory*, protesting 'I am no anthropologist, and these stray notes of mine, gathered mainly from blacks and from a few observant whites in many days and many ways of roaming, are no attempt to set a figure in mosaic, but only a bower-bird's playground of shining bits and pieces, facets of the aboriginal mind.' Here Hill realises her work as folk ethnographer is inevitably thwarted – that it is 'Impossible, now, to read the Rosetta Stone'–because of the erosion of Aboriginal culture by white settlement.[4] To me, this is where the strength of her vision lies: in its imperfect nature. As much as Hill's perspective is backward-looking in fixing Aboriginal culture in the past, she is also startlingly farsighted in recognising white colonisation's damaging effects on Australia's first people. This is especially the case in her unpublished material in the Fryer Library, where she expresses a counter-history – or at least a counterpoint – throughout to standard, mainstream Australian history by recounting Aboriginal and settler stories from the past.

Invasion reverberates as a theme throughout Hill's notes – 'the white man's invasion', 'the Christian invasion of the Great South Land', 'the last of the first of the invaders'.[5] According to Tom Griffiths, Hill's contemporary Eleanor Dark also used 'invasion', along with 'we stole the land', to refer to British colonisation in an earlier draft of *The Timeless Land,* until her publisher challenged the suitability of its usage during wartime, fearing it might expose Australia's weaknesses to the 'enemy'. Dark documented her background research for her book in the Mitchell Library in notebooks like Hill, including a specific one recording 'customs and traditions of Australian Aborigines, organised alphabetically into sections on "Ceremonies", "Kinship" and "Language". Eleanor was captivated,' Griffiths observes, 'but she also felt the burden of this scholarly mission, "a type of mental effort which doesn't come naturally to me" and ultimately left her "with a sort of loathing of my desk."'[6] Why Hill didn't feel this sort of loathing relates to her belief in her ethnographic mandate and her investment in preserving 'swiftly vanishing' old Australia. Griffiths says that Dark 'was decades ahead of Australia's historians in realising that the big story about British colonisation at Port Jackson was that of the encounter between settlers and Aborigines', suggesting that Aboriginal people's declaration of a Day of Mourning in Sydney in 1938 may have influenced her telling of 'a story of the white settlement partly from the black man's point of view'.[7]

Hill was in Sydney's Mitchell Library at the time, researching Flinders, which may be when she became aware of the idea of white settlement as invasion. Much of her unpublished material documents the struggles of white explorers like Sturt, Stuart and Leichhardt, along with Flinders, and their French counterparts, Baudin and de Freycinet, in encountering Australia. She was also fascinated with James Cook and began planning a novel based on his life, similar in flavour to *My Love Must Wait,* in the lead-up to the bicentenary of the *Endeavour*'s first landing at Botany Bay in 1970. She attempted to humanise Cook as a national icon, chipping away at that 'wooden figure-head, an effigy ciphered with dates and latitudes' – a process that led her to query some of his exploits. 'First use of the cynical word "dispersed"', she wrote in the margin of her transcription of Cook's journal entry in Cooktown. The word 'dispersal' also appears in her records of some pioneering legends; she recalled how 'skulls and bones could be found about the spring' twenty-five years after a massacre and how English 'gentleman riders' in the Kimberleys of the 1880s were 'leading the punitive raids against the cattle-killers, taking the girls to be "stock-boys", house-lubras and wives'. Nor are all of these tales from Australia's wild west; Hill heads her account of Melbourne's white settlement: 'The Dispossessed. Batman's Treaty with the Yarra Tribes'.[8]

Hill's background notes for 'Johnnie Wise-cap' elaborate similar themes: 'The natives of Australia have never been recognised as having any legal title to their tribal lands ... In the N.T. long leases of large areas, many tribes not a square foot to call their own of well-defined countries that had been theirs from time immemorial.' Her insights here are highly prescient for the 1950s – if anything, more in keeping with the struggle for land rights and native title accompanying the self-determination era.[9] Hill conceived 'Wise-cap' as 'a complete history of the aboriginal race since the Christian invasion of Australia', according to the following schema in her notes:

Purposes

History of white man's treatment of aborigines.

Stone age compared with civilization.

Contrast of life and love of black woman and white.

Historic picture of settlement and pearling.

Aboriginal life, language, lore and legend.

Wholesale exploitation for white man's gain.

Vanished race.

A comedic Gothic romance in the tradition of *Frankenstein* set in late 19th-century Australia, 'Wise-cap' queries what vision of Australia is possible in the aftermath of colonisation by exploring the predicament of an albino Aboriginal man unable to fit into either traditional Aboriginal or white settler societies. The book opens with the discovery of a mysterious man of indeterminate racial identity, 'a cracked old combo outside of everything', in the Kimberley. He is in fact a full-descent Aboriginal man lacking dark pigment: Hill's inspiration for 'Johnnie Wise-cap' came from an 1893 *Argus* article, the 'Story of Nungun', about an 'Albino discovered by A. McPhee, 200 miles from the coast in the far north, taken to Melbourne and exhibited'. Like Nungun, Wise-cap is kidnapped by an unscrupulous pearler and taken to Melbourne to be exhibited as a freak at the Bourke Street Palace of Varieties. An anthropologist, Professor von Weinckel, hears of Johnnie's servitude and is appalled, paying the bond to free him. He invites Johnnie to live with him and his daughter, Erika, a bluestocking linguist with some Batesian preoccupations, in his suitably Gothic mansion on Gotham Road, Kew. After being given a makeover as a Victorian gentleman, Johnnie is happily employed translating Aboriginal lore and language for Erika in exchange for learning English and German.

Somewhat predictably, Johnnie and Erika fall in love, and Professor von Weinckel is aghast when he learns that they intend to marry. When he asks Erika what she will do if their children 'are blackfellows', telling her it will 'ruin your life', she replies that rather than having children, she and Johnnie intend to sail the world, compiling dictionaries. The professor chokes and dies shortly after this revelation, which Johnnie believes is his fault – not only because of Erika's shock announcement about their engagement but because he accidentally pointed the death-bone at von Weinckel during a 'semi-scientific evening' when Johnnie was persuaded grudgingly to perform a corroboree dance for guests.

Fearing Erika's wrath at her father's death, Johnnie deserts Kew, 'swinging a boomerang instead of a cane'. After walking across the continent via Uluru back to the Kimberley, he marries a local Aboriginal woman and is later to be found inscribing lines from Heine alongside rock art in a bizarre expression of cultural hybridity. 'Wise-cap' stops short of its final two envisaged chapters: Louise Campbell suggested to me that Hill may have failed to complete the manuscript because she was squeamish about depicting sexual relations between Johnnie and Erika, which was where the story was headed, should they reunite and set sail on their joint dictionary-writing venture.[10]

Although Erika and Johnnie never consummate their union, 'Wise-cap' was subversive for the 1950s, when Hill wrote the manuscript, in suggesting that a highly educated white woman might pair up with a black man – unlike the *Loneliness*, where the only woman (Mrs Witchetty) to do so is seen as an amusing working-class curio. Their union also reverses the trend for portraying doomed or exploitative relationships between white men and Aboriginal women in novels by Hill's contemporaries such as Prichard's *Coonardoo* and Herbert's *Capricornia*. In imagining a relationship between an Aboriginal man and a white woman, 'Wise-cap' gestures towards a more diverse vision of Australia, although it also reflects anxieties about the hybrid's future survival from the assimilationist era, which was at its height during the 1950s. By Ernestine Hill's death in 1972, its view of hybridity had dated radically as civil rights activism by urban Aboriginal people 'now the rage' and the publication of Aboriginal writers' work gathered momentum during the 1960s. As literary academic Adam Gall writes, while 'Hill's work is so concerned with futurity … imagining Aboriginality as "fast disappearing" has largely, though not comprehensively, given way to quite different, if still contestable, accounts of indigenous futures'.[11] So too did her self-appointed role as wirra-toting scribe and proxy for Aboriginal women, who, far from disappearing, became strong and vocal advocates and recognised writers in the decades following her.

Hill was not alone in her fascination with what the 'white Aborigine' or hybrid might portend, not only within the then 'wicked', newsworthy predicament of mixed-descent Aboriginal people she saw on the fringes of settler society during her travels, but in tales she heard of interracial boundary dwellers, such as Mrs Witchetty, of two white women rumoured to be living in Arnhemland during the 1920s and of a blue-eyed man, like Johnnie, 'living with the Arnhemland blacks, looking like a half-caste in hell'.[12] These stories intrigued her because they suggested social experiments in peaceful co-existence and the possibility of settlers grafting as hybrids onto the landscape. This theme was a staple outlier of the colonial imagination, epitomised by Eliza Fraser, the shipwrecked Scot who lived with the Badtjala people in Queensland, who inspired enduring interest, from popular accounts in the mid-19th century to Sidney Nolan's nightmarish paintings of her experience, to the raunchy film of the same name and Patrick White's *A Fringe of Leaves* in 1976. David Malouf's 1993 novel, *Remembering Babylon*, narrates the story of Gemmy Fairley, a British cabin boy who lives with Aboriginal people for sixteen years but struggles to adapt and is ostracised by pioneers on his return to white society. Nevertheless, the spectre of cultural appropriation in which white Australians profit yet again from Aboriginal dispossession has never been too far from non-Indigenous forms of hybridity, most dramatically in the adoption of pseudonymous Aboriginal identities such as Elizabeth Durack's use of the nom de plume of Eddie Burrup and Leon Carmen's authorship of *My Own Sweet Time* under the name of Wanda Koolmatrie.

Germaine Greer's 2003 *Quarterly* essay, 'Whitefella jump up', presents one of the most provocative expressions of desire for a hybrid Australian identity. Greer calls for Australia to recognise itself as an Aboriginal country and for all Australians to declare themselves Aboriginal as a means of unshackling the stranglehold of white settler identity, admonishing readers to try 'saying it to yourself in the mirror: "I live in an Aboriginal country".' It is, she acknowledges, a challenge that is difficult to implement without reinforcing white imperialism or inadvertently enacting another form of cultural appropriation. 'Any such assumption could well be seen by Aboriginal people as the last and most terrible co-option, a final annihilation,' Greer writes. 'More vexing is the question of whether blackfellas would let us become Aboriginal, whether they would adopt us.'[13]

It is an enticing idea, one that persists through hybrid imaginings such as Hill's notion of an Australia wrested in Aboriginal and settler cultural history, traditions and language. It speaks of a longing to be grounded in what Europeans saw as a hostile physical landscape and a culture they found quite other, freighted with a vision of how Australia could be reconceived. Historian Inga Clendinnen offers another turn on this motif in her image of dancing with strangers, of British First Fleeters dancing with the original Australians at Sydney Cove, as a space of curious play that initially existed between Aboriginal and settler cultures. She admonishes us to accept our intertwined identity: 'Despite our long alienation, despite our merely adjacent histories, and through processes I do not yet understand, we are now more like each other than we are like any other people.'[14] This could extend, as Hill thought, to how we envisage a national literature. In his book *Australia Day*, journalist Stan Grant suggests in terms that echo and amplify this conjoined vision that, rather than classifying Australian authors as black or white, we reconfigure our literary culture as an 'unbroken tradition' of 'Australian stories, ancient and modern, and all efforts at recognition – a need to be seen. It is indeed a fleeting project, an attempt to capture a people – a people always changing – in a time and place.'[15]

Hill's own bicultural ethos, reflected in her attempt to preserve Aboriginal and settler stories in her mosaic of fragments, anticipates this vision of a fleeting project seeking to capture something of an ever-changing people. Despite its shortcomings – which she acknowledges are part of any literary historical project, post-colonisation – her perspective is a remarkable one. Hill sought to express something not only of an Australia she had seen from her earliest days as a reporter, taking notes in the campfire's shadows on the threshold between cultures, but of what it could become, spun from the fibres of its histories and mythologies.

Beyond Ernestine Hill and her ethnographic aspirations is the more challenging figure of Daisy Bates. 'Hill and Bates mark a shift in the movable feast that was the amateur ethnologist,' cultural theorist Liz Conor observes of the historical passage their lives spanned from the days of explorers' and pioneers' notetaking and journalling about Aboriginal people and culture to the development of anthropology as an academic discipline. 'The emphasis both authors place are on documenting as a means to preserve the mythologies of black primitivism and white pioneering is key to their freelance entrepreneurship since, as Meaghan Morris argues, "writing is really the border that separates white from black, life from death, and history from oblivion."'[16]

Bates's manuscripts, her efforts to document Aboriginal languages and cultures to save them from what she thought was certain oblivion, did not lie fallow indefinitely at the National Library. Despite being critical of the 'negativism' and 'sentimental tosh' Bates peddled about Aboriginal people, in 1969 professor of anthropology AP Elkin commented there was 'much gold to be garnered' from her papers, although he thought her lack of scientific training was evident insofar as her 'reports on kinship and totemism were tantalizingly incomplete'.[17] In 1974 British social anthropologist Professor Rodney Needham stated that it was 'very desirable that a scholar competent in the analysis of Australian social organization, and familiar with the history of anthropological investigation in the continent, should edit these papers for publication'.[18] Notably, it was a female scholar, Isobel White, who first engaged substantially with Bates's collection by editing her lost manuscript, *The Native Tribes of Western Australia*, during the early 1980s.

With the advent of native title legislation in the 1990s, Bates's ethnographic work took on fresh relevance. Information that Fanny Balbuk passed on to Daisy Bates at Ma'amba Reserve about the Bibbulmun – Noongar people in the south-west – featured in a landmark native title case. On 19 September 2006 Justice Wilcox of the Federal Court of Australia found in *Bennell v Western Australia* that Noongar people held native title over parts of Perth – the first determination to recognise a claim over a capital city.[19] Bates's description of the territory and practices of the people she called the 'Bibbulmun Nation' played a central role in establishing the existence of a single Noongar society in the south-west in this claim. Her field notes, along with those of fellow folk ethnologists such as EM Curr and RH Mathews, continue to be used to support claims in the National Native Title Tribunal.

The survey work that Bates conducted for the Western Australian government, compiling Aboriginal vocabularies and grammars, has had a new lease of life in the digital age through Bates Online. This project, led by associate professor Nicholas Thieburger in collaboration with the National Library of Australia, has digitised 21 000 pages of Bates's manuscripts in a searchable database linking vocabulary, phrases and sentences to their originary locations and language groups on maps.[20] It is a significant contribution to existing linguistic and ethnographic work, given that less than fifty out of an estimated 300 Australian Indigenous languages are spoken today, providing a resource not only for researchers such as linguists and botanists, but for Aboriginal people, especially in remote areas, to reconnect with their family histories and heritage.[21]

Through these evolving uses of her manuscripts, Bates's ethnographic work has had renewed, even restorative, value in preserving Aboriginal languages and cultures. It is perhaps fitting that her material should be repurposed in these ways, given that in some respects she was a woman ahead of her time, an unconventional self-taught scientist and curious about the potential of new media such as radio broadcasts and film documentaries for cultural transmission. She deserves some credit for her perspicacity and dedication in preserving this material when it was widely assumed that Aboriginal people were dying out in the wake of the ravages they'd experienced through frontier conflict, the spread of introduced diseases and dispossession from their homelands. Although Bates's ministrations to Aboriginal people were often self-seeking and paternalistic, she expressed more sympathy for their plight than many of her contemporaries.

Nevertheless, Bates's casting as a mythic malevolent figure, 'Daidj Bate mamu', is understandable because of the damaging ways in which she represented Anangu's cultural practices and of how she treated mixed-descent Aboriginal people. Ernestine Hill may have seen her as the ultimate exemplar of the white hybrid bluestocking living on the boundary between cultures, but to postcolonial, Anglo-Celtic feminists such as me, Bates is unsettling to have as a foremother.

While writing this book, I made several visits to the National Library to read material from Bates's extensive collections. She often seemed elusive as I leafed through her copious manuscripts, which recalled Hill's bowerbird nest for me – a mess of shining and not-so-shining bits and pieces. After satisfying my more routine biographical queries, I fell into a habit of pulling out a box of Bates's notebooks from her camps at random at the end of each day; I figured I would never get through all of her collection's ninety-odd boxes but that this was a way of immersing myself in slabs of her life. The lists of words in Aboriginal dialects, snatches of local stories and logs of visitors to her camp in her notebooks are interspersed with longer diary-style observations, which I often found revealing. Sometimes I was confounded by their contents, like the screeds of vitriol she directed at half-castes, Germans and trade unionists, among others. At other times, I caught glimpses of a daily existence beyond her flagrant, alienating rhetoric – that of the anthropologist's quiet life of observation. Daisy might describe an episode like camping overnight with an Aboriginal couple on a clifftop near Fowlers Bay, hunting and skinning lizards, cooking tea and damper with them, then searching for meteorites on the beach below with the woman the next day. Or she might savour the simple, natural pleasures of living on the Nullarbor Plain: 'Often a little strange wind comes, alights for just a moment and is gone just as though a fan were waved from some other sphere.'[22] Fleeting moments that reflected a genuine delight in people and place.

At the end of my last trip to the National Library, I retrieved a box of Bates's Ooldea notebooks I'd looked at several years earlier but which I wanted to reread, interested in whether I'd find anything fresh after visiting her campsite at the soak. Just before closing time, I fished out the last three pages from the bottom of the box. They featured a careful typescript in Pitjantjatjara with an occasional stage direction in English – 'they come gliding half stepping waving wands between their hands. Women ... ' accompanied by a pencilled diagram of two circles stacked vertically and joined by cross-hatching. I couldn't be certain but I felt it was the number eight dance, or something very similar, that the women had told me about at Fowlers Bay.[23] It was as if the arcs of my two journeys – through the archives and along the Eyre to Ooldea – had suddenly met, and I was hearing something both ways, from the women and Bates, about coming together to dance.

14

Inside the breakwind

*'... they come gliding half stepping waving wands
between their hands. Women ...'*[1]

Much later than I would have liked, I returned to Yalata. I drove down the Stuart Highway from Alice Springs beneath whimsical desert clouds, the detritus of cumulus formations blown up from the south, to Port Augusta. Turning onto the Eyre, I passed through countryside that had once registered to me as little more than a bland agricultural landscape but now possessed a welcoming familiarity. I picked out landmarks from my past forays with ease, and those of Hill and Bates, across the Bight. Pausing at the Caltex servo in Penong, I could see the original sandstone town-within-the-town against its backdrop of quietly churning windmills. I imagined Daisy, drinking cups of tea on the verandah of Mrs Nieass's store, writing heated letters to Ernestine about the white farmers taking over the area, urging her to visit. After Penong, I recognised an otherwise unremarkable stretch of highway as Bookabie, where Bates had leapt out of Mrs Nieass's car, chasing after people she called 'her natives'.

I'd broached the Eyre two years earlier, hoping to return to Yalata to check my account of community members' stories with them, but there'd been a death and I'd had to turn back. A year later, when I attempted to visit Yalata again, there'd been another death, this time of a senior man who'd been suggested to me as a guide to Ooldea on my first trip. I struggled to line up a mutually agreeable time between my work commitments and the community's activities, especially given the distance between us. I began to wonder whether I would ever see the Yalata people again, or if I'd just caught them by luck before.

When I finally returned to the community, I didn't recognise anyone in the administration block; its management had changed, and the new manager, whom I'd never met, was away. I hung around in the parking area, hoping to catch sight of someone I knew. I wondered if anyone would remember me – enough time had elapsed and enough strange whitefellas, I imagined, would have passed through the community for this to be possible. I'd spoken to one of the senior women on the phone beforehand, telling her of my visit, and I contemplated making my way to the vacant lot beside the Bryants' house to see if anyone was there. Then, in the way things inexplicably seem to happen in remote communities, Russell appeared, walking between the buildings, hand outstretched, saying, 'It's good to have you back here.'

We returned to the vacant lot where his mother Rita was living by herself in a large khaki canvas tent that looked like military surplus; the army had assisted Yalata with a works program, refurbishing houses and the caravan park. The middle-aged adults who'd been camping last time were inside the house next door to the lot; Russell had relocated with his children to a new place elsewhere in the community.

Outside her tent, Rita stirred up the white embers of the previous night's fire with a stick and flames swirled into life. Why she was in the tent, I wasn't sure. Isobel White described how once, when an Adelaide architect visited Yalata in the 1970s and asked the women what kind of house they'd like, all except one told him they didn't want to leave their wiltjas. 'We'd have to keep it clean,' a woman explained, which was 'greeted with murmurs of agreement'. But 'this does not represent the racist's stereotype of the lazy, feckless Aboriginal woman,' White emphasised. 'Rather it indicates a rejection of white values, particularly those centred around the ownership and careful maintenance of property.'[2] Perhaps Rita preferred living in a wiltja as Aṉangu women had done for generations.

Rita summoned Margaret and Joy, and they directed me to drive through Yalata, pointing out local landmarks and telling me their history, often from when people first camped there. We parked at a bushy patch on the community's edge, where they sat on a sarong from my van that I spread out on the ground. I scrabbled about, trying to start a fire using dead leaves and bark to boil them a cup of tea. We talked, listened, sharing stories, Rita acting as translator, pressing me to learn Pitjantjatjara words: waṟu – fire, inma – song, minyma – mature woman.

Was this what it had been like, I wondered – people volunteering and insisting that you learn language – for Daisy Bates with Joobaitch, Fanny Balbuk, Mr Windlass at Ooldea and others, and for Ernestine Hill in her 'little impromptu wongi' with Aboriginal people on the road? The image western anthropology evokes is of the scientist roughing it at the fringes of the European-known world, painstakingly extracting linguistic and folkloric knowledge from local people. But had it been the other way round, Aboriginal people making contact, eagerly plying them with words, dancing with strangers on the metaphorical shore, inviting the other in?

Bates made a great show of her linguistic prowess – 'master of 188 dialects', her memorial at Pyap boasts. In the *Passing* she presents her exploits as a display of mastery, of acquiring control over Aboriginal people wherever she went, trying to save unfortunate wretches destined to die out. Yet in her notes she describes how elders cared for her wherever she camped, assisting her in recording languages, stories and customs. Perhaps what I found most surprising in researching Bates was that despite all the complaints about her garrulousness, she was also described as a 'great listener'. According to Edith Sinclair: 'she'd just have this little bit of paper and write down a few things to keep it in her memory ... I'm sure she didn't talk and talk to them. She just waited for the information to come from them.'[3] This technique, which Bates claimed distinguished her from her male contemporaries, was essential to her ethnological practice of engaging in everyday conversations with Aboriginal people while camping alongside them for decades.

In describing Anangu's relationship with Bates, the Yalata women echoed this idea of a simple exchange: that they had been learning 'both ways', protecting her as she protected them. 'Both ways' is a term I'm familiar with from Aboriginal educational contexts, used to indicate the sharing of western and Indigenous knowledge, about which I've sometimes been sceptical because of how it might mask a power differential. Bates, for example, capitalised on knowledge she learned from Aboriginal people in trying to build her reputation as an ethnologist and a protector, blindsiding them by publishing scurrilous articles about cannibalistic practices and predicting their demise. Hill assisted Bates by mythologising her as Kabbarli, the great white grandmother, incorporating Daisy's version of the story in this process: that she was protecting Anangu rather than it happening both ways. Part of the long shadow, as Lisa Waller puts it, cast by the Kabbarli myth is a maternal authority role for settler women like me in the Indigenous arena, especially in remote areas where middle-class professionals often deliver services, manage administration or conduct research and implement government policies in Aboriginal communities.

Sitting with the Yalata women, hearing their stories not only about Bates but their own history, I wanted to cast off the great white mother mantle and return to an earlier, childlike state of simply listening and learning from them. In *Trapped in the Gap*, medical anthropologist Emma Kowal queries the motives of white anti-racists – as she calls left-wing, middle-class professionals like me who work in remote Indigenous contexts – when we indulge the fantasy of role reversal, ostensibly giving up our power and becoming like children. Of how we often revel in episodes on bush trips and in remote communities when Indigenous locals display their knowledge by showing you where to find bush medicine, taking you hunting or inviting you to participate in inma. Or in their practical and mechanical know-how, as when the Yalata people helped me out when I bogged the four-wheel-drive at Ooldea Soak. 'In these moments we feel the unadulterated delight of cross-cultural exchange,' Kowal writes, 'and the relief of oppressiveness shed, if only temporarily ... Through this imaginary inversion, the White anti-racist is cleansed of stigma. The White anti-racist that most comfortably inhabits the anti-racist fantasy space is neither overbearing father nor tender mother, but fervent child.'[4] Fumbling my way around Yalata, trying to learn scraps of Pitjantjatjara, slotting into the role of daughter while letting Rita boss me around, I wondered whether it was possible to shift the dynamic beyond the deadlock of mother and child to one of cultural friendship?

The last night of my stay, Rita instructed me to buy trays of chicken and chops, vegetables and flour from the community store for a cook-up on the vacant lot. She made damper while I fried meat in pans over her campfire and wrapped vegetables in foil, placing them in the ashes. Only about five people were around but once the chicken was roasted, another twenty or so appeared then disappeared just as quickly when the food was gone. A neighbour brought a roo tail in foil and buried it among glowing coals. You'll know it's cooked, Rita told me, when you hear the fat sizzling.

While I sat at the campfire outside Rita's tent, Sharon, her eldest, and her husband Sean Kelly pulled up in a LandCruiser. They welcomed me warmly, especially Sean, or the 'camel man', who reminded me how we'd lain on our fronts and scooped out sand from beneath the bogged four-wheel-drive on the soak's flanks. On this occasion, Sean was quite the raconteur, regaling those left around the fire with stories about life when people had camped along the East–West line, before Maralinga.

One story he told, unprompted by me, was about Lewis Lasseter, the knockabout inventor and prospector who died in 1931 while attempting to locate a massive gold reef he reported seeing decades earlier in central Australia. Lasseter quarrelled with fellow team members, struck out on his own and perished several months later near Shaws Creek in the Petermann Ranges. The whereabouts of the reef, if it exists, remains unknown but still inspires quests to find it.[5] Lasseter's story has never exerted the imaginative pull over me that it has for some people; I've tended to dismiss it as Depression fare, a cautionary masculine pioneering tale. Although I haven't studied it extensively, I was familiar with its broad brushstrokes, and the camel man told me some twists I hadn't heard before. During Lasseter's last days in the Petermann Ranges, when he had starved to a scarecrow and was mad with sandy blight, an Aboriginal woman had helped him, leading him to water, pointing out what plants to eat.

Here Sean paused before saying 'like Daisy Bates', indicating he'd understood the crux of my interest in her life at Ooldea. Daisy Bates had had someone too, a friend, not a lover, showing her how to survive at the soak.

Lasseter had written a letter, Sean continued, and given it to Aṉangu, begging them to take it to the Bush Telegraph Station in Alice Springs to summon a rescue party and lead them back to where he was. But the people had never heard of the Bush

Telegraph Station or the name Alice Springs, and they went on their way, travelling as they always did, in the opposite direction, taking Lasseter's unread letter with them, and he died.

The people began telling stories about Lasseter after his death, the camel man said, along with the ones they'd always told to children round the fire at night to lull them to sleep. I was fascinated to hear how Lasseter had become a skein of local mythology: that his tale had had another life among Anangu as a story about a white man failing to survive in the country's centre. The promise of the hybrid, the white Indigene, was always part of the attraction of Bates's as well as Lasseter's story for Hill; they were both tales, as the camel man hinted, about lone whites who'd relied on Aboriginal people in attempting to live in unfamiliar country.

After the cook-up, Rita invited me to sleep overnight by the fire outside her tent. No doubt Ernestine Hill would have accepted the offer, but it was mid-winter, the temperature had been zero overnight on the Bight and I'd left my warm bedding in a donga at the caravan park on the community's edge. So I bailed, saying 'Another time'.

Rita asked me to heap coals from the fire onto a small pile inside her tent before I left. A shovel leant against the wall near her camp bed; crowbars and shovels have supplemented the wana, the women's digging stick, in community life. The tent was a tall, canvas bell-shaped affair rather than a small, nylon, A-shaped one, and I could almost stand upright beneath its peak. Rita told me this was how Anangu had heated wiltja in the old days. I picked up the shovel and scooped white-orange coals from the fire then tipped them onto a patch of grey embers on the ground inside the tent. The pile I heaped was remedial, like all my bushcraft efforts, and one of her sons tended it into a neater, more effective stack. The next morning, I found imprints like kisses melted on the soles of my Dr Martens; I must have walked on stray hot coals the night before.

Inside the breakwind

I thought of Bates, another woman happier to live in a tent, cooking potatoes among her campfire's ashes inside the breakwind, imitating the Spinifex people's ways. After travelling to meet these people on the Nullarbor's edge, I felt I understood the appeal of going off script in this way for a highly intelligent and independent woman whose marriages had failed, who'd been an inattentive mother to her only child, whom men had thwarted professionally. Bates had discovered not only material for her intellectual preoccupations but a fresh relevance in camping alongside Aboriginal people. She'd set herself apart from other whites but she was never truly alone. Anangu had accepted her, drawing her into their lives. Aboriginal women had joined her inside the breakwind, carting water to her tent from the siding. They'd called out to her in the evening, asking her to join them dancing, snaking in and out of a figure-of-eight formation. Children had chased after her on the Trans, wanting to play games with her and eat treats in her camp. An Aboriginal man had been her friend and protector, walking with her on the sandhills, telling her the names of plants, animals and stars, instructing her where to go and not go. They'd named her 'kabbarli', placing her as a grandmother within their networks, but she had betrayed them, distorting this role for her own self-seeking purposes, obscuring how much she had relied on them.

Like Bates, I'd experienced a warmer welcome from Anangu than from anyone else I'd met on the road. I had felt out of place as a middle-aged thinking and writing woman, travelling alone without a friend, partner or dependants, much more misfit than missionary by the time I arrived at Yalata. I was struck by the warmth and openness with which community members, especially the women, had met me. I was scared of abusing their hospitality and generosity, given their history of betrayal – by white fettlers on the Trans line, by Bates, then the missionaries by the soak; through the theft of their children and being 'shoved' and 'eased' off their country to escape Maralinga's toxic mist. Much of their history was echoed in Indigenous people's experience across the country and, rather than disappearing as Bates, Hill and others had predicted, they had proved highly resilient.

I had journeyed across the continent and halfway back again, trying to untangle the threads of the Kabbarli mythology. However troubling some of its strands were, I thought it better that Bates's story be remembered rather than forgotten, for what it revealed about European women's complicated history of relating to Aboriginal people. Nor did I think it possible, or desirable, to attempt to return to a childlike state predating contact between first and other Australians; nor did I want to erase this story's stigma for settler women like me. But my encounters with Aṉangu had left a question hanging: could we be friends, despite this history?

Within the stories Aṉangu had told me about Bates and Lasseter were fleeting snatches of a way beyond relating as either mother or child: that of friendship and interdependence. Ernestine Hill's vision of a national literary history interwoven from Aboriginal and settler mythologies had also possessed an idea of mutuality. She had known this enterprise was inevitably thwarted; that it was impossible to complete this history's mosaic because of the damage done to Aboriginal people and cultures. But her vision was nevertheless compelling for what it expressed of the mourning and longing for wholeness at the country's heart.

Notes

Prologue
1. E Taylor to E Salter, 8 February 1969, NLA MS 6481/2/5.
2. A glossary of Pitjantjatjara words is provided in the notes on page vii of this book.
3. D Bates to W Campion, 19 July 1928, SRSA GRG24 6/570, No. 409/1914.
4. E Hill, interviewed by M Bonnin, 30 March 1972, UQFL633.
5. Sources for the Prologue include: D Bates, *The Passing of the Aborigines*, John Murray, London, 1938, Chs 15 and 16, hereafter abbreviated as *Passing*; E Hill, *Kabbarli: A Personal Memoir of Daisy Bates*, Angus & Robertson, Sydney, 1973, Ch. 6; 'Woman of Ooldea', *West Australian*, 25 June 1932, p. 4; 'On the old Trans line', UQFL18.D.12; 'Ooldea Water', UQFL18.D.1; and T Gara, 'Ooldea soak', *Journal of the Anthropological Society of South Australia*, vol. 26, no. 4, June 1988, pp. 1–11. Racially pejorative terms such as 'gin', 'blacks' and 'natives' feature in early-to-mid-20th-century writing by Ernestine Hill, Daisy Bates and others. Inverted commas are used to signal their first reference in the text; their offensive nature should be assumed for subsequent references.

Introduction
1. D Bates to E Hill, 12 April 1945, UQFL18.D.2.
2. Bates to Hill, 17 October 1946, UQFL18.D.2.
3. Bates to Hill, 12 April 1945, UQFL18.D.2.
4. E Hill to G Mackaness, 26 July 1945, NLA MS 534/471.
5. Bates to Hill, 17 February 1947, UQFL18.D.2.
6. Bates to Hill, 21 March 1947, UQFL18.D.2.
7. Bates to Hill, 15 May 1947, UQFL18.D.2; JA Carrodus to E Hill, 16 November 1948, UQFL18.D.4
8. Hill to G Mackaness, 1 December 1947, NLA MS 534/471.
9. E Hill, 'Australia's Home Notes', NLA MS 3392, p. 1; R Hill, 'Notes by Robert Hill on his mother's Ernestine Hill's "Notes of a Journey – Melbourne to Perth" on which she visited Daisy Bates for the last time (c. 1947)', NLA MS 8392, p. 1.
10. R Hill, p. 2.
11. E Hill, *The Great Australian Loneliness*, 2nd edn, Robertson & Mullens, Melbourne, 1942, p. 7 (hereafter abbreviated as *Loneliness*).
12. *Loneliness*, p. 7.
13. *Loneliness*, p. 340.
14. Hill, 'From the first old Centre notebook 1932', UQFL18.A.72.
15. UQFL18.A.33.20.
16. UQFL18.A.26.4.

17 Hill, 'Grand Kangaroo', 18.A.73; M Durack, 'E Hill', *Walkabout*, vol. 18, no. 3, 1952, pp. 8–9.
18 E Hill to R Hill, 17 March 1971, UQFL18.E.1.
19 M Thomas, *The Many Worlds of RH Mathews*, Allen & Unwin, Sydney, 2011, pp. 44–45.
20 D Bates to Professor Fitzherbert, 7 September 1931, BSL MSS 572.994 B321.
21 E Hill, *The Territory*, 3rd edn, Angus & Robertson, Sydney, 1963, p. 348.
22 *Loneliness*, p. 182.
23 E Hill to Coy Bateson, 10 March 1944, UQFL18.E.2.
24 I White, 'Introduction' to D Bates, I White and National Library of Australia, *The Native Tribes of Western Australia*, National Library of Australia, Canberra, 1985, p. 2.
25 E Hill, *Kabbarli: A Personal Memoir of Daisy Bates*, Angus & Robertson, Sydney, 1973, p. 2.

1 A confirmed wanderer
1 D Bates, *The Passing of the Aborigines*, John Murray, London, 1938, p. 115 (hereafter referred to as *Passing*).
2 E Hill, *The Great Australian Loneliness*, 2nd edn, Robertson & Mullens, Melbourne, 1942, p. 7 (hereafter abbreviated as *Loneliness*).
3 B Spencer, *Vagabondage*, UWA Publishing, Perth, 2014 (Kindle loc. 248).
4 *Loneliness*, p. 210.
5 B Garner, *Born in a Tent*, UNSW Press, Sydney, 2013, pp. 237–38.
6 E Hill to G Mackaness, 1 December 1947, NLA MS 534/471.
7 E Hill to Coy Bateson, Letter 25, 12 July 1947, UQFL18.E.1.
8 E Hill, 'Nullarbor. Eucla', UQFL18.D.12.120.
9 Watson family, 'Along the Eyre Highway with E Hill', photograph album, SLSA PRG 1527/3/1-55.
10 Matthew Flinders quoted in 'Streaky Bay – our history', District Council of Streaky Bay, 2 May 2006, Internet Archive Wayback Machine, <web.archive.org/web/20070829230659/http://www.streakybay.sa.gov.au/site/page.cfm?u=274>, viewed 22 April 2020.
11 R Hill, 'Notes by Robert Hill', NLA MS 8392, p. 1.
12 D Bates to E Hill, 15 November 1945, UQFL18.D.2.
13 *Passing*, p. 4.
14 D Bates, 'XIII, 9: Compilation of records on Aborigines; Work of Mrs Bates from 1904 – various accounts', NLA MS 365/66/2.
15 Bates, NLA MS 365/66/8.
16 D Bates to JG Murray, 25 June 1938, NLS ACC. 13328/38, DA 8.
17 Bates, NLA MS 365/66/4.
18 RH Mathews to D Bates, 7 February 1907, NLA MS 365/97/370.
19 Bates, NLA MS 365/66/9.
20 Bates, NLA MS 365/66/9.
21 *Passing*, p. 115.
22 D Bates to G King, 17 January 1913, ML MS 1492.
23 D Bates, 'Section XIII. General notes on Aborigines. Part 6.(d)', NLA MS 365/64/497.

24 DM Bates, *Minutes of Evidence of Royal Aborigines Commission*, SA Government, Adelaide, 1916, 29 July 1914, p. 31.
25 D Bates, 'Rough notes', NLA MS 365/66/52.
26 Bates, 'More about the Aborigines: Why they are dying out', *Brisbane Courier*, 20 February 1930, p. 14.
27 SA Protector F Garnett to the SA Premier, 9 February 1928, GRG24 6/570 409/1914.
28 D Bates to T Gill, 28 September 1919, RGS (SA), SLSA MS 9c.
29 Chief Protector W South to H Jackson, Commissioner for Public Works, 14 October 1920, SRSA GRG1/323, 845/1919.
30 D Bates to A Hore-Ruthven, 19 July 1928, SRSA GRG 52/1/1930/56.
31 'Our aboriginals. Smoothing the pillow of dying race. Missionary's efforts', *Cairns Post*, 6 May 1925, p. 4.
32 CA Wiebusch to South, 19 January 1915, SRSA GRG24 6/570, 409/1914.
33 South to Jackson, 17 November 1919, GRG1/323 File 845/1919.
34 Garnett to Jackson, 17 January 1931, SRSA GRG24 6/570, 409/1914.
35 C Mountford, 'Notebook and diaries', 15 September 1940, SLSA PRG 1218/11/3.
36 C Mountford, *Brown Men and Red Sand: Wanderings in Wild Australia*, Robertson & Mullens, Melbourne, 1948, p. 97.
37 Mountford, 1948, p. 98.
38 Bates, 'Cannibal Aborigines', *Australasian*, 26 May 1928, p. 67.
39 H Basedow, *Notes on Some Native Tribes of Central Australia*, David M Welch, Virginia, 2008, p. 41; B Reece, 'AP Elkin interviewed about Daisy Bates', *Australian Aboriginal Studies*, 2007, no. 1, pp. 131–37. See also: 'Cannibal theory discounted. The Ooldea blacks', Adelaide *Register*, 21 February 1928, pp. 10–11.
40 Bates, 'Section XII 2 G 8', NLA MS 365/60/1.
41 T Gara, '"As familiar with the wild creatures as I am with my own family history": Daisy Bates on the Nullarbor Plain, 1912–35', unpublished paper, 2003, p. 10.
42 Gara, 2003, p. 10.
43 Hill, 'Cannibal notes', UQFL18.D.7.17.
44 South to Jackson, 14 October 1920, SRSA GRG1/323, 845/1919.
45 Const. Lodge to Insp. Giles, 19 July 1930, SRSA GRG52/1/1930/56.
46 Precis of letter from Bates to South, n.d. 1919, SRSA GRG1/323, 845/1919.
47 File note – Commissioner of Public Works, SA Records, 16 March 1920, SRSA GRG1/323, 845/1919.
48 South to the 'Women's Non-Party Association', 2 February 1920, GRG1/323, 845/1919.
49 British Commonwealth League, British Commonwealth League Conference Report, 1927, p. 29.
50 C Cooke, 'The work and aims of the Anti-Slavery and Aborinines [sic] Protection Society', n.d., GRG 52/32/45.
51 JW Bleakley, *(Report) [on] the aboriginals and half-castes of Central Australia and North Australia*, Parliamentary Paper No. 21, Commonwealth of Australia, Canberra, 1929, p. 9.
52 A Lock to M Bennett, August 1929, GRG 52/32/31.

53   Lock to Bennett, August 1929, GRG 52/32/31.
54   Hill, 'Notes and Suggestions DMB', UQFL18.D.11.37.
55   Bates to King, 11 January 1915, ML MS 1492.
56   Bates to South, 15 September 1915, GRG24 6/570, 409/1914.
57   Bates, *Minutes of Evidence of Royal Aborigines Commission*, p. 32.
58   Bates to South, 15 September 1915, GRG24 6/570, 409/1914.
59   Bleakley, 1929; A Holland, 'Wives and mothers like ourselves: Exploring white women's intervention in the politics of race, 1920s–1940s', *Australian Historical Studies*, no. 117, 2001, pp. 292–310; M Lake, 'Frontier feminism and the marauding white man', *Journal of Australian Studies*. no. 49, 1996, pp. 12–20; R McGregor, *Imagined Destinies: Aboriginal Australians and the Doomed Race Theory, 1880–1939*, 2nd edn, Melbourne University Press, Melbourne, 1998.
60   WD Walker, quoted in McGregor, 1998, p. 131.
61   Bates to JG Murray, 25 June 1938, NLS ACC. 13328/38, DA 8.
62   D Bates, Letter to the Editor, *Sunday Times*, 2 October 1921.
63   Gara, 2003, p. 11.
64   E Hill, 'Cannibalism on East-West', *Sunday Sun*, 19 June 1932, p. 2.
65   L Behrendt, *Finding Eliza: Power and Colonial Storytelling*, University of Queensland Press, Brisbane, 2016, pp. 42–4.
66   D Bates to J Cleland, 2 June 1931, SUA MSS 572.994 B32c.
67   Bates to Cleland, 5 August 1930, SAM AA23/1/3.
68   Hill, *Sunday Sun*, 19 June 1932, p. 1.
69   Hill, 'Cannibal notes', UQFL18.D.7.17.
70   *Loneliness*, pp. 7–8, 36.
71   E Hill, *Kabbarli: A Personal Memoir of Daisy Bates*, Angus & Robertson, Sydney, 1973, pp. 103, 104 (hereafter referred to *Kabbarli*).
72   E Hill, 'Woman of Ooldea', *West Australian*, 25 June 1932, p. 4.
73   Hill, 'From the first old Centre notebook 1932', UQFL18.D.7.18.
74   South to Jackson, 14 October 1920, SRSA GRG1/323, 845/1919.
75   Bates to Cleland, 6 February 1931, SAM AA23/1/3.
76   Bates to JG Murray, 25 June 1938, NLS ACC. 13328/38, DA 8.
77   Bates to Cleland, 6 February 1931, SAM AA23/1/3.
78   Bates to Cleland, 13 June 1930, SAM AA23/1/3.
79   *Kabbarli*, p. 25.
80   NLA MS 365 86/217–26.
81   *Kabbarli*, p. 56.
82   NLA MS 365 86/217–26.
83   Bates to Cleland, 6 February 1931, SAM AA23/1/3.
84   D Bates to W Hurst, 29 May 1926, NLA MS 7374, 595/ENV4.
85   All references in the preceding three paragraphs are from D Bates, *My Natives and I*, ed. PJ Bridge, Hesperian Press, Perth, 2004, pp. 1–5.
86   Hill, 25 June 1932.

2   A wandering sickness

1   E Hill to M Durack, 28 April 1948, UQFL18.E.6.
2   E Hill, *The Great Australian Loneliness*, 2nd edn, Robertson & Mullens, Melbourne, 1942, p. 17 (hereafter abbreviated as *Loneliness*).

3   *Loneliness*, p. 13.
4   D Bates to A Fairbairn, 31 December 1913, NLA MS 9037.
5   R Macfarlane, *The Old Ways: A Journey on Foot*, Penguin, London, 2012, p. 314.
6   TW Adorno, *The Culture Industry: Selected Essays on Mass Culture*, Routledge, London, 2001 p. 190.
7   E Hill, 'Lugger that is link with lonely outposts', *Sunday Mail*, 3 September 1933, p. 21.
8   E Hill, *The Territory*, 3rd edn, Angus & Robertson, Sydney, 1963, p. 350.
9   E Hill to R Foster, 12 July 1972, UQFL18.F.1.
10 E Hill, interviewed by M Bonnin, 14 March 1972, UQFL633.
11 E Hill to H Drake-Brockman, 18 August 1963, NLA MS 1634/3/14.
12 Margaret Lynam, Queensland Department of Education records, 1882–98, 26 July 1898, SLWA MN71 7273/EH1/1, 26 July 1898; 'Ernestine Hemmings: Queensland's Girl Poet: Great Gift of Song: Tardy Recognition', *Sun*, 18 June 1916, p. 21.
13 Hill to Foster, 12 July 1972, UQFL18.F.1.
14 R Foster, 'Ray Hemmings', UQFL18.F.1.
15 'Ernestine Hemmings', 18 June 1916.
16 'Genius unspoiled. Ernestine Hemmings, girl poet. Pegasus as a legal librarian', *Sunday Times*, 3 February 1918, p. 13.
17 'Genius unspoiled', 3 February 1918.
18 E Hill to T Keleher, 3 February 1917, SLQ OM73-06, Box 8850.
19 'Genius unspoiled', 3 February 1918.
20 E Hemmings 'Australian poetesses', *WA Record*, 20 July 1918, p. 8.
21 'Ernestine Hemmings', 18 June 1916.
22 E Hill, 'J.F.A. Introductions', UQFL18.C.22.3.
23 R Hill, interviewed by M Bonnin, 30 May 1972, UQFL633.
24 E Hemmings. 'The City of everlasting no. A first impression,' *WA Record*, 26 January 1918, p. 8.
25 S Young, *Paper Emperors: The Rise of Australia's Newspaper Empires*, NewSouth, Sydney, 2019, p. 551.
26 B Griffen-Foley, *The House of Packer: The Making of a Media Empire*, Allen & Unwin, Sydney, 1999, p. 5; A Manning, *Larger than Life: The Story of Eric Baume*, Reed, Artarmon, 1967, pp. 57.
27 *Bulletin*, quoted in Griffen-Foley, p. 6.
28 'Genius unspoiled', 3 February 1918.
29 F Packer, 'Great newspaper man passes on,' *Australian Women's Weekly*, 21 April 1934, p. 14.
30 L Campbell, personal communication, 18 June 2015.
31 C Ferrier, *As Good as a Yarn With You*, Cambridge UP, Sydney, 1994, p. 183.
32 T Afford to M Bonnin, 26 May n.d., UQFL633.
33 M Bonnin, *A Study of Australian Descriptive and Travel Writing, 1929–1945*, unpublished PhD thesis, University of Queensland, Brisbane, 1980, p. 22.
34 R Foster to M Durack, 20 October 1972, SLWA MN 0071 7273A/RF/MDM.
35 M Van Velzen, *Call of the Outback,* Allen & Unwin, Sydney, 2016, p. 255.
36 B Griffen-Foley, *Sir Frank Packer: A Biography*, Sydney University Press, Sydney, 2014, p. x.

37 L Campbell, personal communication, 18 June 2015; Van Velzen, p. 23.
38 R Hill, interviewed by M Bonnin, 30 May 1972.
39 Hemmings, 26 January 1918.
40 Bonnin, 1980, p. 22.
41 B Davis to R Foster, 19 July 1977, MLMSS 7638/3.
42 R Hill to M Bonnin, 25 July 1972, UQFL633.
43 I Foster to M Durack, n.d. 1973, no. 52, SLWA MN71 7273A/RF/MDM.
44 M Durack, 1952, p. 9.
45 M Durack, 1952, p. 8.
46 Bonnin, 1980, p. 23.
47 R Hill, interviewed by M Bonnin, 30 May 1972.
48 E Hill to M Durack, 28 April 1948, UQFL18.E.6.
49 *Loneliness*, p. 34.
50 E Hill, interviewed by M Bonnin, 18 July 1972, UQFL633.
51 P Kelley, interviewed by M Bonnin, 9 August 1972, UQFL633.
52 E Hill, 'Road to gold', *Chronicle,* 27 October 1932, p. 52.
53 E Hill, 'From the first old Centre notebook 1932', UQFL18.A.72.2.
54 *Loneliness*, p. 48.
55 E Hill to L Campbell, 16 November 1967, UQFL18.E.3.
56 R Foster, 'Notes on Ernestine Hill by Irene Foster', UQFL18.F.1.
57 E Hill, 'Granites is Gold City in embryo', *Mail*, 15 October 1932, p. 3.
58 C Madigan, *Central Australia*, Oxford University Press, Melbourne, 1944, p. 280.
59 *Loneliness*, p. 310.
60 FE Baume, *Tragedy Track: The Story of The Granites*, 1933; Hesperian Press, Perth, 1994, p. ix.
61 E Hill, 'Bank for Granites gold', *News*, 31 October 1932, p. 5.
62 Hill, 27 October 1932.
63 Baume, 1994, p. viii.
64 Baume, 1994, p. 1.
65 Madigan, 1944, p. 241.
66 E Hill, 'Trek from Granites. Begging lifts: 20 lose work', *News*, 22 November 1932, p. 1.
67 Robert Hill notes, sighted 18 June 2015.
68 S Harlow, 'The 1932 Rush to The Granites', *Journal of Northern Territory History*, no. 6, 1995, p. 26.
69 *Loneliness*, p. 312.
70 Baume, 1994, p. viii.
71 Madigan, 1944, p. 240.
72 Baume, 1994, p. ix.

3 Great wide spaces
1 E Hill, 'Frenchmen', UQFL18.A.19.38.
2 B Salt, 'Australia reinvented: A nation divided according to its interests', *The Australian,* 24 November 2016, <www.theaustralian.com.au/australia-reinvented-a-nation-divided-according-to-its-interests/news-story/6b19bbc5175f4e5b620e6d28d2c90d1f>, viewed 6 January 2020.
3 Salt, 2016.

4   Hill, UQFL18.A.19.38.
5   R Ward, *The Australian Legend*, Oxford University Press, Melbourne, 1958, p. v.
6   P White, 'The Prodigal Son', in *Patrick White Speaks*, Jonathan Cape, London.
7   K Tennant to M Bonnin, 29 July 1972, UQFL633.
8   A Johnson, 'American servicemen find Ernestine Hill in their kitbags: *The Great Australian Loneliness*', in T Dalziell and P Genoni (eds), *Telling Stories: Australian Life and Literature 1935–2012*, Monash University Publishing, Melbourne, 2013, p. 86.
9   R McGregor, *Environment, Race and Nationhood in Australia: Revisiting the Empty North*, Palgrave Macmillan, New York, 2016, p. 1.
10 E Parke, 'Northern Australia boundary prompts identity crisis for WA towns, as shires seek planning change,' 24 September 2015, <www.abc.net.au/news/2015-09-24/northern-australia-boundary-prompts-identity-crisis-for-wa-towns/6802116>, viewed 5 December 2018.
11 E Hill to M Durack, 14 January 1940, UQFL18.E.6.
12 M Morris, '*The Great Australian Loneliness*: On writing an inter-Asian biography of Ernestine Hill', *Journal of Intercultural Studies*, vol. 35, no. 3, 2014, p. 246.
13 MP Durack diary, 1 November 1930, UQFL F1472.
14 MP Durack, diary, 31 October 1930.
15 E Hill, *The Great Australian Loneliness*, 2nd edn, Robertson & Mullens, Melbourne, 1942, p. 132 (hereafter abbreviated as *Loneliness*).
16 M Dewar, 'Snorters, Fools and Little 'Uns: Sexual Politics and Territory Writing in the South Australian Period', NT State Library, Darwin, Occasional Paper No. 32, p. 4.
17 *Loneliness*, pp. 122–23; Hill, 'Australian ways and sayings', UQFL13.A.24.11; *Loneliness*, pp. 124, 133.
18 *Loneliness*, p. 217; Hill, 'The rim of Arnhem Land: Where white women are unafraid', *Chronicle*, 19 October 1933, p. 2; *Loneliness*, pp. 220, 223.
19 G & V Apsley, *The Amateur Settlers*, Hodder & Stoughton, London, 1926, p. 189; *Loneliness*, pp. 226, 131.
20 JW Bleakley, *(Report) [on] the aboriginals and half-castes of Central Australia and North Australia*, Parliamentary Paper No. 21, Commonwealth of Australia, Canberra, 1929; *Loneliness*, pp. 143, 144, 145.
21 *Loneliness*, pp. 212, 271, 273, 271, 274.
22 *Loneliness*, pp. 226–28.
23 *Loneliness*, pp. 229–31, 232, 102, 333.
24 Hill, 'Yellow Ochre. Armatjira', UQFL18.A.54.11.
25 B Scambary, 'My country, mine country: Indigenous people, mining and development contestation in remote Australia', CAEPR, ANU, Canberra, Research Monograph No. 33, 2013, p. 49.
26 *Loneliness*, p. 301.
27 *Loneliness*, p. 331.
28 Bleakley, 1929, p. 7.
29 *Loneliness*, p. xxx.
30 B Niall, *True North: The Story of Mary and Elizabeth Durack*, Text Publishing, Melbourne, 2012, pp. 39–41.
31 Niall, 2012, p. 25.

32 *Loneliness*, p. 123.
33 M Durack, *Kings in Grass Castles*, Vintage, Sydney, 2008, p. 294.
34 Hill, 'Murray – scourge of the Myalls. Man who keeps white men safe in wilds', *Northern Standard*, Darwin, 3 March 1933, p. 5.
35 *Loneliness*, p. 164.
36 MP Durack to E Hill, 5 October 1939, UQFL18.E.4.
37 *Loneliness*, p. 170.
38 Hill, 'Problem of Aborigine: Appeal to women of Australia', *Advertiser*, 20 June 1934, p. 8.
39 M Bennett, 'Whites and natives: Allegations of slavery', *West Australian*, 17 May 1932, p. 12.
40 E Hill, 'White and natives: The position in the Kimberley', *West Australian*, 26 May 1932, p. 16.
41 RS Schenk, 'The Native Question. Is the Race Doomed?', *West Australian*, 21 June 1932, p. 3.
42 M Bennett, Letter to the Editor, *West Australian*, 21 June 1932, p. 3.
43 *Loneliness*, p. 340.
44 Hill to M Durack, 14 January 1940, UQFL18.E.6.
45 'Australian idyll', *Sydney Morning Herald*, 25 May 1940, p. 10.
46 'New book on Australia by Ernestine Hill', *Air Mail*.
47 'A woman on the north', *Bulletin*, 2 June 1937, p. 2.
48 R Foster to M Bonnin, 28 June 1972, p. 2.
49 'Review of *The Great Australian Loneliness*', *Spectator*, 12 March 1937, p. 32.
50 PR Stephensen, *The Publicist*, March 1941, p. 16.
51 HM Green, *A History of Australian Literature*, Angus & Robertson, Sydney, 1962, vol. 2, p. 304.
52 F Clune to H Lamond, 2 March 1948, MLMSS 605; Clune to Lamond, 23 January 1948, MLMSS 605; Clune to Lamond, 6 January 1948, MLMSS 605; Lamond to Clune, 11 January 1948, MLMSS 605.
53 Green, 1962, p. 304.
54 'A woman on the north', p. 2.
55 'A woman on the north', p. 2; Morris, 2014, p. 245.
56 R Foster, 'Notes on Ernestine Hill by Irene Foster', UQFL18.F.1.
57 C Ferrier, *As Good as a Yarn with You*, Cambridge UP, Sydney, 1994, p. 183.
58 'Son given exemption to help mother finish book', *Telegraph*, 10 October 1943.
59 Hill, 'Cruise of the Silver Gull', *Advertiser*, 10 March 1934, p. 9.
60 S Young, *Paper Emperors: The Rise of Australia's Newspaper Empires*, NewSouth Publishing, Sydney, 2019, p. 332.
61 Young, 2019, p. 332.

4 An uneasy alliance
1 E Hill to D Bates, 28 November 1934, NLA MS 365/97.
2 Hill to Bates, 27 December 1934, NLA MS 365/97.
3 E Hill, '650 miles to receive honor. Mrs. Daisy Bates in Adelaide', *Advertiser*, 23 May 1934, p. 14.
4 E Hill, *Kabbarli: A Personal Memoir of Daisy Bates*, Angus & Robertson, Sydney, 1973, p. 135 (hereafter referred to *Kabbarli*).

5   Hill to Bates, 27 December 1934, NLA MS 365/97.
6   *Kabbarli*, 1973, pp. 135–38.
7   Hill to Bates, 27 December 1934, NLA MS 365/97.
8   Hill to Bates, 28 November 1934, NLA MS 365/97.
9   AE Gerard, *History of the United Aborigines Mission*, United Aborigines Mission, Adelaide, 1944, p. 3.
10 Gerard, 1944, p. 38.
11 A Lock to C Cooke, 16 December 1929, SRSA GRG52/32/35; A Lock to M Bennett, August 1929, SRSA GRG52/32/31.
12 AH O'Kelly & Board of Enquiry, *Finding of the Board of Enquiry concerning the killing of natives in Central Australia by Police Parties and others, and concerning other matters*, unpublished report, 1929, NLA MS 744.
13 J Bleakley to Minister for Home and Territories, 15 October 1928, NAA A431 50/2768, Part 1, quoted in CE Bishop, '"a woman Missionary living amongst naked blacks": Annie Lock, 1876–1943', unpublished MA thesis, ANU, Canberra, 1991, p. 32.
14 AH O'Kelly & Board of Enquiry, p. 2.
15 'The Aboriginal Anti-Feminist', *Register*, 9 January 1929, p. 8.
16 Lock to Bennett, August 1929, SRSA GRG52/32/31.
17 'The Aboriginal Anti-Feminist', p. 8. Similar accusations were later directed at Olive Pink about her friendship with her Warlpiri assistant, Johnny J Yannarilyi.
18 A Lock to W South, 10 June 1934, SRSA GRG 52/1/1933/44.
19 *Kabbarli*, 1973, p. 148.
20 D Bates, 'Notebook 6g. Native Camp, Ooldea', p. 38, NLA MS 365/70/297.
21 D Bates, *The Passing of the Aborigines*, John Murray, London, 1938, p. 115 (hereafter referred to as *Passing*), p. 198.
22 A Lock to J Sexton, 5 September 1934, SRSA SRG 139/324.
23 A Lock to W Penhall, 16 October 1934, SRSA GRG 52/1/1933/44.
24 Hill to Bates, 28 November 1934, NLA MS 365/97.
25 *Kabbarli*, 1973, p. 137.
26 D Bates to W Howie, November 1943, SLSA PRG 878 D.4623/28.
27 *Passing*, 1938, p. 242.
28 Tom Gara comments that although contemporary Aboriginal elders do not believe that 'their male ancestors told Daisy Bates restricted information or gave her their sacred boards', the stories correspond with material recorded by male anthropologists in the area and her letters to Cleland, Hale and Tindale document the provenance and bequeathing of the boards: Gara, '"As familiar with the wild creatures as I am with my own family history": Daisy Bates on the Nullarbor Plain, 1912–35', unpublished paper, 2003, pp 4–5.
29 *Passing*, 1938, p. 243.
30 *Passing*, 1938, p. 242.
31 'Future of natives. Own areas essential. Rations are necessary', *Adelaide Mail*, 23 May 1936, p. 18.
32 E Hill, 'Problem of Aborigine. Appeal to women of Australia', *Advertiser*, 20 June 1934, p. 8.
33 M Gilmore, *Diaries of Dame Mary Gilmore 1940–49*, 5 February 1943, NLA MS 614.

34 *Kabbarli*, 1973, p. 138.
35 Bates to Hill, 15 November 1946, UQFL18.D.2.
36 E Wolff to E Salter, 19 September 1969, NLA MS 6481/2/5.
37 *Kabbarli*, 1973, pp. 135, 141–42, 154.
38 E Hill to Charles Bateson, 11 September 1966, UQFL18.E.8.
39 *Kabbarli*, 1973, pp. 150, 154.
40 Mrs D Bates, interviewed by Bob Smart, SLSA D 7761 (T), p. 8.
41 Hill to Bates, 28 November 1934, NLA MS 365/97.
42 *Kabbarli*, 1973, p. 154.
43 B Polkinghorne to E Riddell, 30 October 1970, SLSA PGR 1038/25.
44 Wolff to Salter, 19 September 1969, NLA MS 6481/2/5.
45 M Morris, 'Media and popular modernism around the Pacific War: An inter-Asian story', *Memory Studies*, vol. 6, no. 3, 2013, p. 364.

5 The Passing of the Aborigines

1 CA Lyon, 'Strangest, and greatest, woman in the empire', *Australian Women's Weekly*, 17 December 1938, p. 47.
2 M Lamshed, 'Natives always see the joke', *Advertiser*, 30 August 1932, p. 9.
3 E Hogan, A Antonia and H Craig, 'More than an amanuensis: Ernestine Hill's contribution to *The Passing of the Aborigines*', *Journal of the Association for the Study of Australian Literature*, vol. 3, no. 18, 2018, p. 5.
4 SC Brown to JG Murray, 21 December 1937, NLS ACC. 13328/38, DA 8.
5 To avoid confusion, 'John Murray' is used to refer to 'John Murray Publishing'; 'Sir John' for 'Sir John Murray V' and 'Grey Murray' for 'John Grey Murray VI.'
6 D Bates to JG Murray, 17 August 1938, NLS ACC. 13328/38, DA 8.
7 EML, 'Reader's report on *The Passing of the Aborigines*', NLS ACC. 13328/38, DA 8.
8 Bates to JG Murray, 24 October 1938, NLS ACC. 13328/38, DA 8.
9 B Reece, 'Introduction' in D Bates, *My Natives and I*, PJ Bridge (ed.), Hesperian Press, Perth, 2004, p. xvii.
10 E Hill, *Kabbarli: A Personal Memoir of Daisy Bates*, Angus & Robertson, Sydney, 1973, p.154 (hereafter referred to as *Kabbarli*).
11 E Hill to Charles Bateson, 17 March 1970, UQFL18.E.8.
12 D Bates to Sir John Murray, 17 June 1935, NLS ACC. 13328/38, DA 8.
13 EL Grant Watson, *But to What Purpose: The Autobiography of a Contemporary*, Cresset, London, 1946, p. 105, quoted in I White, 'Introduction' to D Bates, I White and National Library of Australia, *The Native Tribes of Western Australia*, National Library of Australia, Canberra, 1985, p. 7.
14 Grant Watson, pp. 105–106.
15 D Bates, *The Passing of the Aborigines*, John Murray, London, 1938, Chapter IX, 'Isles of the Dead', (hereafter referred to as *Passing*).
16 I White, 'Daisy Bates: Legend and reality', in J Marcus (ed.), *First in their Field: Women and Australian Anthropology*, Melbourne University Press, Melbourne, 1993, p. 59.
17 A Lang to A Radcliffe-Brown, NLA MS 2300/22.
18 D Bates to John Mathew, NLA MS 365 3197/25.
19 Nevertheless, the Victorian government had published another untrained

ethnologist's work, Edward M Curr's four volumes, *The Australian Race: Its Origins, Languages, Customs*, in 1886–87 at a cost of £4000: see White, 1985, p. 14.
20 Bates to Mathew, 17 February 1913, quoted in White, 1985, p. 27.
21 Bates to Mathew, 17 February 1913.
22 Bates to J Murray, 9 September 1940, NLS ACC. 13328/38, DA 8.
23 White, 1993, p. 53.
24 I White to B Polkinghorne, 18 September 1983, SLSA PGR 1038/25.
25 Bates to J Murray, 18 September 1940, NLS ACC. 13328/38, DA 8.
26 Bates to J Murray, 4 February 1944, NLS ACC. 13328/38, DA 8.
27 Bates to JG Murray, 27 August 1943, NLS ACC. 13328/38, DA 8.
28 Bates to JG Murray, n.d., NLS ACC. 13328/38, DA 8.
29 Bates to J Murray, 4 February 1944, NLS ACC. 13328/38, DA 8.
30 E Witcombe to E Durack, 4 May 1988, NLA MS 7739/33/5.
31 Bates to J Murray, 4 February 1944, NLS ACC. 13328/38, DA 8.
32 APA Burdeu to JG Murray, 15 December 1938, NLS ACC. 13328/38, DA 8.
33 C Duguid to JG Murray, 1 February 1939, NLS ACC. 13328/38, DA 8.
34 W Morley to JG Murray, 21 February 1939, NLS ACC. 13328/38, DA 8.
35 Bates to JG Murray, 15 April 1939, NLS ACC. 13328/38, DA 8.
36 Bates to JG Murray, 25 June 1938, NLS ACC. 13328/38, DA 8.
37 Lyon, 1938, p. 47.
38 G Innes, 'Queen of the orphaned world', *Herald*, 3 December 1938, p. 40.
39 'Kabbarli', *Manchester Guardian*, 23 December 1938, p. 5.
40 'Study of Aborigines by Australian idealist offers much, yet …', *Adelaide Mail*, 21 January 1939, p. 26.
41 'Faithful friend of a vanishing race', *Sydney Morning Herald*, 31 December 1938, p. 8.
42 'Kabbarli, who quelled an Aboriginal revolution', *Advertiser*, 31 December 1938, p. 18.
43 Bates to JG Murray, 24 October 1938, NLS ACC. 13328/38, DA 8.
44 Bates to JG Murray, 17 June 1938, NLS ACC. 13328/38, DA 8.
45 For a more in-depth discussion of this computational stylistics investigation, see Hogan, Antonia and Craig, pp. 1–17.
46 J Burrows and DH Craig, 'Lyrical drama and the "Turbid Mountebanks": Styles of dialogue in Romantic and Renaissance tragedy', *Computers and the Humanities*, vol. 28, no. 2, 1994, pp. 63–86.
47 Hogan, Antonia and Craig, p. 12.
48 Hill to Campbell, 17 March 1970, UQFL18.E.3; *Kabbarli*, 1973, p. 143.
49 Reece, 'Introduction' in Bates, 2004, p. xvi.
50 E Hill to R Foster, 7 November 1971, UQFL18.E.5.
51 B Reece, 'AP Elkin interviewed about Daisy Bates', *Australian Aboriginal Studies*, 2007, no. 1, p. 131.
52 R Hughes, 'The remarkable story of Mrs Daisy Bates', *Sunday Times*, 15 January 1939; R Firth, 'The Australian Aborigines', Letter to the Editor, *Sunday Times*, 22 January 1939.
53 Bartholomew to JG Murray, 5 October 1956, NLS ACC. 13328/38, DA 8.
54 J Curtain to K Pinnock, 5 February 1973, NLS ACC. 13328/38, DA 8.
55 Bates to JG Murray, 17 June 1938, NLS ACC. 13328/38, DA 8.

56 I Tindall to E Salter, 11 July 1969, MS 6481/2/5.
57 Bates to JG Murray, 17 August 1938, NLS ACC. 13328/38, DA 8.
58 E Sinclair, interviewed by E Witcombe, 1980, NLA TRC 5607.
59 B Garner, *Born in a Tent*, NewSouth Publishing, Sydney, 2013, p. 16.
60 E Hill to A Mackaness, 6 November 1942, MS 534/371.
61 E Hill, *Water into Gold*, Robertson & Mullens, Melbourne, 1958, p. vi.
62 *Kabbarli*, 1973, p. 155.
63 M Bonnin, 18 July 1972, UQFL633.
64 Bates to JG Murray, 24 October 1938, NLS ACC. 13328/38, DA 8.
65 Bates to JG Murray, 20 July 1939, NLS ACC. 13328/38, DA 8.
66 Bates to JG Murray, 11 September 1939, NLS ACC. 13328/38, DA 8.

6 A wraith, flitting by
1   E Hill to Coy Bateson, 4 April 1944, UQFL18.E.2.
2   E Hill, 'Nullarbor. Eucla.', UQFL18.D.12.86.
3   See, for example, R Traister's discussion of the historical value of postponing marriage for women in *All the Single Ladies: Unmarried Women and the Rise of an Independent Nation*, Simon & Schuster, New York, 2016, ch. 7, 'For richer: Work, money and independence'.
4   B Spencer, *Vagabondage*, UWA Publishing Kindle edition, Perth, 2014 (Kindle loc. 707, 710–11).
5   Hill to Coy Bateson, 4 April 1944, UQFL18.E.2.
6   L Campbell, personal communication, 18 June 2015.
7   D Bates, *The Passing of the Aborigines*, John Murray, London, 1938, p. 198 (hereafter referred to as *Passing*).
8   D Bates to G King, 24 February 1910, ML MS 1492.
9   D Bates to E Hill, 17 February 1947, UQFL18.D.2.
10 E Hill to A Mackaness, 6 November 1942, MS 534.
11 E Hill, interviewed by M Bonnin, 30 March 1972, UQFL633.
12 R Hill, 'Notes by Robert Hill', NLA MS 8392.
13 E Hill to H Drake-Brockman, 30 September 1939, NLA MS 1634/3/13.
14 Hill to Drake-Brockman, 29 August 1946, NLA MS 1634/3/13.
15 Hill to Drake-Brockman, 27 May 1938, NLA MS 1634/3/13.
16 Hill to Drake-Brockman, 16 August 1940, NLA MS 1634/3/13.
17 E Dark to M Bonnin, 14 August 1972, UQFL633; K Tennant to M Bonnin, 29 July 1972, UQFL633.
18 Hill to Drake-Brockman, 3 December 1938, NLA MS 1634/3/13.
19 M Gilmore, 14 February 1940, NLA MS 614.
20 M Gilmore, 3 February 1940, NLA MS 614.
21 Hill to Drake-Brockman, 3 December 1938, NLA MS 1634/3/13.
22 E Hill to G Mackaness, 22 October 1939, NLA MS 534/471.
23 M Gilmore to G Mackaness, 24 October 1939, NLA MS 534/380.
24 M Gilmore, 3 February 1940, NLA MS 614.
25 R Hill, interviewed by M Bonnin, 18 July 1972, UQFL633.
26 Gilmore to G Mackaness, 24 October 1939, NLA MS 534/380.
27 Hill to Drake-Brockman, 30 September 1939, NLA MS 1634/3/13.
28 Hill to Drake-Brockman, 26 September 1940, NLA MS 1634/3/13.

29 R Foster to S Deamer, 7 December 1939, UQFL633.
30 Hill to Drake-Brockman, 16 August 1940, NLA MS 1634/3/13.
31 E Hill to S Deamer, 28 December 1939, UQFL633.
32 S Deamer, 'Editorial introduction', *ABC Weekly*, 6 January 1940, p. 4.
33 E Hill, 'E Hill's Page for Women', *ABC Weekly*, 6 January 1940, p. 29.
34 J Baker, *Australian Women War Reporters: Boer War to Vietnam*, NewSouth, Sydney, 2015, p. 10.
35 E Hill, 'Sister Susie in uniform', *ABC Weekly*, 29 June 1940, p. 16.
36 E Linn, Letter to the Editor, *ABC Weekly*, 10 Jan 1940, p. 20.
37 E Hill to M Durack, 14 January 1940, UQFL18.E.6.
38 S Deamer, 'Editorial page', *ABC Weekly*, 15 June 1940, p. 3.
39 Hill, 'Long trail of romance', *ABC Weekly*, 23 March 1940, pp. 64–65.
40 Hill to G Mackaness, 5 October 1941, NLA MS 534/471.
41 Hill to Deamer, 18 December 1941, UQFL633.
42 Hill to Deamer, 27 December 1941, UQFL633.
43 Baker, 2015, pp. 53, 54.
44 Hill to M Durack, 14 January 1940, UQFL18.E.6.
45 M Bonnin, *A Study of Australian Descriptive and Travel Writing*, 1929–1945, unpublished PhD thesis, University of Queensland, Brisbane, 1980, p. 51, n. 51.
46 Hill to G Mackaness, 5 October 1941, NLA MS 534/471; 'Record price for novel', *Sydney Morning Herald*, 11 May 1946, p. 4.
47 A Johnson, 'American servicemen find Ernestine Hill in their kitbags: *The Great Australian Loneliness*', in T Dalziell and P Genoni (eds), *Telling Stories. Australian Life and Literature 1935–2012*, Monash University Publishing, Melbourne, 2013, p. 89.
48 'Record price for novel'.
49 Hill to G Mackaness, 5 October 1941, NLA MS 534/471.
50 'Ernestine Hill's novel inspires modern song hit. My Love Must Wait', article typescript, February 1945, UQFL633.
51 Hill to G Mackaness, 4 December 1940, NLA MS 534/471.
52 'Two historical novels', The Red Page, *Bulletin*, 7 January 1942, p. 2.
53 Hill to G Mackaness, 4 December 1940, NLA MS 534/471.
54 T Griffiths, *The Art of Time Travel: Historians and Their Craft*, Black Inc., Melbourne, 2016, p. 19.
55 E Dark, quoted in Griffiths, 2016, p. 34.
56 Griffiths, 2016, pp. 16–41; S Grant, *Australia Day*, HarperCollins, Sydney, 2019, pp. 55–59.
57 Hill to G Mackaness, 17 January 1942, NLA MS 534/471.
58 C Ferrier, (ed.), *As Good as a Yarn With You*, Cambridge University Press, Sydney, 1994, p. 271.
59 Hill to Drake-Brockman, 11 September 1940, NLA MS 1634/3/13.
60 Hill to G Mackaness, 11 June 1942, NLA MS 534/471.
61 Hill to G Mackaness, 5 October 1941, NLA MS 534/471.
62 Hill to G Mackaness, 11 June 1942, NLA MS 534/471.
63 Hill to Coy Bateson, Letter 8, n.d. 1942, UQFL18.E.2.
64 Hill to G Mackaness, 14 March 1942, NLA MS 534/471.
65 HM Collingwood, 'American Bombardment Group', *Western Mail*, 27 January 1944, p. 6.

66 Johnson, in Dalziell and Genoni (eds), p. 89.
67 Hill to Drake-Brockman, 4 August 1942, NLA MS 1634/3/13.
68 Hill to G Mackaness, 11 June 1942, NLA MS 534/471; M Gilmore, 10 June 1942, NLA MS 614.
69 M Gilmore, 1 June 1942, NLA MS 614.
70 Hill to Drake-Brockman, 26 September 1940, NLA MS 1634/3/13.
71 'New Commissioners are keen on job', *ABC Weekly*, 11 July 1942, pp. 19, 22.
72 M Gilmore, 5 March 1944, NLA MS 614.
73 E Hill to CJA Moses, 14 January 1944, NAA: SP1489/1, ERNESTINE HILL.
74 E Hill to A Tully, 11 May 1955, SLWA MN71 7273A/EH1/8L.
75 E Hill, 'Before the white man came', NAA: SP300/1, ERNESTINE HILL, pp. 3, 5.
76 'ABC appointee knows her Australia', *The Listener In*, 20–26 June 1942, p. 17.
77 M Gilmore, 17 March 1943, NLA MS 614.
78 Hill to A Mackaness, 6 November 1942, MS 534/371.
79 E Hill to J Curtin, n.d., NAA M1415, 431.
80 Hill to Curtin, 18 December 1943, NAA M1415, 431; 'Son given exemption to help mother finish book', *Telegraph*, 10 October 1943.
81 M Gilmore, 5 February 1943, NLA MS 614.
82 M Gilmore, 1 July 1942, NLA MS 614.
83 M Gilmore, 16 October 1942, NLA MS 614.
84 M Gilmore, 10 June 1942, NLA MS 614.
85 Hill to Drake-Brockman, 5 June 1943, NLA MS 1634/3/13.
86 M Gilmore, 22 October 1942, NLA MS 614.
87 Hill to A Mackaness, 6 November 1942, MS 534/371.
88 Hill to Curtin, 4 January 1942, NAA: M1415, 431.
89 S Alderman, Reid and Brazel to HV Evatt, 13 September 1943, NAA: SP1489/1, ERNESTINE HILL.
90 Hill to Curtin, 16 January 1943, NAA: M1415, 431.
91 Curtin to Hill, 20 January 1943, NAA: M1415, 431.
92 'Before Mr. R J. Coombe, S.M.', *Advertiser*, 6 October 1943, p. 8.
93 'Authoress seeks son's exemption,' Adelaide *News*, 5 October 1943, p. 3.
94 'Son given exemption to help mother finish book'.
95 'Authoress seeks son's exemption'.
96 HV Evatt to S Alderman, Reid and Brazel, NAA, 24 November 1943, NAA: SP1489/1, ERNESTINE HILL.
97 Hill to Curtin, 18 December 1943, NAA: M1415, 431.
98 Capt FS Kidd to G Mackaness, 14 March 1944, NLA MS 534/371.
99 Kidd to G Mackaness, 14 March 1944, NLA MS 534/371.
100 Hill to A Mackaness, 9 March 1944, MS 534/371.
101 Gilmore to G Mackaness, 2 January 1944, NLA MS 534/380.
102 Hill to Coy Bateson, 10 March 1944, UQFL18.E.2.
103 Hill to Coy Bateson, 4 April 1944, UQFL18.E.2.
104 Hill to Drake-Brockman, 26 March 1944, NLA MS 1634/3/13.
105 M Gilmore, 11 March 1944, NLA MS 614.
106 Gilmore to G Mackaness, 12 February 1944, NLA MS 534/380.
107 Kidd to G Mackaness, NLA, 14 March 1944, NLA MS 534/380.

108 Hill to Coy Bateson, 10 March 1944, UQFL18.E.2.
109 M Gilmore, 20 May 1944, NLA MS 614.
110 Kidd to G Mackaness, NLA, 14 March 1944, NLA MS 534/380.
111 Hill to Coy Bateson, 4 May 1944, UQFL18.E.2.
112 Hill to Coy Bateson, 30 October 1944, UQFL18.E.2.
113 Hill to M Durack, 9 November 1944, SLWA MN71 7273A/EH1/7F.
114 Hill to Coy Bateson, 1 January 1945, UQFL18.E.2.
115 Hill to Curtin, 18 December 1943, NAA: M1415, 431.
116 Hill to M Durack, 9 November 1944, SLWA MN71 7273A/EH1/7F.
117 M Gilmore, 5 February 1943, NLA MS 614.
118 Hill to Coy Bateson, 1 January 1945, UQFL18.E.2.
119 Hill to Drake-Brockman, 26 September 1940, NLA MS 1634/3/13.
120 Hill to Coy Bateson, 1 January 1945, UQFL18.E.2.
121 R Hill to E Hill, n.d. 1944, UQFL 633.
122 Hill to M Durack, 2 January 1945, UQFL18.E.6.
123 'Flying Doctor helps authoress', *Western Grazier*, 14 January 1944, p. 3.
124 R Hill to M Bonnin, 25 July 1972, UQFL 633.
125 Hill to M Durack, 26 January 1945, UQFL18.E.6.
126 Hill to Drake-Brockman, 26 March 1944, NLA MS 1634/3/13.

7   Derelict on the Nullarbor
1   A Brooks, interviewed by M Hinchcliffe, 1980, NLA TRC 1883.
2   'Daisy Bates' life with the blacks', Adelaide *News*, 10 March 1945, p. 2.
3   Brooks, interviewed by Hinchcliffe, 1980.
4   D Bates to E Hill, 17 October 1946, UQFL18.D.2; 'D Bates' life with the blacks', p. 2.
5   B Polkinghorne to I White and E Witcombe, n.d., SLSA PRG 1038/25.
6   M Gilmore to G Mackaness, 28 January 1945, NLA MS 534/380.
7   E Hill to H Drake-Brockman, 3 December 1938, NLA MS 1634/3/13.
8   M Gilmore, 3 July 1944, NLA MS 614.
9   M Gilmore, 17 March 1944, NLA MS 614.
10 C Ferrier, *As Good as a Yarn With You*, Cambridge University Press, Sydney, 1994, p. 271.
11 M Gilmore, 3 July 1944, NLA MS 614.
12 E Bates to JG Murray, 12 March 1939, NLA NLS ACC. 13328/3, DA 8.
13 D Bates, interviewed by Russell Henderson, 18 February 1941, TRC 160.
14 E Bates to J Murray, 4 February 1942, NLS ACC. 13328/38, DA 8.
15 Bates to J Murray, 9 September 1940, NLS ACC. 13328/38, DA 8.
16 'Mrs. Bates to write story of native "spirit babies"', *Advertiser*, 15 March 1941.
17 Bates to J Murray, 17 June 1935, NLS ACC. 13328/38, DA 8.
18 G Kinnaird, 'Reader's report no. 59 on *Stone Age Myths and Legends*', 1938, NLS MS, ACC. 13328/38, DA 8.
19 JG Murray to Bates, 28 November 1944, NLS ACC. 13328/38, DA 8.
20 ER Bartholomew to J Murray, 23 August 1945, NLS ACC. 13328/38, DA 8.
21 JG Murray to SC Brown, 5 October 1948, NLS ACC. 13328/38, DA 8.
22 Bates to JG Murray, 27 August 1943, NLS ACC. 13328/38, DA 8.
23 J Murray to Bates, 28 November 1944, NLS ACC. 13328/38, DA 8.

24 D Bates to W Howie, 27 February 1943, SLSA PRG 878 D.4623/5.
25 Polkinghorne to White and Witcombe, n.d., SLSA PRG 1038/25.
26 Bates to Howie, 27 February 1943, SLSA PRG 878 D.4623/5.
27 Brooks, interviewed by Hinchcliffe, 1980.
28 Bates to J Murray, 4 February 1942, NLS ACC. 13328/38, DA 8.
29 Bates to J Murray, 6 June 1941, NLS ACC. 13328/38, DA 8.
30 Bates to J Murray, 14 July 1942, NLS ACC. 13328/38, DA 8.
31 Bates to W Hurst, 5 July 1944, NLA MS 7374, B595/ENV4.
32 Bates to J Murray, 4 February 1942, NLS ACC. 13328/38, DA 8.
33 Bates to J Murray, 20 October 1944, NLS ACC. 13328/38, DA 8.
34 Bates to J Murray, 14 July 1942, NLS ACC. 13328/38, DA 8.
35 Bates to Howie, 5 June 1944, SLSA PRG 878 D.4623/36; D Bates to M Hosking, 21 December 1944, BSL MSS 572.994 B32t.
36 Bates to J Murray, 6 June 1941, NLS ACC. 13328/38, DA 8.
37 Brooks, interviewed by Hinchcliffe, 1980.
38 Bates to Howie, 27 February 1943, SLSA PRG 878 D.4623/5.
39 Bates to Howie, 2 February 1944, SLSA PRG 878 D.4623/31.
40 Brooks, interviewed by Hinchcliffe, 1980.
41 LE Randell to E Salter, 29 July 1969, NLA MS 6481/2/5.
42 Witcombe to Polkinghorne, 11 April 1988, SLSA PRG 1038/25.
43 White to Polkinghorne, 18 September 1983, SLSA PRG 1038/25.
44 Witcombe to Polkinghorne, 11 April 1988, SLSA PRG 1038/25.
45 E Hill to B Polkinghorne, 16 December 1968, SLSA PRG 1038/25.
46 Polkinghorne to White and Witcombe, n.d., SLSA PRG 1038/25.
47 S de Vries, *Desert Queen: The Many Lives and Loves of Daisy Bates*, HarperCollins, Sydney, 2008, p. 10.
48 In discussing a possible diagnosis for Bates, de Vries suggests in an aside '(It is likely that D's obsessions with Aboriginal infant cannibalism, which she wrote about in her popular articles, as well as her illogical prejudice against half-caste children, arose from this disease.)': de Vries, 2008, p. 169.
49 J Bedford, 'The secret life of Daisy Bates and the Breaker', *National Times*, 11–17 November 1983.
50 B Polkinghorne to E Riddell, 30 October n.d., PRG SLSA 1038/25.
51 M Carnegie and F Shields, *In Search of Breaker Morant: Balladist and Bushveldt Carbineer*, HH Stephenson, Melbourne, 1979; A Queale to M Carnegie, 17 March 1980, MLDOC 3213; M Carnegie, 'Did Daisy bloom briefly for Breaker Morant?', *West Australian*, 5–6 April 1980; J Bedford, 'The secret life of Daisy Bates and the Breaker', *National Times*, 11–17 November 1983.
52 de Vries, 2008, pp. 85–92. Elsewhere, de Vries credits Nick Bleszynski with the first mention of Bates's marriage to Ernest Baglehole in *Shoot Straight, You Bastards!: The Truth Behind the Killing of 'Breaker' Morant*, Random House, Sydney, 2003, a detail that he had learned from Eleanor Witcombe and cited without her permission. (See S de Vries, 'The story of the writing of Desert Queen, the first biography to tell the truth about Daisy Bates', unpublished typescript, 2010, UQFL421, Box 10, pp. 7–8.) Needless to say, there are no records of Bates's marriage to Baglehole within the manuscripts that Witcombe donated to the National Library.

53 E Witcombe, MS 7739/1/1; Richard Griffith's *Primary Valuation of Ireland* and consultation with Roscrea historian, Kathleen Moloughney, provide the basis for much of Witcombe's reconstruction of Bates's youth – sources that Reece and de Vries also use in their biographies of Bates.
54 B Reece, *Daisy Bates: Grand Dame of the Desert*, National Library of Australia, Canberra, 2007, p. 13.
55 Reece, 2007, p. 17.
56 E Witcombe, MS 7739/1/1.
57 According to Reece, there is no evidence for Bates's attachment to the Outram family (Reece, 2007, p. 172, n. 14). The Outram family did not corroborate this story when Salter and Australian historian Jim McJannett contacted them seeking confirmation. Salter, however, accepted Bates's version and included a glowing account in her book.
58 J Blackburn, *Daisy Bates in the Desert: A Woman's Life Among the Aborigines*, Secker & Warburg, London, 1994, p. 32.
59 L Sussex to E Hogan, personal communication, 11 November 2019; L Sussex, *Women Writers and Detectives in Nineteenth-Century Fiction: The Mothers of the Mystery Genre*, Palgrave Macmillan, New York, 2010, p. 129.
60 Y Smaal, 'Queer relationships in nineteenth-century Australia', 15 October 2017, <www.auswhn.org.au/blog/queer-19th-century/>, viewed 8 November 2019; S Trevor, 'Love in the age of convicts', 27 December 2013, <www.tracesmagazine.com.au/2013/12/love-in-the-age-of-convicts/>, viewed 8 November 2019.
61 Edith Sinclair, interviewed by Eleanor Witcombe, 1980, NLA TRC 5607.
62 White to Polkinghorne, 18 September 1983, PRG SLSA 1038/25.
63 Sinclair, interviewed by Witcombe, 1980.
64 Sinclair, interviewed by Witcombe, 1980.
65 Mrs D Bates, interviewed by Bob Smart, SLSA D 7761 (T).
66 Sinclair, interviewed by Witcombe, 1980.
67 V Wood to E Witcombe, 26 June 1981, NLA MS 7739/33/3.
68 Bates, quoted in Witcombe, 'Daisy Bates' Notes', p. 14, NLA MS 7739/1/1.
69 Witcombe, 'Daisy Bates' Notes'.
70 E Louttit to E Salter, 11 July 1969, MS 6481/2/11.
71 Bates to Hill, 17 October 1946, UQFL18.D.2.
72 Polkinghorne to Riddell, 30 October n.d., SLSA PRG 1038/25.

8 The lady living over the hill
1 D Bates, 'Ooldea etc dialects Oct. 16th 1940', NLA MS 365/60/11.
2 E Hill to Coy Bateson, 13 September 1947, UQFL18.E2
3 D Bates, *The Passing of the Aborigines*, John Murray, London, 1938, pp. 242–43.
4 Bates, 'Ooldea etc dialects Oct. 16th 1940', NLA MS 365/60/11.

9 Gypsying to windward
1 E Hill, 'Australia's Home. Notes', NLA MS 8392, p. 1.
2 D Bates to WT Haslam, 27 March 1946, NLA MS 6481/2/11.
3 D Bates to T Gill, June 1946, RGS (SA), SLSA MS 9c.
4 D Bates to K Symon, 1 October 1946, BSL MSS 0015.
5 D Bates to E Hill, 17 October 1946, UQFL18.D.2.

6   Bates to Gill, June 1946, RGS (SA), SLSA MS 9c; Bates to Hill, 17 October 1946, UQFL18D.2.
7   Bates to Symon, 1 October 1946, BSL MSS 0015.
8   Bates to Haslam, 27 March 1946, MS 6481/2/11; L Nieass to D Bates, 20 February 1947, BSL MSS 572.994 B32t/10.1.
9   R Hill, 'Notes by Robert Hill', NLA MS 8392, p. 1.
10 E Hill to Coy Bateson, 26 August 1947, UQFL18.E.2; Vida Thompson, interviewed by Aileen Treagus, SLSA OH 541/14, 6 October 1999; Bates to Hill, 21 March 1947, UQFL18.D.2.
11 Thompson, interviewed by Treagus, 1999; W Mathews to E and B Hill, 16 November 1947, UQFL18.D.2.
12 Bates to Hill, 7 February 1947, UQFL18.D.2.
13 Bates to Hill, 15 November 1945, UQFL18.D.2; D Bates to J Murray, 12 September 1942, ACC. 13328/38, DA 8; D Bates to JG Murray, 30 December 1945, ACC. 13328/38, DA 8.
14 E Wolff to E Salter, 19 September 1969, NLA MS 6481/2/5.
15 Bates to Hill, 12 April 1945, UQFL18.D.2.
16 Bates to Hill, 15 November 1945, UQFL18.D.2.
17 Bates to Hill, 15 May 1947, UQFL18.D.2.
18 Bates to Hill, 17 October 1946, UQFL18.D.2.
19 Bates to Hill, 1 March 1947, UQFL18.D.2.
20 Bates to Hill, 15 November 1945, UQFL18.D.2; Bates to Hill, 15 November 1946, UQFL18.D.2.
21 D Bates to W Hurst, 2 November 1933, NLA MS 7374 B595/ENV4.
22 Bates to Hurst, 16 January 1941, NLA MS 7374 B595/ENV4.
23 Bates to Hurst, 11 March 1941, NLA MS 7374 B595/ENV4.
24 Bates to Hurst, 4 July 1937, NLA MS 7374 B595/ENV4.
25 J Atlas, *The Shadow in the Garden: A Biographer's Tale*, Knopf Doubleday Kindle Edition, New York, 2018, p. 48.
26 Bates to Hill, 17 October 1946, UQFL18.D.2.
27 Bates to Hill, 18 December 1946, UQFL18.D.2.
28 Bates to Hill, May 1948, UQFL18.D.2.
29 E Hill to B Polkinghorne, 20 April 1970, SLSA PRG 1038/25.
30 J van Loon, *The Thinking Woman*, NewSouth, Sydney, 2019, p. 207.
31 Bates to Hill, 24 December 1946, UQFL18.D.2; Bates to J Murray, 12 December 1946, NLS ACC. 13328/38, DA 8.
32 E Hill to M Gilmore, 8 January 1947, NLA MS 727.
33 E Hill to H Drake-Brockman, 25 January 1946, NLA MS 1634/3/13.
34 AD Mackenzie, *RACV Radiator*, 1936, quoted in J Davidson and P Spearitt, *Holiday Business: Tourism in Australia since 1870*, Miegunyah Press, Melbourne, 2000, p. 176.
35 E Hill to KS Prichard, 22 July 1950, NLA MS 6201/10/4.
36 J Pilgrim, 'Across the "Bight" with Ernestine Hill: Australia's foremost travel-writer tells of the adventurous years', *The Land*, 24 October 1947.
37 E Hill, 'Australia's Home. Notes', p. 1.
38 Hill to Coy Bateson, 26 August 1947, UQFL18.E.2; R Hill, p. 1.
39 S Wolff, 'Sam Fullbrook: Delicate Beauty review – Australia evoked in living

colour', *Guardian*, 1 April 2014, <www.theguardian.com/artanddesign/australia-culture-blog/2014/apr/09/sam-fullbrook-delicate-beauty-review-australia-evoked-in-living-colour>, viewed 28 January 2018.
40 P Millett, 'Notes on correspondence from Irene Foster to MDM', SLWA MN71 7273A/RF/MDM 5083, p. 2.
41 Hill to Coy Bateson, 26 August 1947, UQFL18.E.2.
42 Thompson, interviewed by Treagus, 1999, p.10.
43 R Hill, p. 1.
44 D Bates to W Howie, 20 October 1947, SLSA PRG 870 D.4623/81.
45 Hill to Coy Bateson, 26 August 1947, UQFL18.E.2.
46 R Hill, p. 2.
47 Hill to Coy Bateson, 26 August 1947, UQFL18.E.2.
48 L Campbell, personal communication, 18 June 2015. A photograph with Bates's handwriting on the back in the Hill Collection appears to corroborate this story's provenance: Robert Hill notes that it is of an Aboriginal man who died in Bates's arms and whose bamburoo he gave to the WA Museum in 1972–73 – UQFL18.G.29 18/1764.
49 E Hill, *Kabbarli: A Personal Memoir of Daisy Bates*, Angus & Robertson, Sydney, 1973, p. 164 (hereafter, *Kabbarli*).
50 Hill to Coy Bateson, 13 September 1947, UQFL18.E.2.
51 E Hill to G Mackaness, 19 October 1947, NLA MS 534/432.
52 Hill, 'Australia's Home. Notes', p. 1.
53 Hill to Drake-Brockman, 26 March 1947, NLA MS 1634/3/14.
54 Hill to G Mackaness, 19 October 1947, NLA MS 534/432.
55 Hill to G Mackaness, 19 October 1947, NLA MS 534/432; Hill to Coy Bateson, 19 October 1947, UQFL18.E.2.
56 C Ferrier, *As Good as a Yarn With You*, Cambridge University Press, Sydney, 1994, p. 181.
57 Hill to Drake-Brockman, 7 May 1948, NLA MS 1634/3/14.
58 *Kabbarli*, pp. 169, 170.
59 Bates to J Murray, 3 March 1948, NLS ACC. 13328/38, DA 8.
60 Bates to Hill, n.d. 1948, UQFL18.D.2.
61 Bates to Hill, 18 May 1948, UQFL18.D.2.
62 Hill to G Mackaness, 30 June 1948, MS 534/432.
63 *Kabbarli*, pp. 169–70.
64 J Preece to JG Murray, 10 November 1948, NLS ACC. 13328/38, DA 8.
65 *Kabbarli*, p. 170.
66 JG Murray to Preece, 23 November 1948, NLS ACC. 13328/38, DA 8.
67 JG Murray to Bates, 19 December 1945, NLS ACC. 13328/38, DA 8.
68 JG Murray to ER Bartholomew, 7 December 1945, NLS ACC. 13328/38, DA 8.
69 Bartholomew to JG Murray, 15 October 1945, NLS ACC. 13328/38, DA 8.
70 Preece to JG Murray, 16 June 1949, NLS ACC. 13328/38, DA 8.
71 Preece to John Murray, 24 April 1951, NLS ACC. 13328/38, DA 8.
72 Margaret Kelsh, interviewed by Aileen Treagus, SLSA OH 541/11, 5 October 1999; Rae Brewster, personal communication, 2016.
73 W Mathews to E and B Hill, 16 November 1947, UQFL18.D.2.
74 D 7761 (T) Mrs Daisy Bates, interviewed by Bob Smart.

75 Hill to Drake-Brockman, 2 October 1950, NLA MS 1634/3/14.
76 Hill to Polkinghorne, 16 December 1968, SLSA PRG 1038/25.
77 *Kabbarli*, p. 171.
78 Preece to Bartholomew, 23 May 1949, NLS ACC. 13328/38, DA 8.
79 Preece to JG Murray, 12 April 1951; Preece to JG Murray, 10 November 1948, NLS ACC. 13328/38, DA 8.
80 JG Murray to A Gowrie, 24 June 1949, NLS ACC. 13328/38, DA 8.
81 Preece to JG Murray, 16 June 1949, NLS ACC. 13328/38, DA 8.
82 Preece to J Murray, 24 April 1951, NLS ACC. 13328/38, DA 8.
83 Preece to JG Murray, 17 April 1952, NLS ACC. 13328/38, DA 8.
84 Preece to JG Murray, 16 April 1952, NLS ACC. 13328/38, DA 8.
85 B Ker Wilson, *Tales Told to Kabbarli: Aboriginal Legends Collected by Daisy Bates*, Angus & Robertson, Sydney, 1972; B Ker Wilson, 'Afterword', de Vries, pp. 272–75.
86 *Kabbarli*, p. 173.
87 B Raine to E Hill, 22 April 1951, UQFL18.24.D2.
88 Hill to Drake-Brockman, 2 May 1951, NLA MS 1634/3/14.
89 Raine to Hill, 22 April 1951, UQFL18.24.D2.
90 *Kabbarli*, p. 173.

10 The great-great-grandmother of that welfare mob
1 D Bates, *The Passing of the Aborigines*, John Murray, London, 1938, Chapter IX, 'Isles of the Dead'.
2 M Brady, 'The politics of space and mobility: Controlling the Ooldea/Yalata Aborigines, 1952–1982', *Aboriginal History*, vol. 23, 1999, p. 6.
3 C Mattingley, *Maralinga's Long Shadow: Yvonne's Story*, Allen & Unwin, Sydney, 2016, p. 70.
4 Bates's original water tank was not found in a 1988 archaeological survey of the site: S Colley, S Rockwell, T Gara and S Cane, 'The archaeology of Daisy Bates' campsite at Ooldea, South Australia', *Australian Archaeology*, no. 28, 1989, p. 88.
5 Mattingley, 2016, p. 67.
6 L Graham, 'Memories of Daisy Bates', in A Peng (ed.), *Women of the Centre*, Pascoe Publishing, Apollo Bay, 1990, pp. 68, 72 and 69.
7 United Aborigines Mission, *The United Aborigines Messenger*, vol. 4, no. 45, 1 June 1936, <nla.gov.au/nla.obj-580845612>, viewed 3 January 2020.
8 Mrs DM Bates, 29 July 1914, *Minutes of Evidence of Aborigines Royal Commission*, SA Government, Adelaide, 1916, par. 3535.
9 B Lomas, *Queen of Deception: The True Story of Daisy Bates*, Brian Lomas, Kalamunda, 2015, Ch. 18.
10 Edith Sinclair, interviewed by Eleanor Witcombe, 1980, NLA TRC 5607.
11 E Tantjingu Williams and E Wani Wingfield, *Down the Hole, Up the Tree, Across the Sandhills ... Running from the State and Daisy Bates*, IAD press, Alice Springs, 2000, pp. 26 and 40. Wingfield's official birthdate is 1932; the editor suggests it was earlier because she was school age when she travelled through Ooldea with her family, which Bates left in mid-1935. But if her birthdate was closer to 1932, then Bates would not have been at Ooldea when Wingfield passed through on the Trans.

12 Bates is remembered with 'appreciation and affection' by some people at Yalata and Oak Valley who knew her during the 1930s: E Tanjingu Williams and E Wani Wingfield, 2000, p. 48.
13 Tom Gara, interviewed by Aileen Treagus, SLSA OH 541/16, 1 November 1999.
14 Preece to J Murray, 24 April 1951, NLS ACC. 13328/38, DA 8.
15 L Waller, 'Singular influence: Mapping the ascent of Daisy M. Bates in popular understanding and Indigenous policy', *Australian Journal of Communication*, 2010, vol. 37, no. 2, p 13.
16 D Bates to W Hurst, n.d., NLA MS 7374, B595/ENV4.
17 E Hill, *Kabbarli: A Personal Memoir of Daisy Bates*, Angus & Robertson, Sydney, 1973, p. 1.
18 'Keeping alive the memory of a remarkable woman', *Advertiser*, 16 November 1954, p. 2.
19 E Hill to H Drake-Brockman, 21 November 1954, NLA MS 1634/3/14.
20 E Hill, 'The friend from the dreaming: Her memorial in Ooldea', UQFL18.D.10.3.

11 A surrealist's madness
1 E Hill to H Drake-Brockman, 26 March 1944, NLA MS 1634/3/13.
2 G Standing, 'The Precariat and Class Struggle', *RCCS Annual Review* (online), no. 7, 2015, pp. 4 and 6.
3 ABS, Glossary, 2049.0 – Census of Population and Housing: Estimating homelessness, 2016, 14 March 2018.
4 E Hill to G and A Mackaness, 8 January 1948, NLA MS 534/471.
5 Hill to G Mackaness, 3 May 1952, NLA MS 534/471.
6 Hill to G Mackaness, 20 May 1947, NLA MS 534/471.
7 Hill to G Mackaness, 30 November 1948, NLA MS 534/471.
8 Hill to G Mackaness, 19 October 1947, NLA MS 534/471.
9 Hill to Drake-Brockman, 25 January 1946, NLA MS 1634/3/14; E Hill, *The Territory*, 3rd edn, Angus & Robertson, Sydney, 1963, p. 1.
10 'Lucky dip', *Times Literary Supplement*, 22 August 1952; K McConagher, 'Northern Territory Saga: Exploration and Adventure', *The Age*, 26 January 1952, p. 7; C Ferrier, *As Good as a Yarn With You*, Cambridge University Press, Sydney, 1994, p. 274.
11 Ferrier, 1994, p. 181.
12 R Hill, interview with M Bonnin, 30 May 1972, UQFL633.
13 *The Territory*, pp. 377, 380 and 381. Hill's italics.
14 *The Territory*, p. 133.
15 Hill, 'Murray – Scourge of the Myalls. Man who keeps white men safe in wilds', *Northern Standard*, 3 March 1933, p. 5.
16 E Hill, 'The old woman's eye', UQFL18.A.29.3.
17 E Hill to M Durack, 9 November 1944, SLWA MN71 7273A/Hill1/7E.
18 *The Territory*, pp. 421 and 424.
19 E Hill, 'Australia's Home. Notes', NLA MS 8392, p. 1.
20 Hill, 'Nullarbor', 18.D.12.27.
21 Hill, 'Nullarbor', 18.D.12.27.
22 E Hill to AG Mitchell, 18 November 1964, UQFL18.E.10.

23 S Hawke, *A Town is Born: The Fitzroy Crossing Story*, Magabala Books, Broome, p. 23.
24 E Hill, *Kabbarli: A Personal Memoir of Daisy Bates*, Angus & Robertson, Sydney, 1973, p. 165. She was not alone in her nostalgia for this era. Aboriginal commentators such as Oodgeroo Noonuccal expressed similar sentiments about cultural loss during the age of equality and citizenship rights – 'No more boomerang No more spear; Now all civilized – colour bar and beer.' Noel Pearson also chronicled the largely northern narrative of social upheaval following the pastoral era and the development of a culture of Aboriginal unemployment, alcohol and welfare dependency in *Up from the Mission*, Black Inc., Melbourne, 2009, pp.156–59.
25 E Hill to A Tully, 18 December 1964, SLWA MN71 7273A/Hill1/8P.
26 E Hill to B Polkinghorne, 20 April 1970, SLSA PRG 1038/25.
27 Hill to Tully, 9 December 1962, SLWA MN71 7273A/Hill1/8O.
28 E Hill to M Durack, 28 April 1945, SLWA MN71 7273A/Hill1/7K.
29 R Hill, Notes on letters, 1955–59, p. 6, UQFL18.E.1.
30 P Millett to L Campbell, 12 September 2003, SLWA MN71 7273A/Hill1/9F.
31 R Hill, Notes on letters, 1955–59, p. 6, UQFL18.E.1.
32 Hill to Tully, 11 May 1955, SLWA MN71 7273A/EH1/8L; Hill to Coy Bateson, 12 January 1954, UQFL18.E.2; Hill to M Durack, 9 October 1953, SLWA MN71 7273A/Hill1/7W.
33 B Niall, 2012, pp. 129–37.
34 Hill to M Durack, 3 May 1955, SLWA MN71 7273A/Hill1/7Y; Hill to Tully, 11 May 1955, SLWA MN71 7273A/EH1/8L.
35 Hill to R Hill, 22 August 1955, UQFL18.E.1.
36 Hill to Coy Bateson, 6 December 1955; 8 February 1956; April 1956, UQFL18.E.2.
37 R Hill, interview with M Bonnin, 30 May 1972, UQFL633.
38 Hill to R Hill, 10 September 1951, UQFL18.E.1; R Hill, Notes on letters, 1955–59, p. 11, UQFL18.E.1.
39 Hill to Coy Bateson, 6 December 1955; September 1956, UQFL18.E.2.
40 Foster to M Durack, n.d. 1973, Letter no. 52, SLWA MN71 7273A/RF/MDM 5083.
41 R Hill, interview with M Bonnin, 30 May 1972, UQFL633; Hill to Coy Bateson, 8 February 1956, UQFL18.E.2; R Hill, Notes on letters, 1955–59, p. 11, UQFL18.E.1.
42 E Hill to M Durack, 14 July 1953, SLWA MN71 7273A/Hill1/7V; E Hill to Coy Bateson, 15 March 1961, UQFL18.E.2.
43 E Hill to R Hill, 22 August 1955, UQFL18.E.1; E Hill to L Campbell, 10 January 1947, UQFL18.E.3; Hill to R Hill, 1 July 1958, UQFL18.E.1; Hill to Campbell, 12 November 1965, UQFL18.E.3.
44 Hill to Coy Bateson, 18 November 1956, UQFL18.E.2; R Hill to E South, 9 January 1969, UQFL18.E.3; Hill to Coy Bateson, 7 March 1956, UQFL18.E.2; E Hill to R Foster, 14 February 1970, UQFL18E.5; Hill to R Hill, 22 August 1955, UQFL18.E.1.
45 A Queale to M Durack, 9 January 1973, SLWA MN71 7273A/EH1/10B.
46 E Hill to KS Prichard, 28 August 1960, NLA MS 6201/10/4; Hill to Coy Bateson, 17 August 1960, UQFL18.E.2; E Hill to H Drake-Brockman, 20 July

1960, NLA MS 1634/3/14; Hill to Coy Bateson, 26 April 1961, UQFL18.E.2; Hill to Campbell, 4–6 November 1962, UQFL18.E.3.
47 Hill to Drake-Brockman, 31 July 1960, NLA MS 1634/3/14.
48 B Davis to E Hill, 29 August 1958, UQFL18.E.11.
49 Hill to Charles Bateson, 24 September 1964, UQFL.13.E.8.
50 Davis to Hill, 17 May 1955, UQFL18.E.11.
51 Hill to R Hill, 22 August 1955, UQFL18.E.1.
52 Hill to Drake-Brockman, 1 August 1951, NLA MS 1634/3/14; Hill to Drake-Brockman, 25 May 1955, NLA MS 1634/3/14.
53 Davis to Hill, 15 March 1963, UQFL18.E.11.
54 Hill to Coy Bateson, 23 January 1961, UQFL18.E.2.
55 R Hill to M Bonnin, 25 July 1972, UQFL633.
56 R Foster to M Durack, 15 May 1973, Letter no. 46, SLWA MN71 7273A/RF/MDM 5083.
57 E Hill to R Hill and J Scrivener, 31 March 1966, UQFL18.E.1; Hill to Charles Bateson, 1 March 1960, UQFL18.E.3; R Hill, Notes on letters, 1966–73, p 3, UQFL18.E.1.; Hill to Campbell, 10 February 1966, UQFL18.E.3. At 5 foot 4 inches, Hill's BMI would have been around 14, placing her in the 'underweight – severe thinness' category.
58 E Hill, *Paul Johns' Statement about Lasseter – as told to Ernestine Hill*, Scrivener Press, Adelaide, 1968.
59 R Hill, 'Notes on letters, 1966–73', p. 5, UQFL18.E.1.

12 This little breathlessness
1 E Hill to Charles Bateson, 20 June 1971, UQFL18.E.10.
2 Hill to R Hill, 5 March 1971, UQFL18.E.1.
3 Hill to Drake-Brockman, 18 August 1963, NLA MS 1634/3/14.
4 S Fullbrook, n.d. 1971, AGNSW MS 2005.4, box 3, vol. 18.
5 S Wolff, 'Sam Fullbrook: Delicate Beauty review – Australia evoked in living colour', *Guardian*, 1 April 2014.
6 E Hill to R Foster, 14 Feb 1970, UQFL18.E 5.
7 S de Vries, *Desert Queen: The Many Lives and Loves of Laisy Bates*, HarperCollins, Sydney, 2008, p. 264.
8 Hill to R Hill, 17 March 1971, UQFL18.E.1; Hill to Foster, 6 April 1971, UQFL18.E.5.
9 Hill to Charles Bateson, 6 December 1970, UQFL18.E.8; Hill to Campbell, 27 January 1971, UQFL18.E.3; Hill to Charles Bateson, 6 December 1970, UQFL18.E.8; Hill to R Hill, 17 March 1971, UQFL.13.E.1.
10 Hill to Charles Bateson, 3 February 1971, UQFL18.E.8; Hill to Charles Bateson, 5 June 1971, UQFL18.E.8; Hill to Foster, 29 January 1972, UQFL18.E 5.
11 Hill to Foster, 29 January 1972, UQFL18.E.5.
12 E Hill, interview with M Bonnin, 18 July 1972, UQFL633.
13 M Bonnin, 1980, p. 9.
14 Hill to Foster, 12 March 1972, UQFL18.E.5; E Hill to AC Cawley, 30 Jan 1960, UQFL18E.10; E Hill to AG Mitchell, 18 November 1964, UQFL.18.E.10; Hill to Foster, 28 June 1972, UQFL18.E.5.
15 M Bonnin, 21 March 1972, UQFL633.

16 M Bonnin to R Foster, 25 April 1972; 13 April 1972; E Hill, interview with M Bonnin, 21 March 1972, UQFL633.
17 Hill to Foster, 29 January 1972, UQFL18.E.5; Hill to R Hill, October 1957, UQFL18.E.1; Hill to Cawley, 30 Jan 1960, UQFL18.E.10.
18 Hill to Davis, 20 November 1968, UQFL18.E.10.
19 Bonnin to Foster, 13 April 1972, UQFL633.
20 E Hill to B Polkinghorne, 20 April 1970, SLSA PRG 1038/25.
21 Hill to Polkinghorne, 16 December 1968, SLSA PRG 1038/25; Hill to Foster, 30 September 1970, UQFL18.E.5.
22 B Polkinghorne to R Foster, 5 July n.d., UQFL18.E.10.
23 R Helpmann to E Hill, 9 March 1970; Hill to Helpmann, 12 March 1970, UQFL120.
24 B Polkinghorne to E Riddell, 30 October n.d., SLSA PRG 1038/25.
25 Charles Bateson to Hill, 10 December 1970, UQFL120.
26 Hill to Charles Bateson, 20 June 1971, UQFL18.E.10.
27 L Campbell to E Witcombe, 30 June 1980, UQFL120.
28 Witcombe, 'Daisy Bates' Notes', pp. 29–35, NLA MS 7739/1/1.
29 Charles Bateson to Hill, 24 February 1971, UQFL120.
30 Hill to Charles Bateson, 20 June 1971, UQFL18.E.10.
31 B Davis to R Foster, 19 July 1977, MLMSS 7638.
32 M Brown, 'The myth of Daisy Bates', *Credit Union Quest*, March 1971, n.p.
33 M Durack, 'Australian legend in retrospect', review of *The Passing of the Aborigines*, *Age*, 14 January 1967, p. 20.
34 Hill to Charles Bateson, 11 September 1966, UQFL18.E.10; E Hill to I Giddy, 6 December 1968, UQFL18.E.11.
35 Hill to Charles Bateson, 11 September 1966, UQFL18.E.10.
36 R Hill to Foster, 23 August 1972, UQFL18.E.5.
37 A Queale to M Durack, Saturday, n.d., SLWA MN71 7273A/Hill1/10E; Charles Bateson to R Hill, 27 August 1972, UQFL18.E.8; Davis to Foster, 19 July 1977, MLMSS 7638/3.
38 I Giddy to R Hill, 18 May 1973, UQFL18.E.11.
39 Ellison, Moschella & Co. to TG Matthews, 30 November 1972, UQFL18.E.11.
40 Charles Bateson to Davis, 20 January 1973; 6 February 1973, UQFL18.E.11.

13 A fleeting project
1 E Hill, *The Territory*, 3rd edn, Angus & Robertson, Sydney, 1963, p. 348.
2 E Hill, 'Road for Cook', Australia Day 1965, UQFL18.A.36.23.
3 E Hill, 'Grand kangaroo', UQFL18.A.52.15 and 14. Elsewhere in her notes, however, she comments that 'lubra', a word for Aboriginal woman still in common use in the mid-sixties, had, along with 'gin', become recognised as a term of contempt used by white men – a sign of the cultural shift that took place through the emergence of civil rights movements in her life's last decade: 'Aboriginal women', UQFL18.A.49.
4 *The Territory*, 1963, p. 348.
5 E Hill, 'Folk-lore Fancy', UQFL18.A.40; 'Johnnie Wise-cap', UQFL18.A.33.458; 'Road for Cook', Australia Day 1965, UQFL18.A.36.23.

6　T Griffiths, *The Art of Time Travel: Historians and Their Craft*, Black Inc., Melbourne, 2016, pp. 31, 34.
7　E Dark, quoted in Griffiths, 2016, p. 34.
8　E Hill, 'Cook', UQFL18.A.34.42; 'Captain Cook, Bligh – Banks', UQFL18.A.33.21; 'Kimberley Notes', UQFL18.A.36.9; 'Orphan Waters. Book', UQFL18.A.40.6; 'Cook', UQFL18.A.35.17.
9　For a more detailed textual discussion of 'Johnnie Wise-cap', see E Hogan, '"Impossible, now, to read the Rosetta Stone": Cultural hybridity and loss in the Ernestine Hill Collection', D. Hecq and J. Novitz (eds), *Inhabitation: Creative Writing with Critical Theory*, Gylphi, 2018.
10　L Campbell, personal communication, 12 March 2015.
11　A Gall, 'Ernestine Hill and the North: Reading race and Indigeneity in *The Great Australian Loneliness* and *The Territory*,' *Journal of Australian Studies*, vol. 37, no. 2, 2013, p. 198.
12　*The Territory*, 1963, p. 387.
13　G Greer, 'Whitefella jump up: The shortest way to nationhood', *Quarterly Essay*, no. 11, Melbourne, Black Inc., 2003, pp. 14, 19–20 and 41.
14　I Clendinnen, *Dancing with Strangers*, Text, Melbourne, 2003, p. 288.
15　S Grant, *Australia Day*, HarperCollins, Sydney, 2019, p. 63.
16　L Conor, *Skin Deep: Settler Impressions of Aboriginal Women*, UWA Publishing, Perth, 2016, p. 230.
17　AP Elkin, cited in Reece, 'AP Elkin interviewed about Daisy Bates', 2007, p. 131.
18　R Needham, cited in White, 1985, p. 2.
19　V Hughston SC, 'Native Title and the Bennell Decision', *Indigenous Law Bulletin*, 2007, vol. 6, no. 26, p. 18.
20　N Thieburger, 'Daisy Bates in the digital world', in *Language, Land and Song: Studies in Honour of Luise Hercus*, PK Austin, H Koch and J Simpson (eds) EL Publishing, London, 2016, pp. 102–14; 'Bringing back languages from scraps of paper', <pursuit.unimelb.edu.au/articles/bringing-back-languages-from-scraps-of-paper>, viewed 19 May 2020.
21　See also P Monaghan, 'Tracing the new: Processes of translation and transculturation in Wirangu', in Austin, Koch and Simpson, 2016, pp. 555–66, for discussion of how Wirangu engage with and reincorporate Bates's material within their cultural traditions.
22　D Bates, 'Notebook 6 (c): Ooldea notes', NLA MS 365/69/45.
23　D Bates, 'Notebooks 6 (g, h, k, j, l): Ooldea notes', NLA MS 365/70/337.

14　Inside the breakwind
1　D Bates, 'Notebooks 6 (g, h, k, j, l): Ooldea notes', NLA MS 365/70/337.
2　I White, 'From camp to village', in RM Berndt (ed.), *Aborigines and Change: Australia in the '70s*, Australian Institute of Aboriginal Studies, Canberra, 1977, p. 104.
3　Edith Sinclair, interviewed by E Witcombe, 1980, NLA TRC 5607, 1980.
4　E Kowal, *Trapped in the Gap: Doing Good in Indigenous Australia*, Berghahn Books, New York, 2015, p. 147.
5　Luke Walker's documentary *Lasseter's Bones* provides an interesting investigation of what happened to Lasseter.

Abbreviations

Kabbarli *Kabbarli: A Personal Memoir of Daisy Bates*
Loneliness *The Great Australian Loneliness*
Passing *The Passing of the Aborigines*
'Wise-cap' 'Johnnie Wise-cap'

References

MANUSCRIPTS AND RECORDS

National Archives of Australia (NAA)
Mrs Ernestine Hill [correspondence with the Australian Broadcasting Commission, Sydney], 1942–45, NAA: SP1489/1, ERNESTINE HILL.
Personal Papers of Prime Minister Curtin, NAA: M1415, 101; NAA: M1415, 431.
Mrs DM Bates. Proposed enquiry re: Aboriginal Affairs, NAA: A1, 1935/1066.
Ernestine HILL [ABC press cuttings and written publicity], NAA: SP1011/2.
Ernestine Hill – 'Before the White Man Came' [broadcast 18 Jan 1943] [Box 12] NAA: SP300/1.
Ernestine Hill – re exemption of son from Military Service, NAA: A472, W16168.

National Library of Australia (NLA)
Papers of Daisy Bates, 1833–1990, MS 365.
Papers of Daisy Bates, 1905–1921, MS 2300.
Daisy Bates Letters, 1901–51, MS 9037.
Papers of Henrietta Drake-Brockman, MS 1634.
Diaries of Dame Mary Gilmore, MS 614.
Papers of Mary Gilmore, 1883–1962, MS 727.
Typescripts and photographs, Ernestine Hill, MS 8392.
Notes by Robert Hill on his mother's Ernestine Hill's 'Notes of a Journey – Melbourne to Perth' on which she visited Daisy Bates for the last time (c. 1947), NLA MS 8392.
Papers of William Hurst, 1918–1956, MS 7374.
Correspondence and literary manuscripts of George Mackaness, 1918–62, MS 534.
Papers of Katharine Susannah Prichard, MS 6201.
Papers of Elizabeth Salter, 1922–1980, MS 6481.
Papers of Eleanor Witcombe, MS 7739.

AH O'Kelly & Board of Enquiry, *Finding of the Board of Enquiry concerning the killing of natives in Central Australia by Police Parties and others, and concerning other matters*, unpublished report, 1929, MS 744.

Mrs D Bates, interviewed by Russell Henderson, 18 February 1941, ABC, TRC 160.
Edith Sinclair, interviewed by Eleanor Witcombe, 1980, NLA TRC 5607.
Alvis Brooks, interviewed by Marian Hinchcliffe, 1980, NLA TRC 1883.

National Library of Scotland (NLS)
Papers of Daisy Bates, ACC.13451, 13328.
Daisy Bates Bookfiles, ACC.13328/38, DA 8.

State Library of New South Wales (MLMSS)
Daisy May Bates correspondence, 1910–1942, MLMSS 1492.
Frank Clune correspondence, 1947–1954, MLMSS 605.
Beatrice Davis papers, 1952–1989, Rene Foster, 1973–1977, concerning Ernestine Hill, MLMSS 7638/3.
Constance Robertson further papers, 1902–1964, and associated family papers, 1904–1986, MLMSS 8060.
Editions Tom Thompson (ETT) and ETT Imprint records, ca. 1950–1999, ML MSS 8879.
Paul Johns' Statement about Lasseter – as told to Ernestine Hill, by Ernestine Hill. Decorated with Serigraphs by Jacqueline Hill. Scrivener Press, Elizabeth, SA, 1968, MLMSS 7638/21.
A Queale to M Carnegie, 17 March 1980, MLDOC 3213.

Barr Smith Library, University of Adelaide (BSL)
Daisy Bates Papers, BSL MSS 572.994 B32t/10.1.
Lesley Kilmeny Symon, Letters from Daisy Bates 1941–1946, BSL MSS 0015.
Letters 1931–32 Ooldea, E–W line to Professor Fitzherbert, BSL MSS 572.994 B32l.

Mortlock Library, SA State Library of South Australia (SLSA)
'Along the Eyre Highway with E Hill', SLSA PRG 1527/3/14.
Papers of Daisy May Bates, 1863–1951, SLSA PRG 878 D.4623.
Mountford, Charles P (Charles Pearcy), 1890–1976, Notebook and diaries, SLSA PRG 1218/11/3.
Polkinghorne (Family) – Letters and papers relating to Daisy Bates, SLSA PRG 1038/25.
Mrs Daisy Bates, interviewed by Bob Smart, D 7761 (T).
Tom Gara, interviewed by Aileen Treagus, SLSA OH 541/16 1 November 1999.
Margaret Kelsh, interviewed by Aileen Treagus, SLSA OH 541/11, 5 October 1999.
Vida Thompson, interviewed by Aileen Treagus, SLSA OH 541/14, 6 October 1999.

South Australian Museum (SAM)
Daisy Bates Collection, Letters to Hale, Tindale and Cleland Collection, AA23/1/3/1–15.

State Records of South Australia (SRSA)
Aborigines Department Correspondence Files, SRSA GRG24 6/570, 409/1914; SRSA GRG1/323, 845/1919; SRSA GRG52/1/1930/56, GRG52/1932/31, GRG52/1932/35, GRG 52/1/1933/44, SRG139/324.

References

Papers of Constance Ternent Cooke, SRSA GRG52/32/1–4574.

State Library of Queensland (SLQ)
Ernestine Hill Papers 1917–1922, Ernestine Hemmings to Timothy Keleher, OM73-06.

University of Queensland, Fryer Library (UQFL)
F1472	MP Durack diary, 1930.
F272	Irene Foster letters.
UQFL18	Ernestine Hill Collection.
UQFL120	Louise Campbell Collection.
UQFL421	Susanna de Vries Collection.
UQFL633	Margriet Bonnin Papers.

Ernestine Hill, interviewed by Margriet Bonnin, 14 March 1972.
Ernestine Hill, interviewed by Margriet Bonnin, 30 March 1972.
Ernestine Hill, interviewed by Margriet Bonnin, 18 July 1972.
Robert Hill, interviewed by Margriet Bonnin, 30 May 1972.
Patricia Kelley, interviewed by Margriet Bonnin, 9 August 1972.

Battye Library, State Library of Western Australia (SLWA)
Durack Family (Papers of Mary Durack Miller) MN71
Bess Durack IM Diaries/memoirs/letters/articles, 7273A/BIM-D.
Correspondence to and from Irene Foster, 7273A/RF/MDM.
Correspondence to and from Ernestine Hill, 7273A/EH.
Correspondence to and from Alan Queale, 7273A/QUEALE doc.

BOOKS, THESES AND UNPUBLISHED MANUSCRIPTS
Adorno, TW, *The Culture Industry: Selected Essays on Mass Culture*, Routledge, London, 2001.
Apsley, G & V, *The Amateur Settlers*, Hodder & Stoughton, London, 1926.
Atlas, J, *The Shadow in the Garden: A Biographer's Tale*, Knopf Doubleday Kindle Edition, New York, 2017.
Baker, J, *Australian Women War Reporters: Boer War to Vietnam*, NewSouth, Sydney, 2015.
Basedow, H, *Notes on Some Native Tribes of Central Australia*, David M Welch, Virginia, 2008.
Bates, D, *My Natives and I*, P Bridge (ed.), Hesperian Press, Perth, 2004.
———, *The Passing of the Aborigines*, John Murray, London, 1938.
Bates, D, White, I and National Library of Australia, *The Native Tribes of Western Australia*, National Library of Australia, Canberra, 1985.
Baume, FE, *Tragedy Track: The Story of The Granites*, 1933; Hesperian Press, Perth, 1994.
Behrendt, L, *Finding Eliza: Power and Colonial Storytelling*, University of Queensland Press, Brisbane, 2016.

Bishop, CE, 1991 '"a woman Missionary living amongst naked blacks": Annie Lock, 1876–1943', unpublished MA thesis, ANU, Canberra, 1991.

Blackburn, J, *Daisy Bates in the Desert: A Woman's Life Among the Aborigines*, Secker & Warburg, London, 1994.

Bleakley, JW, *(Report) [on] the aboriginals and half-castes of Central Australia and North Australia*, Parliamentary Paper No. 21, Commonwealth of Australia, Canberra, 1929.

Bleszynski N, *Shoot Straight, You Bastards!: The Truth Behind the Killing of 'Breaker' Morant*, Random House, Sydney, 2003.

Bolam, A, *The Trans-Australian Wonderland*, University of Western Australia Press, Perth, 1978.

Bonnin, M, *A Study of Australian Descriptive and Travel Writing, 1929–1945*, unpublished PhD thesis, University of Queensland, Brisbane, 1980.

British Commonwealth League, *British Commonwealth League Conference Report*, 1927 <digital.library.lse.ac.uk/objects/lse:cak649yez/read/single#page/100/mode/1up>; viewed 2 January 2020.

Bruder, J, *Nomadland: Surviving America in the Twenty-First Century*, W W Norton, New York and London, 2017.

Carmen, L, *My Own Sweet Time* by Wanda Koolmatrie (pseudonym), Magabala Books, Broome, 1994.

Carnegie, M and F Shields, *In Search of Breaker Morant: Balladist and Bushveldt Carbineer*, HH Stephenson, Melbourne, 1979.

Clendinnen, I, *Dancing with Strangers*, Text, Melbourne, 2003.

Cole, A, Haskins, V and Paisley, F (eds), *Uncommon Ground: White Women in Aboriginal History*, Aboriginal Studies Press, Canberra, 2005.

Conor, L, *Skin Deep: Settler Impressions of Aboriginal Women*, UWA Publishing, Perth, 2016.

Curtis, A, *Kabbarli*, Heinemann, Melbourne, 1983.

Davidson, J, and P Spearitt, *Holiday Business: Tourism in Australia since 1870*, Miegunyah Press, Melbourne, 2000.

de Vries, S, *Desert Queen: The Many Lives and Loves of Daisy Bates*, HarperCollins, Sydney, 2008.

Durack, M, *Kings in Grass Castles*, Vintage, Sydney, 2008.

Durack, M, *Keep Him My Country*, Constable, London, 1955.

——, *Kings in Grass Castles*, Constable, London, 1959.

——, *The Rock and the Sand*, Constable, London, 1969.

Ferrier, C (ed.), *As Good as a Yarn With You: Letters Between Franklin, Prichard, Devanny, Barnard, Eldershaw and Dark*, Cambridge UP, Sydney, 1994.

Gall, A, 'Re-imagining Australian modernity: Performative and non-performative Indigenisation in three white Australian cultural texts', in R West-Pavlov and J Wawrzinek (eds), *Frontier Skirmishes: Literary and Cultural Debates in Australia after 1992*, Universitätsverlag Winter GmbH Heidelberg, Heidelberg, 2010, pp. 217–30.

Garner, B, *Born in a Tent*, NewSouth Publishing, Sydney, 2013.

Gerard, AE, *History of the United Aborigines Mission*, United Aborigines Mission, Adelaide, 1944.

Grant, S, *Australia Day*, HarperCollins, Sydney, 2019.

References

Grant Watson, EL, *But to What Purpose: The Autobiography of a Contemporary*, Cresset, London, 1946
Green, HM, *A History of Australian Literature*, Angus & Robertson, Sydney, 1962.
Griffen-Foley, B, *The House of Packer: The Making of a Media Empire*, Allen & Unwin, Sydney, 1999.
———, *Sir Frank Packer: A Biography*, Sydney University Press, Sydney, 2014.
Graham, L, 'Memories of Daisy Bates', in A Peng (ed.), *Women of the Centre*, Pascoe Publishing, Apollo Bay, 1990.
Griffiths, T, *The Art of Time Travel: Historians and Their Craft*, Black Inc., Melbourne, 2016.
Hatfield, W, *Sheepmates*, Robertson and Mullens, Sydney, 1935.
Hawke, S, *A Town is Born: The Fitzroy Crossing Story*, Magabala Books, Broome, 2013.
Herbert, X, *Capricornia*, Angus and Robertson, Sydney, 1938.
Hill, E, *Peter Pan Land and Other Poems*, Hibernian Newspaper Company, Brisbane, 1916.
———, *Water into Gold*, 1937, Robertson & Mullens, Melbourne, 1958.
———, *The Great Australian Loneliness*, 1937, 2nd edn, Robertson & Mullens, Melbourne, 1942.
———, *My Love Must Wait*, 1941, Angus & Robertson, Sydney, 1967.
———, *Australia, Land of Contrasts*, Sydney Ure Smith (ed.), John Sands, Sydney, 1943.
———, *Flying Doctor Calling*, Angus & Robertson, Sydney, 1947.
———, *The Territory*, 1951, 3rd edn, Angus & Robertson, Sydney, 1963.
———, *Kabbarli: A Personal Memoir of Daisy Bates*, Angus & Robertson, Sydney, 1973.
Idriess, I, *Lasseter's Last Ride*, Angus & Robertson, Melbourne, 1931.
James, B, *No Man's Land: Women of Northern Territory*, Collins, Sydney, 1989.
Johnson, A, 'American servicemen find Ernestine Hill in their kitbags: *The Great Australian Loneliness*', in T Dalziell and P Genoni (eds), *Telling Stories: Australian Life and Literature 1935–2012*, Monash University Publishing, Melbourne, 2013, pp. 84–90.
Jones, P, *Ochre and Rust: Artefacts and Encounters on Australian Frontiers*, Wakefield Press, Adelaide, 2011.
Kent, J, *Beatrice Davis: Backroom Girl of Modern Literature*, Macmillan, Melbourne, 2013.
Ker Wilson, B, *Tales Told to Kabbarli: Aboriginal Legends Collected by Daisy Bates*, Angus & Robertson, Sydney, 1972.
Kowal, E, *Trapped in the Gap: Doing Good in Indigenous Australia*, Berghahn Books, New York, 2015.
Langley, E, *The Pea Pickers*, Angus & Robertson, Sydney, 1942.
Lennon, J, *I'm the One that Know This Country!*, Aboriginal Studies Press, Canberra, 2000.
Lomas, B, *Queen of Deception. The True Story of Daisy Bates*, Brian Lomas, Kalamunda, 2015.
Macfarlane, R, *The Old Ways: A Journey on Foot*, Penguin, London, 2012.
McGregor, R, *Imagined Destinies: Aboriginal Australians and the Doomed Race Theory, 1880–1939*, 2nd edn, Melbourne University Press, Melbourne, 1998.
———, *Environment, Race and Nationhood in Australia: Revisiting the Empty North*, Palgrave Macmillan, New York, 2016.

Madigan, C, *Crossing the Dead Heart*, Georgian House, Melbourne, 1946.
Madigan, C, *Central Australia*, Oxford University Press, Melbourne, 1944.
Malouf, D, *Remembering Babylon*, Random House, Sydney, 1993.
Manning, A, *Larger than Life: The Story of Eric Baume*, Reed, Artarmon, 1967.
Marcus, J, *The Indomitable Miss Pink: A Life in Anthropology*, UNSW Press, Sydney, 2001.
Mattingley, C, *Maralinga's Long Shadow: Yvonne's Story*, Allen & Unwin, Sydney, 2016.
Monaghan, P, 'Tracing the new: Processes of translation and transculturation in Wirangu', in PK Austin, H Koch and J Simpson (eds), *Language, Land and Song: Studies in Honour of Luise Hercus*, EL Publishing, London, 2016, pp. 555–66.
Morris, M, *Identity Anecdotes: Translation and Media Culture*, London, Sage Publications, 2006.
Mountford, C, *Brown Men and Red Sand: Wanderings in Wild Australia*, Robertson & Mullens, Melbourne, 1948.
Niall, B, *True North: The Story of Mary and Elizabeth Durack*, Text Publishing, Melbourne, 2012.
Pearson, N, *Up from the Mission*, Black Inc., Melbourne, 2009.
Prichard, KS, *Coonardoo*, Angus & Robertson, Sydney, 1929.
Reece, B, *Daisy Bates: Grand Dame of the Desert*, National Library of Australia, Canberra, 2007.
Reece, B, 'Introduction' in D Bates, *My Natives and I*, PJ Bridge (ed.), Hesperian Press, Perth, 2004, p. xi–xxxiii.
Salter, E, *Daisy Bates: The Great White Queen of the Never-Never*, Coward, McCann & Geoghegan, New York, 1972.
Sheridan, S, 'Women Writers', in Laurie Hergenhan (ed.), *The Penguin New Literary History of Australia*, Penguin Books, Ringwood, 1988, pp. 319–36.
———, *Along the Faultlines: Sex, Race and Nation in Australian Women's Writing*, Allen & Unwin, Sydney, 1995.
South Australia, *Minutes of Evidence of Aborigines Royal Commission*, SA Government, Adelaide, 1916.
Spencer, B, *Vagabondage*, UWA Publishing Kindle edition, Perth, 2014.
Sussex, L, *Women Writers and Detectives in Nineteenth-Century Fiction: The Mothers of the Mystery Genre*, Palgrave Macmillan, New York, 2010.
Tantjingu Williams, E and E Wani Wingfield, *Down the Hole Up the Tree Across the Sandhills ... Running from the State and Daisy Bates*, IAD press, Alice Springs, 2000.
Thieburger, N, 'Daisy Bates in the digital world', in PK Austin, H Koch and J Simpson (eds), *Language, Land and Song: Studies in Honour of Luise Hercus*, EL Publishing, London, 2016, pp. 102–14.
Thomas, M, *The Many Worlds of RH Mathews*, Allen & Unwin, Sydney, 2011.
Traister, R, *All the Single Ladies: Unmarried Women and the Rise of an Independent Nation*, Simon & Schuster, New York, 2016.
Van Loon, J, *The Thinking Woman*, NewSouth, Sydney, 2019.
Van Velzen, M, *Call of the Outback*, Allen and Unwin, Sydney, 2016.
Ward, R, *The Australian Legend*, Oxford University Press, Melbourne, 1958.
White, I, 'From camp to village', in RM Berndt (ed.), *Aborigines and Change: Australia in the '70s*, Australian Institute of Aboriginal Studies, Canberra, 1977, pp. 100–105.

References

———, 'Introduction' to D Bates, I White and National Library of Australia, *The Native Tribes of Western Australia*, National Library of Australia, Canberra, 1985.

———, 'Daisy Bates: Legend and reality', in J Marcus (ed.), *First in Their Field: Women and Australian Anthropology*, Melbourne University Press, Melbourne, 1993, pp. 47–65.

———, 'Daisy Bates: Legend and reality', in J Marcus (ed.), *First in their Field: Women and Australian Anthropology*, Melbourne University Press, Melbourne, 1993, pp.47–65.

White, P, *A Fringe of Leaves*, Jonathan Cape, Sydney, 1976.

———, 'The Prodigal Son', in *Patrick White Speaks*, Jonathan Cape, London, 1990.

Young, S, *Paper Emperors: The Rise of Australia's Newspaper Empires*, NewSouth Publishing, Sydney, 2019.

JOURNAL AND NEWSPAPER ARTICLES

'ABC Appointee Knows Her Australia', *The Listener In*, 20–26 June 1942, p. 17.

ABS, 'Glossary', 2049.0 – Census of Population and Housing: Estimating homelessness, *2016, 14 March 2018*, <www.abs.gov.au/AUSSTATS/abs@.nsf/Latestproducts/2049.0Glossary12016?opendocument&tabname=Not>, viewed 30 December 2019.

'An Aboriginal albino', *Argus*, 27 January 1890, n.p.

'The Aboriginal anti-feminist', *Register*, 9 January 1929, p. 8.

A Special Reporter, 'Daisy Bates' life with the blacks', *News*, 10 March 1945, p. 2.

'Australian idyll', *Sydney Morning Herald*, 25 May 1940, p. 10.

'Authoress seeks son's exemption', *News*, 5 October 1943, p. 3.

'A woman on the north', *Bulletin*, 2 June 1937, p. 2.

Bates, D, Letter to the Editor, *Sunday Times*, 2 October 1921.

———, 'Cannibal Aborigines', *Australasian*, 26 May 1928, p. 67.

———, 'More about the Aborigines: Why they are dying out', *Brisbane Courier*, 20 February 1930, p. 14.

Bedford, J, 'The secret life of Daisy Bates and the Breaker', *National Times*, 11–17 November 1983.

'Before Mr R. J. Coombe, S.M.', *Advertiser*, 6 Oct 1943, p. 8.

Bennett, M, 'Whites and natives: Allegations of slavery', *West Australian*, 17 May 1932, p. 12.

———, Letter to the Editor, *West Australian*, 21 June 1932, p. 3.

J Bleakley to Minister for Home and Territories, 15 October 1928, NAA A431 50/2768, Part 1.

Bonnin, Nancy, interviewed by Roberta Bonnin, Brisbane, March 2017, <espace.library.uq.edu.au/view/UQ:57379>, viewed 10 February 2018.

Brady, M, 'The politics of space and mobility: controlling the Ooldea/Yalata Aborigines, 1952–1982', *Aboriginal History*, vol. 23, 1999, pp 1–14.

Brown, M, 'The myth of Daisy Bates', *Credit Union Quest*, March 1971, n.p.

Burrows, J and DH Craig, 'Lyrical drama and the "Turbid Mountebanks": Styles of dialogue in Romantic and Renaissance tragedy', *Computers and the Humanities*, vol. 28, no. 2, 1994, pp. 63–86.

'Cannibal theory discounted. The Ooldea blacks', Adelaide *Register*, 21 February 1928, pp. 10–11.

Carment, D, 'Writing the mining history of Australia's Northern Territory,' *Journal of Northern Territory History*, No. 7, 1996, pp. 1–7.
Carnegie, M, 'Did Daisy bloom briefly for Breaker Morant?', *West Australian*, 5–6 April 1980.
Collingwood, HM, 'American Bombardment Group', *Western Mail*, 27 January 1944, p. 6.
Colley, S, Rockwell, S, Gara, T and Cane, S, 'The archaeology of Daisy Bates' campsite at Ooldea, South Australia', *Australian Archaeology*, no. 28, 1989, pp. 78–91.
'Daisy Bates' life with the blacks', *News*, 10 March 1945, p. 2.
Deamer, S, 'Editorial introduction', *ABC Weekly*, 6 January 1940, p. 4.
———, 'Editorial page', *ABC Weekly*, 15 June 1940, p. 3.
de Vries, S, 'The story of the writing of Desert Queen, the first biography to tell the truth about Daisy Bates', unpublished typescript, 2010, UQFL 421, Box 10.
Dewar, M, 'Snorters, fools and little 'uns: Sexual politics and Territory writing in the South Australian period', NT State Library, Darwin, Occasional Paper No. 32.
Drake, H, 'Whites and natives', *West Australian*, 30 May 1932, p. 14.
Durack, M, 'Ernestine Hill', *Walkabout*, vol. 18, no. 3, 1952, p. 89.
———, 'Australian legend in retrospect', *The Age*, 14 January 1967, p. 20.
'Ernestine Hemmings: Queensland's girl poet: Great gift of song: Tardy recognition', *Sun*, 18 June 1916, p. 21.
'Faithful friend of a vanishing race', *Sydney Morning Herald*, 31 December 1938, p. 8.
Firth, R, 'The Australian Aborigines', Letter to the Editor, *Sunday Times*, 22 January 1939.
'Flying Doctor helps authoress', *Western Grazier*, 14 January 1944, p. 3.
'Future of natives. Own areas essential. Rations are necessary', *Adelaide Mail*, 23 May 1936, p. 18.
Gall, A, 'Ernestine Hill and the North: Reading race and Indigeneity in *The Great Australian Loneliness* and *The Territory*,' *Journal of Australian Studies*, vol. 37, no. 2, 2013, pp. 194–207.
Gara, T, 'Ooldea Soak,' *Journal of the Anthropological Society of South Australia*, vol. 26, no. 4, 1988, pp. 1–11.
———, '"As familiar with the wild creatures as I am with my own family history": Daisy Bates on the Nullarbor Plain, 1912–35', unpublished paper, 2003, pp. 7–14.
'Genius unspoiled. Ernestine Hemmings, girl poet. Pegasus as a legal librarian', *Sunday Times*, 3 February 1918, p. 13.
Greaves, R, 'A "grim and fascinating" land of opportunity: The walkabout women and Australia', *Journal of the Association for the Study of Australian Literature*, vol. 14, no. 15, pp. 1–12.
Greer, G, 'Whitefella jump up: The shortest way to nationhood', *Quarterly Essay*, 11, Black Inc., Melbourne, 2003.
Harlow, S, 'The 1932 rush to The Granites', *Journal of Northern Territory History*, no. 6, 1995, pp. 23–33.
Hemmings, E, 'Australian poetesses', *WA Record*, 20 July 1918, p. 8.
———, 'The City of Everlasting No. A first impression,' *WA Record*, 26 January 1918, p. 8.

References

Hill, E, 'White and natives: The position in the Kimberley', *West Australian*, 26 May 1932, p. 16.
———, 'Cannibalism on East-West', *Sunday Sun*, 19 June 1932, p. 2.
———, 'Woman of Ooldea', *West Australian* 25 June 1932, p. 4.
———, 'White "grandmother" of Ooldea: Work of Mrs Daisy among the Aborigines,' *Daily News*, 23 July 1932, p. 13.
———, 'Granites is Gold City in embryo', *Mail*, 15 October 1932, p. 3.
———, 'Road to gold', *Chronicle*, 27 October 1932, p. 52.
———, 'Bank for Granites gold', *News*, 31 October 1932, p. 5.
———, 'Trek from Granites. Begging lifts: 20 lose work', *News*, 22 November 1932, p. 1.
———, 'Murray – scourge of the Myalls. Man who keeps white men safe in wilds', *Northern Standard*, 3 March 1933, p. 5.
———, 'Lugger that is link with lonely outposts', *Sunday Mail*, 3 September 1933, p. 21.
———, 'The rim of Arnhem Land: Where white women are unafraid', *Chronicle*, 19 October 1933, p. 2.
———, 'Cruise of the Silver Gull', *Advertiser*, 10 March 1934, p. 9.
———, '650 miles to receive honor. Mrs. D Bates in Adelaide', *Advertiser*, 23 May 1934, p. 14.
———, 'Problem of Aborigine: Appeal to women of Australia', *Advertiser*, 20 June 1934, p. 8.
———, 'Ernestine Hill's page for women', *ABC Weekly*, 6 January 1940, p. 29.
———, 'Long trail of romance', *ABC Weekly*, 23 March 1940, pp. 64–65.
———, 'Sister Susie in uniform', *ABC Weekly*, 29 June 1940, p. 16.
———, 'The friend from the dreaming: Her memorial in Ooldea,' UQFL18.D.10.3.
Hogan, E, 'Into the loneliness', *Meanjin*, vol. 76, no. 3, 2017, pp. 116–25.
———, '"Impossible, now, to read the Rosetta Stone": Cultural hybridity and loss in the Ernestine Hill Collection', in D Hecq and J Novitz (eds), *Inhabitation: Creative Writing with Critical Theory*, Gylphi, 2018.
Hogan, E, Antonia, A and Craig, H, 'More than an amanuensis: Ernestine Hill's contribution to *The Passing of the Aborigines*', *Journal of the Association for the Study of Australian Literature*, vol.3, no. 18, 2018, pp. 1–17.
Holland, A, 'Wives and mothers like ourselves: Exploring white women's intervention in the politics of race, 1920s–1940s', *Australian Historical Studies*, no. 117, 2001, pp. 292–310.
Hughes, R, 'The remarkable story of Mrs Daisy Bates', *Sunday Times*, 15 January 1939.
Hughston, V, SC, 'Native Title and the Bennell Decision', *Indigenous Law Bulletin*, 2007, vol. 6, no. 26, p. 18.
Innes, G, 'Queen of the orphaned world', *Herald*, 3 December 1938, p. 40
'Kabbarli', *Manchester Guardian*, 23 December 1938, p. 5.
'Kabbarli, who quelled an Aboriginal revolution', *Advertiser*, 31 December 1938, p. 18.
'Keeping alive the memory of a remarkable woman', *Advertiser*, 16 November 1954, p. 2.
Lake, M, 'Frontier feminism and the marauding white man', *Journal of Australian Studies*, no. 49, 1996, pp. 12–20.
Lamshed, M, 'Natives always see the joke', *Advertiser*, 30 August 1932, p. 9.

Linn, E, Letter to the Editor, *ABC Weekly*, 10 Jan 1940, p. 20.
'Lucky dip', *Times Literary Supplement*, 22 August 1952.
Lyon, CA, 'Strangest, and greatest, woman in the empire', *Australian Women's Weekly*, 17 December 1938, p. 47.
McConagher, K, 'Northern Territory saga: Exploration and adventure', *The Age*, 26 January 1952, p. 7.
Morris, M, 'Media and popular modernism around the Pacific War: An inter-Asian story', *Memory Studies*, vol. 6, no. 3, 2013, pp. 359–69.
——, '*The Great Australian Loneliness*: On writing an inter-Asian biography of Ernestine Hill', *Journal of Intercultural Studies*, vol. 35, no. 3, 2014, pp. 238–49.
'Mrs. Bates to write story of native "spirit babies"', *Advertiser*, 15 March 1941.
'New book on Australia by E Hill', *Air Mail*, n.d.
'New Commissioners are keen on job', *ABC Weekly*, 11 July 1942, pp. 19, 22.
'Our aboriginals. Smoothing the pillow of dying race. Missionary's efforts', *Cairns Post*, 6 May 1925, p. 4.
Packer, F, 'Great newspaper man passes on,' *Australian Women's Weekly*, 21 April 1934, p. 14.
Parke, E, 'Northern Australia boundary prompts identity crisis for WA towns, as shires seek planning change,' 24 September 2015, <www.abc.net.au/news/2015-09-24/northern-australia-boundary-prompts-identity-crisis-for-wa-towns/6802116>, viewed 5 December 2018.
Pilgrim, J, 'Across the "Bight" with Ernestine Hill: Australia's foremost travel-writer tells of the adventurous years', *The Land*, 24 October 1947.
'Record price for novel', *Sydney Morning Herald*, 11 May 1946, p. 4.
Reece, B, 'AP Elkin interviewed about Daisy Bates', *Australian Aboriginal Studies*, 2007, no.1 , p. 131–37.
——, '"You would have loved her for her lore": The letters of Daisy Bates', *Australian Aboriginal Studies*, 2007, no. 1, pp. 51–70.
'Review of *The Great Australian Loneliness*', *Spectator*, 12 March 1937, p. 32.
Salt, B, 'Australia reinvented: A nation divided according to its interests', *The Australian*, 24 November 2016, <www.theaustralian.com.au/australia-reinvented-a-nation-divided-according-to-its-interests/news-story/6b19bbc5175f4e5b620e6d28d2c90d1f>, viewed 6 January 2020.
Scambary, B, 'My country, mine country: Indigenous people, mining and development contestation in remote Australia', CAEPR, ANU, Canberra, Research Monograph No. 33, 2013, p. 49.
Schenk, RS, 'The native question. Is the race doomed?', *West Australian*, 21 June 1932, p. 3.
Smaal, Y, 'Queer relationships in nineteenth-century Australia', 15 October 2017, <www.auswhn.org.au/blog/queer-19th-century/>, viewed 8 November 2019.
'Son given exemption to help mother finish book', *Telegraph*, 10 October 1943.
Standing, G, 'The precariat and class struggle', *RCCS Annual Review* (online), no. 7, 2015, <journals.openedition.org/rccsar/585>, viewed 30 April 2019.
Stephensen, PR, *The Publicist*, March 1941, p. 16.
'Study of Aborigines by Australian idealist offers much, yet …', *Adelaide Mail*, 21 January 1939, p. 26.
Sullivan, V, 'Speculative fiction is a powerful political tool': From *War of the Worlds*

References

to *Terra Nullius*', *Guardian*, 22 August 2017, <www.theguardian.com/books/australia-books-blog/2017/aug/22/speculative-fiction-is-a-powerful-political-tool-from-war-of-the-worlds-to-terra-nullius>, viewed 8 August 2019.

Taffe, S, 'Behind the mulga curtain and beyond the grave: Mary Montgomerie Bennett's leadership in Aboriginal Affairs, 1930–1961', in *Seizing the Initiative: Australian Women Leaders in Politics, Workplaces and Communities*, eScholarship Research Centre, The University of Melbourne, 2012.

Thieburger, N, 'Bringing back languages from scraps of paper', <pursuit.unimelb.edu.au/articles/bringing-back-languages-from-scraps-of-paper>, viewed 16 March 2020.

Trevor, S, 'Love in the age of convicts', 27 December 2013, <www.tracesmagazine.com.au/2013/12/love-in-the-age-of-convicts/>, viewed 8 November 2019.

'Two historical novels', The Red Page, *Bulletin*, 7 January 1942, p. 2.

United Aborigines Mission, *The United Aborigines Messenger*, vol. 4, no. 45, 1 June 1936, <nla.gov.au/nla.obj-580845612>, viewed 3 January 2020.

Waller, L, 'Singular influence: Mapping the ascent of Daisy M Bates in popular understanding and Indigenous policy', *Australian Journal of Communication*, 2010, vol. 37, no. 2, pp. 1–14.

Witcombe, E, 'From sainthood to scandal: The murky legend of the mysterious Daisy Bates', *Weekend Australian*, 2–3 April, 1988, p. 4

Wolff, S, 'Sam Fullbrook: Delicate Beauty review – Australia evoked in living colour', *Guardian*, 1 April 2014, <www.theguardian.com/artanddesign/australia-culture-blog/2014/apr/09/sam-fullbrook-delicate-beauty-review-australia-evoked-in-living-colour>, viewed 28 January 2018.

FILMS

Blom, D, D Malouf and J Tulip, *Invocation to earth, an opera; Prelude, for orchestra; Daisy Bates, a documentary essay for television*, [microform] / Diana Blom, 1973.

Smart, R (dir.), *Bitter Springs*, Umbrella Films, Sydney, 1950.

Taylor, A (dir.), *Kabbarli: A film about Daisy Bates*, Ronin Films, Mitchell, ACT, 2003.

Walker, L (dir.), *Lasseter's Bones*, Umbrella Films, Sydney, 2012.

Acknowledgements

This book was supported by an Australia Council for the Arts – Projects for Individuals and Groups Grant 2016, the Peter Blazey Fellowship 2017 and the Hazel Rowley Literary Fellowship 2019. I am very grateful for the work and support of these donors and organisations, without which I would have found the research for this book difficult to conduct as an independent scholar and writer.

I am deeply thankful to Phillipa McGuinness at NewSouth Publishing for her insightful and empathetic steering in taking on this 'vast and wandering work'. Thanks also to Emma Hutchinson, Elspeth Menzies and the team at NewSouth for their enthusiastic support of this project, to Tricia Dearborn for her patient, thoughtful and sharp-eyed editing of the manuscript, and Lisa White for her arresting cover design.

A very warm thanks to Yalata Anangu Aboriginal Community for welcoming me at their campfire, sharing their stories so generously and taking me to Ooldea, especially Margaret May, Mima Smart, Joy West, Rita, Russell and Sharon Bryant, and Sean Kelly. Thanks also to Desley Culpin, David White and Sharon Yendall for their assistance in facilitating my visits.

I'm very grateful to Louise Campbell for meeting with me and answering my questions about Ernestine Hill with interesting and informative emails over the years. I owe a huge debt to Margriet Bonnin for her foundational research into Australian travel writing during the 1930s and 1940s, and I'm grateful to Roberta Bonnin

Acknowledgements

for making her sister's papers about Ernestine Hill available at the Fryer Library. Alexis Antonia and Hugh Craig at the University of Newcastle's Centre for Literary and Linguistic Computing kindly responded to my request to undertake a computational stylistic analysis of the authorship of *The Passing of the Aborigines*, and were tirelessly patient in giving their time, knowledge and expertise. Thanks also to Tom Gara and Nic Thieburger for fielding my queries about their Daisy Bates research. Many librarians provided significant support for this book's research, especially Simon Farley and Kerri Klumpp at the Fryer Library, University of Queensland; Isobel Johnstone and Eva Bernroider at the National Library of Australia; Kirsty McHugh at the National Library of Scotland; and Shane Agius at the South Australian Museum. I also wish to thank the following for their assistance and permissions: Rae Brewster at Streaky Bay Museum, Patsy Millett, Peter Bridge at Hesperian Press, Sam van der Plank at Monash Publishing and Afroditi Forti at Berghahn Books. All reasonable efforts were taken to obtain permission to use copyright material in this book, but in some cases copyright could not be traced. The author welcomes information in this regard.

Special thanks to Jo Case for commenting on an early draft of the manuscript, and encouraging me to apply for grants I never thought I'd get. Thanks also to Lucy Sussex, Angus Gordon, Delia Falconer and Aviva Tuffield for helping me sound out ideas during the project's early stages. Corridor chats with Peter Browne, Jock Given and Brian McFarlane at Swinburne Institute for Social Research also played a formative role. Ken Gelder and Amanda Morris kindly shared their time and resources with me at the Australian Centre, University of Melbourne. Warm thanks to Laurencia Grant and Lisa Gray for their loyal support in Alice Springs, and Alice Woods of the Alice Springs Collection for her enthusiastic assistance.

I am thankful to Ellie Rennie and Julian Thomas for employing me on the Australian Research Council linkage project, Home Internet for Remote Indigenous Communities, at Swinburne Institute for Social Research, which enabled me to continue travelling to Central Australia. Initial research for this book was seeded by the Swinburne University Research Output Scheme. I am also grateful to Foong Ling Kong, Trish Grieg and the Hansard Unit at the Parliament of Victoria, and Clare Fisher, Kate Gilbert and the team at Alice Springs Public Library for providing me with employment and camaraderie in the book's later stages.

My sincere thanks to the following people for their support: my family – Enid Gordon, Claire and Mark Hogan-Gibbons. And my friends and colleagues: Simeon Barlow and Ronn Morris, Sally Bolton, Alecia Buchanan and Matt Johnson, Marg Carew and Simon Murphy, Laura Carroll, Janis Constable, Martin Cowling and Pomme Chanapat Maneedul, Mel Cranenburgh, Tracy Crisp, Andrew Crouch, Tandy Culpepper, Angela ni Dhalaigh, Jeremy Dore, Bronwyn Druce, Fiona Dyball, Catriona Elek and Simon Kenny, Heather Elliott, Kathleen Epelde, Wendy Feather, Caren Florance, Kate Francis, Russell Goldflam, Kerryn Goldsworthy, Robin Gregory, Robyn Grey-Gardner, Richard Harling, Jocelyn Hedley, Indigo Holcombe-James, Ana Hutchinson, Carly Ingles, Alina Iser, Meredith Jones, Sonja Kurtzer, Amanda Lawrence, Nici Lindsay and Ross Hamilton, Melody Lord and Mark Whybro, Esther Lukabyo, Jane McCredie, Deepika Mathur, Philip Morrissey, Kathy Moylan, Meg Mundell, Naomi Parry, Jenny Petersen and Fiona Stewart-Darling, Andrew Preston, Jane Schleiger, Rochelle Siemienowicz, Tracey Stevens, Margaret Stuart, Dale Wakefield, Kim Waldock, Mary-Helen Ward, Sandy Webster and Gillian Wood.

Thanks also to Sam, Nonna and family at the Factory Café, West Brunswick, and Mel at The Bakery, Alice Springs, not only for providing great food and coffee but warm ports of call on writing days.

Finally, I wish to acknowledge my cat Lulu for her constant companionship during the writing of this book and on some of my later trips in the van.

Index

ABC Weekly 2, 3, 178–82, 186, 188, 190, 192, 260
Aboriginal-settler relationships 101, 373–74
    Aboriginal activism 319–20, 352–53, 355, 358
    Aboriginal culture and white romanticism 103–106
    assimilation policies 43, 104, 358
    cultural appropriation 208, 353, 359–60
    doomed race theories 10, 30, 34, 35, 40, 87, 97, 105, 146, 154, 303–304, 317–18, 353, 358, 363
    half-castes/hybridity 40–43, 94, 96–97, 105, 358–60
    Hill and 97–98, 103, 303, 358
    invasion terminology 352–55
    Kabbarli mythology influence 285, 301, 302, 303, 304, 369
    massacres 101–102, 122–23, 316, 355
    miscegenation 42–43, 94–97, 124, 300–301
    native title 356, 362
    Northern Territory 315–16
    pastoralists 27–28, 101–102, 104–106, 145, 147, 180, 320
    post-war diaspora 318–19
    violence 92–93, 101–102, 122–23, 147, 315–17, 355
Aboriginal and Torres Strait Islander Commission (ATSIC) 83
Aborigines Protection League 40, 146
Aborigines Uplift Society 145

Adelaide 1–4, 21, 23, 31, 32–33, 40, 45, 78, 79, 84, 107, 112, 118–21, 128–34, 143, 148, 155, 156–57, 165, 188, 192, 194–97, 204–207, 220, 229–30, 231, 238, 242, 251, 253, 267–71, 274–75, 277–78, 292, 297, 298, 304, 331–33
    Queen Adelaide Club 1, 128, 157, 247, 267
    Trent Hospital 247
Adelaide Festival 343
    Writers' Week 335
Adelaide Women's Club 128
Adorno, Theodor 58
Advertiser (Adelaide) 1–2, 71, 75, 89, 111–12, 118, 119–20, 128–32, 135–36, 145, 148, 149, 152, 178, 188, 194, 205, 207, 209, 257, 258, 272, 303, 305, 348
Afford, Max 68, 186
Afford, Thelma 68
Age (Melbourne) 60, 314, 347
Albrecht, Pastor 7
Aldred, Doreen 264
Alice Springs 77–78, 79, 82, 84, 88–90, 266, 366
Alice Springs Telegraph Station 316, 371
Anangu people xiv, 33–34, 35–36, 52, 115–16, 119, 122, 125, 206, 212, 230, 239, 241, 243–44, 280–82, 291, 302, 368, 369, 372–73
    Maralinga tests and 280–81, 289–90, 296
Angus & Robertson 70–71, 183, 202, 259, 277, 328–31, 344, 346, 350
anthropology
    Aboriginal kinship system 28, 30

Index

Aboriginal languages 7, 28, 30, 361–63, 368
  anthropological practice 143, 284
  Bates and Aboriginal anthropology 5, 9–12, 27–33, 124, 138–43, 145, 153–54, 263, 303–304, 364–65
  Bates's contribution 361–63
  emergence of Australian anthropology 9, 30, 137, 363, 369
  'ethnomania' 9–10
  folk ethnography 271, 354, 363–65
  Hill's ethnographic contribution 341–42, 353–55
Anti-Slavery and Aboriginal Protection Society, London 40
Antonia, Alexis 150
Apsley, Viola 94
  The Amateur Settlers 94
Archibald, JF 64–65
Archibald Prize 335–37
Argus (Melbourne) 254, 255, 357
Arnhem Land 6, 92–93, 118, 159
Art Gallery of New South Wales 336–37
Art International 337
Associated Newspapers 68, 72, 78, 80, 90, 110, 111
Association for the Protection of Native Races 146
Atlas, James 256
Australasian 36, 254
The Australian 350
Australian Dried Fruits Association 135, 158
Australian Frontier see The Great Australian Loneliness
Australian Worker 65, 176

Badtjala people 359
Baglehole, Ernest 222–24, 225
Baker, Jeannine 179, 181
Balbuk, Fanny xii, 29, 230, 362, 368
Barnard, Marjorie 175
Bartholomew, ER 209, 251, 269, 275
Basedow, Herbert 37, 147, 267
Bates, Arnold Hamilton 27, 50, 51–52, 160–61, 201–202, 227, 274–75, 278, 295–96

Bates, Daisy
  Aboriginal languages work xv–xvi, 2, 28–30, 32, 138, 361–63, 368
  Aboriginal people, relationship with 11–12, 39–40, 229–30, 243–44, 368–69, 373
  Anangu responses to cannibalism claims by 242, 292, 297
  arrival in Australia 48–49
  attitude to sex 226–27
  Batesian mythology 218–25, 303–304, 345–46
  bush writing 125
  cannibalism claims 12, 25–26, 35–33, 43–46, 147, 155, 242, 292, 297
  death and interment 277–78
  diaries and letters 144–45, 254–56
  duality 228–29
  health 13, 27, 32, 153, 204, 214–17, 219–21, 249, 262–63, 266, 276, 295
  Hill, relationship with 11, 12–13, 44–47, 52–54, 130–34, 251–59, 265–66, 271–74
  impact on Aboriginal people 292, 297–98, 300–303
  Irish origins 53–54, 223–25
  letters to Hill 1–5, 9, 119, 251–57, 259, 265–66
  lobbying by 26, 31–32
  Lock and 124–25, 129
  London *Times* commission 27–28
  marriages 49–52, 128–29, 222–23, 225–28, 295
  memoirs 1–2, 8, 46, 119–20, 128–37
  miscegenation views 12, 24, 39, 42–43, 242, 287, 292, 297, 298, 299–301, 304
  missionaries, views on 124
  'More about the Aborigines. Why they are dying out' 33
  'Ngar'galulla Law: The Country of the Spirit Babies' 143–44, 207–208, 210, 251, 252, 265, 266–69, 273, 277

417

paranoia 144, 160, 215, 220, 221, 222, 268, 272–73
'The Passing of a Race: Australia's Stone-Age Nomads' 208, 209–210
psychology 228–29
responses to cannibalism claims by 25, 25, 36, 37, 38, 44, 147
self-mythology as Kabbarli 48, 136, 141, 214, 230, 248, 301, 304, 369, 373–74
siblings 224
son 27, 50, 51–52, 160–61, 201–202
stolen generation and 287–88, 292, 297–98, 300–302
will 159, 275–76
Yalata people memories 236–43
Bates, Jack 27–28, 32, 48, 49–52, 160, 222, 225, 227, 228
Bates Online 362–63
Bateson, Catherine Roy 'Coy' (nee Foster-Lynam) 63, 64–65, 67, 69, 71, 197, 199, 262, 319, 323, 325, 335, 344, 349
Bateson, Charles 'Harry' 344, 346, 348, 349–50
Battams, Mary 121
Battarbee, Rex 7
Baume, Eric 77–78, 79–81, 108, 109, 111, 285
  Tragedy Track 80, 81, 108
Beagle Bay 28, 36, 51, 345
Behrendt, Larissa 44
  Finding Eliza: Power and Colonial Storytelling 44
Bennell v Western Australia 362
Bennett, Mary 40, 41, 43, 104–105, 122, 123, 300, 303
Bibbulmun people 4, 23, 29, 30, 47–48, 52, 126, 362
Birdsville 201, 206
Bleakley, JW 40, 41, 42, 99, 122–23
  The Aboriginals and Half-Castes of Central Australia and North Australia 40, 94, 99
Blom, Diana 222
Bolam, Anthony 33

Bonnin, Margriet 68, 69, 70, 72, 73–74, 175, 338–39, 340–42
Bonnin, Nancy 339–40
Bookabie 248, 366
Borderland 27, 124
Borroloola 3, 6
Brady, Maggie 280–81
  'The politics of space and mobility' 280–81
Brewster, Rae 23–26, 272
Bridge, Timothy 223
Brisbane 60–65, 338–41, 349
British Association for the Advancement of Science 31, 143, 165
Broken Hill 84, 180, 189, 198, 202
Brooks, Constable Alvis 211–12, 215, 216–18, 222, 241
Brooks, Fred 122
Broome 6, 8, 70, 143, 207–208, 323
Brown, Max 347, 348
Brown, May 'Wolfram Queen' 79
Brownrigg, Captain Robert 224
Bruder, Jessica 310–11
  Nomadland 310–11
Bryant, Rita 235–41, 282–83, 297, 298, 367–68, 370–72
Bryant, Russell 231–32, 282–84, 286–97, 367
Buderim Mountain 334–38, 340
Bulletin 64, 65, 107, 109, 133, 174, 183, 184
Burdeu, APA 145–46
Burke, Inspector 216, 218
Butler, Mary Anne 311

Cairns 323
Caledon Bay crisis 92–93, 118
Campbell, Louise 67, 69, 111, 172, 172, 339, 340, 345, 357–58
Canberra 9, 23, 88, 118, 121, 189, 192, 196, 207, 254
Canning Stock Route 322
Carmen, Leon 359
  My Own Sweet Time 359
Carnegie, Margaret 222
  In Search of Breaker Morant: Balladist and Bushveldt Carbineer 222

Index

Catholic Advocate 62, 65
Catholic Leader 349
Cawley, Professor AC 339, 341
Ceduna 34, 82–83, 231, 235, 263, 264, 319
central Australia 6–7, 13, 20, 36, 41, 53, 76–77, 79, 83–85, 87, 88, 89, 316
Chapman, CH 76–77, 79
Chauvel, Charles 183, 329
   Jedda 329
Cleland, Professor JB 37–38, 44–45, 48, 157, 305
Clendinnen, Inga 360
Clune, Frank 76, 108, 178
Colebrook Children's Home 298–99
Coleman, Claire G. 311
Commonwealth Literary Fund (CLF) 177, 205, 248, 262, 267, 328, 332, 342
Commonwealth-State Native Welfare Conference 1937 104
Coniston massacre 122–23, 316
Conor, Liz 361
Coober Pedy 281, 302
Cook, James 355
Cooke, Constance 39–41, 121, 122
   'The status of Aboriginal Women in Australia' 41
Cooktown 326–27, 355
Coolgardie xi, 76, 167, 264–65, 313, 314
Cooper, William 146
Cordillo Downs Station 197, 199, 200–201, 202
Courier Mail (Brisbane) 135
Cousins, Walter 183, 184, 259
Cowra 199
Craig, Hugh 150
Cundeelee 235, 281
Curr, EM 362
Curtin, John 188, 192, 194–96, 199–200
Curtis, Allan 222
   Kabbarli 222
Curtis Brown, Spencer 118, 135, 136, 208, 209, 303

Daily Mail 65
Daisy Bates; Invocation to Earth (authors D Malouf/J Tulip) 222
Daisy Chain 219–20, 222
Dampier, William 111
Dark, Eleanor 175, 183–85, 354–55
   The Timeless Land 183–85, 354
Darwin 87, 91, 93, 95, 123, 180, 202, 259, 321
   refugee crisis 181–82
Davis, Beatrice 70–71, 328, 329–31, 341, 346, 348, 350–51
de Vries, Susanna 220, 222–23, 225
   Desert Queen: The Many Lives and Loves of Daisy Bates 220
Deamer, Sydney 178–81, 186–87, 260
Depression x, 75–77, 85, 100, 133–34, 371
Dewar, Mickey 92
Dillon, Mary 224
Dorre and Bernier Islands 140–41, 145, 263
Doubleday 182, 187
Down the Hole, Up the Tree, Across the Sandhill: Running from the State and Daisy Bates (authors ET Williams/ EW Wingfield) 301–302
Drake-Brockman, Henrietta 20, 76, 172, 174, 178, 185, 188, 193, 197, 273, 334, 340
Duguid, Dr Charles 146
Duhig, Archbishop 62
Duke of Gloucester 125–26
Dumas, Sir Lloyd 111, 119–20, 129, 135, 136, 205, 208, 221, 303, 305
Durack, Bess 91, 322
Durack, Elizabeth 101, 261, 313, 322, 359
Durack, Mary 72, 73, 76, 91, 100–101, 111, 200, 203, 321–24, 335, 344–45, 347, 348
   Kings in Grass Castles 101, 323
   The Rock and the Sand 345
Durack, Michael 101
Durack, Michael Patrick 72, 91, 100–101, 103, 104
Durack, Patsy 101
Dwyer, Bridget 223–24
Dwyer, Daisy May *see* Bates, Daisy
Dwyer, Francis 224

Dwyer, James 223
Dwyer, William 223

East-West Line xi, 25, 33, 38, 39–41, 116, 117, 121, 125, 281, 298, 300–301, 371
Easton, WR 91
Eckermann, Ali Cobby 311
Edwards, Yvonne 297
Elkin, AP 37, 157, 361–62
Endeavour 355
Eucla xv, 26, 30, 31, 34, 45, 58, 165, 166–67, 173, 277, 299
Evatt, HV 195
Examiner (Launceston) 67, 69, 70
Eyre Highway x, 20, 56, 82, 115, 117, 165, 167–68, 231, 233, 280, 366

Far North Queensland 90, 128, 318, 323, 326, 357
Fellowship of Australian Writers (FAW) 174, 175, 176, 188, 315
Firth, Raymond 149, 153–54
Fitzherbert, Professor 157
Flinders, Matthew 21, 110, 159, 182–85, 355
Forbes, Jackie 'Witchetty' 95–96, 358, 359
Forrest, John xiv, 29
Forrest River Mission 101
Foster, Irene 'Rene' 71, 75, 107, 109, 178, 197, 325, 331–32, 335, 339, 341–42, 349, 350
Foster-Lynam, Kitty 69, 70, 71, 112, 178, 188, 193, 201
Foster-Lynam, Margaret 'Madge' *see* Hemmings, Madge
Fowlers Bay 31–32, 34, 42, 165, 231, 233–35, 243, 248, 263–64, 282, 289, 292, 364, 365
Frame, Janet 311–12
Franklin, Miles 68, 109–110, 185, 205–206
Fraser, Eliza 44, 53, 359
Fuel Board 259, 264
Fullbrook, Sam 335–37

Gall, Adam 358
Gara, Tom 38, 43, 290, 302
Gardner, John 7
Garner, Bill 19, 157–58
    Born in a Tent 19
Gauera 31, 262
Gibney, Bishop Matthews 26, 28
Gillard, Julia 170
Gilmore, Dame Mary 174, 175–77, 192–93, 198, 205–206, 257, 328, 331, 347, 348
government policies 86–87, 155, 303
    activism 146–47
    influence of Bates 303
    protectionist era 26, 31–35, 42, 140–41, 145
    racial purity 87
    'Tombs of the living dead' (WA) 140–41
    'Vanishing race' initiative 28–29
    war and post-war 318–20
Gowrie, Lady 148
Gowrie, Lord 148
Graham, Lorna 298–99
The Granites 76–81
Grant, Stan 185, 360
    Australia Day 360
Grant Watson, EL 138–39, 142
Great Australian Bight xi–xii, xv, 11, 21, 26, 30, 30–34, 83, 116, 149, 160, 165–68, 173, 221, 234, 260, 262, 282, 299, 319, 322, 366, 372
The Great Australian Loneliness 2, 5–7, 9, 10, 17, 46, 81, 85, 87–92, 94–101, 106, 158, 182, 184, 187–88, 313, 314, 317, 329
    computational stylistic testing 150–51
    reviews 106–109
Great War xi, 33, 62, 85, 198, 201
Green, Harry 297–98, 301
Green, HM 108–109
Green, Marion 297–98, 301
Greer, Germaine 359–60
    'White Fella jump up' 359–60
Grey, Beatrice 110
Griffen-Foley, Bridget 69

The House of Packer 69
Griffiths, Tom 184–85, 354
   The Art of Time Travel 184
Grimshaw, Beatrice 178
Groverman, Sergeant 213, 216–17

Hamilton, Vera (Joan Pilgrim) 172, 200, 260, 264
Hanson, Pauline 155
Harlow, Sue 79
Harris, William 43
Hartog, Dirk 111
Hasluck, Paul 305
Hatfield, William 76, 85, 178
   Sheepmates 85
Hawke, Steve 320
Hay, Frederick 101
Heinrich, HA 123
Helpmann, Sir Robert 222, 342–43, 344–46
Hemmings, Ernestine *see* Hill, Ernestine
Hemmings, Madge 60–61, 69, 71, 112, 176, 177, 186, 193
Hemmings, Ray 60–62
Hemmings, Robert 59–61
Henderson, Russell 206
Hepburn, Katharine 343–45
Herald (Melbourne) 75, 78, 135, 148, 337
Herbert, Xavier 99–100, 187, 358
   Capricornia 100, 187, 358
Hermannsburg mission 7, 123
Hewson, Ethel Maud 67
Hill, Ernestine
   ABC employment 2, 3, 178–82, 186, 188–92, 196, 199–200, 260
   Aboriginal/white relationships, views 41–42, 352–54, 360
   About Lasseter 76, 333
   'Along the Eyre Highway with Ernestine Hill' 20
   Archibald Prize portrait 335–37
   'Australian poetesses' 63
   'Australia's Home' 20
   Bates, relationship with 11, 12–13, 44–47, 52–54, 130–34, 251–59, 265–66, 271–74
   Batesian mythology promotion 303–305, 369
   bush/travel writing 75–78, 85–86, 180
   'Cannibalism on East-West' 45–47, 76
   childhood 59–63
   death 349–50
   emotional and physical health 3, 194–200, 326–27, 332, 333–40, 348–49
   fake gold rush 76–80
   Fuel Board sponsorship 259, 264
   financial concerns 176–78, 192, 326, 337, 347–48
   Flying Doctor Calling 89, 202, 329
   international readership 187, 194, 314
   'Johnnie Wise-cap' 323, 325, 328–29, 342, 350, 355–58
   journalism 1–3, 6–8, 10, 45–47, 63–75, 180–82
   Murray River commission 135, 158
   'Murray – Scourge of the Myalls' 102, 316
   Ooldea with Bates x–xvi
   Packer, Robert Clyde 'RC', relationship with 66–73, 110–11, 134, 202, 257, 324
   Peter Pan Land 62
   poetry 61, 62, 64–65, 133
   reticence 174–75
   son, absconsion with 194–97
   son, relationship with 201–202, 321–25, 330–33
   son's paternity 67–70
   Water into Gold 158
   white exploration 355
   'Women of Ooldea' 47, 305
   work on 'Ngar'galulla Law' 251–52, 263, 265, 266–70
Hill, Jackie *see* Scrivener, Jackie
Hill, Robert David 'Bob' 3, 4, 9, 23, 65, 67–71, 73, 79, 112, 172, 173, 177–78, 188, 193–94, 200–201, 203, 206, 259, 261, 262–64, 314, 315, 329, 340, 349
   conscription battle 194–99, 256

daughter Celeste 332
marriage 330–33, 340
relationship with Hill 201–202, 321–25, 330–33
son Luke 'Lui' 331, 332
Hinde, John 178
HMS *Investigator* 21
Hope, AD 84
Hurst, William 254–55, 304
Hyde, Matron Ruby 299, 301

Idriess, Ion 75–76, 85, 108–109, 120
Lasseter's Last Ride 76, 85
Men of the Jungle 109
Indian Pacific 115, 286
Ingamells, Rex 267

James, Florence 178
Jarrold & Son 158, 175
John Murray Publishing 136–38, 145–47, 153, 154, 155, 208–10, 251, 267–69, 275–76, 303
Johns, Paul 76, 333
Johnson, Anna 86, 182, 187
Joobaitch 4, 29–30, 230, 243, 250, 368
Joynton Smith, James 66

Kabbarli 8, 46, 89, 129, 132, 133, 136, 152, 272, 277, 278–79, 319, 348, 351
Kalgoorlie xi, 33, 83, 84, 167, 213, 231, 233, 265, 310, 323
Kaytetye people 123, 316
Kelley, Patricia 74
Kelly, Sean 286, 293–95, 371
Kelly, Sharon 283, 286, 294–95, 371
Kelsh, Margaret 271–72
Ker Wilson, Barbara 277
Tales Told to Kabbarli: Aboriginal Legends Collected by Daisy Bates 277
Kidd, Captain 196–97, 198, 199
The Killing Times 101
the Kimberley 28, 45, 51, 72–73, 91, 101–104, 174, 318, 355–57
'King Billy' 236
King George V 126
King, Georgina 173

Koonibba mission 34, 287, 319
Kowal, Emma 369–70
Trapped in the Gap 369–70

Lamond, Henry 108
Lamshed, Max 103, 135–36, 208
Lane, William 176
Lang, Andrew 30, 138, 142, 143–44
Langley, Eve 312
The Pea Pickers 312
Lasseter, Lewis Harold 76, 371–72
Laverton 29, 40, 104, 122
Leichhardt, Ludwig 85
Lindsay, Norman 65
Lingiari, Vincent 320
Linn, Eva 179–80
Lock, Annie 41, 121–26, 128, 243, 297–99, 300, 301
Lodge, Constable 38
Lomas, Brian 300
Queen of Deception 300
London *Times* 27
Louttit, Ellen 229
Loxton 155–56, 160
Lucinda 74
Lyons, JA 126–27

Ma'amba Reserve xii, xv, 29–30, 47, 52, 230, 243, 250, 362
MacDougall, Walter 280–81
Macfarlane, Robert 58
Mackaness, Alice 192, 194, 197, 198, 312
Mackaness, George 3, 4, 176–77, 183, 186, 197, 198, 312
Macquarie 50
Madigan, Cecil 78–79, 81
Crossing the Dead Heart 83
Magnetic Island 327, 330
Malouf, David 222, 359
Remembering Babylon 359
Maralinga nuclear tests 11, 115, 116, 280–82, 291, 296–97, 371, 374
Martelli, Dean 28
Mathew, John 143
Mathews, RH 29–30, 227, 362
Mathews family 249, 261–62, 273
Mattingley, Christobel 297

Index

May, Margaret 235–43, 368
McConagher, Ken 314
McConnel, Ursula 11
McCulloch, Allan 337
McGregor, Athol 123
McKay, Claude 66
Mears, Gillian 311
Mee, Arthur 136, 146, 147
Melbourne 4, 6, 13, 20, 21, 40, 64, 69, 77, 89, 156, 169, 180, 254, 259–60, 284, 298, 309, 318, 322, 325, 329, 343, 355
Menzies, Robert 158
Miller, Horrie 323, 324
Miller, John 323–24
Minmilla 25, 26, 45–46
Mitchell Library 159, 174, 175, 176, 177, 354, 355
Mitchell, Professor AG 339
Moorehead, Alan 154
Morley, William 146–47
Morris, Meaghan 90, 109, 133, 361
Moses, CJA 197
Mount Margaret mission 40, 104, 122
Mountford, Charles 36, 147, 159
  Brown Men and Red Sand 36, 83
Mudge, Mrs 248
Mundrabilla 318–19
Murchison 322
Murdoch, Keith 78
Murrant, Edwin Henry (Breaker Morant) 49, 222, 225, 227
Murray, Constable George 41, 102, 122–23, 316, 317
Murray, John Grey 136–37, 144, 156, 158, 159, 207, 209, 267–70, 275, 276 *see also* John Murray Publishing
Murray, Sir John 136–37, 143, 145, 207, 213, 214, 267 *see also* John Murray Publishing
Murray, Sir George 118
My Love Must Wait 23, 174, 177, 182–87, 192, 259, 328, 329
  reviews 183–84
'My Natives and I' 1, 130, 135, 136, 152, 223, 347–48

National Council of Women 128
National Library of Australia (NLA) 143, 156, 176, 207, 219, 341, 350, 361, 362, 363–64
National Native Title Tribunal 362
National Service Office 194, 196
The Native Tribes of Western Australia 143, 149, 219, 362
Needham, JS 34
Needham, Professor Rodney 362
Nellie 319
Niall, Brenda 101
Nieass, Mrs 248, 266, 366
Nolan, Sidney 359
north-west Australia 27, 28, 32, 50, 73, 101, 111, 137, 138–41, 145, 147, 149, 207–208, 227, 345
northern Australia 6, 13, 41, 75, 87, 94, 107, 274, 313, 318
Nullarbor x–xii, xiv, 1, 4, 10, 13, 17, 20, 46, 56, 58, 82–84, 115–17, 119, 155, 161, 165, 167, 169, 171, 204–30, 231, 239, 243, 257, 267, 274, 281, 283, 297, 309, 319, 333, 364, 373
Nullarbor Regional Reserve 281
Nyan-ngauera 37, 45
Nyoongar people 29

Ohlsen, Louis 139
Oodgeroo Nocnuccal (Kath Walker) 339
Oodnadatta 40, 299
Ooldea x–xvi, 4, 5, 11, 12, 13, 25, 33–39, 43, 44–48, 52–53, 77, 115–27, 157, 210, 212–13, 221, 231, 232, 236–41, 248, 254, 280–95, 297–98, 300–301, 302, 304, 364–65
  memorial for Bates 304–305
Ooldea Films 345
Our North, Our Future: White Paper on Developing Australia 2015 88
outback travel 17–26, 55–53, 82–83, 88–89, 115–18, 156, 165–71, 231–34, 259–65, 282–95, 309–313, 366–74
  Hill 17, 19, 58–59, 71–75, 77, 88–93, 158, 172, 259–65, 312–13, 318–22, 325–27
  older underclasses 310–11

women 12, 19, 55–56, 169–74, 309–312
Overland Telegraph xi, 316
Oxford University Press (OUP) 154, 209, 251, 275

Packer, Frank 67, 69, 78, 110, 111
Packer, Kathleen 67
Packer, Kerry 69
Packer, Robert Clyde 'RC' 66–70, 71, 78, 110–11, 257, 325
Palmer, Nettie 178
Palmer, Vance 178
Palmer, Yvonne 191–92
Park, Ruth 178
The Passing of the Aborigines 2, 18, 127, 128–30, 140, 144, 145–48, 303, 345
   authorship 130–32, 137–38, 150–53, 205–206, 208–209, 256–57, 272, 347–48
   computational stylistic testing 150–52
   editing 135–36
   Hill, role of 150–53
   immersion journalism 149–50
   influence of 153–55
   reviews 148–49
Pearl Harbor 181
Penong 248, 266, 273, 366
Perth xii, xiv, xv, 20, 27–30, 32, 45, 50, 51, 52, 55, 73, 100, 126, 138, 174–75, 231, 259, 262, 265, 322–23, 331, 332, 334, 338, 362
   Karrakatta Club xii, 129
Pila Nguru *see* Spinifex people
Pink, Olive 11, 41, 43, 53
Pitjantjatjara language 238–40, 283, 364, 368, 370
Polkinghorne, Barbara 205, 219, 220, 222, 230, 256, 342
Port Augusta xi, 20, 33, 38, 56, 83, 211, 213, 215–18, 242, 247, 366
   hospital 204, 217–18, 299
Preece, John 267–68, 269–71, 273, 274–77
Prichard, Katharine Susannah 68, 99, 109, 185, 265, 314–15, 335, 358

Coonardoo 99, 358
Prior, Sian 311
Pyap 155–60, 206, 236, 275–76, 368

Quarterly 359–60
Queale, Alan 327, 349
Queensland University Fryer Library 339–40
   Ernestine Hill Collection 5, 6–11, 71, 98–99, 252–53, 316, 350, 352–54

Radcliffe-Brown, Alfred 138–39, 142–44, 208, 284
Raine, Beatrice 167, 267, 274, 278, 279
Randell, Laurel E 218
Reece, Bob 43–44, 137, 153, 224, 254
Register (Adelaide) 39, 123, 124
remote Australia 6, 11, 12–13, 42, 58, 72, 82–91, 106, 124, 172, 174, 190–91, 197, 257–58, 286, 288, 317–20
   bushmen mythology 10, 75, 85, 92, 101, 108, 317, 318
   definitions 87–88
   diversity 6, 90–91, 95, 190–91, 358
   isolation 13, 89–90, 92–93, 172–74, 257
   travel in *see* outback travel
   travel writing genre 85–86
   women in 13, 39–42, 47, 91–100, 104, 123–24, 179–80, 190, 257, 304
Review of Reviews 27
Riddell, Elizabeth 219
RMS *Maloja* 110
Robertson, Constance 200, 335
Robertson & Mullens 85, 106, 158 *see also* Angus & Robertson
Rose, Jessie 223
Royal Commission into the condition of Aborigines in South Australia 31, 42, 299
Royal Flying Doctor Service 202
Royal Geographical Society 30
Ruxton, Miss 52
Rymill, Mrs 128

Index

Salt, Bernard 84
Salter, Elizabeth 222, 223, 236, 277, 290, 342–43, 344, 346–48
   Daisy Bates: The Great White Queen of the Never-Never 222, 223
Schenk, RS 105
Scrivener, Jackie 329, 331, 332, 338, 340
Scrivener Press 332
Scrivener, Stella 334, 338
Second World War 181, 186–87
Shields, Frank 222
   In Search of Breaker Morant: Balladist and Bushveldt Carbineer 222
Silver Gull 110
Sinclair, Edith 157, 207, 226–27, 369
Sitwell, Edith 342
Smart, Mima 235, 237–38, 242
Smith, Eleanor 172, 322, 330
Smith's Weekly 64–66
South Australian Museum 37, 46, 127
south-west Australia x, xv, 13, 19, 29, 30, 235, 310, 362
South, William 33, 34, 35, 38, 39, 42, 47
Spencer, Baldwin 42, 43
Spencer, Beth 18, 170, 311
   Vagabondage 311
Spinifex people 120–21, 238–39, 280–81, 283, 373
Spurling, Stephen 74
SS *Almora* 48, 53
SS *Stuttgart* 27, 28
Standing, Guy 311
Standish, Ann 288
Stead, WT 27, 124, 137
Stephenson, PR 107, 189
Streaky Bay 3–4, 8, 13, 19–21, 34, 82, 204, 230, 247–51, 257, 259–63, 266, 271–74
Streaky Bay National Trust Museum 23–26
Strehlow, Ted 37, 147
Stretton, EJ 167
Stuart Arms Hotel 77, 80, 81
Stuart Highway 321, 366
Sturt's Stony Desert 197, 200
Sun (Sydney) x–xi, xvi, 45–47, 67, 70, 72, 75, 111, 135

Sunday Times 43, 52, 66, 154
Sunshine Coast 334–35
Sydney 50, 64–67, 70, 72, 78, 174–87, 192, 196, 202, 206, 223, 225, 323, 326, 343, 355
Sydney Morning Herald 106, 111, 149, 200
Sydney University 139

Tarcoola 38–39, 115, 121, 204, 213, 216–17, 241, 281
Tennant, Kylie 86, 175, 182
terra nullius 83
The Territory 8, 59, 177, 184, 185, 202, 252, 259, 265, 313–18, 322, 329
   reviews 314
Thieburger, Nicholas 362
Thomas, Harold 277
Thomas, Martin 9
   The Many Worlds of RH Mathews 9
Thomas, Northcote 30
Thompson, Beverley 248, 249
Thompson, Cyril 248, 249, 250
Thompson, Natalie 248, 249
Thompson, Vida 25, 248–50, 262
Thompson, W 74
Thomson, Donald 93, 119
Thursday Island 60, 326, 327, 328
Tindale, Norman 191
Tindall, Isabell 155–56
Townsville 48, 60–61, 66, 326
Treagus, Aileen 272
Tully, Anne 190, 323

United Aborigines Mission (UAM) 41, 121–22, 280, 290–91, 297
   History of the UAM 121
University of Adelaide's Board for Anthropological Research 37
University of Newcastle's Centre for Literary and Linguistic Computing 150
University of Queensland 339–40

van Loon, Julienne 258
   The Thinking Woman 258

Walkabout 75, 174, 329, 340
Walker, WD 42
Waller, Lisa 303, 369
Wandervogel 58
Ward, Russel 85
    The Australian Legend 85
Watts, Edith *see* Sinclair, Edith
Wave Hill walk-off 320
West Australian 75, 105
West, Joy 238, 368
Westall 4–5, 21–23, 249–50, 261
Western Mail 100, 135
White Australia 6, 8, 88, 94, 95, 97–98
White, Isobel 11, 143, 219, 226, 227, 237, 302, 362, 367–68
White, Patrick 85, 359
    A Fringe of Leaves 359
    Voss 85

Wiebusch, Pastor 34–35
Wiluna 322
Witcombe, Eleanor 218–19, 220, 221, 222, 223, 226, 300, 345–46
Wolff, Elizabeth 132–33, 155, 251
Women's Non-Party Association 39, 41
Women's Weekly 132
Woods, Violetta 228
Woomera Rocket Range 280
Wright, Judith 339
Wynbring Siding 116, 119, 204–205, 207, 210–16, 219, 238, 240–43, 247, 254, 287, 298–301

Yalata 11, 116–17, 231–42, 280–86, 292, 295, 296–98, 300–302, 366–74
Yolŋu people 92–93
Yuldilgabbi xiv, 35

www.ingramcontent.com/pod-product-compliance
Lightning Source LLC
Chambersburg PA
CBHW051534230426
43669CB00015B/2590